THE ESSENTIAL
New York Times
Grilling
COOKBOOK

MORE THAN 100 YEARS OF
SIZZLING FOOD WRITING AND RECIPES

Edited by
PETER KAMINSKY

Foreword by
MARK BITTMAN

STERLING EPICURE
New York

STERLING EPICURE
New York

An Imprint of Sterling Publishing
387 Park Avenue South
New York, NY 10016

ISBN 978-1-4027-9324-0

Library of Congress Cataloging-in-Publication Data

The essential New York times grilling cookbook : more than 100 years of sizzling food writing and recipes / edited
by Peter Kaminsky ; foreword by Mark Bittman ; other contributors include Craig Claiborne, Pierre Franey, Florence
Fabricant, Steven Raichlen, Molly O'Neill, Julia Moskin, and many more.
     pages cm
  Includes index.
  ISBN 978-1-4027-9324-0
  1. Barbecuing. I. Kaminsky, Peter. II. Title: Grilling cookbook.
  TX840.B3E85 2014
  641.5'784--dc23

                                                                    2013026602

Distributed in Canada by Sterling Publishing
c/o Canadian Manda Group, 165 Dufferin Street
Toronto, Ontario, Canada M6K 3H6
Distributed in the United Kingdom by GMC Distribution Services
Castle Place, 166 High Street, Lewes, East Sussex, England BN7 1XU
Distributed in Australia by Capricorn Link (Australia) Pty. Ltd.
P.O. Box 704, Windsor, NSW 2756, Australia

Designed by Christine Heun

For information about custom editions, special sales, and premium and corporate purchases,
please contact Sterling Special Sales at 800-805-5489 or specialsales@sterlingpublishing.com.

Manufactured in the United States of America

2 4 6 8 10 9 7 5 3 1

www.sterlingpublishing.com

Contents

CHAPTER 4

Pork 117

Fish and Shellfish 211

CHAPTER 9

Desserts and Breads

CHAPTER 10

Marinades, Rubs, and Sauces

FOREWORD

In his introduction to this comprehensive and unusual (I'll get to that) collection, Peter Kaminsky delightfully details the history of *The Times*'s writing about grilling and barbecue. (The latter, as aficionados know, is a very different thing from the former.) What's left to me is to praise what's here, detail why I believe it to be unique (a word we're not really allowed to use at *The Times*), and single out some of my favorites.

The collection is unusual—and truly unique—because it spans so much time and so many different personalities. I was literally enamored of Craig Claiborne when I was in my 20s; he was nothing short of a demigod to me, and at a time when "barbecue" meant burgers and franks, he affected my restaurant-eating and cooking life like no one else. But when I finally met him (I was nearly 40 by then, and he almost 70) I wasn't surprised to find out that, aside from a love of food and the craft of writing about it, we had little in common.

Later on I came to admire other *Times* food writers, but I would say most especially Florence Fabricant—FloFab. She and I have been colleagues of sorts for going on 20 years. (I was a late bloomer.) Yet again, our styles could hardly be more different.

There have been new additions to the roster, too (I include Julia Moskin among these, even though she's been on staff for something like ten years at this point), which has allowed us all to discover new approaches and a greater variety of wisdom. I might single out Steven Raichlen, along with John Willoughby and Chris Schlesinger, grilling specialists who brought super-knowledgeable credibility to this kind of writing in *The Times* pages over the course of the last quarter-century or so.

The same could be said for almost everyone represented here: I know most of them, and have shared meals and stories with them. We come from different places, different backgrounds, and even different eras. The only common ground here is grilling, writing, and *The Times*.

Which means what? That in every single year represented, the Magazine, Living and Dining editors of *The Times* made an effort, every grilling season, to pull together the best grilling (and, yes, barbecue) recipes they could find. Some years this was a few recipes, some years 20 or 30 or more. (There was a summer not long ago when I was told that I personally was contributing too many grilling recipes. Who knew there was such a thing?)

The point is this: over some 90 years, *The Times* has run thousands of recipes for outdoor cooking. What's here is far from all of them, but a selection of 200 chosen— wisely (if immodestly; several of my own pieces are included), I might add—by Peter, himself a longtime contributor and an important part of not only the food sections but the paper in general for many years.

.

And we are not talking only about recipes here. Unlike many collections, this one features full stories, stories that often contain information and tips that can be valuable once the cooking process begins, even before the grill is lit, stories that could stand by their own, without recipes at all. So when seen as a kind of "greatest hits" of *Times* writing about grilling, this collection becomes even more unusual. One of the earlier pieces, by John Willig (page 302), begins thus:

"One of the most alarming aspects of these troubled times is not, as one might be led to believe, the rock 'n' roll singer or Khrushchev or even Brigitte Bardot. It is the spread of outdoor cooking and the way people now regard it as an Art."

Kinda great, no? And if you swap a couple of names it could have been written yesterday. (Be sure to check it out; it's a great read.)

None of this is to say, of course, that the recipes and general cooking instructions aren't the stars here; I believe that they are. You've got a fine DIY guide to barbecue sauces by Dena Kleiman (who, I do believe, got it right); the great Molly O'Neill's essential guide to the basics of grilling vegetables, and the Lee brothers' take on hobo packs; a comprehensive piece by Ms. Fabricant on grilling fish with, of course, terrific recipes; and Ms. Moskin writing what amounts to all about jerk.

It is indeed a stunning collection, filled with joys and surprises, a delight to browse through or read almost as you would a novel. It spans more than a century and a half, and though there is an ostensible focus on New York, what we can see here is the true evolution of the "barbecue" or "cook-out" into an understanding of the difference between barbecuing and grilling and the progression of the foods of choice. Whereas they were once almost exclusively hot dogs and hamburgers—and as American as both—they're now as varied as roasted eggplant, grilled mackerel, and barbecued tofu, and they come from every place on earth.

Mark Bittman

INTRODUCTION: LIGHT MY FIRE

The New York Times, born on September 18, 1851, has covered barbecue from Day One. Actually make that Day Four Hundred and Two, October 25, 1852, to be exact. In a short piece that ran without a byline, mention is made of a barbecue thrown by the Whig Party at which supporters of Daniel Webster's candidacy for president refused to let Congressman Daniel Jenifer speak unless he promised not to vote for Webster's rival, General Winfield Scott, hero of the recent war with Mexico and eventual loser to Franklin Pierce. There is no mention of what was served at the barbecue.

Throughout the nineteenth century, *The Times* continued to write about barbecue, most often in the context of political events and great public gatherings. Not a word about gastronomy. No recipes, no side dishes, no discussion of the virtues of vinegar-based vs. mustard-based vs. tomato-based sauces (an age-old debate that still ignites the passions of partisans of these three traditions of Southern barbecue). If Rome can be said to have purchased the support of its citizens through bread and circuses, American political parties, especially at election time, employed a barbecue strategy that combined pork and politics, beef and braggadocio.

For example, in 1876 the paper ran a piece about a Republican rally in Myrtle Avenue Park in Brooklyn where 50,000 people gathered for speeches and roast oxen. When you consider that Danny Meyer's annual barbecue fest, the Big Apple Block Party, attracts 20,000 'cue fanatics, it's quite clear that cooking over wood fire has long been a big draw in the Big Apple.

It really is a hoot to look through these early years of the paper's coverage of outdoor grilling as spectacle. On December 15, 1910, a "special to *The New York Times*" appears under the headline "Buffalo Bill's Last Buffalo," wherein the famous Wild West impresario was invited to the ranch of Major Gordon (Pawnee Bill) Lillie to dispatch "an unruly old buffalo." Buffalo Bill "executed the death sentence with one shot." I have my doubts about the kill shot, but it made good copy. Likewise, the headline is a head-scratcher: how did the editor who wrote it have the foresight to know it was Bill's last buffalo seven years before Bill died?

The first mention I could find of the actual food served at these massive gatherings appeared in 1897 when the National Stock Growers Convention in Denver drew a mid-sized crowd (that is, 10,000) for a bill of fare that included:

Eight beeves	Half A Ton of Cheese
Four Elk	Two Thousand Loaves of Bread
Four Buffaloes	Two Hundred Opossums
Twenty-Five Sheep	Thirty Barrels of Yams
Two Bears	One Hundred Kegs of Beer
Twelve Antelope	

Opossums? Did Andrew Zimmern's great grandparents live in Denver?

In the nineteenth century, food, chefs, restaurants, and recipes were not heavily covered in *The Times*. Some may write this off to the fact that cooking was still considered "women's work" and therefore somehow not worthy of notice in a journal that carried news of the goings on of potentates, the rise and fall of empires, the building of great fortunes, the grim toll of war. The basic biological operation of eating did not rise to the same level of gravitas. Moreover, ours was not yet a culture with an insatiable appetite for celebrity. Chefs were everyday working stiffs, blue collar guys (always guys, never gals). Gladiatorial cooking competitions had not yet elevated them to the status of superstars.

But, with or without reportage, Americans grilled at every opportunity. Fourth of July celebrations in the Northeast and Northwest often featured the first salmon of the year, grilled over open fires. At rodeos, church suppers, and harvest festivals, whole hogs, steers, and lambs—long smoked or grilled over wood fire—were served. In the Deep South, until quite recently, the tobacco harvest was the occasion for a festive "pig pickin'" where the consumption of a pit-roasted whole hog was one of the few times when groups of whites and blacks dined together. Twenty generations of American sportsmen, from John Audubon to Teddy Roosevelt to Brett Favre, set off to forest, wetland, and stream to hunt deer, shoot duck, and catch fish, all of which involved wood-fire cookery of the day's harvest. As the great convoys of Conestogas moved westward over plains teeming with bison, antelope, sage hens, and waterfowl, the pioneers cooked over fire. Likewise the legions of laborers who laid the track of the transcontinental railroad availed themselves of the plentiful wildlife of the mountains and prairies.

Americans have barbecued as long as there has been an America, humankind even longer. Our distant ancestors going back hundreds of thousands of years grilled, smoked, roasted, and broiled. The link between food and fire is as old as humanity, perhaps a little older. Harvard paleobiologist Richard Wrangham theorizes that cooking over fire is what made us human. Compressing his elegant argument into a few sentences, he writes that once humans tamed fire and began cooking their food, it was no longer necessary for our forebears to have massive intestinal tracts to digest food **that already had been partially processed by cooking. We were free to devote our life force to evolving bigger brains that were** conveniently supplied with the energy that is highly concentrated in cooked meat. In that respect, love of barbecue is chiseled into our DNA.

Perhaps we should take a moment here to say what it is that we are talking about when we talk about barbecue. When I grew up in a tract home in New Jersey in the 1950s, a barbecue was a kind of flimsy metal box on unstable legs where my dad cooked burgers, dogs, steaks, and—in recognition of our Russian heritage—the occasional *shasklik* or shish kebab.

For me, a child of the suburbs, barbecue was cooking that you did over charcoal—later charcoal briquettes—on a piece of metal equipment. The act of cooking was barbecuing.

Down South, as I have been reminded many times, barbecue is a noun referring to the meat of a pig that has been cooked at a low temperature in a smoke-filled chamber until the pork reaches a magical point of unctuous succulence (185 degrees, when collagen melts), and the meat is then shredded and dressed with a sauce that is usually a combination of sweet, sour, and spicy. Why these sauces are held to be such closely guarded secrets has always been a mystery to me. You take some common condiments and throw in some other kitchen staples and slather it on. Not a whole lot of mystery there. On this subject Craig Claiborne wrote, "In the United States, the national American barbecue sauce consists of a dark red blend of tomato ketchup, Worcestershire sauce and brown sugar with variations that include vinegar, hot pepper and butter. Europeans generally regard this combination as (choose one) vulgar, naive, unsophisticated, barbaric, amusing."

Which brings me to the subject of the immortal Craig Claiborne. Food writing in *The New York Times* can be demarcated by the terms B.C. and A.C., as in Before Craig and After Craig. True, there had been the occasional food story as well as recipes, often sent in by readers, throughout the 1920s, 1930s, and 1940s. But that was the era of home-ec and wholesome—that is, unimaginative—cooking: not much about barbecue. When Claiborne arrived at *The Times* in 1957, there was a confluence of food trends in American culture. The suburbanization of the postwar decades gave millions of us tidy homes on quarter-acre plots where it was practical to cook outdoors in a way that was impossible in the crowded tenements of our grandparents' time. The oft-lampooned image of paterfamilias in apron, Bermuda shorts, and high black socks incinerating burgers and dogs on the backyard grill made good fodder for *New Yorker* cartoons, and except, perhaps, for the high black socks, it wasn't far off the mark. But in recipe after recipe and story after story, Craig and his cooking compatriot, Pierre Franey, began to turn to more elegant food from the grill: recipes that relied less on powerhouse sauces and more on purity of ingredients and careful but not complicated techniques.

Craig and Pierre were mindful that gastronomic chefs in Europe weren't particularly adept as grillers. Pan roasting was the way one achieved a nice crust on a steak or a piece of fish. But outside of the Michelin temples of haute cuisine, everyday Europeans were masterful at grilling whole lambs, swordfish, beefsteaks, pork loins, and even vegetables. In their work, Craig and Pierre rediscovered a world of rustic cookery that immigrants had for the most part left behind in Europe and which their children and grandchildren once again learned through these two pioneers.

Craig and Pierre also inspired a generation of women who took it to heart when Craig wrote "it seems a perfect occasion to demolish the age-old shibboleths surrounding the art of summer grilling. For example, barbecuing does not require charring food beyond recognition; barbecuing is not just 'Dad's job.'" Actually, a more on-the-money comment is found in a column written in 1956 contrasting the male and female egos at the grill (page 350).

The author observed "the well known phenomenon that when a woman puts on an apron she feels like a maid, but when a man puts on an apron he feels like a chef (and looks like a maid)." Bingo!

Florence Fabricant did much to put that misconception to rest as she sought out ethnic recipes in the 1970s, some of which you'll find in these pages. Moira Hodgson also manned (or "womaned") the front line of fire cookery in those early years. They were the first in a chain of talented female writers who fanned the flames of our infatuation with the grill. A great debt is owed to Molly O'Neill; year after year her recipes in *The New York Times Magazine* gave home grillers inspiration for what to cook on Sunday.

In our time, the most numerous contributions from The Times family of writers come from the ubiquitous Mark Bittman. His "101 Fast Recipes for Grilling" (page 1) just begins to plumb the depths of his grilling adventures, which are chronicled throughout this book. In fact, we could have easily done one book exclusively devoted to recipes from Claiborne and Franey and another, thicker, volume covering the Bittman oeuvre. And don't let me forget restaurant critics emeriti Mimi Sheraton, Bryan Miller, and Sam Sifton, who demonstrate they, too, can cook as well as consume and critique.

There are recipes from prominent chefs as well, Jacques Pepin, Alfred Portale, Adam Perry Lang, Zakary Pelaccio, Susan Spicer, Francis Mallmann, and Dean Fearing among them, who have shared grilling recipes with *Times* writers and readers. So too has barbecue maven and bestselling author Steven Raichlen. Right alongside them you will find contributors, many of them my favorites, from everyday folks who like to grill. From the tailgate capital of America (the parking lot of Arrowhead Stadium in Kansas City, Missouri), there's the McSparin brothers' prime rib (page 73). And, cholesterol-fears-be-damned, we had to include the infamous and caloric Bacon Explosion (page 152) of Jason Day and Aaron Chronister.

In short, it was not a hard task to look through the archives of *The Times* and come up with more than 200 varied, well-thought-out, and delicious recipes. Volumes 2 through 10, anyone?

With that said, open up the book, pick a recipe, and fire away!

Peter Kaminsky

PREVIOUS PAGE: Fish, vegetables, and fruit on the grill; **OPPOSITE:** Duck à l'orange, *see tip number 32 page 3;*

ABOVE: Beef Tartare Burger, *see page 44.*

ABOVE: Greek-Style Fish with Marinated Tomatoes, *see page 217.*

ABOVE: Grilled Lobster, *see page 254*; **ABOVE LEFT:** Halibut with Indian Rub and Corn Salsa, *see page 214*.

ABOVE RIGHT: Grilled Clams, *see page 25*.

E

ABOVE: Curry-Spiced Lamb Burgers, *see page 58*;

OPPOSITE: Grilled Sardines, *see page 229*.

ABOVE: Bacon Explosion, *see page 152*.

TOP: New Yorkers grilling Jerk Chicken; **ABOVE:** Jerk Chicken, *see page 195*.

ABOVE: Grilled Pork Loin with Wine-Salt Rub, *see page 129.*

TOP: Steak prepared with a rub, *see page 332*;

ABOVE: Braised and Grilled Pork Ribs, *see page 140*.

OPPOSITE TOP: Shu Mai-Style Burger, *see page 59*; **OPPOSITE BOTTOM**: Japanese Burger with Wasabi Ketchup, *see page 57*; **ABOVE**: Crusty Macaroni and Cheese, *see page 288*.

TOP: Grilled Leeks with Romesco Sauce, *see page 14*; **BOTTOM**: Grilled Lamb and Figs on Rosemary Skewers, *see page 158*; **OPPOSITE**: Grilled Peaches with Dukkah and Blueberries, *see page 300*.

ABOVE: Grilled Rose-Water Poundcake, *see page 312.*

101 Fast Recipes for Grilling

Mark Bittman, June 29, 2010

There, in all of their Fourth of July glory, are 101 grilling ideas begging to be tried. A vast majority take less time to prepare and grill than it takes to watch your coals turn white. (If you use gas, they're still almost as fast as heating up the grill.) Some of them feature ingredients like corn, eggplant and tomatoes, which will be better a month from now, at least in the Northeast. But there are also suggestions for foods in season right now that not everybody thinks of putting on the grill. Please note that salt and pepper are (usually) understood.

Vegetables and Fruits

1.   A winter dish, summer style: Brush thick slices of fennel bulbs with olive oil and grill over not-too-high heat. Cut oranges in half and grill, cut-side down. Put fennel on a bed of arugula or watercress; squeeze grilled oranges over top. Garnish with fennel fronds.

2.   Best grilled artichokes: Cut artichokes in half, scoop out the choke, parboil until tender. Grill, cut-side down, until lightly browned; grill a couple of halved lemons, too. Combine the juice from the grilled lemons with melted butter and spoon over the artichokes. Finish with parsley.

3.   Tahini tofu steaks. Thin tahini with lots of lemon juice and some minced garlic. Cut a brick of firm tofu into four slabs and brush with sesame oil. Grill over a moderate fire, turning a few times, until marked and crisp outside and custardy inside. On the last turn, baste with the tahini sauce. Serve on thick tomato slices with a drizzle of soy sauce and chopped basil, Thai if possible.

4.   Spice-rubbed carrots: Roll peeled carrots in cumin, salt, pepper and brown sugar. Char, then move them away from direct heat and cover the grill until carrots are tender.

5.   Grill bread; grind in a food processor to make coarse bread crumbs. (You can add garlic and/or parsley and/or Parmesan, or not.) Grill asparagus until tender. Top with bread crumbs and olive oil.

6.   Brush slices of beet with olive oil and grill slowly until tender and lightly browned. Top each slice with a little goat cheese and some salad greens.

7.   For perfectly ripe tomatoes only: Grill tomatoes, any size, until hot and lightly charred but not bursting. Drizzle with olive oil, sprinkle with salt and pepper, and serve with fresh mozzarella (or, even better, burrata) and grilled bread.

8.   Halve and grill radicchio (or Belgian endives); drizzle cut sides with honey or plain vinaigrette, pesto or parsley pesto. Or just brush with oil and finish with a little grilled prosciutto.

9.   Grilled guacamole: Halve and pit avocados; lightly char them, then scoop out the flesh. Grill halved red onion, too. Chop, combine, add tomatoes, lime, garlic and spices if you like.

10.   Grill corn. Serve with mayo with minced garlic, pimentón and parsley.

11.   Grill more corn. Serve with curry-powder-laced yogurt and minced onion.

12.   Grill corn again. Serve with coconut milk, cilantro and mint.

13.   Root vegetable of your choice: Slice celeriac—or jicama, big potatoes, daikon or yams—and grill slowly, until very tender and browned. Drizzle with olive oil or melted butter and sprinkle with chopped rosemary or sage and olive oil.

14.   Choose another root. Slice it, but this time char lightly and leave it crunchy. Chop and toss with chopped cilantro, a pinch of cayenne and juice of grilled lime.

15.   Rub thick zucchini slices with a mixture of fresh or dried dill, yogurt, olive oil and lemon. (Or use pesto or parsley pesto.) Grill slowly.

16.   More shopping than cooking: Grill an array of radishes on little skewers, four to six each. Serve with butter, salt and bread.

17.   Halve Belgian endives. Brush with olive oil, sprinkle with salt and pepper and grill over moderate-to-low heat, turning once or twice, until soft and browned. Finish cut-side up and sprinkle with grated Parmesan; close the grill to melt cheese.

18.   Lightly char whole or halved heads of baby bok choy; drizzle with soy sauce and top with chopped scallions.

19.   Peel and thickly slice a not overly ripe mango. Brush very lightly with neutral oil and grill just until softened; sprinkle with cilantro and/or mint and lime juice (you might as well grill the lime first, too).

20.   Grill pineapple (or anything, really, from pork to tofu to eggplant). Make a sauce of half-cup peanut butter, a tablespoon (or more) soy sauce, a dash (or more) sriracha chili sauce, a handful of basil or mint and enough warm water to thin. (I'm tempted to say, "Throw away the pineapple and eat the sauce," but the combination is sensational.)

21.   Waldorf salad revisited, sort of: Grill cut apples until browned but not mushy; grill chunks of Napa or savoy cabbage, also left crisp; grill halved red onion. Chop or shred all together with blue cheese, walnuts and a little yogurt.

22.   Cut a slit in as many ripe figs as you like; stuff with herbed goat cheese (or cream cheese mixed with chopped nuts) and grill slowly. Appetizer or dessert? Your call.

23.   Grill red, orange and/or yellow peppers; toss with olives, capers, balsamic vinegar and olive oil.

24.   Quick grilled pickle: Rapidly char thick slices of cucumber; toss with salt, vinegar and sugar; let sit for 15 minutes, then drain.

25.   Charred salsa verde. Toss whole husked tomatillos, scallions and jalapeños in olive oil and grill until charred. Remove the blackened skin from the chilies and chop or blend everything with diced avocado, lime juice and cilantro. Eat with chips or top grilled chicken with it.

Meat

26.   Mideast lamb chops: Shoulder cuts are the best and the cheapest; just don't burn them. Marinate them briefly in yogurt, lemon, cardamom and mint. Serve with lemon and parsley.

27.   Midwest pork chops: Again, shoulder; again, don't burn. Marinate briefly in spicy mustard, chopped garlic and apple cider.

28.   Six-minute steak (or maybe four): Salt skirt steak and grill it, quickly. Top with queso fresco, thinly sliced red onion (you could grill it first, if you like) and the juice of grilled lime.

29.   Six-minute steak, plus a little marinating time: Soak skirt steak in a mixture of soy, lime juice, garlic, ginger and sugar (or mirin) before grilling. (The time it takes to heat the grill is long enough.)

30.   Smear chicken leg quarters (or thighs) with a paste of garlic, chopped rosemary (thyme, too, if you like), olive oil and the juice of grilled lemon. Grill away from heat, covered; crisp briefly over high heat.

31.   Steak au poivre: Sirloin strip is ideal. Press lots of cracked black pepper into both sides, sprinkle with salt and grill over fairly high heat, about three to four minutes on each side. Slice quarter-inch thick before serving.

32.   Crisp (and better) duck à l'orange: Score the skin of duck breasts and press rosemary leaves, salt and pepper into both sides. Grill skin-side down over low-ish heat until crackly, then turn and grill briefly. Serve with grilled orange halves.

33. Smear hanger, skirt, flatiron or other steak with mustard. Grill and serve with grilled shallots.

34. Brush chicken thighs—boned or not—with basil, parsley or cilantro pesto. Boneless and skinless thighs can be grilled over direct heat; thighs with skin should be started away from heat.

35. Fast lamb leg: Use steaks cut from the leg, and rub them with a mix of warm spices: cumin, coriander, cinnamon and turmeric. Grill quickly, serve hot.

36. Spread flank steak or butterflied lamb leg with garlic, parsley and lemon zest. Roll and tie, or fold. (Or grill without further fuss, adding more paste occasionally.)

37. Moist grilled chicken breast? Yes: Pound chicken breast thin, top with chopped tomato, basil and Parmesan; roll and skewer and grill over not-high heat until just done.

38. Call it grilled chicken Parm: Pound breast thin, top one side with sliced tomato, mozzarella and Parmesan; fold in half, seal with a toothpick or skewer and grill for a few minutes on each side.

39. Pork (or veal) saltimbocca: Pound pork or veal cutlets thin; top with ham (prosciutto preferably) and cheese (maybe Gruyère). Roll, cook on skewers and serve with pickles.

40. Slice pork shoulder thin. Fry lots of sesame seeds, minced garlic, fresh minced chili in sesame oil; off heat, stir in some soy sauce. Grill the pork fast over high heat, smearing with the sesame paste right after flipping. Serve with lettuce leaves and cilantro, basil and/or mint for wrapping.

41. Bacon-wrapped hot dog. You know you want one.

Fish and Shellfish

42. Grill thick onion slices; puree in a blender with olive oil and lemon juice. Grill scallops for about four minutes; serve with the vinaigrette.

43. Salmon tartare with grilled stuff: Lightly grill radishes, scallions, lime halves and, if you like, plantain disks. Serve the plantains under, and the other things next to, chopped raw salmon (preferably wild) seasoned with salt and pepper.

44. Grill sardines or mackerel; serve with a squeeze of grilled lemon, grapefruit or both.

45. Stuff whole gutted trout with slices of lemon and chopped marjoram or oregano. Wrapping in bacon is optional. One per person is best.

46. Not so easy, but so impressive: Stuff squid bodies with chopped chorizo (optional), garlic-toasted bread crumbs, lemon zest and parsley. Close with toothpicks. Char quickly over a very hot fire.

47. Shrimp, Part 1: Rub with chili powder and salt, and grill quickly. Finish with cilantro and the juice of grilled lime halves.

48. Shrimp, Part 2: Rub with olive oil, salt and cumin. Finish with the juice of grilled lemon halves; garnish with chopped marjoram, if you have it, parsley if you don't.

49. Shrimp, Part 3: Rub with curry powder. Drizzle with warm coconut milk and chopped mint, basil and/or cilantro.

50. Grilled tuna niçoise: Brush tuna with olive oil and grill; keep it rare. (You might grill some new potatoes while you're at it.) Serve with more olive oil, lemon juice, cherry tomatoes, olives, grilled red onion and parsley. Green beans and hard-cooked eggs are optional.

51. Grilled clams on the half shell: Get them shucked (or cook in the microwave or on the grill until opened); top with bread crumbs, parsley, lemon, minced cooked bacon (optional). Grill until topping is hot.

52. You think you don't like bluefish? Grill it, then drizzle with a mixture of chopped fennel fronds (or crushed fennel seeds), melted butter and the juice of grilled grapefruit or orange.

53. White fillets with spice: Mix salt, sugar, chili powder and paprika. Rub on sturdy white fish fillets (make sure the grill grates are clean and well oiled).

54. Buy shucked oysters. Top with juice of grilled lemon. Period. (You could grill shallots, mince and make a grilled mignonette, but this is better.)

55. Grill soft-shell crabs, brushing with melted butter and Tabasco. A little charring of the claw tips isn't a bad thing.

56. Simmer octopus tentacles until tender (this may take a couple of hours); cool. Grill; cut into attractive little rounds and drizzle with lemon and olive oil.

57. Grill wild salmon (preferably king or sockeye) until not-well-done. Toss diced cucumbers with fresh dill, olive oil and lemon juice. Serve salmon hot, slaw cold.

Kebabs

58.　Shrimp and chorizo. Serve with lemon or a little vinaigrette.

59.　Lamb and carrots. In last few minutes, brush with miso thinned with a tiny bit of mirin (or sherry, wine or water).

60.　Lamb and onions. Brush with a mixture of cumin and olive oil as they sizzle. You can add bell peppers, too, but somehow the stark minimalism of this is pleasing.

61.　Odd, but good: Strawberries and cherry tomatoes, finished with basil-laced balsamic vinegar.

62.　The New Yawk special: Italian sausage, peppers and onions.

63.　The California special: Figs, with chunks of good bacon.

64.　Kebab or hero? Your choice: Cut brussels sprouts in half; grill slowly on skewers with chunks of sausage. Both slowly crisp as they cook.

65.　Bread salad on a stick: Cubes of bread, black olives and cherry tomatoes. Don't grill too long, and drizzle with basil or thyme or parsley vinaigrette.

66.　Peaches, plums, strawberries and watermelon. Finish with a sprinkle of salt and perhaps a drizzle of balsamic vinegar.

67.　Cubes of mango and chunks of white fish; brush with a mixture of soy, fish sauce, sriracha chili sauce and chopped mint or cilantro. Serve with a mai tai.

68.　Go Hawaiian or Italian: Wrap pineapple or melon in prosciutto. Grill briefly.

Salads

69.　Grilled coleslaw: Lightly char wedges of green and red cabbage and carrots. Let cool, then shred and toss with a little mayo, vinegar, salt and sugar.

70.　Grill halved new potatoes or fingerlings (microwave or parboil first for a few minutes to get a head start), red onions and scallions. Chop as necessary and toss with chopped celery, parsley, mustard and cider (or other) vinegar. I make this annually.

71.　Toss grilled Lacinato kale leaves with a little Caesar salad dressing (or olive oil, lemon and Parmesan) and grilled croutons.

72.　Char iceberg wedges and cherry tomatoes (skewer these first). Top with blue cheese dressing.

73.   Lightly grill ripe figs; brush with balsamic. Chop and toss with arugula and blue cheese. Sprinkle with olive oil.

74.   Steak salad with almost no steak: Halve endives or radicchio; brush with oil and grill. Sprinkle with bits of blue cheese and bits of charred steak.

75.   Ratatouille: Grill chunks of zucchini, yellow squash, mushrooms, eggplant, onion and tomatoes (or use cherry tomatoes), all until lightly browned and perfectly tender. Toss with fresh marjoram or oregano, thyme, basil and olive oil.

Burgers

76.   Greek salad burger: Ground lamb with grated feta, chopped calamatas and a little oregano. Top with tomato, red onion and cucumber.

77.   The pickled onions make it: Soak sliced red onions in diluted vinegar and salt while you prepare everything else. Combine ground lamb with grated carrots and cumin; grill, then top with onions.

78.   Asian burger: Grind pork, combine with grated daikon and a little soy sauce. Brush with hoisin or miso and grill; top with sliced-and-salted cucumbers.

79.   Grind beef, combine with crumbled blue cheese and chopped toasted walnuts. Top, if it doesn't sound too effete, with sliced grilled pear.

80.   A chicken or turkey burger worth eating: Cook and chop bacon; mix with ground chicken (or turkey) and grill.

81.   Another: Grind turkey, combine with chopped basil, shove a cube of mozzarella into the center, grill until well done (the cheese will melt). Top with tomato and more basil.

82.   Grind salmon (actually, it's better if you grind half and chop half) and combine with chopped scallions and soy sauce. Grill medium-rare, top with mayo spiked with ginger, soy and/or lime.

83.   Philly cheesesteak burger: Grind beef and grill with mushrooms and onions; top with aged provolone.

Sandwiches and Breads

84.   Actual grilled cheese: Use good bread, good cheese, tomato slices and maybe a little mustard; brush with melted butter or olive oil and grill with a weight on top.

85. Glorified grilled cheese: Use grilled pineapple, grilled ham, cheese, pickles and mayo; grill with a weight on top.

86. Grill bell peppers until blackened and collapsed; cover, cool and peel. Grill eggplant planks, brushed with olive oil (or pesto if you have it), until very tender. Make a sandwich with balsamic vinegar, mozzarella and basil. This is also good with strip or skirt steak: grill meat until medium-rare, then slice and salt.

87. Grilled quesadilla (simple): Fill a flour tortilla with queso fresco, Monterey Jack or Cheddar; add chicken, shrimp and/or tomato. Fold and grill until cheese melts.

88. Grilled quesadilla (not as simple): Grill and strip corn from the cob; grill red-onion slices and chop them. Combine both with chili powder and bind with a tiny bit of mayo or yogurt. Put between two flour tortillas with cheese and grill. Serve with grilled lime wedges.

89. A different kind of Cuban sandwich: Grill pork steaks (best from the shoulder, about half-inch thick). Put on baguette spread with well-seasoned mashed black beans, queso fresco, chopped red onion (grilled or not), cilantro and lime juice.

90. Grill pork steaks as above; grill red onions. Slice the meat, chop the onions, toss with thinly sliced apples and roll in lavash bread or stuff in pita with yogurt-dill dressing. You can use the meat as an accent, or as the dominant ingredient.

91. Grill sweet Italian sausage and some figs. Combine on a toasted hot dog bun; mustard is optional.

92. Grill split kielbasa or chorizo (the Spanish type). Serve in buns, filled with chopped Manchego and mayo spiked with pimentón. Some chopped dried apricots would be good, too.

Desserts

93. An idea whose time has come: Halve and grill peaches, nectarines or apricots. Brush with barbecue sauce or, if you want to be sophisticated, a mixture of bourbon, sugar and mint, or simple syrup laced with basil.

94. An idea whose time will come in September: Halve and grill pears or apples. When they're done, drizzle with yogurt, honey and a pinch of cardamom.

95. Grilled fruit salad, and why not? Toss grilled watermelon (really good), peaches, plums, pineapple and kiwi with honey, a little salt, lemon juice and tarragon (not much), chervil, basil or mint (or a combo).

96.   Cut grapefruit in half. Sprinkle with brown sugar; grill, cut-side down. You might top this with chopped pistachios or a little honey.

97.   Grilled shortbread or poundcake (store-bought is totally fine) topped with grilled fruit sauce, strawberries in sugar, yogurt, ice cream, whatever.

98.   Grilled angel food cake or poundcake (again, store-bought is fine) topped with Nutella, chocolate sauce, sorbet, etc.

99.   Grilled s'mores: Put graham crackers (or other good quality flat cookie) on foil, top with marshmallows and chocolate and another cracker. Grill until the chocolate and marshmallow begin to melt.

100.   Cut bananas into thick rounds (like scallops almost), char quickly and serve with caramel sauce, brown sugar, vanilla ice cream, Nutella . . . whatever.

101.   Actually, this is a drink: Skewer green olives, then char them a bit. These would be a good garnish for shrimp, chorizo or anything else. But instead, make yourself a fantastic dirty martini.

CHAPTER ONE

Starters

The thing about barbecues, as opposed to dining-room, sit-down meals, is that most people are standing around, having lively party conversations and getting into the mood with a drink or two. Before they get too lubricated or start feeling hunger pangs, you need to serve something fast that can be eaten with fingers or in bite-sized servings. Strong flavors are a must—any combination of salty, sweet, sour, and hot works. Crispy texture helps too. Remember, the one iron rule of barbecue is that it always seems to take longer than planned for main courses to come off the grill. What you don't want is for folks to be standing around the grill, debating if the coals are hot enough or too hot. These starters can forestall those conversations and, very quickly, tide people over until the main event. Check out Melissa Clark's Grilled Clams with Lemon-Cayenne Butter on page 25. They are about the easiest—and tastiest—things to cook you will ever encounter.

Master barbecue grill and charcoal briquettes, circa 1949.

Grilled-Onion Guacamole

The grilled onions in this guacamole add a sweet, buttery component to any paper plate heaped with barbecued beef.

Yield: 4 to 6 servings

2 tablespoons vegetable oil

2 tablespoons fresh lemon juice

1 tablespoon red wine vinegar

1 teaspoon cracked black peppercorns

1 teaspoon ground cumin

¾ teaspoon salt, plus more to taste

1 large red onion, cut into ¼-inch-thick
    slices

3 ripe avocados

1 large tomato

2 cloves garlic, minced

3 serrano chilies, chopped

3 tablespoons chopped fresh cilantro

Fresh lime juice to taste

1. In a small bowl, combine oil, lemon juice, vinegar, pepper, cumin and ¾ teaspoon salt. Place in a shallow dish, add onion and let marinate for 1 hour.

2. Heat a grill until hot. Drain liquid from onion and place on grill. Grill for 3 minutes per side. Chop coarsely.

3. Peel, seed and cut avocados into ½-inch dice. Dice tomato.

4. Combine grilled onion, avocados, tomato, garlic, chilies and cilantro. Season to taste with salt and lime juice. Keep at room temperature until ready to serve.

July 4, 1993: "Food: The Texas Three-Step," by MOLLY O'NEILL;
adapted from DEAN FEARING, Mansion on Turtle Creek, Dallas, Texas

Grilled-Scallion Salad

Gochugaro, Korean chili powder, which contributes heat to this recipe, is difficult to find in most supermarkets, but a substitute of red pepper flakes or not-terribly fiery ground chili powder will give you a similar effect.

Yield: 4 to 6 servings

1 pound scallions, left untrimmed

1 tablespoon sesame oil

⅓ cup rice vinegar

1 to 2 tablespoons gochugaro
   (if substituting with red pepper
   flakes, use less)

1 tablespoon sesame seeds

2 teaspoons sugar

Brush scallions with sesame oil; grill over moderately high heat, turning once, until charred and tender, 5 to 10 minutes. Roughly chop and toss with vinegar, gochugaro, sesame seeds and sugar. Serve immediately.

June 1, 2011: "Eat: Backyard Bulgogi," by MARK BITTMAN

Grilled Leeks with Romesco Sauce

In Catalonia there is an annual ritual called the *calçotada*, an outdoor barbecue that revolves around local spring onions called *calçots*. After harvest, the onions, which look like baby leeks, are grilled, then wrapped in newspapers to steam for a bit. They're served with romesco sauce, the nut-thickened pepper purée that is another regional specialty. For this recipe, I've substituted leeks for the spring onions and reversed the process, steaming the leeks, then finishing them on a wood fire to get the smoky flavor.

Yield: 6 servings

For the romesco sauce

1 medium red bell pepper

6 ounces tomatoes (1 large or 2 roma)

1 large clove garlic, peeled

¼ cup toasted almonds, or a combination of almonds and skinned roasted hazelnuts

1 thick slice (about 1 ounce) baguette or country-style bread, toasted lightly

½ to 1 teaspoon pure ground chili powder or red pepper flakes, to taste (pepper flakes are hotter)

2 teaspoons chopped fresh flat-leaf parsley

½ teaspoon sweet paprika or Spanish smoked paprika (pimentón)

Salt and freshly ground pepper to taste

1 tablespoon sherry vinegar

¼ cup extra virgin olive oil, as needed

For the leeks

6 fat leeks or 12 baby leeks

2 tablespoons extra virgin olive oil

1. Make the romesco sauce. Preheat oven to 425 degrees. Line a baking sheet with foil. Place pepper on foil, and roast 30 to 40 minutes, using tongs to turn pepper every 10 minutes. Pepper is done when skin is brown and puffed. Transfer pepper to a bowl. Cover bowl with a plate or with plastic, and let sit for 30 minutes until cool. Carefully remove skin. Holding pepper over bowl so no juice escapes, separate into halves or quarters, and remove stem, seeds and membranes.

2. Preheat broiler, and cover a baking sheet with foil. Place tomatoes on baking sheet, and place under broiler at highest setting. Broil for 2 to 4 minutes until charred on one side. Turn over, and broil on other side for 2 to 4 minutes until charred. Remove from heat, transfer to a bowl and allow to cool. Peel and core.

3. Turn on a food processor fitted with steel blade, and drop in garlic clove. When garlic is chopped and adheres to side of bowl, stop machine and scrape down side. Add toasted almonds (or almonds and hazelnuts), bread and chili powder or flakes to bowl. Process into a paste. Scrape down side of bowl, and add roasted pepper, tomatoes, parsley, paprika and salt and pepper to taste. Process until smooth. With machine running, add vinegar and olive oil in a slow stream. Process until well mixed, then scrape into a bowl. Taste and adjust seasoning, adding salt as desired. If possible, allow sauce to stand for an hour at room temperature before using.

4.   Cut away dark green ends of leeks. Trim root ends. Cut fat leeks lengthwise into quarters, and rinse thoroughly under cold water to wash away any sand. If your leeks are ½ inch in diameter, they needn't be cut; if they are between ½ inch and an inch, you can just cut them in half.

5.   Bring an inch of water to a boil in bottom of a steamer. Place leeks in steamer, and steam 10 minutes. Transfer to a bowl, and toss with olive oil and salt and pepper to taste.

6.   Prepare a medium-hot grill. Grill steamed leeks for 5 minutes, turning often, just until grill marks appear. Remove from heat, and serve with romesco sauce.

ADVANCED PREPARATION: Romesco keeps for several days in the refrigerator; the garlic will become more pungent. The steamed leeks will keep in the refrigerator for 3 days.

August 30, 2010: "Recipes for Health: Grilled Leeks with Romesco Sauce," by MARTHA ROSE SHULMAN

Mr. Gunning's Barbecue

It Turns a Country Town
Topsy-Turvy and Will Cause a Brisk Demand in
Mount Vernon This Morning for Larger Hats

Mount Vernon had a wild time yesterday. It was a wilder time than it had ever dreamed of, and the wildest ever known to an interior town of New York State. Mount Vernon is a hamlet about 25 miles up on the line of the New York, New Haven and Hartford Railroad. It is a placid place, with few events, so that the oldest inhabitant will henceforth date all future occurrences from the reign of terror that was yesterday caused by "Gunning's Barbecue."

Thomas B. Gunning, Jr., is a very wealthy young Englishman, who last June leased the Allerton Farm, two miles from Mount Vernon, on the White Plains road, and has since been conducting it as a large milk ranch. Mr. Gunning is very eccentric. His house as it appeared yesterday afternoon, when the back door barricade was removed, was redolent of flowers, and beautiful blossoms were everywhere visible from the kitchen to the parlor. This is its perpetual state, and arises from the fact that upon taking possession Mr. Gunning leased the capacious conservatory and greenhouses to a nurseryman on condition that he would pay him $1 a day rental and six dozen roses daily all the year round. The nurseryman has made a profitable contract, being allowed to eke out the lacking roses, upon occasion, with other flowers. Mr. Gunning being passionately fond of flowers is satisfied as well.

On Friday last it occurred to Mr. Gunning that yesterday would be his twenty-eighth birthday, and he instantly became desirous of celebrating it in some memorable fashion. Having passed the most of his life since he left college in England in the Argentine Republic on an immense stock farm he determined to have such a barbecue as he had often witnessed on the Rio de la Plata. To think was to act. He summoned his secretary, and the next afternoon two hundred printed invitations were issued as follows:

You are cordially invited to a
GRAND BARBECUE AND DRINKS FOR THE CROWD,
in honor of free America and her sovereign people, to be given at the
Coach House of A. M. Allerton, Esq., on the White Plains road, Mount Vernon,
on Tuesday, March 29, 1887, at 9 o'clock A. M.
Carriages will be waiting at the depot, where you will please meet them.
Returning carriages will leave in time for town meeting.
By the order of SMALL MOGUL, MOUNT VERNON, N.Y., MARCH 27, 1887.

The consternation that this sinister proclamation created in the peaceful and conservative circles of Mount Vernon can scarcely be appreciated in a wicked metropolis. A meeting of the Supervisors was instantly called, and the "President of the Village," as Mr. Gunning styles him, declared that he would instantly go out and reason with Mr. Gunning, whose previous eccentricities led everybody to expect Bedlam let loose on this occasion. The Supervisors refused to authorize him, however. It happened that yesterday was election day in Mount Vernon when the destinies of the town were to be potently affected by the choice of a Supervisor, a Town Clerk, and a Constable. Consequently the Supervisors, fearing that their President would utilize the barbecue for political purposes, sent one of their own number. Mr. Gunning received him politely, said he was an alien, knew little about politics and cared less, and was going to have a barbecue because he liked 'em.

His preparations were of two widely different kinds. The first related to the reception and entertainment of his guests; the second to the defense of his wife and household against them. He began by chartering all the horses, carriages, trucks, and furniture vans in Mount Vernon. There are only two livery establishments there, and he paid them $100 apiece. The opposing candidates flew to him in despair, declaring that they must have some vehicles for election purposes. It made no difference to him. He needed them for his guests.

For the barbecue he bought 200 loaves of bread, a dozen boxes of cake, 180 gallons of whisky, a barrel of Jamaica rum and 40 gallons of brandy. A portion of this he had made into 40 gallons of milk punch. He had an ox slaughtered which, when dressed, weighed 720 pounds. He further, in order that music might lend its sensuous softness to the scene, purchased 100 tin horns. Then he had the large coach house cleared and everything made ready.

To defend his house from his guests he first carefully inspected the arsenal, which consists of four Winchester rifles and two six-shooters. Then he had all the doors and windows barricaded except the back door, which he used for exit and entrance during the gladsome merry-making. He planned that Mrs. Gunning and the maids should take refuge in the tower, which is a rectangular observatory on the top of the country house, and which overlooks the scene. Not satisfied with this he mobilized his troops by organizing a pitchfork brigade. For three hours on Sunday afternoon he had six of his men, three of them Germans, who had served in the German Army, and one of them a Hungarian of bellicose experience, standing in line in the barnyard armed with pitchforks and learning the pitchfork drill. His coachman was formerly in the Sixteenth Lancers, and fought with them in Zululand. He superintended the drill, and put the pitchforkers through the lancers' manual of thrust, parry, and the lateral movements until Mr. Gunning was satisfied with their proficiency.

The only cloud that marred the preparations was the sudden discovery on Sunday evening at dinner time that nobody knew how to barbecue an ox. Nothing dismayed,

Mr. Gunning undertook it. He always arrays himself in evening dress for dining, and consequently he wore evening dress when the difficulty was announced. He put on first a "poucho," which is a fiery red blanket with a black border, and has a hole cut in it to put one's head through. With this over his dress suit and a crush hat on he went out to the barnyard, had an oven built next to the stone fence, and a fire lighted, which soon made a bed of coke coals. Then he caused a pole to be thrust through the ox, which was placed over the coals. All night long the enthusiastic host superintended the roasting. At 9 o'clock yesterday morning the guests began to arrive. The house was barricaded and the wife and maids were safely in the tower.

"I had no fears at first," he said last evening, "but after they got started I was deathly afraid they would set the place on fire." Instead of 200, 300 men appeared. The coach house was crammed. The ox, which was brought in on the shoulders of eight men, received some perfunctory attention, but not much. The barrels of whisky were broached, and the fun began. Norman A. Lawlor, Mr. Gunning's attorney, made a speech of welcome, which was enthusiastically applauded in the interjections of all languages, for all nationalities were represented. They came from the highways and the byways, and they reveled. G. H. Cameron, a real estate dealer, tried to talk, but created little interest. The liquor question was the absorbing topic of discussion. Whisky flowed in rivers. They gulped it down from dippers, buckets, and pans. The more they gulped the more they yelled. Every man who thought he could sing tried to. The common ambition was to make a noise. When the tin horns were passed around the roof began to loosen. Indignant artists overlooked in the distribution raided the pan house and converted the milk pans into drums, which they hammered with clubs. They stamped and beat the sides of the barns till the noise was deafening. Mr. Gunning superintended everything with placid dignity, modestly declining to make a speech.

By 11:30 200 of the 300 were wildly, insanely drunk. They would wander off and fall down on their backs and yell to high heaven because they couldn't do anything else. Inside the coach house pandemonium reigned. A group of Italians in one corner were the ugliest and fell to fighting. Mr. Gunning jumped into the fight, broke his whip over the head of one of his guests and knocked the other down. A second fight started soon afterward, and he stopped that by seizing one of the contestants by the ears and locking him up in a box stall. The outlook had become so threatening that several appealed to him to adjourn the happy gathering, and he finally consented. One hundred men, more or less sober, then began to load 200 men more or less drunk into wagons. Finally all were loaded in, and the procession of 30 vans started for town yelling, fighting, blowing horns, and beating pans. Mr. Gunning then put a violet in his buttonhole and informed his wife and the maids that they might come down. Fearing to go himself he sent his secretary to report proceedings in Mount Vernon.

Mount Vernon was prepared. Its doors were closed and its shutters up. Five minutes after the procession of wagons arrived and dumped its load on the open space next to the station there were only six fights visible from the window of Dr. Casey's office. Five minutes later only one fight was visible, but everybody was in it. Noses were punched, cheeks hammered, and eyes blackened, everybody yelling like an Indian. The good citizens backed up the constables and hustled the fighters to the lockup, but it had only four cells. If any two men were put in a cell the lockup was endangered, to say nothing of the men. Consequently no more than four could be taken there and the fight wore itself out. Nobody was seriously hurt, however, for there were no weapons and all the fighters were too drunk to do much injury. "A regular Donnybrook Fair, you know," said Mr. Gunning mildly. "Oh! It was no end of fun."

In his flower-hung residence the host last evening awaited the return of his secretary.

"Do you really think, Hellmann," he asked, "that it will be safe for Mrs. Gunning or myself to go to town for a few days?"

"Safe!" said Hellmann. "Why, you're the most popular man in the county. They'd take the horses from your carriages and drag it themselves to honor you."

Mr. Gunning smiled a bland smile and was ease.

March 30, 1887

Barbecued Eggplant and Pine Nut Appetizer

Yield: 8 servings

2 medium eggplants

2 tomatoes

⅓ cup fresh lemon juice

1½ teaspoons salt

Freshly ground black pepper to taste

2 cloves garlic, finely chopped

½ cup olive oil

¼ cup pine nuts

¼ cup finely chopped scallions, including
   green part

3 tablespoons chopped fresh parsley

Small squares of pumpernickel or
   flat bread

1.　Prick eggplants all over with a fork and place over hot coals on a barbecue grill, turning frequently until all sides are scorched. A skewer inserted through each eggplant makes turning easier.

2.　Wrap eggplants in foil and cook over coals until soft. Spear tomatoes on a skewer or fork, and cook over coals until skins wrinkle.

3.　Peel eggplants and tomatoes and place in a bowl. Mash with a fork or potato masher.

4.　Beat in lemon juice, salt, pepper, garlic, oil and pine nuts. Chill. Sprinkle with scallions and parsley and serve with the pumpernickel squares or flat bread.

July 14, 1972: From "Weekend Cookout: Grilled Eggplants"

Piquant, Savory Corn Fritters
with Sautéed Vegetables

Time: 1 hour   **Yield:** 8 appetizer servings

3 ears fresh corn, shucked and kernels
    cut off cobs (1 cup)
1 cup all-purpose flour
2 teaspoons baking powder
½ teaspoon salt, plus more for seasoning
¾ cup soda water
Tabasco sauce to taste
¼ teaspoon freshly ground black pepper,
    plus more for seasoning to taste
2 cups green beans, trimmed
3 ears fresh corn in husks
2 tablespoons olive oil
2 ounces smoked bacon, diced

1½ cups okra
1 cup chopped onions (about ½ large onion)
1 teaspoon fresh thyme leaves
2 large tomatoes, peeled, seeded and
    diced
1 tablespoon minced garlic
2 tablespoons red wine vinegar
2 tablespoons butter
1 tablespoon chopped fresh tarragon
1½ quarts vegetable oil
3 scallions, including green part, chopped

1. In a bowl, combine 1 cup of corn kernels, flour, baking powder, ½ teaspoon salt and soda water. Stir to blend. Add Tabasco sauce and black pepper. Stir, and set batter aside.

2. Blanch green beans in boiling water. Chill.

3. Place 3 ears of corn (in husks) on a preheated barbecue grill, and cook, turning periodically, for 10 minutes. Let cool; then, shuck corn, remove kernels and set aside.

4. Place a large sauté pan over medium-high heat. Add 1 tablespoon of olive oil and bacon. Cook for 1 minute, stirring. Add okra. Cook, stirring, for 1 minute. Add onions. Stir. Add thyme and tomatoes. Add toasted corn, and stir; then, green beans and garlic. Add vinegar. Stir and reduce heat to medium. Cook for 3 minutes. Add butter and tarragon, and stir to blend. Salt and pepper to taste. Keep sauce warm.

5. Heat vegetable oil in a wok or deep fryer to 340 degrees. Drop a tablespoon of fritter batter into oil. Cook until golden brown, about 4 to 5 minutes. Remove with a slotted spoon, and drain on paper towels. Repeat with remaining batter.

6. Before serving, add scallions to vegetable sauce and reheat. Distribute over the center of each plate, and surround with fritters.

July 27, 1994: From "Great Cooks: Susan Spicer: Bold Flavor for Sultry Days,"
by BRYAN MILLER with PIERRE FRANEY;
recipe by SUSAN SPICER, Bayona, New Orleans, Louisiana

Grilled Pizza with Italian Cheeses and Bitter Greens

Time: 30 minutes

Yield: 2 to 3 servings as an appetizer, 1 serving as a main course

6 ounces pizza dough (recipe follows)

4 tablespoons extra-virgin olive oil

1 clove garlic, minced

¼ cup shredded bel paese or Italian fontina cheese

3 tablespoons freshly grated Parmigiano-Reggiano cheese

1 ripe medium tomato, peeled, seeded and coarsely chopped

8 arugula leaves (see note)

1. Prepare a hot charcoal fire with coals mounded in center. Punch dough down. Oil a baking sheet, and stretch dough out on it to form a 10- to 12-inch circle ⅛-inch thick.

2. Gently lift dough, using both hands, and drape it onto grill over hottest part of fire. Within a minute, dough will puff slightly, and bottom will stiffen. As soon as grill marks appear on underside, turn dough over with tongs, and move it to edge of grill, away from heat.

3. Quickly brush dough with 1 tablespoon of oil. Scatter garlic over dough. Sprinkle on cheeses, followed by tomato. Arrange arugula leaves on top. Drizzle with remaining 3 tablespoons oil.

4. Slide pizza back over coals. Cook pizza, rotating frequently, for 30 to 60 seconds, or until bottom is slightly charred and cheeses bubble. Serve at once.

NOTE: Watercress, shredded radicchio or sautéed rape (also known as broccoli rape) can be substituted for the arugula.

Pizza Dough

Time: About 17 minutes, plus 2 hours for rising
Yield: Enough dough for 4 pizzas

1 envelope active dry yeast or 1 cake
   yeast
1 teaspoon sugar
1 cup warm water
2¼ teaspoons kosher salt

¼ cup johnnycake meal (see note)
3 tablespoons whole wheat flour
1 tablespoon extra virgin olive oil, plus oil
   for greasing and brushing
2½ to 3 cups unbleached white flour

1. In a bowl dissolve yeast and sugar in water. After 5 minutes, stir in salt, johnnycake meal, whole wheat flour and oil. Gradually stir in enough white flour to form a soft but not sticky dough. Knead until smooth. (Dough can also be made in a food processor.)
2. Place dough in an oiled bowl, brush top with oil and cover with plastic wrap. Let dough rise in a warm place for 1 to 2 hours or until doubled in bulk. Punch dough down.
3. Let dough rise again for 40 minutes or until doubled in bulk. Punch down. If dough is sticky, knead in a little more flour.

NOTE: Johnnycake meal is made from stone-ground white-cap flint corn. It can be ordered online from www.graysgristmill.com. Or use another type of stone-ground cornmeal.

July 19, 1989: STEVEN RAICHLEN;
adapted from Al Forno, Providence, Rhode Island

Self-Opening Grilled Clams

Of all the grilling gurus in my life, from my fire-happy mother (who thinks nothing of grilling lamb chops in January) to the big-time grilling maven Waldy Malouf (with whom I wrote a cookbook), the grill master who made the deepest impression was my childhood pediatrician, Dr. Arthur Ruby.

Dr. Ruby was a close family friend and partner in gustatory delights. In winter he brought over pots of gelatinous *p'tcha* (stewed calves' feet) that we ate with challah to sop up the shimmering, garlicky broth.

Summertime meant weekends at the Rubys' second home in Cold Spring, New York, where Dr. Ruby had a stone grill built into the patio.

Our Saturday-night dinner menu never varied. After nibbling on baked brie strewn with canned fried onions, there were always clams, grilled until their pink bellies were steaming hot and slightly smoky, but still raw, with a crisp bite and soft center.

Then, Dr. Ruby artfully grilled a two-inch-thick porterhouse until it was salt-crunchy and charred on the outside but still bloody within. Fresh corn, tomato salad with basil, and hot bread and butter rounded out the offerings.

Naturally, the star of the meal was that steak. But the flavor I most associate with those hot, hammock-swinging days is that of briny, smoky clams.

Dr. Ruby had a particular way of preparing them. He would scrub them well and shuck each one. Then he would carefully lay the clams directly on the grill, taking care not to spill precious drops of clam juice into the fiery grate. Exactly one minute later, the clams were ready. We slurped them down, burning our fingers on the hot shells.

Although I've craved grilled clams every time I think about the Rubys, I never did try to make them at home. The idea of shucking the clams, then transferring them to the grill always seemed like one step too many. But what if I just threw the clams on the grill grate and let them open as they cooked: Would I lose all the clam juice? If I grabbed them as they opened, would I be able to preserve some, if not all, of their tasty liquor? It was worth trying at least once.

As the grill preheated, I stirred together a quick garlic-cayenne-lemon butter—the kind of savory, zesty, creamy sauce that could make a two-by-four delectable.

Then I stood by the grill, tongs in one hand, bowl in the other, carefully transferring the just-opened clams to the bowl to catch their juices. It took all of five minutes, less time than it took the mosquitoes to find me.

I poured the butter over the clams and sprinkled on some chopped chives, and dived in.

The clams were tender and plump, and there was enough clam juice in the bottom of the bowl to meld with the seasoned butter. They were nothing like what we had at Dr. Ruby's, with one tactile exception. The shells burned my fingers as I scooped them up. But caught up in the garlicky whirl, I couldn't have cared less.

Grilled Clams with Lemon-Cayenne Butter

Yield: 2 servings

1 large clove garlic, minced

Large pinch kosher salt, more to taste

4 tablespoons (½ stick) unsalted
   butter, melted

2 teaspoons fresh lemon juice, more
   to taste

Pinch cayenne pepper

2 dozen littleneck clams, scrubbed

Chopped fresh chives for serving

1. Using a mortar and pestle, or on a cutting board using flat part of a knife, mash together garlic and salt until a paste forms. Scrape paste into a small bowl and stir in butter, lemon juice and cayenne. Taste and make sure salt and lemon are balanced.

2. Preheat grill. Place clams directly on grill grate or on a large baking pan in a single layer. Cover grill and let clams cook for 2 minutes. Open grill and check clams, using tongs to remove any that have opened, and transfer them to a large bowl. Be careful not to spill the clams' juices when transferring them. Close grill lid and check every 30 seconds, removing clams as they open.

3. Pour lemon-cayenne butter over clam bowl and toss lightly. Serve hot, garnished with chives.

August 26, 2009: MELISSA CLARK

Grilled Clams with Fried Garlic

Time: 15 minutes, plus grill preparation
Yield: 4 appetizer servings; 2 light main-course servings

24 littleneck clams, well scrubbed
¾ cup extra virgin olive oil, plus more to
    brush on clams
Juice of 1 lemon

8 cloves garlic, thinly sliced lengthwise
    (remove any green shoots in center)
½ teaspoon red pepper flakes

1.   Prepare a grill for direct grilling over high heat.

2.   Lightly brush clams on both sides with olive oil. Arrange them on grate, cover and cook until shells pop open, 3 to 6 minutes. (You could grill clams on foil to catch juices.)

3.   Pour lemon juice into a baking dish large enough to hold clams in one layer. Transfer clams to dish with tongs, trying not to spill their juices.

4.   Heat ¾ cup olive oil in a small skillet on the grill. When hot, add garlic and cook until golden brown, 1 to 2 minutes. Add pepper flakes, and stir for 15 seconds. Pour this over clams.

5.   Transfer clams to 4 deep bowls. Whisk juices in baking dish for 1 minute and pour over clams.

June 28, 2011: From "For These Chefs, Even Fire Can Be Improved,"
by STEVEN RAICHLEN; adapted from Etxebarri, Axpe, Spain

When the Park Is Your Kitchen

To touch-football players, the park grill may be an obstacle or, at best, a goal post. But to us, it is one of the country's great gestures of civic generosity. Like a bus shelter in a downpour, the park grill makes you glad to pay taxes. Here in this beautiful place, it seems to say, is your own personal kitchen. Entertain!

Park grills—those sturdy steel fireboxes fixed to poles—are widespread. We have seen the same nearly identical park grill on the beaches of San Diego Bay, at Interstate rest areas in Tennessee and on the shore of Wolfe's Pond Park on Staten Island.

From manufacturer to manufacturer (there are at least three in the United States today), the two-part design of the park grill consists of a heavy steel-plate firebox, open at the top and at the front, and an adjustable grate with a handle at each side that can be positioned at three heights above the coals. Two steel brackets at the front edge of the grill prevent anyone from walking off with the grate.

The grill is a homely appliance, but whether brand new or—more likely—coated with a fine layer of rust, this utilitarian icon is likely to see decades of use and weather before it must be replaced.

The best and worst feature of a New York City park grill is its location.

"Park grills are fine, but they become victims of their own popularity," said Henry J. Stern, who was the parks commissioner from 1983 to 2001. "Parks don't take reservations, so who gets the grill? And do they get to use it all day? An hour at a time? There's no system."

The Parks and Recreation Department reports a total of 370 grills in the five boroughs—the Bronx having the most at 200, Manhattan the fewest at 25. With eight million people in the city, we calculate one measly grill for every 21,621.6 New Yorkers. Not surprisingly, an informal survey of park-grillers in Manhattan showed that if you want to use a city-owned grill on a sunny summer weekend, you had better be an early riser. Possession is apparently ten-tenths of the law in city parks.

"I got here at 7 a.m., and there were people here already," said Bernadette Smith, 53, a nurse and cooking-class veteran. It was 4:30 p.m. on a warm Saturday in Thomas Jefferson Park in East Harlem, and Ms. Smith was setting three picnic tables and preparing three grills for her father's ninetieth-birthday party.

She had stood guard all morning and much of the afternoon beside her grills, but had paid a neighbor to watch them during the middle of the day, while she prepared the rest of the meal at her apartment.

On another day, the 12 grills in the East River Park between Eighth Street and Tenth Street had been claimed by 8 a.m. Rico Colon, 33, a former chef's assistant, had arrived in the park at 5 in the morning and secured three tables and the three grills on which he planned to cook a menu of pork chops, chicken, steak, kebabs and chicken wings for his nephew's second-birthday party that afternoon. Because he expected more than 30 family members and friends, he had supplemented the park grills with his own.

Our first grilling excursion of the year was Prospect Park in Brooklyn, within view of the band shell, shaded by a grove of elms. After sizing up our site, we designed a simple three-course menu for six, taking into account the standard park grill's cooking area (14 by 18 inches) and features (three rack levels). And because this kind of effort is as much about packing as it is about cooking, our menu was designed to minimize the material and equipment we would have to haul in and out of the park.

By the time the fire gets going, the guests are usually starving, so we knew we wanted a quick-grilling appetizer (see Ginger and Chili Grilled Shrimp, page 30). At home, we had marinated peeled shrimp for an hour in a simple tart and spicy marinade of buttermilk, minced jalapeño and grated ginger, then threaded the shrimp and cubes of fresh mango onto wooden skewers, which we had soaked in water for 10 minutes, so they would not ignite on the grill. We packed the skewers in a gallon-size freezer bag to transport to the site.

The entree, we reasoned, should be as easy as hamburgers (or even easier), but with zing. And the simplest protein we know is our grandmother's marinated flank steak—a recipe whose source she has long forgotten, but which we like to think was inspired by her childhood in Japan and her golden years in the South: pour a half-cup of bourbon, a half-cup of soy sauce (not the reduced-sodium "junk," she advises) and a half-cup of water into a freezer bag, add the steak, seal shut and marinate for two hours in the fridge. She broils it in the oven. We would grill it outdoors. (See recipe on page 83.)

We loaded the cooler and a bag of the essentials: matches, tongs, a sturdy spatula, oven mitt, garbage bags, paper towels, a cutting board and a scouring sponge. And a 15-pound bag of easy-lighting charcoal.

We placed about 8 to 10 pounds of charcoal briquettes in the left corner of the grill, set the pile ablaze and refitted the grate at its lowest setting to sterilize the grill.

In midsummer, the grates of most park grills are nicely seasoned from use and require only a brushing with cooking oil. If we encounter some surface rust, we polish it off with the sponge, then swab it with a damp paper towel.

After nearly 15 minutes, the flames had subsided, and we pulled the grate forward again to distribute the briquettes to give a high, hot area on the left about three deep and a lower, not-as-hot area only one coal deep. We set two hobo packs (see recipe, page 274) side by side on the low coals and placed a few coals from the high side around and between the packs.

We replaced the grate and brushed it with olive oil, then grilled the shrimp in batches on the high heat for between four and six minutes on each side, until they were pink, opaque and striped with a few picture-perfect grill marks.

We speared a wedge of lime at the end of each skewer, handed one to each guest and set the flank steak down on the hottest part of the grill.

As the hobo packs steamed away and the steak sizzled, the guests took to the shrimp skewers like candy. The peppery, lightly charred bits of shrimp worked nicely with the fruity, tropical ginger and mango, and it made a truly portable dish—no plates or utensils were necessary, only paper towels.

Just before the steak went on, we added a few hickory chips to the coals to boost the aromatic quality of the smoke and chase off the faint petroleum flavor of easy-lighting charcoal briquettes. The flank had browned beautifully on both sides by the time the hobo packs were ready to come off the coals.

We pulled the steak out and then coordinated retrieving the hobo packs. While one person carefully removed the hot grill grate, another lifted the packs out of the coals with a stout grilling spatula and tongs—both of which are indispensable in this setting. We put the foil packs on the picnic table and allowed them to cool for a moment while we sliced the steak.

We cut a slit into the top of the still-steaming hobo packs and assembled the plates with slices of steak, the vegetables dressed with spoonfuls of its mustardy braise and a simple green salad we had made earlier.

One hobo pack emerged a shade al dente, but the other had cooked perfectly through; both had an impressively three-dimensional flavor for such a primitive oven.

As long as the grill was still hot, we thought we would try grilling some white peaches and plums we had brought along for dessert. We cut each into halves, removed the pits, then allowed the cut surfaces to air-dry for a few minutes to increase their browning potential.

We placed the fruit, cut sides down, on the greasiest part of the grill for about 5 to 10 minutes, until the halves visibly softened at the edges and began to hiss. Then we flipped them, moving them to the edge of the grill, allowing them to warm on their skins until we were ready.

About 20 minutes later, they had softened into a puddinglike cup of grilled peach nectar, with a savory note from all the meats that had gone before.

To our minds, the park grill experiences were an unqualified success. There were a few hitches: the time we forgot the olive oil for brushing the grill was annoying; the time we brought too little charcoal even more so. But we have fired up many park grills, in a variety of locations, and found that it is hard to beat the vaguely Thoreau-like thrill of cooking with an acre of elbow room.

Ginger and Chili Grilled Shrimp

Time: 15 minutes, plus 1 hour's marinating

Yield: 6 servings

½ cup low-fat buttermilk

1 tablespoon grated fresh ginger

2 jalapeños, minced

2 cloves garlic, crushed

1 teaspoon kosher salt

½ teaspoon freshly ground black pepper

18 jumbo shrimp (about 1¼ pounds), peeled and deveined, tails left on

2 ripe mangos, peeled, seeded and cut into 1-inch dice

1 small lime, cut into 6 wedges.

1. Pour buttermilk into medium bowl, and add ginger, jalapeños, garlic, salt and pepper. Whisk to combine. Add shrimp, and toss thoroughly with a wooden spoon to coat. Marinate 1 hour in refrigerator.

2. Soak 6 wooden skewers in water for 10 minutes. Thread 3 shrimp and 2 pieces of mango onto each skewer, alternating shrimp and mango.

3. Prepare a fire in the grill. When flames have subsided and coals are glowing, grill shrimp 4 to 6 minutes on each side, until shrimp are opaque. Serve each skewer with a wedge of lime.

June 30, 2004: MATT LEE and TED LEE

Shrimp Mojo de Ajo

Yield: 4 servings

For the marinade

2 tablespoons annatto (achiote) seeds

3 tablespoons black peppercorns

3 cloves garlic, peeled

2 allspice berries

2 serrano chilies, trimmed

1 small bunch fresh cilantro

¼ cup fresh orange juice

¼ cup fresh lemon juice

½ cup white vinegar

For the salsa

4 tomatoes, peeled, seeded and diced

6 scallions, including green and white parts, diced

1 tablespoon sugar

1 tablespoon grated orange zest

2 tablespoons fresh lemon juice

1 serrano chili (or ½ jalapeño), trimmed, with seeds

1 tablespoon salt

For the shrimp and avocado

8 jumbo shrimp (or 24 medium shrimp), peeled and deveined, if desired

1 large ripe avocado

1. Soak annatto seeds in 1 cup water for 1 hour. Drain seeds, discarding water.

2. Build and light a medium-sized charcoal fire in a barbecue, or preheat broiler.

3. Place peppercorns, soaked annatto seeds, garlic, allspice berries, chilies and cilantro in a food processor fitted with a steel blade. Add orange juice and pulse until mixture is coarsely chopped. Add remaining marinade ingredients and process until mixed.

4. To make salsa, place all ingredients except the salt in a food processor fitted with a steel blade and pulse until puréed. Taste for seasoning, then add plenty of salt to taste.

5. Set grill about 3 inches above coals.

6. Thread two jumbo shrimp on each of four bamboo skewers. Dip shrimp in achiote marinade, then place on grill until shrimp are firm to touch and slightly darkened on outside—this should take no longer than 5 minutes. Watch shrimp carefully, and turn them once during cooking. If you use smaller shrimp, thread an equal number on skewers and dip them in the marinade.

7. While shrimp are cooking, peel, pit and quarter avocado lengthwise. Cut quarters lengthwise into thin slices.

8. To serve, place equal amounts of salsa in center of four dinner plates. Fan out avocado slices in center of salsa and place skewers of shrimp (or individual shrimp) on top.

September 3, 1989: "Food: Beyond the Burrito,"
by SUSAN HERRMANN LOOMIS;
adapted from DAVID SCHY, formerly of Hat Dance, Chicago, Illinois

French Thoughts on U.S. Barbecue

I have never believed that old canard about "no accounting for taste." A preponderant liking for one food or another is almost invariably traceable to childhood patterns or the "learned" taste of adulthood. What has long fascinated me, however, are the marked differences in taste at the international level.

Take the obvious example like outdoor grilling and barbecuing, the "official" season for which begins on Memorial Day. In the United States, the national American barbecue sauce consists of a dark red blend of tomato ketchup, Worcestershire sauce and brown sugar with variations that include vinegar, hot pepper and butter. Europeans generally regard this combination as (choose one) vulgar, naive, unsophisticated, barbaric, amusing.

We were recently feasting on an assortment of skewered foods—beef, seafood and kidneys—hot off a charcoal grill, and we were discussing with Charles Chevillot the principles and virtues of grilling and barbecuing. He is a scion of the family that has owned the Hotel de la Poste in Burgundy and is the proprietor of two estimable restaurants in Manhattan, La Petite Ferme and Les Tournebroches, the latter of which specializes in grilled dishes. "The trouble with the ketchup sauce," he said with a pronounced French accent, "is it tends to disguise flavors." He ladled another spoonful of bearnaise sauce on the brochette of kidneys and added, "So much that you can't taste the natural flavor of the foods."

Mr. Chevillot is fairly well known for the purity in taste of several specialties.

When he grills meats or seafood *en brochette*, he does not marinate the foods even briefly. He coats the foods lightly with a neutral oil before adding them to a hot grill, but simply to prevent them from sticking. Salt and pepper are added at the last moment. He prefers white pepper to black pepper since it is less forceful in flavor.

Mr. Chevillot, who is rail-thin and, with his rimless glasses, resembles a Gallic Woodrow Wilson, is a bachelor in his mid-40s. He states that he had rarely grilled anything in his life until he came to this country.

"But that's how I celebrated my becoming an American citizen in 1965," he recalled. "I have an apartment with a backyard in Greenwich Village, and on that day I gave a big party, a cook-out. A lot of people came and we grilled hamburgers and hot dogs."

Thus, for the grilling season, a sampling of foods to be cooked simply, hurriedly over charcoal and served with sauce béarnaise.

Brochette de Rognon de Veau
(Veal Kidney on Skewers)

Yield: 4 servings

2 veal kidneys, trimmed of all fat

8 slices bacon

2 tablespoons peanut, vegetable or
  corn oil

Salt and freshly ground pepper to taste

Sauce Béarnaise (recipe follows)

1. Heat grill.

2. Place kidneys on a flat surface and carefully cut away and discard part but not all of white core that runs down center. Cut kidneys crosswise into cubes. There should be about 48 pieces.

3. Cut bacon into 1½-inch pieces.

4. Arrange kidney pieces on skewers, interlarding each two pieces with a piece of bacon.

5. Place skewered foods in a flat dish and brush all over with oil.

6. Place brochettes on grill and cook about 3 to 4 minutes on one side. Sprinkle all over with salt and pepper to taste and turn brochettes to cook on other side, about 3 to 4 minutes. Serve immediately with béarnaise sauce.

Sauce Béarnaise

Yield: About 1 cup

½ pound (2 sticks) butter

2 tablespoons finely chopped shallots

2 tablespoons tarragon vinegar

1 teaspoon crushed peppercorns

1 teaspoon dried tarragon

2 egg yolks

1. Put butter in a small, heavy saucepan and let it melt slowly. A film will rise to top. Skim off this film carefully.

2. Heat shallots, vinegar, peppercorns and tarragon in another small, heavy saucepan and cook until all liquid evaporates. Remove from heat and let saucepan cool slightly.

3. Add egg yolks and 1 tablespoon cold water to shallots.

4. Return saucepan to stove and, using very low heat, stir yolk mixture vigorously. Do not overheat or eggs will curdle. Remove saucepan from heat and place it on a cold surface. Add melted butter, ladle by ladle, stirring rapidly. Do not add it too rapidly.

Brochettes de Fruits de Mer (Seafood on Skewers)

Yield: 4 servings

12 jumbo shrimp, peeled and deveined

8 large sea scallops

16 (1½-inch) cubes monkfish (about
½ pound)

16 (1½-inch) cubes swordfish (about
½ pound)

2 tablespoons peanut, vegetable or
corn oil

Salt and freshly ground pepper to taste

Sauce Béarnaise (page 33)

1. Heat grill.

2. On each of four metal skewers, arrange alternately three shrimp, two scallops, four pieces of monkfish and four pieces of swordfish.

3. Place skewered foods in a flat dish and brush all over with oil.

4. Place brochettes on grill and cook about 4 to 5 minutes on one side. Sprinkle all over with salt and pepper to taste. Turn skewers and cook about 4 to 5 minutes on other side. Turn often as necessary, but take care not to overcook. Serve immediately with béarnaise sauce.

May 23, 1979: CRAIG CLAIBORNE

Diners and Dinner, Close to the Flame

Some American cooks believe that grilling is the national pastime. But it's also a passion in Korea and Japan, where cooks enjoy a particularly cozy relationship with the fire.

In Korean restaurants the grill is in the middle of the table, where everyone can reach it.

"Cooking together and serving other people are part of the barbecue experience," said Max Han, who runs an online guide to Korean-American culture at newyorkseoul.com. "It's one of the ways we Koreans feel *jeong*, a bonding, a connection that's very important in our culture."

More and more, though, New Yorkers are seeing takes on a Japanese version of grilling, *robatayaki* (or *robata* for short), in refined but rustic Japanese restaurants where food is cooked in front of the customer and served with excruciating simplicity.

Robatas ("ro" means hearth, or fireplace) are descended from simple beach restaurants where fishermen cooked their catch over an open fire, with only an oar as a cooking utensil. (Robata chefs still use a wooden paddle to pass food to customers.)

Traditional robatas have a horseshoe-shaped bar wrapped around a hearth; ingredients like whole fish, chunks of prime meat, shiny green shishito peppers, corn on the cob and enokitake mushrooms are set on ice, and customers pick. Chefs thread the food onto long metal skewers using delicate techniques like the stitch and the fan.

"A robata is a place of great ceremony and also great noise," said Steven Raichlen, a grilling expert who has traveled widely in Japan, referring to the boisterous shouting of orders between the cook and the waiters.

While Japanese grilling is preoccupied with pristine ingredients and ever-fattier beef, Korean grilling is dedicated to garlicky, spicy marinades and smoky flavor. Charcoal is considered a necessity for good grilling in both countries, something to which American grill snobs can relate.

Kom Tang Soot Bul in Midtown is one of the few Korean restaurants using only wood charcoal in table grills. (Most have switched to gas, or gas and ceramic charcoal.)

Kom Tang and most other restaurants in New York that grill with charcoal use the American hardwood variety. But chefs who have cooked with imported Japanese *bincho-tan* are fascinated by it. Made from oak, it is so hard it rings when you knock two pieces together. Mr. Raichlen said it burns at 1,200 degrees while American charcoal burns at about 800.

"There is literally no smoke" from the *bincho-tan*, said Scott Ubert of Ono. "It's hotter and adds no flavor to the food. It's totally different from what we think of as grilling."

Mr. Raichlen said the absence of smoke flavor and the clean quality of the food are prized in Japanese cooking. To Americans used to sauces, spice rubs and wood smoke, high-end Japanese grilled food can seem a little plain. Served with just salt, pepper and hot pepper mix (*shichimi*)—with an occasional lemon wedge for a gamy piece like liver or gizzard—the food must speak for itself. New York chefs avoid this by devising inauthentic but appetizing dipping sauces.

Japanese grilling is hardly new to the United States. Manhattan, especially the East Village, has long been well stocked with cheap and raucous *yakitori* places that specialize in skewers and beer. But newer restaurants that focus on grilled organic chicken and imported Japanese mushrooms are arising, often using the more expensive charcoal.

Small Japanese grills are often designed for skewers: narrow and rectangular so the ends of the bamboo are not exposed to the heat. Americans call such a grill a hibachi, but the Japanese call it a *konro*.

Teppanyaki, introduced by the Benihana restaurants in 1964, is cooked on a griddle called a *teppan*. But that does not qualify as grilling to American cooks, for whom the occasional smoky flare-up when juice and fat drip on the coals is part of the fun.

That's probably why Korean barbecue is already a favorite with New York carnivores: it's experienced through the eyes, nose and fingers, as well as the mouth.

Chicken Yakitori

Time: 1 hour for soaking skewers, plus 45 minutes for preparation and grilling
Yield: 4 to 6 appetizer servings or 4 main course servings

1½ pounds skinless, boneless chicken
 thighs, trimmed of excess fat
1 large bunch scallions, 1 reserved, others
 trimmed and cut into 1½-inch lengths
1 cup soy sauce
¾ cup sugar
½ cup mirin

1 clove garlic, lightly crushed and peeled
1 (¼-inch) slice fresh ginger, lightly
 crushed
1 (½-inch-by-2-inch) strip lemon zest
Vegetable oil to brush on grill
Toasted sesame seeds for garnish.

1. Soak 16 (6-inch) bamboo skewers in cold water for 1 hour, then drain.
2. Rinse chicken under cold water and pat dry with paper towels. Cut into uniform 1½-inch pieces. On each skewer, thread alternating pieces of chicken and scallions, pressing them together. Cover and refrigerate until ready to grill.
3. Lightly crush white part of reserved scallion. Slice green part into thin rings and reserve. In a small saucepan, combine soy sauce, sugar, mirin, scallion white, garlic, ginger and lemon zest. Place over medium heat and bring to boil. Reduce heat and simmer until syrupy, 5 to 10 minutes. Strain into small bowl and cool to room temperature. If desired, reserve some as a dipping sauce.

4. Heat a grill or hibachi. Brush and oil grill rack, and place yakitori on grill so that ends of skewers are not over direct heat. Sear meat by continually turning skewers for about 2 minutes. Baste with sauce and turn occasionally until chicken is cooked, 8 to 10 minutes. When chicken is done it should feel firm and be coated with a shiny glaze.

5. To serve, place skewers on a platter and sprinkle with scallion rings and sesame seeds. If desired, serve reserved sauce in a small bowl as a dipping sauce.

May 4, 2005: JULIA MOSKIN; adapted from How to Grill, *by STEVEN RAICHLEN (Workman, 2001)*

Crisp and Unctuous Pork Belly

Adam Perry Lang, the chef and owner of Daisy May's BBQ in Manhattan, builds flavor whenever possible, and this pork belly calls for a marinade, a bourbon glaze (preferably applied with a bundle of herbs), and a dressing applied directly to the cutting board: you squeeze lemon on the board and add olive oil, chives and pepper, so that the resting slab of pork draws in even more flavor.

Mr. Lang suggests serving slices of the belly in a bun with applesauce and mustard, the latest iteration of the pork bun. It's also good on watercress or arugula, tossed with a sharp dressing.

Mr. Lang drove home one point: Never use a spray bottle to douse flares from dripping fat. Instead, he suggests moving the food to a cooler corner of the grill, or stacking meat so that it's exposed to less heat. "A lot of people fear the flame," Mr. Lang said. "I tell them: Don't. Because when you're cooking on wood the flavor is like nothing else."

Time: 6½ hours, plus at least 12 hours' marinating and 2 hours' resting
Yield: 8 servings

For the marinade
¼ cup extra virgin olive oil
¼ cup fresh lemon juice
¼ cup cider vinegar
10 cloves garlic, halved
2 tablespoons fresh rosemary leaves
2 tablespoons fresh thyme leaves
2 tablespoons sliced serrano chili
2 tablespoons kosher salt
1 tablespoon coarsely ground black
    pepper.

For the pork
1 (4-pound) piece pork belly, skin on
2 tablespoons unsalted butter
¼ cup bourbon
¼ cup packed brown sugar
2 tablespoons roughly chopped fresh flat
    leaf parsley
1 tablespoon cider vinegar
½ teaspoon red pepper flakes
¼ cup extra virgin olive oil
1 tablespoon fresh lemon juice
2 tablespoons chopped fresh chives
Salt and freshly ground pepper to taste

1. In a blender, pulse marinade ingredients until roughly chopped. Transfer to a 1-gallon freezer bag and add pork belly and 1 cup water. Squeeze to remove air, then seal and refrigerate at least 12 hours.

2. When ready to cook, preheat oven to 275 degrees. Place pork in a 13-by-9-inch baking dish with marinade, butter and water to cover. Cover with heavy-duty foil, crimping edges tightly. Braise in oven 5 ½ hours; let rest in pan, covered, 2 hours.

3. Meanwhile, simmer bourbon in a small pan over medium heat until alcohol aroma fades. Stir in brown sugar, parsley, vinegar and pepper flakes. Cover and set aside.

4. Heat a grill. Carefully remove pork from pan and place in a grilling basket. Grill skin side down over medium-low heat for 15 to 20 minutes, until skin is crisp and golden. Remove from heat and brush skin side with one quarter of bourbon glaze, then return to heat, skin side up, for another 5 minutes. Remove pork from heat once more and brush meat side with one quarter of glaze, then return to heat, meat side up, for another 5 minutes. Repeat with remaining glaze on both sides.

5. Dress a cutting board with half the olive oil, lemon juice and chives, and salt and pepper to taste. Place pork skin side up on cutting board and let rest for 10 minutes. Sprinkle with remaining olive oil, lemon juice and chives, and salt and pepper to taste. Cut into 1-by-4-inch pieces and serve.

May 20, 2009: From "Grilling over Wood as a Sweaty, Smoky Sport," by OLIVER SCHWANER-ALBRIGHT; adapted from Serious Barbecue, *by ADAM PERRY LANG (Hyperion, 2009)*

CHAPTER TWO

Burgers

There is nothing more basic to a cookout than burgers, but the world of burgers is much richer than a quarter pound of beef on a bun. The basic rule is if it can be chopped and shaped into a patty, it can be a burger. Pork, lamb, turkey, shrimp, salmon, tuna, even vegetables can be "burger-ized." Rather than relying on the predictable effect of ketchup and mustard, you'll find that capers, roasted peppers, anchovies, onions, garlic, in fact almost any savory ingredient, can be added to the mix to create an ingenious new riff on the burger. Bittman's Beef Tartare Burger (page 44) proves there's new life in the beef burger. Martha Rose Shulman's Portobello Mushroom Cheeseburgers (page 65) demonstrate that you don't need meat to create a burger that satisfies.

The hamburger is as quintessentially American as pasta is Italian or paprika dishes are Hungarian.

Happy Birthday, Hamburger!

No one knows for sure when the hamburger made its debut. *The Oxford English Dictionary* traces the first report of a Hamburg steak, as it was called then, to 1889, which would make this the centennial year of the first official sighting.

Readers of *The Walla Walla* (Wash.) *Union* learned about the hamburger on January 5, 1889, according to the dictionary, in an article that described how patrons at a restaurant in Walla Walla were asked if they would have one of the following: "porkchopbeefsteakhamandeggshamburgsteakorliver."

The Dictionary of American English traces the first mention of the Hamburg steak to 1884 in an article in *The Boston Journal*. If that is correct, we have missed the centennial by five years. But it is also possible that we may have missed it by 153 years: an entry in *American Gastronomy*, written by Louis Szathmary in 1974, says the hamburger's opening performance was recorded as early at 1836 on a Delmonico's menu. In which case we have not only ignored the centennial, we have missed the sesquicentennial by three years.

None of these esteemed publications even deigns to mention three other contenders for the title of inventor of the hamburger: Fletcher Davis in Athens, Texas, sometime before 1904; Frank Menches at the Summit (N.Y.) County Fair of 1892 and Louis Lassen of Louis' Lunch in New Haven, Connecticut, in 1900.

Centennial or not, the celebration of the hamburger is in order, especially at a time when the nostalgia craze is sweeping the food business, when comfort foods and diners rather than roasted red pepper purees and temples of haute cuisine set the trend.

It is generally agreed that the Hamburg steak made its way to America from the German city of Hamburg. The city traded with Latvians, Estonians and Finns and adopted the Baltic love of scraped raw beef. Somewhere between its first appearance in an American restaurant and its Hamburg origins, the Hamburg steak was cooked.

In all likelihood Nancy Ross Ryan, writing in the February 6, 1989, issue of *Restaurants & Institutions*, has the most plausible explanation of how it came about. "The hamburger," she wrote, "probably was a case of spontaneous combustion."

The name was not changed to hamburger until sometime around the beginning of the twentieth century when it also acquired its bun. Without its roll it was, and still is, known in pretentious restaurants as chopped steak. Sometime around the turn of century the Salisbury steak made a brief run at unseating the hamburger as the ground beef of choice in this country. The Salisbury steak was named after Dr. J. H. Salisbury, a British physician who prescribed it for its health benefits on a three-times-a-day regimen. A mixture of chopped beef, minced onion, parsley, salt and pepper, it was shaped into ovals and broiled. My only early memories of the Salisbury steak are as a gray, overcooked piece of meat, sunken in library-paste gravy and accompanied by watery mashed potatoes.

By 1921 the fast-food hamburger was well on its way. The White Castle chain, promoting carry-out food, suggested that its customers "Buy 'em by the Sack." And at five cents apiece, people did. Called "the slider," the White Castle version of a hamburger is cooked on a hot griddle over a layer of onions. The steam from the onions cooks the hamburger, which explains their steamed flavor.

"By the 1930's Americans were calling hamburgers 'Wimpy burgers,'" says John Mariani in *The Dictionary of American Food and Drink* (Ticknor & Fields, 1983). Wimpy burgers were inspired, he wrote, "by an insatiable hamburger addict named J. Wellington Wimpy from the Popeye comic strip." In England, Wimpie is a synonym for hamburger.

The next phase in the maturation—some would say degradation—of the hamburger began in the 1950's with the arrival of McDonald's, where one pound of ground beef became 10 patties. Serious hamburger aficionados know that only four hamburgers should be made from a pound of ground beef.

Beyond that there is little agreement on how a hamburger should be made and what should go in it. Unlike classical dishes, like hollandaise sauce, there is no right recipe. Ingredients and cooking methods are intensely personal matters. Ground beef and nothing else says one school. A little cream or an ice cube in the middle to keep it moist, says another.

Salt and pepper after cooking? Chopped raw onions mixed in with the ground beef? There is an advocate for every viewpoint. Topped with ketchup, mayonnaise, pickle, relish, tomato, barbecue sauce, meat sauce, pizza sauce, sautéed onion, American cheese, cheddar cheese, Roquefort, Swiss cheese, wrapped in bacon, dipped in flour or topped with nothing at all. Take your choice.

The late twentieth-century hamburger has also come topped with peanut butter and sprouts, stuffed with carrots and seasoned with curry or cumin. There is no end to the ignominy of the poor thing. Sautéed? Grilled? Broiled? Everyone has a different opinion. Never less than one-and-a-half-inches thick, says one expert. Never more than a quarter-inch thick says another. Made with ground chuck? No. Made with ground sirloin. Charred on the outside, raw in the center. Medium rare all over. Well done. Yes, there are those who prefer their hamburger cooked dry. They like their steaks the same way. And they put ketchup on cottage cheese.

To me the best hamburger is made with six ounces of ground beef that is about 20 percent fat. It is cooked over a charcoal grill, dark brown on the outside and pink everywhere else. If there is a bun, it is fresh and toasted and when the two halves are clapped together, the juice is liable to dribble down on the front of your blouse.

Running a close second to this plain, unadorned burger is one stuffed with soft goat cheese. There are those who would say that stuffing a hamburger with goat cheese is as ignominious as topping it with sprouts.

March 1, 1989: MARIAN BURROS

Beef Tartare Burger

Time: 30 minutes   **Yield:** 4 burgers

1½ pounds fatty sirloin or chuck, cut into
    1-inch chunks

1 shallot, peeled

1 medium clove garlic, peeled

1 tablespoon capers

2 anchovy fillets (optional)

½ cup chopped fresh parsley

½ teaspoon Tabasco sauce, or more
    to taste

2 teaspoons Worcestershire sauce

Salt and pepper to taste

Chopped medium-cooked egg, capers,
    whole anchovies, diced sweet white
    onion, chopped fresh parsley and
    peeled lemon slices for garnish
    (optional)

1.   The heat should be medium-high and grill rack about 4 inches from fire. Put beef, shallot, garlic, capers and anchovies, if using, in a food processor and pulse until coarsely ground—finer than chopped, but not much. Put it into a bowl with parsley, Tabasco sauce and Worcestershire sauce, and sprinkle with salt and pepper. Mix gently, then taste and adjust seasoning. Handling the meat as lightly as possible to avoid compressing it, shape it into 4 or more burgers.

2.   Grill about 3 minutes on each side for rare and another minute per side for each increasing stage of doneness.

3.   Garnish with chopped egg, capers, anchovies, onion, parsley and lemon if desired.

May 25, 2010: "The Minimalist:
For the Grill, Burgers Beyond the Basic,"
by MARK BITTMAN

Broiled Chopped Beefsteak
Scandinavian-Style

The calendar never stops me from cooking outdoors at my home on eastern Long Island. I have been known to wade through a few inches of snow to get to my patio barbecue grill. I recently prepared a quick weekend lunch with some chopped shoulder of beef and herbs. Among the best cuts of beef for grilling or barbecuing is a cut from the shoulder; it has just the right percentage of fat to be moist without being greasy. I never buy ground beef in packages, preferring instead to have a butcher chop it on the spot. That way I know exactly what I am getting. About 1½ pounds of ground shoulder, or round steak, should feed four. I call this recipe Scandinavian-style because of the sauce, which contains a lot of dill.

Yield: 4 servings

1½ pounds fresh chopped lean round steak

1 tablespoon butter

4 ounces mushrooms, thinly sliced

1 tablespoon finely chopped shallots

2 tablespoons red wine vinegar

2 tablespoons capers

½ cup sour cream

Salt and freshly ground pepper to taste

1 tablespoon vegetable oil

2 tablespoons finely chopped fresh dill or cilantro

1. Form 4 hamburgers 3 inches in diameter and about ¾ inch thick. Do not handle them more than necessary or the texture will be ruined.

2. Heat an outdoor grill to high.

3. Meanwhile, heat butter in a skillet. Add mushrooms and cook, stirring, over high heat until lightly browned. Add shallots and cook 15 seconds. Add vinegar and capers and cook and stir briefly. Add sour cream, salt and pepper; bring to a simmer and keep warm.

4. Sprinkle meat with salt and pepper. Brush with oil. Place hamburgers 3 inches from source of heat. Grill meat 3 minutes, then turn and grill for 3 minutes longer or to desired degree of doneness.

5. Transfer hamburgers to warm plates and spoon sauce over them. Sprinkle top with dill and serve.

September 26, 1990: "60-Minute Gourmet,"
by PIERRE FRANEY

Grilled Chili Burger

Yield: 8 servings

2 pounds twice-ground round steak

Salt and freshly ground pepper to taste

1 clove garlic, finely minced

1 teaspoon chili powder, or more to taste

¼ cup bread crumbs

4 teaspoons butter, at room temperature

1. Prepare a charcoal fire. When coals are hot and white ash forms, fire is ready.

2. Place meat in a bowl and add remaining ingredients. Shape into 8 patties.

3. Grill on both sides to desired degree of doneness. Serve on hamburger buns with relishes.

July 4, 1968: "It's the Fourth of the July and That's an Occasion for a Barbecue," by CRAIG CLAIBORNE

In Paris, Burgers Turn Chic

Even if you couldn't be on the Champs-Élysées for Bastille Day on Monday to watch seven parachutists float down in front of President Nicolas Sarkozy, you can still celebrate the greatness of France with a new local tradition.

Eat a hamburger.

Beginning a few years ago but picking up momentum in the past nine months, hamburgers and cheeseburgers have invaded the city. Anywhere tourists are likely to go this summer—in St.-Germain cafes, in fashion-world hangouts, even in restaurants run by three-star chefs—they are likely to find a juicy beef patty, almost invariably on a sesame seed bun.

"It has the taste of the forbidden, the illicit—the subversive, even," said Hélène Samuel, a restaurant consultant here. "Eating with your hands, it's pure regression. Naturally, everyone wants it."

It is a startling turnaround in a country where a chef once sued McDonald's for $2.7 million in damages over a poster that suggested he was dreaming of a Big Mac. Hamburgers were everything that French dining is not: informal, messy, fast and foreign.

But as French chefs have embraced the quintessentially American food, they have also made it their own, incorporating Gallic flourishes like cornichons, fleur de sel and fresh thyme. These attempts to translate the burger, or maybe even improve it, strongly suggest that it is here to stay.

"It's not just a fad," said Frédérick Grasser-Hermé, who, as consulting chef at the Champs-Élysées boîte Black Calvados, developed a burger made with wagyu beef and seasoned with what she calls a black ketchup of blackberries and black currants. "It's more than that. The burger has become gastronomic."

Some of the most celebrated chefs in the city have taken up the challenge. Yannick Alléno, who earned a third Michelin star in 2007 for his precise, rarefied cuisine at Le Meurice, serves a thick, succulent hamburger at his casual restaurant, Le Dali. Mr. Alléno's baker, Frédéric Lalos, a winner of one of the country's fiercest cooking competitions, makes the buns. With smoked bacon, lettuce, dill pickles, mustard, mayonnaise and fries, the burger at Le Dali costs 35 euros, about $56.

Romain Corbière, the chef at Alain Ducasse's restaurant Le Relais du Parc, in a Norman-style manor near Trocadéro, cooks a seasonal burger *à la plancha*. This summer Mr. Corbière, a veteran of Mr. Ducasse's Louis XV in Monaco, is substituting a shrimp and squid patty for the beef burger he served in cooler weather.

L'Atelier de Joël Robuchon offers Le Burger, actually two small burgers topped with slabs of foie gras of almost equal size.

The only thing more surprising than the about-face in chefs' attitudes may be the enthusiasm with which their patrons have devoured these haute burgers.

"I didn't think we would sell so many," said Sonia Ezgulian, guest chef at Café Salle Pleyel, which Ms. Samuel opened last fall in an airy, modernist space inside one of Paris's most prestigious concert halls.

On some days, as many as a third of her customers order the burger, which is offered alongside Mediterranean-inspired dishes like sea bass with fennel confit and pistachios. "Sometimes we say we have no more," she said. "It's just too much."

When a new guest chef replaces Ms. Ezgulian at the end of August, he will keep the burger on the menu. It's in his contract.

It is not as if hamburgers were unknown in Paris. American restaurants here like Joe Allen have long served them. Ms. Grasser-Hermé ate her first in 1961 at the American Legion, 11 years before McDonald's unveiled its golden arches in France. But with few exceptions the local burgers were flat, overcooked and shunned even by American expatriates.

Other forms of ground or chopped beef have been enjoyed here for years as well. Butchers sell kilos of ground meat destined to become steak haché, a pan-seared patty made with lean meat, pressed into an oval, and served without a bun.

And while steak tartare shows up on practically every brasserie menu, chefs now recognize that a hamburger is not simply six ounces of chopped lean beef grilled until crusty.

"No, that would be an error," said Ms. Grasser-Hermé.

"A hamburger is the architecture of taste par excellence," she explained. "The meat needs to be a mix of fatty and lean. Not raw, not rare. It must be medium rare. At the same time the bread needs to be smooth, tepid, toasted on the sesame side. I like to brush the soft side with butter. There needs to be a crispy chiffonade of iceberg lettuce. Everything plays a role."

In developing the Salle Pleyel burger, Ms. Samuel and Ms. Ezgulian felt the weight of tradition. "We're a little terrified of making a mistake," said Ms. Samuel. "We cling to things like the soft buns, sweet-and-sour pickles, onions, tomatoes, cheese. We need these guideposts because we don't have the history, the context. Otherwise, for us, it's not a burger. It's a hot sandwich."

Yet Ms. Ezgulian has taken some liberties. The current version of her burger is a riff on steak tartare. She's kneaded a mixture of chopped sun-dried tomatoes and tangy cornichons and capers into the ground meat. Parmesan shavings stand in for the usual Cheddar.

Céline Parrenin, a co-owner of Coco & Co., a two-level place devoted to eggs that opened in St.-Germain last year, didn't feel any such compunction when she and her business partner, Franklin Reinhard, invented the Cocotte Burger. The Cheddar cheeseburger, with pine nuts and thyme mixed into the meat, sits on a toasted whole-wheat English muffin pedestal. In a wink at the restaurant's egg theme and recalling the time-honored steak à cheval, a fried egg is placed on top.

All the chefs are making hamburgers for the first time, and they are uncertain about the exact cuts of beef they are using. Mr. Alléno, for example, simply relies on his butcher, Yves-Marie Le Bourdonnec, whose shop, Le Couteau d'Argent, is in the Paris suburb Asnières.

For Mr. Alléno's burgers, Mr. Le Bourdonnec delivers a mix of chuck and beef rib. But the butcher thinks the American T-bone steak is an ideal cut. The T-bone does not exist in France, but to make his point, Mr. Le Bourdonnec made his own. He combined a piece of filet, which is tender but less flavorful, with a piece of contrefilet, which is marbled and tasty, but slightly less tender.

Using a long, razor-sharp knife, he sliced the meat into quarter-inch dice, chopped it fine with a cleaver and shaped it into patties, to be cooked rare in a hot skillet filmed with olive oil. No bun, no pickles, no cheese, no special sauce; only a few grains of fleur de sel.

"What you have is texture and the flavor of meat," he said. "No artifice."

"That's not a burger, Papa," pointed out his 13-year-old son, Paul. "There's no bread."

How did the dripping, juicy hamburger come to be one of the signature dishes of Paris? For one thing, expatriate French chefs reinventing American classics in the United States made it safe for their countrymen to try it back home.

"I didn't have this burger culture," said Ms. Samuel. "A hamburger, what's that? I didn't get it. Then I tasted it at DB Bistro Moderne," she said, speaking of Daniel Boulud's restaurant in Midtown Manhattan. "If Daniel hadn't done it, maybe I wouldn't have either. He helped me understand."

Mr. Corbière grew up with burgers, but he didn't think of putting one on the Relais du Parc menu until he tasted Laurent Tourondel's Black Angus burger at BLT Market in New York last October.

Both Mr. Tourondel and Mr. Boulud laughed when they were told that they had helped the hamburger conquer Paris.

"I think it's shocking, but at the same time the French are realizing that a burger is real food, it's good," said Mr. Boulud.

Mr. Tourondel grew up in a small town where, he said "nobody ever saw a burger until 10 years ago. Everybody was against it, but everybody goes to eat it."

Whether the interpretations are classical or whimsical, Americans would probably recognize most of the burgers in Paris. They might be flummoxed, however, by the etiquette associated with eating them.

Ketchup does not automatically come with a burger. If requested, it may appear in a porcelain bowl. At the Café Salle Pleyel, servers do produce a ketchup bottle on demand. At lunch there one recent day, a businessman shook the ketchup onto his plate, then, taking a knife in his right hand, spread the condiment onto a forkful of hamburger in his left hand before lifting it to his mouth.

Alicia Fontanier, the co-owner and chef at the tiny gourmet bar Ferdi on the rue du Mont-Thabor, laments that many of her customers insist on using silverware. Ms. Fontanier is the sister of Maria Luisa Poumaillou, who owns a couple of boutiques down the street, and many of the socialites, expatriate international types and fashionistas who shop there invariably stop in for her burger, the Mac Ferdi, and guarapita de parchita, a potent drink of cachaça and passion fruit juice.

"Eating with your hands is part of the pleasure," Ms. Fontanier said, seated in a dining room decorated chiefly with her 15-year-old son's childhood toy collection. "But nine out of 10 people use knife and fork. I'm happy not to see it. I'm in the kitchen."

At Floors, a three-story diner in a former printing shop near Sacré-Coeur that features custom burgers, Emil Lager, a waiter, said that many of the diners seem self-conscious about ordering.

"Another thing I've noticed is that the muscled guys order the boeuf double with bacon, egg and fries, and a Diet Coke," he said. "Then they share a cheesecake. They don't want to gain weight."

Also, he explained, Parisians don't really understand about drinking a milkshake with the burger. They order it as dessert.

Café Salle Pleyel Burger

Time: 45 minutes   **Yield:** 4 servings

1 medium red onion, finely chopped

1 tablespoon unsalted butter

1 teaspoon ground coriander

Salt and freshly ground black pepper

⅓ cup oil-packed, sun-dried tomatoes
    (2½ ounces), drained and chopped

¼ cup drained capers (1½ ounces)

6 cornichons

¼ cup fresh tarragon leaves

½ cup fresh flatleaf parsley leaves

1½ pounds ground sirloin, chuck or mix

1 tablespoon olive oil

2 ounces Parmesan cheese, thinly sliced
    with a vegetable peeler

4 large sesame-seed hamburger buns

2 dill pickles, thinly sliced lengthwise
    with a vegetable peeler

1. In a small saucepan, combine red onion with butter, coriander and 1 cup water and season with salt and pepper. Bring to a boil, then simmer over medium heat, stirring occasionally, until mixture is reduced to ½ cup, about 30 minutes.

2. Meanwhile, in a small food processor, pulse sun-dried tomatoes with capers, cornichons, tarragon and parsley until finely chopped.

3. In a medium bowl, lightly mix meat with sun-dried tomato mixture and season with pepper. Shape meat into 4 patties about ¾-inch thick.

4. Heat olive oil in a large cast-iron skillet over medium-high heat until just smoking. Add burgers and cook for about 2 minutes on each side for rare or 3 minutes for medium rare. Transfer burgers to a platter and top with Parmesan. Lightly toast buns. Spread a thin layer of onion jam on bottom buns. Top with pickle slices and burgers. Cover with top buns and serve.

July 16, 2008: "In Paris, Burgers Turn Chic,"
by JANE SIGAL; adapted from SONIA EZGULIAN

Balkan Burgers
(Pljeskavica)

Americans might think themselves masters of the all-beef patty, and Germans may claim bragging rights for its point of origin. But there is no burger passion greater than the one for *pljeskavica*.

Pronounced PLYESS-ka-vee-tsa, this burger as wide as a birthday cake is beloved in Serbia, Croatia, Bosnia and Herzegovina, Slovenia and Montenegro; and more recently in Italy, Germany, Chicago as well as Queens.

Pljeskavica are formed from ground meat and minced onion, pounded thin, then grilled on both sides to a smoky brown. The word *pljeskavica* comes from *pljesak*, a regional word for clapping the hands, the motion used to press the burger into a thin round.

They were originally served flopped onto a plate, but as the American burger assumed global dominance, it became standard to sandwich pljeskavica between the two halves of a fluffy, spongy pita-style bread called *lepinja*.

Pljeskavica passion runs highest in Leskovac, the Serbian city considered the cradle of the dish. Each September, the town holds a weeklong *rostiljijada*, a grilling festival attended by hundreds of thousands of people. The festival's high point is an annual attempt to set a world record for the largest pljeskavica.

In the northern parts of the Balkans, near Romania, pljeskavica is traditionally served with chopped onions and *kajmak*, a thick, tangy clotted cream usually made with sheep's or cow's milk.

In the warmer parts of the region, stretching down the Adriatic just across from Italy, there is *ajvar*, a lush, piquant spread based on roasted red peppers and olive oil. Ajvar is a winter staple throughout the region with the same kind of tangy sweetness that ketchup adds to a burger.

Time: 30 minutes plus at least 4 hours' chilling

Yield: 6 burgers

1 pound ground beef, preferably chuck

1 pound ground veal

1 pound ground pork, preferably neck or
    jowl meat; or ⅓ pound pork belly and
    ⅔ pound regular ground pork

½ cup finely chopped onions, plus
    minced onions for serving

1½ teaspoons salt

1 tablespoon black pepper; or
    2 teaspoons sweet paprika and
    1 teaspoon black pepper

¼ cup sparkling water

6 pita breads, warmed or toasted

Kajmak with Herbs (recipe follows)

Red Pepper–Eggplant Ajvar (page 54)

1. In a large bowl, place meats, ½ cup chopped onions, salt, pepper and sparkling water. Using your hands, lightly combine ingredients. Cover and refrigerate at least 3 hours or overnight.

2. Divide mixture into 6 equal balls. Place one ball between two sheets of plastic wrap and use heel of your hand to pound it to a thin patty, about ¼-inch thick and 6 inches in diameter. Repeat with remaining meat; refrigerate patties about 1 hour.

3. Heat a grill to very hot. Cook patties, turning often, until well browned on both sides, about 5 minutes total. Cut pita breads in half horizontally, and serve burgers between pieces of pita. Sprinkle with onions and spread with kajmak and ajvar as desired.

Kajmak with Herbs

Time: 10 minutes   **Yield:** About 2 cups

4 ounces cream cheese

4 ounces (1 stick) butter

4 ounces ricotta

4 ounces sour cream

1 clove garlic, minced

1 shallot, minced

1 tablespoon chopped fresh parsley

1 teaspoon chopped fresh thyme

1 teaspoon chopped fresh rosemary
    (optional)

Salt and black pepper to taste

1. Bring cream cheese, butter, ricotta and sour cream to cool room temperature. In a mixer or food processor, combine cream cheese and butter and mix until fluffy and smooth. Mix in ricotta and sour cream.

2. Add remaining ingredients and mix or process until thoroughly incorporated. Cover and refrigerate until ready to serve, up to 3 days. Serve with Balkan burgers or as a dip.

Red Pepper–Eggplant Ajvar

Time: 1 hour   **Yield:** About 1½ cups

4 large red bell peppers
1 medium eggplant
6 cloves garlic, unpeeled

½ cup olive oil
Salt and black pepper to taste

1.   Preheat oven to 475 degrees. Place peppers, eggplant and garlic on a baking sheet and roast; remove garlic after 10 minutes and place in a large bowl. Continue roasting peppers and eggplant until blackened and soft, about 20 minutes more, then add to bowl. Cover with plastic wrap and let steam until cool enough to handle. Remove and discard all peels, seeds and stems.

2.   In a food processor, combine pepper flesh, eggplant flesh and garlic with oil and salt and pepper. Pulse until mixture is almost smooth. Taste and season with salt and pepper. Serve with Balkan burgers or as dip.

January 20, 2010: "The Balkan Burger Unites All Factions"
by JULIA MOSKIN; recipe for Balkan Burgers (Pljeskavica)
adapted from VLADIMIR OCOKOLJIC, Kafana, New York City;
recipes for Kajmak with Herbs and Red Pepper–Eggplant Avjar
from JULIA JAKSIC, Employees Only, New York City

Pork-Fennel Burgers

There is undeniable pleasure in a plain beef burger—juicy, tender, and well browned over a backyard grill—but there's even more in a jazzed-up one. If you begin with pork that you buy yourself and grind at home, and continue by adding seasonings aggressively, you're on your way to a summer full of great "burgers" which are, in essence, sausages in burger form.

You need fat: pork shoulder is almost imperative for the correct balance of lean and fat. You need strong spices; as a starting point, you cannot beat fennel seeds and black pepper. And you need adequate salt, an essential to any good burger. Variations, of course, are not just possible but advisable. Chopped fresh fennel or chopped onion are spectacular additions.

When it is cooked over high heat, whether on a grill or in a pan or broiler, until just done, the result is consistently juicy, super flavorful and sublimely tender. And it browns, developing a dark, crisp crust like no beef burger I've ever had.

Time: 30 minutes   **Yield:** 8 burgers

1 fennel bulb, trimmed and cut into large chunks
3 to 4 cloves garlic, peeled
2½ pounds boneless pork shoulder, with some of the fat, cut into 1-inch cubes
1 tablespoon fennel seeds
1 teaspoon caraway seeds (optional)

1 teaspoon salt
½ teaspoon pepper, or more to taste
Peeled orange slices, chopped olives, chopped fresh parsley, chopped roasted red pepper and fennel slices for garnish (optional)

1. Heat should be medium-high and rack about 4 inches from fire. Put fennel and garlic in a food processor and pulse until just chopped; remove to a large bowl. Put pork fat in processor and grind until just chopped; add to bowl. Working in batches, process meat with fennel seeds, caraway if using, and salt and pepper, until meat is just chopped (be careful not to overprocess). Add to bowl and mix well. Shape mixture into 8 patties.
2. Grill about 5 minutes on each side, turning once after 4 or 5 minutes and again as necessary, 8 to 10 minutes total. (They can remain ever-so-slightly pink in the center.)
3. Garnish with orange slices, olives, parsley, roasted red pepper and fennel slices if desired.

May 25, 2010: "The Minimalist: For the Grill, Burgers Beyond the Basic,"
by MARK BITTMAN

A Play Date with Champagne and Burgers

When André and Rita Jammet closed La Caravelle, devotees of classic French food in New York were bereft. So were devotees of the Jammets, who ran the dining room with requisite Gallic elegance limned with an almost familial warmth.

That note of welcome extended to the kitchen; oysters on the half shell were accompanied by squares of brown bread already buttered. A little hug with your appetizer.

The best thing to drink with it was the Jammets' Caravelle Champagne, a brut cuvée that was not too sweet and not too dry and, when it came to those oysters, simply sublime.

After the restaurant closed in the post 9/11 bust for all things French and formal, Mr. Jammet became the manager of the members' dining room at the Metropolitan Club. Mrs. Jammet dried her tears, took her house Champagne in hand and vowed, "I'm going to make you a star."

It was no easy transition from greeting diners at the door to knocking on doors herself, but with her beloved restaurant industry as her focus, and a dog-with-a-bone determination, she succeeded. Mrs. Jammet owns the Caravelle brand, produced by De Castellane, part of the Laurent-Perrier Group, and she distributes it with an importer. In addition to the brut cuvée, she carries a rosé and a blanc de blancs, rated 91 in the *Wine Spectator*.

"I'm on a quest to show that Champagne can go with many more things than people think," Mrs. Jammet said. "The original wise men of Champagne didn't envision drinking it as a contrast with food, only as a marriage. But our palates now are exposed to so many more flavors."

Since those oysters and brown bread are gone forever, I was game to stretch some boundaries. Also, with retail prices being kinder than restaurant markups, La Caravelle is a good buy if you want to experiment at home.

We arranged a tasting at Matsuri, the Japanese restaurant owned by Tadashi Ono, the classically trained French chef who worked at La Caravelle for seven years. A reserved, dignified man who is mindful of tradition and its wisdom, he seemed somewhat skeptical of our experiment. But it's hard to resist Mrs. Jammet and her enthusiasm. The 16 years she devoted to the care and feeding of upper crust New York did nothing to dent her unflappable good humor.

"Champagne works two ways," she said. "It either harmonizes with the flavors or if it's something fatty, it's a welcome contrast to cut the fat. Potato chips are phenomenal with Champagne."

Mr. Ono prepared three dishes: baby back ribs with Japanese barbecue sauce, skirt steak with red miso and Japanese burgers with wasabi ketchup. The skirt steak, which he marinated for three days, was the first to be eliminated.

"Rita's Champagne has such a beautiful nose," he said, "the aroma of this dish could kill it." The ribs worked slightly better, but the eureka moment came with the burger and rosé. The burger was its own eureka; half beef, half pork, it stayed uncannily moist despite being cooked through. Perfection.

Japanese Burgers with Wasabi Ketchup

Time: 30 minutes   **Yield:** 4 servings

For the wasabi ketchup

½ cup ketchup

2 tablespoons soy sauce

1 tablespoon wasabi paste

For the burgers

½ cup panko or other dry bread crumbs

¼ cup whole milk

½ pound ground sirloin

½ pound ground pork

¼ cup finely chopped white onion

1½ teaspoons soy sauce

½ teaspoon salt

¼ teaspoon pepper

Sesame oil for coating hands

4 brioche buns for serving

1. Prepare the wasabi ketchup: Whisk together ketchup, soy sauce and wasabi paste.

2. Make the burgers: Prepare a grill for medium heat. In a large bowl, combine panko and milk and let rest 2 to 3 minutes. Add sirloin, pork, onion, soy sauce, salt and pepper. Knead meat until it becomes sticky and binds together; divide into 4 parts.

3. Lightly dab your hands with sesame oil. Using your palms, roll each portion of meat into a ball, then pat ball flat, shifting it from hand to hand, to form a ½-inch-thick patty. Make a shallow indentation across center of patty with the side of your hand, to keep it from puffing while it grills.

4. Grill burgers, flipping twice, until browned and cooked through, with no pink in the middle, about 10 minutes. Let rest for 2 minutes. Serve on buns, topped with some wasabi ketchup.

June 28, 2011: ALEX WITCHEL;
recipe adapted from The Japanese Grill *(Ten Speed, 2011),*
by TADASHI ONO and HARRIS SALAT

Curry-Spiced Lamb Burgers

Because lamb is the most full flavored of the everyday meats, it makes a more delicious plain burger than beef. Cooked with nothing but salt, it's fantastic. Cooked with a variety of spices, it's a game-changer.

Time: 20 minutes   **Yield:** 4 burgers

1½ pounds boneless lamb shoulder, cut into chunks

1 medium (or ½ large) onion, cut into chunks

1 fresh chili, preferably jalapeño, seeded and minced

1 teaspoon ground coriander

1 teaspoon ground cumin

½ teaspoon turmeric

Salt and freshly ground black pepper to taste

Diced mango, green and red bell pepper, red onion and scallion; and shredded carrot and lettuce for garnish (optional)

1. Heat should be medium-high and rack about 4 inches from fire. Put lamb and onion in a food processor (in batches if your machine is small) and pulse until coarsely ground. Put in a bowl with chili, coriander, cumin and turmeric, and sprinkle with salt and pepper. Mix, handling meat as little as possible, until combined. Taste and adjust seasonings. Handling the meat as lightly as possible to avoid compressing it, shape it into 4 or more burgers.

2. Grill about 3 minutes on each side for rare and another minute per side for each increasing stage of doneness.

3. Garnish with diced mango, green and red pepper, red onion and scallion, and with shredded carrot and lettuce if desired.

May 25, 2010: "The Minimalist: For the Grill, Burgers Beyond the Basic,"
by MARK BITTMAN

Shu Mai-Style Burgers

There are salmon and tuna burgers, and one could easily call a crab cake a crab burger. But because they lack fat, they make nice burgers but not crunchy-crusted, drip-down-the-chin ones.

So why not take a cue from the shu mai dumpling, which mixes shrimp and pork? This gives you uncommon flavor in a burger—not only from the shrimp, but also from the combination of Asian ingredients—with adequate fat.

Time: 30 minutes   **Yield:** 8 burgers

½ pound shrimp, peeled

2 medium cloves garlic, peeled

1½ pounds boneless pork shoulder, with the fat, cut into 1-inch cubes

2 teaspoons soy sauce

¼ cup chopped scallions, plus more for garnish

¼ cup chopped fresh cilantro, plus more for garnish

1 small fresh chili, seeded and minced

1 tablespoon minced fresh ginger

Salt and freshly ground black pepper to taste

Shredded cabbage and pickled pepper for garnish (optional)

1. Heat should be medium-high and rack about 4 inches from fire. Put shrimp and garlic in a food processor and pulse until just chopped; remove to a large bowl. Working in batches, grind pork fat until just chopped (be careful not to overprocess). Add to bowl. Then grind meat until just chopped, again being careful not to overprocess; add to bowl.

2. Mix shrimp, pork fat and meat with soy sauce, scallions, cilantro, chili and ginger; sprinkle with salt and pepper. Shape into 8 patties.

3. Grill about 4 minutes, then turn and cook for a total of 8 to 10 minutes, or until nicely browned and cooked through.

4. Garnish with scallions, cilantro, cabbage and pickled pepper, to taste.

May 25, 2010: "The Minimalist: For the Grill, Burgers Beyond the Basic," by MARK BITTMAN

Salmon Burgers

There were several things that inspired me to create a salmon burger. I knew it would taste good, which is really reason enough. And I figured people would be unlikely to cover it with ketchup, another plus. Then there's the fact that salmon is sold everywhere, and when on sale, it's not much more expensive than ground meat. Finally, the oils contained in salmon are actually supposed to have some health benefits—at least according to the current wisdom—thanks to its high percentage of omega-3 fatty acids.

The creation process, however, was not as easy as I had hoped. When I used hand-chopped or coarsely ground fish, the burger fell apart almost before I got it into the pan. When I ground it fine, it held together well, but the meat became so dense and dry during cooking that even I was reaching for the ketchup bottle after one bite. It was at that point that I began incorporating eggs, mayonnaise, bread crumbs and all the other extra ingredients of "hamburgers" made without meat. My goal, however, was not just a salmon burger—it was a Minimalist salmon burger.

And here are the results of my researches: If you finely grind part of the salmon, it will bind the rest, which can be coarsely chopped to retain its moisture during cooking. Some coarse bread crumbs keep the burger from becoming as densely packed as bad meatloaf. This approach, along with a few simple seasonings, produced a delicious burger in not much more time than it takes to make one from ground round.

As long as you have a food processor, the method is quite simple. About one-quarter of the salmon is finely ground, almost pureed; the machine takes care of that in about 30 seconds. Then the rest of the fish is chopped by pulsing the machine on and off a few times. The only other trick is to avoid overcooking. It's best when the center remains . . . well, salmon color. Two or three minutes a side usually does the trick.

Salmon takes better to a wider variety of seasonings—especially subtle ones—than ground meat. And the two-step grinding process means that those flavorings that you want minced fine, like garlic or ginger, can go in with the first batch of salmon; those that should be left coarse, like onion or fresh herbs, can go in with the rest. See the flavor variations that follow.

Time: 20 minutes   **Yield:** 4 burgers

1½ pounds skinless, boneless salmon	1 tablespoon capers, drained
2 teaspoons Dijon mustard	Salt and freshly ground black pepper
2 shallots, cut into chunks	Lemon wedges
½ cup coarse bread crumbs	Tabasco sauce

1. Cut salmon into large chunks, and put about a quarter of it in a food processor, along with mustard. Turn machine on, and let it run—stopping to scrape down sides if necessary—until mixture becomes pasty.

2. Add shallots and remaining salmon, and pulse machine on and off until fish is chopped and well combined with the puree. No piece should be larger than ¼ inch or so; be careful not to make mixture too fine.

3. Scrape mixture into a bowl, and by hand, stir in bread crumbs, capers and some salt and pepper. Shape into four burgers. (You can cover and refrigerate burgers for a few hours at this point.)

4. Grill over medium-high heat until the first side is firmed up, about 4 minutes; turn and let finish cooking for just another minute or two. To check for doneness, make a small cut and peek inside. Be careful not to overcook. Serve on a bed of greens or on buns or by themselves, with lemon wedges and Tabasco or any dressing you like.

A Variety of Approaches to Seasoning

The recipe's mustard, shallots and capers are not the only approaches to consider for seasoning these burgers.

While pureeing the first batch of salmon, you can:

- Use a combination of soy sauce (about 1 tablespoon), sesame oil (1 teaspoon) and ginger (1 teaspoon).

- Add a small clove of garlic (don't overdo it, because the garlic will remain nearly raw and strong tasting).

For the coarser, second batch, you can:

- Use ¼ cup onion or scallions, in addition to or instead of shallots.
- Add spice mixtures like curry or chili powder, using 1 teaspoon to 1 tablespoon, depending on your spice capacity.
- Add 1 tablespoon or more of fresh herbs, like parsley, chervil, dill or cilantro.
- Add red or yellow bell pepper (½ cup), seeded and roughly chopped.

With the bread crumbs, try mixing in lightly toasted pine nuts (¼ cup or more) or sesame seeds (about 1 tablespoon).

June 10, 1998: "The Minimalist: Burger
with No Need of Ketchup,"
by MARK BITTMAN

Grilled Tuna Burger with Ginger Mayonnaise

Anyone who has tried to grill a hamburger made from super-lean meat can tell you that you need some fat to hold that burger together.

It's the same with fish. You can make a burger with ground salmon, which contains a load of fat. But you simply cannot grind tuna, which usually has less than 1 percent fat, and expect it to hold together, unless you add some form of "glue," like eggs.

It occurred to me that the very characteristic that makes ground tuna untenable as a burger makes small tuna steaks perfect in that role: tuna is so lean that it offers almost no resistance to the bite. So you can grill a whole small tuna steak and serve it as a burger.

What you will probably get when you ask for tuna is yellowfin, which often yields burger-size steaks; if not, you can always cut up one or two larger ones. Yellowfin can be high in mercury, so some people might want to limit how often they eat it.

You could treat a grilled tuna burger (I'm still calling it that, even though it's really a grilled steak) as you would one made from red meat, and serve it with the usual fixings. It's nice, though, to give it a little bit of a twist and top it with pickled ginger and ginger-laced mayonnaise. It's great if you make the mayo yourself, but even bottled mayonnaise, dressed up with a bit of soy sauce and sesame oil, can be quite enticing.

The result is a lean, delicious, wildly different yet quite familiar substitute for the usual burger.

Time: 20 minutes   **Yield:** 4 servings

4 (5-ounce) tuna steaks, ¾-inch thick

2 tablespoons plus 1 teaspoon soy sauce

Freshly ground black pepper or Sichuan
    peppercorns

½ cup mayonnaise, preferably homemade

1 tablespoon minced fresh ginger

1 teaspoon sesame oil (optional)

Neutral oil, like grapeseed or corn

4 hamburger buns

4 tablespoons pickled ginger (optional)

1. Start a gas or charcoal fire; heat should be moderately high and rack should be clean and about 4 inches from heat source. Brush each steak lightly with 2 tablespoons of soy sauce and sprinkle with pepper. In a bowl, combine mayonnaise, fresh ginger, remaining 1 teaspoon soy sauce and sesame oil if using.

2. Oil grill grates lightly; grill tuna about 2 minutes per side for rare, proportionately longer if you want it better done. Toast buns if you like.

3. Serve fish on buns, spread with some ginger mayonnaise and topped with a bit of pickled ginger if using.

August 2, 2006: MARK BITTMAN

Turkey and Vegetable Burgers

The vegetables in this turkey burger mixture not only contribute lots of vitamins A and C and micronutrients like the carotenoids lutein and zeaxanthin, which have been linked to eye health, they also help to moisten burgers that can otherwise be quite dry. Make sure to buy lean ground turkey breast.

Yield: 6 burgers

1 tablespoon extra virgin olive oil
½ cup finely diced onion
½ cup finely diced red bell pepper
Salt to taste
1 large clove garlic, green shoot removed, minced
⅔ cup finely grated carrot (1 large carrot)

1¼ pounds lean ground turkey breast, preferably organic, from humanely raised turkeys
1 tablespoon prepared barbecue sauce
1 tablespoon ketchup
Freshly ground pepper to taste
Whole-grain hamburger buns and condiments of your choice

1. Heat olive oil over medium heat in a medium skillet and add onion. Cook, stirring, until it begins to soften, about 3 minutes, and add red pepper and a generous pinch of salt. Cook, stirring often, until vegetables are tender, about 5 minutes. Stir in garlic and carrot and cook, stirring, for another minute or two, until carrots have softened slightly and mixture is fragrant. Remove from heat.

2. In a large bowl, mash ground turkey with a fork. Add about ¾ teaspoon kosher salt if desired, and mix in barbecue sauce, ketchup, and freshly ground pepper to taste. Add sautéed vegetables and mix together well. Shape into 6 patties, about ¾ inch thick. Chill for 1 hour if possible to facilitate handling.

3. Prepare a medium-hot grill. Cook patties for 4 minutes on each side. Serve on whole-grain buns, with condiments of your choice.

ADVANCE PREPARATION: You can make this turkey burger mix, shape into patties and freeze for 2 or 3 months. Thaw as needed. The mix will keep for a day in the refrigerator, but check the use-by date on the package of the ground turkey.

January 11, 2010: MARTHA ROSE SHULMAN

Watermelon Burgers with Cheese

Grill a watermelon slice, and it dries out and sobers up, losing its sloppy sweetness, and it takes surprisingly well to savory accompaniments. Add a slice of good melting cheese, a hard roll, a few pickles and a lettuce leaf, and look out: watermelon burgers.

Time: 30 minutes   **Yield:** 4 to 6 servings

1 small watermelon
¼ cup olive oil
1 tablespoon minced onion
Salt and black pepper

4 ounces mozzarella, Monterey Jack, Gruyère or other melting cheese, grated or sliced

1. Heat a charcoal or gas grill to moderately high heat and put rack about 4 inches from flame. Cut watermelon lengthwise, into halves or quarters, depending on size of melon. From each length, cut 1½-inch-thick slices; remove rind from each slice. If there are black seeds, use a fork to remove as many of them as you can without beating the flesh up too much.

2. Mix olive oil with onion and sprinkle with salt and pepper. Brush or rub mixture all over watermelon slices. Grill for about 5 minutes on each side. The flesh should be lightly caramelized and dried out a bit. Sprinkle each slice with cheese, cover grill and cook just until cheese melts, about a minute.

3. Serve on buns, toast or hard rolls with usual burger fixings.

July 10, 2011: "Eat: Throw Another Melon on the Barbie,"
by MARK BITTMAN

Portobello Mushroom Cheeseburgers

Large portobello mushrooms are perfect burger material, just the right size for a meaty and satisfying meal. I like them best with Gruyère cheese on top.

Yield: 4 servings

1 tablespoon red wine vinegar or sherry
    vinegar

Salt and freshly ground pepper to taste

1 clove garlic, green shoot removed,
    minced or pureed

3 tablespoons extra virgin olive oil

4 large portobello mushrooms, stems
    removed

1 (6-ounce) bag baby spinach

4 (½-ounce) slices Cheddar or Gruyère
    cheese

Whole-grain hamburger buns and
    condiments of your choice

1. Whisk together vinegar, salt, pepper, garlic and olive oil. Toss with mushroom caps in a wide bowl. Rub marinade over tops of mushroom caps and place them on a baking sheet, rounded side up. Let sit for 15 minutes. Don't rinse bowl, because you'll use any oil and vinegar residue to dress the spinach.

2. Bring a large pot of water to a boil, salt generously and blanch spinach for 20 seconds. Transfer to a bowl of ice water, drain and squeeze dry. Chop coarsely and toss in bowl with residue of marinade. Set aside.

3. Prepare a medium-hot grill. Season mushrooms as desired with salt and pepper. Place mushrooms on hot grill, rounded side down. Cook them for about 6 to 8 minutes, depending on thickness, until lightly browned, and moist. Turn over and cook for another 6 minutes. Turn over for a minute to reheat top, then flip back over and place cheese on top. Continue to cook until cheese melts.

4. Place a mound of spinach on bottom half of each hamburger bun and place mushrooms, rounded side up, on top of spinach. Top with your choice of condiments and serve.

ADVANCE PREPARATION: You can marinate the mushrooms for up to a day.

January 11, 2010: "Recipes for Health: Burgers Without the Beef,"
by MARTHA ROSE SHULMAN

Sit-Down Comedy

Along with memories of meals that were wonderful, terrible and somewhere in between, a restaurant critic inevitably gathers recollections of dining experiences that, for a variety of reasons, were funny. Some of my favorites follow.

Friends accompanying us to dinner several years ago realized that they knew the woman who owned the restaurant. Careful not to introduce me so they would not have to lie or to blow my cover, they chatted with the proprietor, asking how things were going.

"Just great," she said. "And we're really excited because last week Mimi Sheraton was here." "Did she like it?" I asked. "Yes, very much," she answered. "But you know she always visits several times before writing about a place." "How did you recognize her?" I asked. "My press agent brought her in and introduced her," she said.

Funny but embarrassing is the best way to describe another memorable incident, which occurred when I was searching out the best hamburgers in the city. Because of time limitations, I went to six or eight places a day, taking several bites, evaluating meat, buns and trimmings, making notes and moving on.

On the first day it became apparent that waiters and managers were distressed to find partly eaten burgers left on the plate, so there were streams of questions. The next day I set out with a supply of plastic sandwich bags. When I had eaten enough to make a judgment, I slyly pushed the remains into a sandwich bag and into my handbag and discarded each in the nearest trash basket. After the first few stops, however, I forgot to throw away the uneaten portions and five or six accumulated.

Finding that I was close to Saks Fifth Avenue, where a sale of handbags was in progress, I went in and bought one. Since what I was carrying was a wreck, I thought I'd use my purchase and throw the wreck away. As I emptied the old bag I remembered, too late, the cache of burgers.

"What are those?" asked a particularly snooty saleswoman as the greasy, juice-spattered packets smelling of ketchup and onion tumbled onto the counter. "They're my hamburgers," I replied, with what I like to think was utter aplomb. I carefully placed them in the new bag with my other belongings and left her gaping.

The incident I cherish most occurred a few months ago at a very good, very esoteric Japanese restaurant in SoHo. Small dishes of various fish, poultry and vegetable creations were featured and it was customary to order an assortment. Portions were tiny, and six voracious eaters wielding chopsticks picked each dish clean as soon as it was set down.

One small rectangular blue dish held delicious slices of marinated grilled chicken, with just one piece for each of us. I noticed that the dish still had on it a lettuce leaf and a garnish I had missed. It seemed to be small, pale golden, delicately folded layers that might have been the pickled ginger served with raw fish or sheets of bean curd brushed with flavoring.

I picked up a small morsel with my chopsticks and, after swallowing it, announced that it tasted like paper with soy sauce on it.

My husband, realizing what was happening, said, "You're eating my napkin." He had spilled soy sauce on the table and blotted it up with a folded paper napkin, which he discarded on the empty dish.

If there was any satisfaction in all that, it was in knowing that I could recognize soy-soaked paper when I tasted it. It's a good thing I didn't like it; it might have shown up in a review among recommended dishes.

June 19, 1982: MIMI SHERATON

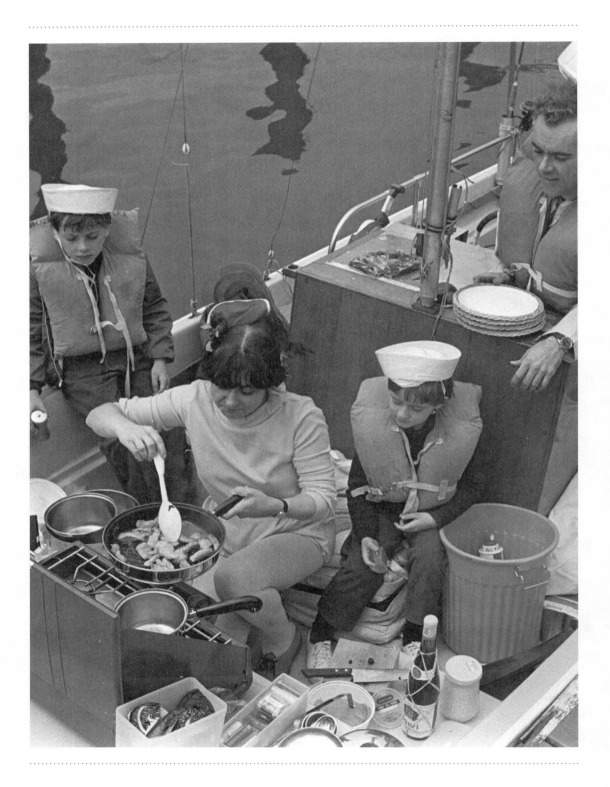

CHAPTER THREE

Beef and Veal

Whether it's a succulent, rare steak with a crunchy char on it or a long-cooked brisket, beef is, for many grillers, the ultimate barbecue meat. Every cut of beef has its own heat and timing requirements, from skirt steak, to filet mignon, to hanger steak, to London broil. Mark Bittman shares his favorite cuts for steak and how to assure success at the grill (page 81). Baltimore Pit Beef Sandwich (page 93) shows why some classics achieve that status. If you want to re-create a meat lovers' Nirvana, check out Craig Claiborne's story about a Brazilian friend re-creating a *churrasco à gaucho* (pages 96–102). Beef in its younger years is veal, which, because it is so lean, can be easily overcooked. Like the white meat of chicken, you want to grill it enough but not dry it out. Moira Hodgson shows how in her recipe Veal Chops with Summer Savory (page 113).

Odette Herrmann stirs a skillet of veal with truffles aboard the *Why Not* in 1968. Robert Jr., left, is ready with a pepper mill, and Mark holds a box of herbs. Robert Herrmann contents himself with looking on hungrily.

Before the Sunday Kickoff, Tailgating with Gusto

They come here to the Arrowhead Stadium parking lots from Independence, Grandview, Boonville and from out in Benton County by the reservoir, all with a passion for food and football. They come dressed in red, driving red vans and red pickups. They light fires in the parking lots before finishing their morning coffee. They are fans of the Kansas City Chiefs, but more than this, they are tailgaters, heartland enthusiasts of al fresco cuisine.

And they are not alone. More than a million people attend National Football League games each weekend. Dan Masonson, a league spokesman, estimates that 400,000 tailgate before kickoff. Hundreds of thousands more—millions maybe—tailgate before college football games and in the infield during Nascar races (race officials estimate that at least 30 percent of the crowds tailgate). Their numbers swell when you take into account Friday night high school games and Saturday college lacrosse matches, amateur soccer and flag-football leagues.

Allocate a six-inch bratwurst for each of these weekend tailgaters—taking two million as a conservative estimate—and you could lay a straight line of sausages from the Meadowlands, the Giants' home, to Ravens Stadium in Baltimore—191 miles.

Todd Wickstrom, who runs Zingerman's Deli in Ann Arbor, Michigan, said sales of foods for grills and picnics increase some 30 percent on the University of Michigan's game days. Tailgate dining costs less and tastes better than eating in the stadium, he said. "You can drink your own beer, eat your own barbecue," he continued, "and then you can go to the game and be full and not have to fight to go through all the lines."

But there is little fast food among die-hard tailgaters. For some fans, the time spent cooking is half the fun. At Louisiana State University, some fans show up 48 hours before kickoff to start tailgating, according to the sports information director, Michael Bonnette. When the Tigers traveled to the University of Arizona, he added, the L.S.U. fans were shocked to discover that tailgating was allowed only five hours before game time. "Our fans just felt like they had gone to another country," he said.

If you had to pick just one tailgate event to attend—and I have attended dozens— Arrowhead's would be the one. Chiefs' fans tailgate with gusto, and eat well while doing so.

With its history as a meatpacking center, Kansas City is the birthplace of one of America's four great barbecue traditions (the others being Texas and the two Carolinas), and on game days the scent of slow-grilled meat hangs like a haze over the more than 300 acres of the stadium's lots. Arrowhead's management recognizes the passion. There are enough Port-a-Potties surrounding the stadium to accommodate 70,000 fans, and special receptacles for disposing of live coals are visible everywhere you look.

Arrowhead is tailgaters' Valhalla. It is also the site of a lineup that suggests a pickup-truck version of the Oklahoma land rush.

At 6:30 a.m. on a recent Sunday, as the Chiefs slumbered before their first home game against the San Diego Chargers, there were lines a half-mile long outside the stadium. The parking lots open at 9 a.m., but arriving three hours early is necessary for those prepared to jockey for the best spots, close to the stadium.

Lucy Long, an assistant professor of popular culture at Bowling Green University in Ohio, had told me that tailgating was male-dominated. "It's a chance to show off," she said, "through the money spent purchasing expensive gourmet food or through culinary prowess." But there at the wheel of the seventh van in the line was Deborah Davis, who with her husband, Richard, heads a competitive barbecue team called Butt Head Barbecue. They had begun their preparations the night before, as I learned during a visit to their farm in Adrian, Missouri. The Davises have devoted a room of their modern barn to a well-equipped kitchen whose décor of football helmets, autographed pictures and banners makes it look like a shrine to the Chiefs and the University of Missouri football team.

Mr. Davis had already loaded his large portable smoker with the first of the 18 slabs of ribs he prepares for game days, while Ms. Davis had prepared the *mise en place* for a fresh black bean salsa with Holland tomatoes. "The local ones just didn't happen this year," she said, wincing. A natural chef, she wielded her knife with speed and precision, then moved along to prepare a marinade for barbecued shrimp.

It looked good, and I asked if I might have the recipe. Ms. Davis looked up with a smile, but Mr. Davis answered, "Nope."

I was not surprised. Those who compete in barbecue contests never tell anybody anything. As in football games, the tiniest adjustments can confer an overwhelming advantage.

I had witnessed similar preparations earlier in the day during a visit to another group of Kansas City tailgaters, this one cooking under the name the Gremlin Grill. Run by three brothers, Al, Pat and Brett McSparin, the Gremlin was competing in the summer sun at the Barbecue Blaze Off at the Calvary Baptist Church in Blue Springs, Missouri. ("And You Think It's Hot Here?" read the sign in front of the church.) Pork shoulder was on the menu for the Blaze Off, but the brothers, accompanied by a legion of children, wives and friends, were also starting to smoke a prime rib that they would eat at their Arrowhead tailgate party the next day.

"We've been doing this for about 15 years," Pat McSparin said. "We are die-hard fans."

At 7 a.m. Sunday morning, Al McSparin's teenage son, Tyler, was tossing a football to friends under light pole G-28, the spot the McSparins have held for every game since they began tailgating in 1988. Over in Lot H, Rich Davis did the same at his spot. Lobbing a pigskin is what tailgaters across the country do when they're waiting for the lots to open. From inside the stadium came the booming sounds of the bass and organ introduction to the Spencer Davis Group's "Gimme Some Lovin.'" It was loud enough to make my heart thump.

At 8:58, the stampede commenced. Like an invasion force hitting the beach, the McSparin crew approached in half a dozen vehicles, parked and began to unload gear. By 9:04, two grills had been assembled, and the first puffs of smoke curled upward from them. Seven minutes after that, there were three tents erected above long tables, a cocktail bar and coolers full of cold drinks. As a breakfast offering, someone put a couple dozen chicken kabobs over the fire.

As the McSparins established their family beachhead, the wide plain of the parking lots here was transformed, nearly as quickly, into a tailgating encampment dedicated to the pleasures of food and drink. The air grew thick with smoke as the aroma of thousands of grills hit from all sides.

Fifty feet away from the McSparins, Ken Yarnevich and his friends—some Croatian, some Slovenian, all Chiefs fans—set out a spread of stuffed cabbage and plates of the nutty, buttery pastry, part sweet, part savory, that is known as *povatica*.

One fan had also prepared a marvelous concoction of ground pork and beef in a savory brown sauce. Joe Horvat, who calls himself Joko the Croat, said it was *djuvec*.

Continuing around the lots, I savored more marvels. Here were grills attached to the trailer hitches of pickup trucks and mobile kitchens that might have served Hollywood movie sets. And there in Lot M was Monty Spradling preparing the most perfectly cooked hamburger I have ever tasted. Indeed, so confident was Mr. Spradling in his offering that he served it to me on a bun, unseasoned and with no condiments.

His secret? "The single most important thing here is to use excellent beef from a butcher who grinds aged chuck," he said. "My butcher actually throws a little brisket trimmings into the grinder." And his technique? Simple. "Cook on a hot but not flaming fire for 5 to 6 minutes per side. I only turn once."

Around 10:30 a.m., the combination of smoke, food, music, good spirits and antici-pation of the game began to blend into an irresistible, almost psychedelic haze of bonhomie.

It led me inexorably toward Rich Davis and his ribs. In contravention of the Kansas City barbecue canon (which calls for a sweet red sauce), Mr. Davis served his ribs bare, with only a dry rub for seasoning, and it was among the best I have eaten in the tailgate or barbecue-competition world. I told him I tasted different kinds of peppers as well as cloves and floral sweetness.

"You're right on the peppers," he said, "wrong on the cloves." The sweetness? A true pit master never tells.

Over at the McSparin bacchanal, Al McSparin was finishing his smoked prime rib. I drew myself an ice cold pint of Foster's beer from his keg, mounted on a truck, and dug into an herbaceous, earthy, smoky, salty slab of beef. By the time I was finished, ticket-holders were streaming past me into the stadium, a river of red.

As best as I could tell, the departing fans had doused their fires and gotten rid of the coals, but Pat McSparin was not so sure. "You can always count on some idiot putting his hibachi under the car so that no one will steal it during the game," he said. "Then you have to call the fire department."

Oh, yes, the game. Chiefs 27, Chargers 14.

Gremlin Grill's Prime Rib

Time: About 3½ hours, plus overnight refrigeration   **Yield:** 10 to 12 servings

1 cup extra virgin olive oil

1 cup Cherry Coke

2 tablespoons Worcestershire sauce

1 tablespoon kosher salt

1 tablespoon freshly ground black pepper

Greek Seasoning Blend (page 74)

1 tablespoon dried oregano

1 teaspoon dried thyme

1 teaspoon onion powder

2 tablespoons minced garlic

Approximately 10 pounds boneless
    prime rib

1.   In a bowl, combine olive oil, Cherry Coke, Worcestershire sauce, salt, pepper and 1 tablespoon Greek Seasoning Blend. Add oregano, thyme, onion powder and garlic. Mix well. Place meat in a large roasting pan. Add marinade, and massage meat with it, turning meat to coat it well. Place meat and marinade in an extra-large Ziploc plastic bag (or wrap in a double layer of plastic wrap), and seal well. Refrigerate overnight.

2.   Light a charcoal fire. Soak 4 to 6 cups of hickory or cherry wood chips, or both, in water. When coals are white, divide them, pushing each half to opposite sides of grill. Top each pile with a few wood chips. Position grill rack over coals, and cover grill.

3.   Poke small holes in a large disposable aluminum roasting pan and add meat. Place pan above center of grill, cover grill and adjust ventilation so it is slightly open. Temperature in grill should be about 225 degrees; insert instant-read thermometer through a ventilation hole in grill cover. Adjust ventilation to regulate temperature.

4.   Cook meat until instant-read thermometer inserted in center registers 130 degrees, 2½ to 3 hours. Keep fire going by adding coals to each side every 30 minutes, or as necessary. Add more wet wood chips when needed to keep fire smoking.

5.   Remove meat and wrap in foil. Allow it to come to room temperature, then refrigerate for at least 2 hours or overnight.

6.   To serve, light a charcoal fire. When coals are white, spread evenly across bottom of grill. Cut ¾- to 1-inch-thick steaks from meat, and dust with remaining Greek Seasoning Blend to taste. Grill over very hot coals to taste, about 1 minute per side. Serve immediately.

Greek Seasoning Blend

Time: 3 minutes   **Yield:** ¼ cup

1 teaspoon salt

2 teaspoons dried oregano

1½ teaspoons onion powder

1½ teaspoons garlic powder

1 teaspoon cornstarch

1 teaspoon freshly ground black pepper

1 teaspoon beef-flavored bouillon
    granules

1 teaspoon dried parsley flakes

½ teaspoon ground cinnamon

½ teaspoon ground nutmeg

Combine all ingredients in a bowl, and transfer to an airtight container. Store in a cool, dark place.

September 24, 2003: PETER KAMINSKY;
recipe adapted from AL, PAT, and BRETT MCSPARIN

Thai Beef

Yield: 4 servings

2 teaspoons finely minced garlic

2 teaspoons finely chopped fresh ginger

2 teaspoons finely chopped jalapeños

2 tablespoons soy sauce

1 tablespoon Thai fish sauce (see note)

¼ cup fresh lime juice

¼ cup coarsely chopped fresh cilantro

½ cup corn, peanut or vegetable oil, plus
more for brushing grill

2 pounds fillet of beef, well-trimmed and
in one piece

1. Combine garlic, ginger, jalapeños, soy sauce, fish sauce, lime juice, cilantro and oil in a mixing bowl. Beat to blend. There should be about 1⅓ cups. Reserve a bit more than ⅓ cup of mixture.

2. Put meat in mixing bowl and turn it in marinade. Cover, and refrigerate marinating meat (as well as reserved mixture) overnight.

3. Preheat a well-scrubbed outdoor gas grill to high, or fire coals of a charcoal grill until they are white hot. When ready to cook, brush grill lightly with oil.

4. Put meat on grill and cook 5 minutes. Give meat a quarter-turn, forming a grill pattern, and continue cooking. Turn fillet over, and repeat, giving meat a quarter-turn every 4 to 5 minutes until meat, when pressed with fingers, does not feel flabby. Total cooking time will be from 20 to 35 minutes.

5. Cut beef on bias into slices, each slice about ½ inch thick. Arrange slices, slightly overlapping, on a warm platter and pour over them any juices that have dribbled from meat. Stir reserved sauce and let it come to room temperature. Spoon it over slices.

NOTE: Thai fish sauce, also known as *nam pla*, can be purchased in Asian food stores and well-stocked supermarkets.

July 6, 1986: "Food: Grilling As Art,"
by CRAIG CLAIBORNE with PIERRE FRANEY;
recipe from LAURA THORNE and JEFF TRUJILLO,
formerly of Coast Grill, Southampton, New York

News of Food: Eisenhower's Recipe for Cooking Steak Calls for Throwing It Right on the Fire

By now, we guess, those of voting age or less know that a certain general likes to cook. His wife and severest critic said during the recent Republican convention that Gen. Dwight D. Eisenhower cooks better than she. And just the other day came that report of a breakfast "Ike" prepared at his vacation ranch in Colorado at which one guest was said to have eaten eleven flapjacks.

We were reminded, in reading it, of a recipe for cooking steak outdoors that the general picked up on fishing trips in the Wisconsin woods. He wrote it out three years ago for Mrs. W. G. Wyman, whose husband was then Chief of Staff of the First Army, stationed at Governors Island. It was the general's contribution to a cook-booklet that the women of that post compiled as a means of raising funds for a carillon for the island's chapel.

The recipe, advocating that a steak be cooked right in the charcoal without pan or grill between meat and heat, created interest when it first appeared here on Dec. 3, 1949. It is even more interesting now perhaps, not only because the general has stepped forward in the news, but also because July is a better time than December to talk about any phase of cooking outdoors.

The General's Instructions

Accordingly, a reprint of the directions as the general originally wrote them:

(a) Get a sirloin tip four inches thick. (This make it as thick as it is wide.)

(b) Make a dry mixture of salt, black pepper and garlic powder. Put it in a flat, wide bowl.

(c) Roll and rub the steak in the mixture until it will take up no more.

(d) Two hours before ready to start cooking build, on the ground, a bonfire on which dump a good-sized basketful of charcoal. Keep fire going well until charcoal has formed a good thick body of glowing coals.

(e) Forty minutes before time to eat throw the steak into the fire (use no grates, grills or anything of the kind).

(f) Nudge it over once or twice but let it lie in fire about thirty-five minutes.

(g) Take out, slice slant-wise (about three-eighths inch thick). Serve hot. (One steak will serve three persons generously.)

When we showed this recipe to Marty Snyder, mess sergeant for three years during the war to the Supreme Headquarters Allied Expeditionary Forces, he said it was quite in keeping with the general's tastes.

General Likes Garlic

"He likes his steak with garlic and he likes garlic," said Mr. Snyder, who is recently back from campaigning in Chicago and again heading up his food speciality business (Boneless Turkey, Inc.). He recalled how, when he was with SHAEF in England, he had come on a farmer plowing up wild garlic, and how, with the general's palate in mind, he had asked for some.

"Scrounging was part of our business," Mr. Snyder went on. "We were always trying to get something fresh and different for the general's table—a few eggs, lobsters from a fisherman in Portsmouth. When we got to France, it was easier. The French wanted coffee so badly they were willing to give up fresh lettuce or peaches for it."

Baked beans ("no tomato sauce, slow-baked with sorghum syrup," Mr. Snyder said) and hominy ("as a side dish and not for breakfast") were among the general's favorites. He allowed that beans were inevitable at an Army mess, and that that might have been one reason, besides the general's liking for them, that they were served along with frankfurters, to Winston Churchill when he came for lunch one day.

But what seemed to delight Mr. Snyder was the real interest the general showed in food and its preparation. His inspection of the kitchen was not "the white glove kind." He did not run his finger along a shelf to see whether it had been kept clean, but rather, Mr. Snyder said, would lift the cover off a pot on the stove and stir up the contents to see what was cooking.

When he got to Paris, Mr. Snyder had put under his supervisory eye the kitchens of the hotels the Army took over.

French Deliberate Cooks

"Those French chefs proved to me that French cooking is the greatest in the world," he said. "It is deliberate cooking, you know, all planned out even days in advance."

It was, in fact, a French chef in the Scribe Hotel who gave Mr. Snyder the idea for the boneless turkey rolls that he has been manufacturing recently.

" 'Gone With the Wind' was being shown, and Gen. Charles de Gaulle had been invited to the movie," Mr. Snyder said. "There was to be a small buffet for the officers afterward. They wanted no one in the room to serve them, so they'd be free to talk, I suppose. The question came up, 'How can we serve roast turkey if there is no one to carve it?' The chef suggested boning and cooking the birds and presenting them in aspic—*a galantine de volaille.*"

When he got back home, Mr. Snyder Americanized the galantine. Now he turns out large round loaves of cooked and raw turkey that have had good success with airlines and restaurants. At retail they may be had only at Charles' Bon Voyage, 340 Madison Avenue; Vendome, 415 Madison Avenue, and Bamberger's in Newark.

Mr. Snyder used to ship his boneless turkey to the general when he was in France. Now he is confident that after November, around the first of next year, he'll be addressing it to a famous residence in Washington, D.C.

July 9, 1952: JANE NICKERSON

Filet of Beef with Roquefort Butter

An impressive platter of tender filet of beef covered with a delicate melted butter and Roquefort cheese sauce

Yield: 6 servings

¼ pound (1 stick) unsalted butter, at
    room temperature
2 tablespoons Roquefort cheese, at room
    temperature
3 tablespoons finely chopped red onion
1 tablespoon finely chopped fresh chives
1 tablespoon finely chopped fresh parsley
1 tablespoon finely chopped shallots
2 teaspoons finely minced garlic

Salt to taste, if desired
Freshly ground pepper to taste
6 filets mignon (about 7 ounces each)
2 tablespoons peanut, vegetable or
    corn oil

1. Combine butter, cheese, onion, chives, parsley, shallots, garlic, salt and pepper. Beat well to blend.

2. Spoon mixture into center of a length of waxed paper and roll into a neat sausage shape, about 1½ inches thick. Chill thoroughly.

3. Meanwhile, preheat a charcoal grill and preheat oven to 350 degrees.

4. Place each filet on a flat surface and pound lightly with a mallet to flatten slightly. Sprinkle both sides with salt and pepper and brush both sides with a little oil.

5. Place filets on heated grill and cook, turning once, about 3 to 4 minutes on each side, or to desired degree of doneness. Place steaks on 6 ovenproof dinner plates.

6. Cut butter roll into 6 individual slices. Arrange one slice of butter on each steak. Place in oven about 2 minutes or less or until butter is melted. Serve immediately.

June 26, 1985: "Sophistication Spices Southern Food,"
by CRAIG CLAIBORNE; recipe from
La Residence, Chapel Hill, North Carolina

Barbecued Steak au Poivre

Yield: 6 to 10 servings

3 (1½-pound) boneless shell steaks
    (about 3 inches thick), trimmed of
    excess fat and gently pounded
1 tablespoon coarse salt
¼ cup crushed black peppercorns (or half
    black, half white if desired) (see note)

¼ cup finely chopped shallots
½ cup dry red wine
½ cup beef stock, homemade or canned
4 tablespoons (½ stick) unsalted butter,
    at room temperature

1. Dust steaks with coarse salt. Lay crushed peppercorns on a flat surface and press steaks over them to coat on all sides.

2. Grill steaks for about 20 minutes total. The best method is to cook on one side for about 4 minutes to sear, then flip and sear other side for 4 minutes. The flat rim should be seared also by standing steaks on their sides for several minutes. Keep rotating until steaks reach desired doneness.

3. While steaks are grilling, combine in a saucepan shallots, red wine and beef stock. Reduce over medium-high heat to one-third of volume. Remove cooked steaks to a warm serving platter. Swirl butter into sauce and pour over steaks. Slice steaks on bias in platter, allowing juices to combine with sauce.

NOTE: Crush peppercorns by placing them on a flat, hard surface and cracking them gently with a heavy, flat-bottomed skillet.

July 2, 1986: "Cooks Move Beyond Humble Hot Dog,"
by BRYAN MILLER

The Best Cuts for Grilling Steak

If you can buy prime beef (this essentially means it is fat-laced, or well marbled), you are ahead of the game. Fat means flavor. But a good cut of choice grade is often the equal of prime. Aging, of course, also improves flavor and tenderness. But even if you find prime meat that is well aged, and even if you spend a lot of money on organic, natural, specialty or so-called gourmet steaks, you won't be eating anything special unless you buy the right cut.

So, what is the right cut? To some degree it's a matter of opinion. Some people will argue for flank, but I don't believe any steak that must be sliced thin to be chewable qualifies as terrific. Others (myself included) like skirt, with the caution that it is easy to overcook. But almost everyone agrees that sirloin strip and rib-eye are best.

Sirloin strip, also called shell, club, New York or top loin, is cut from the loin, usually boneless and a wonderful individual steak. The loin also yields T-bone (or porterhouse, or the famous Italian Fiorentina), a bone-in steak comprising the top loin and the supremely tender but nearly tasteless tenderloin. The advantages of the porterhouse are that it has the bone, it can be cut thick and it serves several people.

To me, the ideal is rib-eye. The center of the rib, it is tender and often nicely fatty, and it can be delicious even when it is from a commercial, anything-but-special animal.

Which brings us to grilling, the way to perfect or ruin a steak. But before delving into a 20-year-old argument about gas versus charcoal, let's get that steak ready for the grill.

If you like a steak with crust—and who doesn't—it is best to start with a dry exterior. You can get one by putting the steak on a rack over a pan in the fridge, uncovered. Leave it there, turning it once a day or so, for a couple of days. I like this method, which might be described as passive-aggressive: you don't have to do much, and it's very effective. (Alternatively, pat it dry with paper towels before grilling.)

For fast, even cooking, it also helps to have the steak at room temperature before grilling. If you're using a rub, put it on at the last minute. As for timing, you can't cook by a clock, but most one-inch-thick steaks started at room temperature will brown in three to four minutes a side and be cooked to medium-rare after seven or eight minutes.

For greater precision, you have three options, in order of preference:

- You can gain experience and cook by touch and sight.
- You can use an instant-read thermometer: 125 degrees is rare, 130 degrees is medium-rare.
- You can cut into the meat and check. This is inelegant, but not all that bad. Meat is not a balloon that pops when cut into; you may lose a little juice, but it's better to cut into a steak, which causes minor damage, than to overcook it, which destroys it.

O.K., now: gas versus charcoal. Charcoal gives you a better crust, and hardwood charcoal is preferable to briquettes. But it's also more of a hassle, and once you start the fire you're committed to a cooking time. Gas is more convenient. And to my surprise I found the results were not that different. If you use charcoal you can sear the steak beautifully. If you use gas you must cover the grill, and the crust is not nearly as attractive. But the timing is about the same. Either way, the taste is terrific, as long as you start with the right cut.

August 22, 2007: "The Minimalist: For the Best Cuts, Here Are the Rubs," by MARK BITTMAN

Grilled Flank Steak

The flank turns out to be an ideal cut for a group because it tapers evenly at both ends and is thick in the middle (and becomes even thicker as the fire's heat contracts the muscle).

When the steak is rare in the middle, it offers a proportion of medium and well-done slices at the ends that closely matches the popularity of each doneness among our friends.

Time: 15 minutes, plus 2 hours' marinating   **Yield:** 6 servings

½ cup bourbon

½ cup soy sauce

1½ pound flank steak

1.   In small bowl, whisk together bourbon, soy sauce and ½ cup water to make a marinade. Pour marinade into a gallon-size self-sealing food storage bag. Put steak in bag, and turn it over several times so entire cut is coated. Marinate in refrigerator 2 hours, turning steak once after an hour. Pour off marinade, and blot steak dry with paper towels.

2.   Prepare a fire in a grill. When flames have subsided and coals are glowing, grill steak 4 minutes on one side for rare, 5 minutes for medium rare. Turn steak, and grill 3 or 4 minutes more, to taste.

3.   Transfer steak to a cutting board, lightly cover with foil and let rest 5 minutes. Slice steak crosswise into ⅛-inch-thick slices.

June 30, 2004: "When the Park Is Your Kitchen,"
by MATT LEE and TED LEE

The Texas Three-Step

The Texas horizon goes on forever, punctuated by the occasional oil rig, the lackadaisical cattle herd and, every once in a while, flat urban sprawl. And everywhere (at least on weekends, as sunset approaches), there are discrete plumes of smoke rising like tumbleweed across the big blue sky.

Barbecue smoke is to the Texas skyline what cathedral spires are to European capitals: sacred things, icons of identity. Barbecue fanatics speak of it more like religion than cooking. In Texas, says Dean Fearing, chef of the Mansion on Turtle Creek in Dallas, "Barbecue is God."

In addition to being an article of faith, barbecue is a way of life, according to Stephan Pyles, the chef and former co-owner of the Baby Routh restaurant in Dallas. "Down here, it's a ritual that's bred in the bone, then developed from childhood on."

Both Fearing and Pyles are speaking, of course, of Texas-style barbecue, which is beef that is marinated in a myriad of idiosyncratic "mops," then slowly cooked in an open pit, preferably over mesquite. In the barbecue belt that stretches from the Lone Star State through the Midwest and Southwest, Texas-style is king; in the belt that stretches from the Carolinas through Kentucky and Tennessee, "barbecue" means pork that's been marinated and cooked in either an open or a closed pit.

Having grown up in eastern Kentucky, Fearing had an epiphany when, at age 16, he tasted Texas barbecue for the first time. "From that moment on, my fate was sealed," he says, "I spent the next 10 years trying to duplicate the flavor, that smokiness, the contrast between the meaty, charred flavors, with the sweet, sloppy sauce and the punchy condiment."

But flavor is only one aspect of Texas Barbecue; ritual is another.

"Barbecue is a happening," Pyles says. "Barbecue is a big spread, a lot of cooperation. Somebody grills some meat, somebody else does some barbecue. There's always tamales and a couple styles of beans, potato salad, chilied mashed potatoes, vegetables, pickles, condiments. . . ."

Until recently, the barbecue creed (and the menu) were slow to change. But Pyles, who is also the author of *The New Texas Cuisine*, and Fearing, author of *The Mansion on Turtle Creek Cookbook*, have pushed the envelope. In addition to refining barbecue's basic elements in their restaurant kitchens, each has grown increasingly ecumenical, adding elements of Mexican, Latin American and even Asian cooking to the Texas barbecue fold.

"Even perfect can get better," says Fearing, who began his experimentation by devising such nontraditional condiments as the watermelon pico de gallo that is served at the Mansion on Turtle Creek (see page 348 for the recipe).

"The best thing to eat after a barbecue is watermelon, so I figure, why not add some of it during the meal?" Grilled onions in guacamole is another of his newfangled condiments that add a sweet, buttery component to any paper plate heaped with barbecued beef (see recipe on page 12).

Excess is as integral to Texas barbecue as smoke, and Pyles piles it on. In addition to the beef, his table is laden with pork chops with tamarind, game hens layered with bacon and jalapeño (page 199), a jicama coleslaw (crunchier and tangier than cabbage slaw; see page 289), corn bread, two kinds of tortilla, lots of cold beer, iced tea, lemonade, watermelon, homemade pecan ice cream or a big ripe fruit shortcake.

Between them, these two barons of barbecue have created the state-of-the-art banquet. "Think of it as the ultimate church supper," says Fearing, who, reflecting on his previous remarks, hastens to add, "Maybe barbecue isn't God; maybe it's just God's work."

Barbecued Flank Steak

Yield: 4 servings

½ cup olive oil

1 medium-size onion, thinly sliced

3 cloves garlic, finely chopped

3 serrano chilies, seeded and finely
 chopped

2 tablespoons chopped fresh cilantro

½ cup fresh lime juice

1 tablespoon salt

1 flank steak (about 1¼ pounds)

1½ cups Bacon Fat Barbecue Sauce
 (page 86)

Warm tortillas

1. Combine olive oil, onion, garlic, chilies, cilantro, lime juice and salt in a large, shallow dish. Add flank steak and marinate in the refrigerator for 8 hours or overnight, turning from time to time.

2. Heat a grill, adding wood chips if desired. Remove flank steak from marinade and place on hot grill. Cook for 3 minutes. Turn and cook for 3 minutes. Use a brush to coat flank with some of the barbecue sauce. Turn and coat other side. Continue cooking, brushing on sauce and turning every 3 minutes until meat is cooked to medium rare, about 18 minutes total.

3. Slice meat across grain into thin strips. Serve with warm tortillas, Grilled-Onion Guacamole (page 12) and Watermelon Pico de Gallo (page 348).

Bacon Fat Barbecue Sauce

Yield: About 1½ cups

1 tablespoon bacon fat or vegetable oil

1 large yellow onion, cut into ¼-inch dice

1 cup ketchup

¼ cup Worcestershire sauce

1 tablespoon malt vinegar

2 tablespoons molasses

2 teaspoons Creole mustard

1 teaspoon hot red pepper sauce

½ teaspoon salt, plus more to taste

1 teaspoon fresh lemon juice, plus more
   to taste

Heat fat or oil in a medium saucepan over medium heat. Add onion and cook until soft, about 5 minutes. Add remaining ingredients and stir to combine. Simmer for 15 minutes. Keep warm until ready to serve.

July 4, 1993: MOLLY O'NEILL;
recipes adapted from DEAN FEARING,
Mansion on Turtle Creek, Dallas, Texas

In Seoul, Let the Eating Begin

Even as South Korea modernizes and the people adopt Western dining habits—even with Wendy's and Burger Kings dotting Seoul—the native cuisine remains intact. Visitors will find that the dishes served in restaurants and homes are based on recipes hundreds of years old, the cuisine of a culture that dates back some 5,000 years.

This cuisine is spicy, primarily because in the seventeenth century the Koreans discovered red pepper. "The Chinese and the Japanese were introduced to red pepper around the same time, but it was the Koreans who took pepper and ran with it," said Dr. Laurel Kendall, a curator in the department of anthropology at the American Museum of Natural History in New York. It is red pepper, together with ginger, garlic, green onions, soy sauce, sesame oil, sesame seeds and sugar, that gives many Korean meat, seafood and vegetable dishes their distinctive, hearty flavor. In the course of a typical five-dish meal, all those spices will be represented.

But the diversity of Korean cuisine depends on more than spices and such varied cooking techniques as grilling, boiling, frying, steaming and braising. It derives from the sheer variety of ingredients Korean chefs use, even in the United States.

South Korea, about the size of Portugal, occupies the southern half of a peninsula that has the Yellow Sea to the west and the Sea of Japan to the east. From these seas come 75 varieties of fish, including corvina, croaker, pollack, red snapper, mackerel and anchovies. There are 20 kinds of shellfish, among them oysters, clams, crabs, mussels, shrimp, abalone and conch. In southernmost Korea, where the food is particularly salty and spicy, the people dry and salt tiny shrimp and anchovies, and sometimes cook with a shrimp or anchovy sauce instead of soy sauce, said Keum Dong Kong, the chef at Woo Lai Oak Restaurant in New York City.

To most South Koreans, however, meat means beef. Few parts of the steer go uneaten. There is bulgogi, the famous Korean barbecue of marinated beef lavishly strewn with toasted sesame seeds; or skewers of beef, rice cakes and peppers, or braised beef ribs cooked with carrots and gingko nuts.

Ginseng root, while used primarily as a medicine, is also used as an ingredient in some recipes for skewered barbecued beef, boiled chicken and other dishes.

The number of meat or fish dishes increases with a person's wealth, but for all South Koreans the basics in each meal of the day are rice, a soup of vegetables in a beef or chicken stock and kimchi. Kimchi, a pickled, fermented vegetable—usually Chinese cabbage but often including turnips, radishes, bean sprouts and cucumbers—is such a staple of the Korean diet, and appears in so many forms, that in Seoul it has its own museum.

In the villages the women, who do all the cooking (although professional chefs are men), go from home to home helping each other with the kimchi. In the cities all the women in a family pitch in, with one chopping the cabbage and another shredding the ginger. Myung

Sook Gong, the wife of Ro Myung Gong, the Korean Consul General in New York City, says she eats kimchi not just with Korean food but even with spaghetti.

Breakfast was once the largest and most important meal of the day and is still the meal for celebrating holidays, birthdays and weddings. Food is offered to the ancestors before the meal, and then eaten by the descendants. But the tradition of the leisurely breakfast is eroding, a victim of a fast-paced life and mass-produced food. In the 1970's South Korea began producing commercially processed foods—sliced bread, jams, instant coffee, eggs in cartons and more.

"Young people have an American breakfast, and older people have a Korean breakfast," Mrs. Gong said.

Dinner, she added, is fast becoming the main meal. It remains the one meal, however, at which the local cuisine still stars. South Koreans may eat American breakfasts and an occasional French or Italian or Japanese lunch. But at home, it is home cooking they covet.

Bulgogi (Korean Barbecued Beef)

This is usually served with rice or by wrapping a few slices of beef in a lettuce leaf together with rice and a very small amount of Korean pepper sauce or Chinese chili.

Time: About 20 minutes   **Yield:** 6 to 8 servings

1½ pounds beef tenderloin or flank steak

3½ tablespoons soy sauce

1½ tablespoons sugar

5 tablespoons scallions, chopped on the
    diagonal

1 teaspoon minced garlic

1½ tablespoons toasted crushed
    sesame seeds

1 large onion, thinly sliced

2 tablespoons sesame oil

2 tablespoons rice wine

¼ teaspoon black pepper

2 tablespoons sherry

1. Slice beef into pieces 1½ inches square and ⅛ inch thick. It is easiest to slice the meat thin when it is partly frozen.

2. Mix beef with other ingredients.

3. Grill all meat and onion slices over a charcoal fire until it is just brown on the outside and pink inside. This will take 2 to 4 minutes.

September 14, 1988: ELAINE LOUIE;
recipe adapted from MYUNG SOOK GONG

Marinated London Broil
with Béarnaise Sauce

Yield: 4 to 6 servings

2½ pounds London broil

2 cups Rory's Marinade (recipe follows)

1½ cups Béarnaise Sauce (page 90)

1. Place London broil in a dish large enough to hold meat and its marinade. Pour marinade over steak and refrigerate overnight, turning once in a while.

2. When ready to cook, remove London broil from its marinade and place it over hot coals. Grill to desired doneness, turning once, about 7 to 8 minutes on each side for rare. Serve with Béarnaise sauce.

Rory's Marinade

Yield: 2 cups

1 cup vinegar

1 teaspoon dried oregano

1 teaspoon dried basil

1 bay leaf

1 teaspoon dried sage

1 teaspoon dried thyme

1 teaspoon dried rosemary

1 tablespoon Dijon mustard

1 teaspoon Tabasco sauce

1 teaspoon minced garlic

½ onion, minced

1 egg yolk

1 cup vegetable oil

Salt and pepper, to taste

1. In a mixing bowl, combine vinegar with all herbs, mustard, Tabasco sauce, garlic and onion.

2. Stir in egg yolk and whip in oil, a little at a time, until thick and smooth. Season with salt and pepper.

Béarnaise Sauce

Yield: About 1½ cups

1 shallot, or 2 scallions, including some
    greens, minced

2 teaspoons dried tarragon

2 tablespoons wine vinegar

2 tablespoons white wine

3 egg yolks

18 tablespoons butter, melted

1 teaspoon fresh lemon juice

Dash Tabasco sauce, to taste

Dash Worcestershire sauce, to taste

Salt and pepper to taste

1. In a small saucepan, combine shallot or scallions, tarragon, vinegar and wine. Bring to a boil and reduce over medium heat until there is no liquid left in pan. Set aside.

2. Bring some water to a boil and lower heat to medium. In a metal mixing bowl, whisk egg yolks and place bowl over steaming pot. Whisk yolks constantly until thickened.

3. Whisking constantly, add melted butter a drop at a time, as with a mayonnaise. If sauce becomes too thick, add one drop or two of water to thin it.

4. When all butter is incorporated, remove pan from heat and season with lemon juice, Tabasco sauce, Worcestershire sauce, salt and pepper. Slowly stir in tarragon mixture. Check seasonings.

October 23, 1983: "Tailgate Feasts," by BRYAN MILLER;
recipes adapted from DEBBIE and PATRICK DONAHUE

The Taco Joint in Your Kitchen

You may never have had a really terrific taco, especially if you live on the East Coast. There are a lot of tacos around, certainly, and many of them can be satisfying enough. But the genuine article is often hard to come by—except in Mexico, on the West Coast and in the Southwest, where taco passion runs deep. And when the Westerners travel east, they frequently fall into despair.

They sit around over coffee or tequila, complaining, sharing tips on where they heard there might be a good taco hiding.

Just about anything can be called a taco, which essentially means "sandwich." You take a tortilla and you put some stuff in it and you eat it; that's a taco. (If you roll the tortilla, it's a burrito, which appears to have been created in the American Southwest; if you layer food on top of it, it's an enchilada; if you crisp it up and use it as a kind of plate, it's a tostada; if you cut it into pieces and bake or fry it, it's a chip; and so on.) But taco aficionados have a particular taste, a particular feel in mind. It's about the ingredients, as high quality and as fresh as possible.

The good news is that without too much effort you can, believe it or not, create an admirable taco at home. What that means is not crisp-fried tortillas loaded with some weird ground beef mixture, lettuce and rice, but corn tortillas with some spicy slivered pork, grilled beef or maybe fish or chicken.

Turkey would probably be most traditional; the Native Americans of what is now Mexico not only hybridized corn as we know it but also raised turkeys.

The best tacos start with corn tortillas; flour is a recent adaptation and, while it is not always inappropriate or scorned, there is nothing like a corn tortilla. These are made from the same base as tamales, a slurry of kernels that have been treated with lime (calcium hydroxide, not the fruit) and then cooked and ground into a dough. At that point they are pressed into tortillas of many sizes, at one time by hand and now usually by machine. (Quite popular in both Mexico and Southern California are those that are just three inches across; you can eat 10 of these at a sitting.)

Machine or no, a good taco starts with a good tortilla.

Your best bet is not the supermarket but a Mexican grocery store, or if you're lucky, a bakery. In any case, it should be fresh and have that particular flinty aroma that all corn-lime products have.

One common approach, starting with ground meat and "taco seasoning mix," is a bad idea. Just think about a taco as having a number of components, and take it from there. My favorite, easy to find at taco trucks in Los Angeles or small shops in Mexico, is difficult to make at home. This is the taco al pastor, closer to what we think of as a gyro, with shaved spit-roasted pork or goat. (This was probably introduced by the Spaniards or, even more likely, the Lebanese, who emigrated to Mexico in significant enough numbers beginning in the late nineteenth century so that there are Lebanese neighborhoods in most major cities.) It doesn't really contain anything more than that meat and perhaps a little salsa, and often, a bit of grilled pineapple on top.

More commonly, a good taco is loaded with several components: something crunchy (lettuce or cabbage usually, but chopped onion or salted radish are also good); the protein; some moisture—crema, sour cream or guacamole will do nicely; and maybe cheese. Many people add salsa for brightness as well.

Grilled Carne Asada for Tacos

Carne asada means "grilled meat," which in turn means pretty much anything. But skirt steak is what you most often see made into carne asada (and in many Los Angeles supermarkets, skirt steak is actually called carne asada). Because of its high fat content, it's perfect here. Rub it with a few spices, grill it for a few minutes and pile it into tortillas with a couple of other ingredients to make a legitimate and near-perfect taco.

Time: About 45 minutes   **Yield:** 6 to 8 servings

1 clove garlic, peeled	1 teaspoon ground oregano
2 pounds skirt steak	½ teaspoon cayenne pepper
2 teaspoons ground cumin	Salt and freshly ground black pepper

1. Start a charcoal or gas grill. Crush garlic and rub steak with it. Combine remaining ingredients and rub into steak. Let steak sit until you're ready to grill.

2. Grill steak 3 to 4 minutes per side for medium-rare. Cut into slices and use as soon as possible (hot is best, but warm or room temperature is fine).

July 26, 2006: MARK BITTMAN

Baltimore Pit Beef Sandwich

I spent the first 18 years of my life in Baltimore, and not once did I eat pit beef. I am not particularly proud of this fact, but it does reflect the parochialism of the region's food. I grew up in the suburb of Pikesville, Maryland, and the foods of my childhood embraced the four C's of Baltimore gastronomy: crab, corned beef, coddies (leaden cakes of codfish and potatoes) and chocolate tops (cookies crowned with a rosette of chocolate icing).

Pit beef came from a working-class neighborhood on the east side of town, which for me might as well have been another planet.

Pit beef is Baltimore's version of barbecue: beef grilled crusty on the outside, rare and juicy inside and heaped high on a sandwich. Several things make it distinctive in the realm of American barbecue.

For starters, pit beef is grilled, not smoked, so it lacks the heavy hickory or mesquite flavor characteristic of Texas- or Kansas City-style barbecue. It is also ideally served rare, which would be unthinkable for a Texas-style brisket. Baltimore pit bosses use top round, not brisket, and to make this flavorful but tough cut of beef tender, they shave it paper-thin on a meat slicer.

Then there's the bread: the proper way to serve pit beef is on a kaiser roll or, more distinctively, on rye bread. The caraway seeds in the rye reflect the Eastern European ancestry of many Baltimoreans in this part of town and add an aromatic, earthy flavor to the beef.

The center of Baltimore pit beef is an industrial thoroughfare called Pulaski Highway, also known as Route 40. As you drive east out of the city, you pass truck stops, tractor dealerships and inexpensive motels. Nestled among them are the simple roadside eateries that purvey pit beef.

You could stop at one of the best known, Chaps, a white cinder-block building with picnic table seating. It has been cooking old-fashioned pit beef—over blazing charcoal— since 1987. Or you could head for Big Al's, where every pit beef sandwich comes with a nugget of Italian hot sausage.

For my money, there's no better place to sample pit beef than Big Fat Daddy's in Rosedale, Maryland, next to a country-western dance hall named Little Texas. To call Big Fat Daddy's a restaurant would be stretching. The "dining room" is a yellow and red tent with plastic siding. The pit (a gas and lava stone grill) is housed in a cinder block building not much bigger than a closet. You place your order at the window and dine at a picnic table, watching the traffic rumble by.

Big Fat Daddy's takes its name from Brian Schafer, a ruddy barbecue entrepreneur. He is big, all right, tipping the scales at 280 pounds. But he has shed 65 pounds since he opened the eatery in 1996 and worked 100 hours a week, running the restaurant and a catering business. "I got tired of working for other people," he said. "I thought I could do things a little better."

If perfection lies in attention to detail, the details distinguish Big Fat Daddy's from the other pit beef emporiums. Mr. Schafer rubs his beef with a tangy mixture of seasoned salt, pepper, oregano, garlic powder and paprika, and he lets the meat sit in the rub for three days. (Most Baltimore pit beef is grilled without all this.) When he makes a sandwich, he takes the time to slice a few burnt edges (the charred crust) to mix with the rare beef, thus adding smoke, crunch and flavor.

Most pit beef places serve bottled prepared horseradish, but Mr. Schafer makes his own sauce, a rich, creamy confection of horseradish and mayonnaise.

Regulars may miss the old days, when Big Fat Daddy's grilled its beef over charcoal. Mr. Schafer switched to gas two years ago, he said, because "we got tired of looking like we cooked in a coal mine."

These touches have brought big success. In the summer, Big Fat Daddy's goes through 40 top rounds (each weighing 25 pounds) a week. That is enough to serve 3,000 to 4,000 sandwiches every week.

Baltimore pit beef isn't difficult to prepare at home and makes a nice switch from the usual ribs and brisket for a party. The only real challenge is slicing the beef thin enough. If you have a meat slicer, you will have no problem. If not, a thin-slicing disc on a food processor will do the trick. Cut the roast in pieces small enough to fit into the feed tube. Or, just slice the meat as thin as possible by hand, then chop it with a cleaver.

The recipe here will give you eight two-fisted sandwiches. The rub is based on the seasoning mix used at Big Fat Daddy's. Lettuce and tomatoes are optional.

This Baltimore boy never knew what he was missing.

Time: 1 hour, plus 3 hours' to 3 days' marinating   **Yield:** 8 sandwiches

For the rub
2 tablespoons seasoned salt
1 tablespoon sweet paprika
1 teaspoon garlic powder
1 teaspoon dried oregano
½ teaspoon black pepper

For the sandwich
1 (3-pound) piece top round
8 kaiser rolls or 16 slices of rye bread
Horseradish Sauce (recipe follows)
1 sweet white onion, thinly sliced
2 ripe tomatoes, thinly sliced (optional)
Iceburg lettuce (optional)

1.   Combine ingredients for rub in a bowl, and mix. Sprinkle 3 to 4 tablespoons all over beef, patting it in. Place in a baking dish, and cover with plastic wrap. You can cover beef with rub for a few hours, but for maximum flavor, leave it for 3 days in refrigerator, turning once a day.

2.   Prepare a hot grill. Grill beef 30 to 40 minutes, or until outside is crusty and dark brown and internal temperature is about 120 degrees (for rare). Turn beef often. Transfer to a cutting board; let it rest 5 minutes.

3. Slice beef thinly across grain. Pile beef high on a roll or bread slathered with horseradish sauce. Garnish with onion, tomatoes and sliced lettuce. Serve.

Horseradish Sauce

No ketchup, brown sugar and liquid smoke, as you would find in Kansas City. No Texas-style chili hellfire or piquant vinegar sauces in the style of North Carolina. The proper condiment for Baltimore pit beef is horseradish sauce—as much as you can bear without crying. And speaking of crying, you need slices of crisp, pungent white onion to make the sandwich complete.

Time: 3 minutes   **Yield:** 1½ cups

1 cup mayonnaise

½ cup prepared white horseradish, or to taste

2 teaspoons fresh lemon juice

Salt and black pepper to taste

Combine ingredients in a bowl, and whisk to mix. Adjust seasonings to taste.

June 28, 2000: "How to Say Barbecue in Baltimore,"
by STEVEN RAICHLEN; recipes adapted from
Big Fat Daddy's, Rosedale, Maryland

In the Style of the Gauchos:
A Brazilian Barbecue

Dorothea Elman, a Native of Brazil, Prepares a Cattleman's Dinner

There are many kinds of feasts based to one degree or another on rituals of either a formal or a highly casual nature. They exist in almost every culture and numerous ones come to mind. In China, there are the elaborate "fire pots" or Mongolian hot pots wherein foods, fish, meat and vegetables, are cooked at the table by guests who stand around a communal and decorative steaming device.

There are the simple and traditional raclettes or fondues of Switzerland whereby guests share melted cheese from a single simmering earthenware pot.

And in America there is the enormously convivial, colorful—and, if properly done, backbreaking for the pit-makers—ritual known as a clam-bake.

One of the grandest ritual feasts in the world is of agrarian origins and comes from Brazil. This is the *churrasco à gaucha*, the traditional feast of southern Brazil, specifically from the state of Rio Grande do Sul, the center of the nation's cattle country.

I was recently involved in a highly sophisticated version of the churrasco à gaucha—all of it assembled under the expert guidance of Dorothea Elman, a redoubtable, enthusiastic cook, an old friend and a native of Rio de Janeiro whose husband, Lee, is an investment banker.

"Although the churrasco had basically humble origins—in the beginning it was nothing more than a cattleman's lunch or dinner made of freshly killed beef cooked over an open fire—the meal is tremendously popular in Rio and São Paolo," she said.

The meal she was preparing during the day was to be cooked and consumed late in the afternoon, at long tables situated next to a charcoal pit where the assorted meats—beef ribs, chicken, pork, lamb and sausages—would be grilled over hot ashes.

The time in which the meat would be grilled would be sufficient to unleash the hounds of hunger, the enraged appetite only partially assuaged by morsels of spicy Brazilian sausages wrapped in foil and buried in the hot coals. These are taken with a seemingly innocent, superficially innocuous and irresistible but potent Brazilian elixir known as caipirnha made with the clear distillate of sugar cane, lime and sugar over ice.

The meats, still amber and still sizzling, would be removed from the long skewer and cut, sliced or carved with an ingeniously, seductively seasoned salad of mixed vegetables—bits of broccoli, cauliflower, green beans, zucchini, green peas, carrots and so on blended in a tangy mayonnaise. That tops a platter of buttery farofa (page 102), a splendid dry cereal dish cooked with banana. And to bind the meat together, to give it an exceptional and uncommon fillip, a spicy onion sauce (page 102), made of oil and vinegar, chopped parsley and coriander.

Before noon the pit had been dug. A neat rectangular hole, 4 feet long, 3 feet wide and 14 inches deep. Ten logs would be burned and 40 pounds of charcoal heaped onto that. Gaucho knives, not essential to the ceremony but appropriate, had been shipped by air from Brazil. Long iron skewers had been obtained.

Before the meal began the long tables had been covered with sheets of heavy brown wrapping paper as is done in Brazil.

Forks and knives were provided plus linen napkins, although the *churrasqueira* (that's the female name of the person who cooks the meal; the male is *churrasquiro*) explained that these were civilized conceits; the gauchos use their fingers.

Mrs. Elman told us that she had arranged the feast as a preliminary to celebrating the national day of Brazil. For the feast, to be drunk with the churrasco, there was excellent imported Brazilian beer labeled Brahma Chopp.

Mrs. Elman went about her business of preparing foods and cooking them as well with cool, assured dedication and determination awesome to behold. The meats were threaded or simply impaled on parallel skewers and when the coals in the pit were properly ashen, she shoved the metal bottoms into the earth with a powerful, educated thrust, taking care that the foods on the rods were neatly centered directly over the heat. The skewers were inserted into the earth at a 10- or 14-degree angle, centering the foods about 12 to 14 inches from the heat.

As the meats were seared on one side, the skewers were deftly turned so that the other side would roast. The moment the meats were turned, she would dip a neatly tied and sizable bundle of leaves together to use as a basting "mop." She would swish the mop inside the vessel containing a basting brine made of water, garlic and salt, then onto the meats.

"You wait until the meats are seared on one side before basting them with the brine. After that you must brush them often. And if the flames start in the pit and under the meat, you must extinguish them at all times with a dash of brine from the mop.

"Take care," she added, "that the meats don't burn. Just let them get nice and crisp on the outside and cooked inside."

As the meats were ready for eating, the skewers were removed and the tips wiped off with a clean damp rag. The meats were removed, transferred to a cutting board and sliced or carved and served piping hot.

"There's one thing to remember," Mrs. Elman advised. "If you plan to cook at one of these, don't ever plan to sit with the guests until the end of the meal. That's why the table should be close to the pit. So you can cook and talk at the same time."

Work List for a Churrasco à Gaucha (for 12 to 16 people)

- A pit measuring about 3 feet by 4 feet by 14 inches
- 6 or 8 metal skewers, preferably flat rather than round, each measuring about 4½ to 5 feet in length
- 10 to 12 fireplace logs
- 40 pounds charcoal (preferably pure charcoal or charcoal briquettes)
- Brown paper to cover dining tables
- Forks, knives, napkins—either linen or paper
- A cutting block or slab for preparing meats after they are cooked
- A basting "mop" made of nontoxic leafy branches tied together or a large purchased basting utensil
- Sponge and clean cloths to wipe off the ends of skewers

As Linguicas (The Portuguese Sausages)

Yield: 12 to 16 cocktail servings

3 linguicas (Portuguese sausages), about
   1 pound

1. Cut each length of linguica in half. Wrap each half closely in heavy-duty foil and add to hot coals in a pit.

2. Let sausages cook about 10 minutes on one side. Turn them and cook about 10 minutes on other side.

3. Open up foil and cut sausages into 1- or 2-inch lengths. Serve hot.

As Costelas de Bife (The Beef Ribs)

Yield: 12 to 16 servings

5 (3-pound) slabs prime beef ribs
Salt to taste

Brine (recipe follows)

1. Using a sharp boning knife, cut away most but not all of fat from tops and bottoms of ribs. There will be pockets of fat between the ribs at tips. Discard fat.

2. Rub ribs with salt and arrange slabs of beef on two parallel skewers, threading them through the meaty portions between the ribs. For each two skewers, add two or three slabs or whatever they can accommodate properly.

3. Place ribs when ready over hot coals. Let cook without basting until nicely browned and seared on one side. Turn, repositioning skewers, so that ribs cook on opposite side. Brush seared side with brine. Continue cooking, turning as necessary and brushing with brine. Total cooking time is about 40 minutes, although time will vary depending on size of meat and its proximity to coals. To test for doneness, run a knife into meat between two of the bones.

4. When ready, remove skewers from coals and wipe off pointed ends. Remove ribs and place on a flat surface. Slice between individual ribs and serve.

NOTE: These slabs of prime beef ribs consist of about seven uncut ribs with the main part of the beef removed. There was no problem in ordering them a few days in advance from our local butcher. These are one of the best things about a churrasco. If they are not available, you can use trimmed fillets of beef in one piece or porterhouse or other steaks. Skewer the meat, either the filets or the steaks, before cooking.

A Salmoura (The Brine)

8 cloves garlic, peeled

2 cups kosher salt

1. Combine garlic, ½ cup of salt and 1 cup water in a food processor or blender. Blend thoroughly.

2. Empty brine into a large vessel and add remaining 1½ cups salt and 12 cups (3 quarts) water. Stir to blend thoroughly. Use as a basting brine for barbecues.

As Galinghas (The Chickens)

Yield: 12 to 16 servings

3 chickens (each about 2½ pounds), split down the back and opened up but left whole

1 tablespoon salt

¾ cup olive oil

3 cloves garlic, crushed and peeled

Brine (page 99)

1. Rub chickens all over with salt and place in a deep pan. Add oil and garlic and massage well with fingers. Cover and let stand 3 hours in refrigerator.

2. When ready to cook, use two skewers about five feet long. Run skewers through birds, inserting them left and right through their bodies. Center the three birds on the skewers, bodies touching, neck to tail.

3. Place chickens when ready about 12 to 16 inches above hot coals. Let them cook without basting until nicely browned and seared on one side. Turn them, repositioning skewers over coals. Brush seared side with brine. Continue cooking, turning as necessary and brushing occasionally with brine. Total cooking time for chickens is about 1 hour, although cooking time will vary depending on size of chickens and their proximity to the hot coals.

Porco (The Pork)

Yield: 12 to 16 small servings

1 (4½- to 5-pound) loin of pork loin

Salt to taste

Brine (page 99)

1. Bone pork loin or have it boned by butcher. Have most but not all of surface fat cut away.

2. Using a sharp knife, butterfly large meaty portion of the loin. That is, slice almost but not quite through the meat, opening it up to lie flat. If there is a smaller tenderloin, use that but leave intact. Rub meat with salt.

3. When ready to cook, use two skewers about five feet long. Run skewers parallel through butterflied loin. Skewer tenderloin if there is one. The pork will not occupy all the cooking room on the skewers so other meats may be added as desired.

4. Place meat or meats when ready over hot coals, fat side down. Let cook without basting until nicely browned and seared on one side. Turn, repositioning skewers over coals. Brush seared side with brine. Continue cooking, turning as necessary and brushing with brine. Total cooking time is about 1½ hours, although time will vary depending on size of meat and its proximity to the hot coals.

5. Remove skewers from grill and wipe off pointed ends. Remove meat and place on a flat surface. Cut and slice as desired for serving.

Carneiro (The Lamb)

Yield: 12 to 16 small servings

1 (2¾-pound) loin of lamb
Salt to taste

Brine (page 99)

1. Bone lamb or have it boned. Have most but not all of surface fat trimmed away. Rub meat with salt to taste. Skewer boned loin lengthwise on one skewer. If there is a small fillet of lamb, skewer that as well. The loin will occupy very little space on skewer; therefore, other meats such as the loin of pork may be added to skewer.

2. Place meat or meats when ready over hot coals, fat side down. Let cook without basting until nicely browned and seared on one side. Turn, repositioning skewer over coals. Brush seared side with brine. Continue cooking, turning as necessary and brushing with brine. Total cooking time is about one hour, although time will vary depending on size of meat and its proximity to the coals.

3. Remove skewer from grill and wipe off pointed end. Remove meat and place on a flat surface. Cut and slice as desired for serving.

Mohlo de Cebola (Onion Sauce)

Yield: 12 to 16 servings

6 cups finely chopped onions

3 cloves garlic, peeled

2½ cups olive oil

1⅓ cups red wine vinegar

½ cup finely chopped fresh parsley

⅓ cup finely chopped fresh cilantro

Salt to taste

3 cups cored tomatoes cut into ½-inch cubes

1. Put onions in a mixing bowl. Use three skewers or toothpicks and skewer each clove of garlic. Add them to the bowl.

2. Add oil, vinegar, parsley, cilantro and salt. Blend well.

3. Shortly before serving, add tomatoes. Remove garlic cloves and serve at room temperature.

Farofa

Yield: 12 to 16 servings

¾ pound (3 sticks) butter

5 cups thinly sliced onions

10 to 12 sweet, firm, ripe bananas

4 cups manioc flour (see note)

Salt to taste

1. Heat 6 tablespoons of butter in a large skillet and add onions. Cook, stirring, until wilted. Continue cooking, stirring, until they start to turn golden.

2. Peel bananas and cut them on the bias into ½-inch-thick slices. Heat 10 tablespoons of butter in a saucepan, and add bananas. Cook, stirring gently on occasion, until they start to turn golden.

3. Add manioc flour, and stir gently to blend bananas and flour. Add onions, and stir gently to blend. Cook, stirring occasionally, about 10 minutes or until manioc flour loses its raw taste.

4. Add remaining 8 tablespoons butter and salt and stir gently until butter is blended.

NOTE: Manoic flour is a staple in Brazilian cookery, made from the ground root of the manoic plant.

September 7, 1977: Craig Claiborne;
recipes from DOROTHEA ELMAN

Texas-Style Brisket

For me, barbecue starts with a rub, a vibrant mixture of spices used to coat and flavor the meat before cooking. A good rub will have the ability to enhance the flavor of the meat without camouflaging or overpowering it. The rub here does just that, although it contains only four ingredients: salt, sugar, pepper and paprika.

In Texas, barbecue means beef, especially brisket. This is more challenging to cook than pork shoulder, for brisket is a tough, ornery cut with an inherent tendency to dry out. To prevent this, I choose brisket with a thick layer of fat on top and cook it in a foil pan, which protects the meat on the bottom.

Time: 6 to 8 hours   **Yield:** 8 to 10 servings

1 (5- to 6-pound) piece beef brisket, with
    thick layer of fat
¼ cup Basic Rub for Barbecue (page 104)

5 cups hickory or oak chips, soaked
    in cold water for 1 hour, and then
    drained

1. Preheat grill to 325 degrees, building fire on opposite sides of grill if using charcoal, or on one side or opposite sides if using gas. Season brisket with rub.

2. If using charcoal, every hour for first 5 hours add fresh coals and toss ½ cup wood chips on each mound of coals. If using gas, place wood chips in smoker box, and preheat until you see smoke (depending on model of gas grill, use all 5 cups at once or 1 cup every hour for first 5 hours).

3. Place brisket, fat side up, in foil roasting pan just large enough to hold it. Place pan in center of grill, away from heat.

4. Barbecue brisket until nicely browned, cooked through and very tender, for 5 to 7 hours. If brisket starts to brown too much, tent it loosely with foil.

5. Transfer cooked brisket to cutting board, cover with foil and let rest for 10 minutes, reserving pan juices. With sharp knife, trim and discard any large lumps of fat. Slice brisket thinly across grain. Serve with slices of white bread, spooning pan juices over top.

Basic Rub for Barbecue

Time: 5 minutes   **Yield:** 2 cups

½ cup kosher salt

½ cup sugar

½ cup ground black pepper

½ cup paprika

Combine ingredients in a bowl, and whisk them all together to mix. Store in an airtight jar.

May 26, 1999: "Time and Smoke,
the Soul of Barbecue," by STEVEN RAICHLEN

Smoky Brisket

This traditional American barbecue is time-consuming, but it would be difficult to find a better way to flavor and prepare barbecued brisket.

Yield: 6 servings

1 (4-pound) piece of brisket

For the dry mop

½ cup sweet paprika

3 tablespoons salt

2 tablespoons freshly ground pepper

For the wet mop

⅔ cup water

1½ tablespoons instant espresso crystals

2 cups ketchup

¾ cup Worcestershire sauce

¼ pound (1 stick) butter

For the barbecue sauce

1 medium-size onion, pureed

¼ cup olive oil

4⅓ cups tomato puree

2 cups water

¾ cup dark brown sugar

2 bay leaves

2 cubes beef bouillion

3 tablespoons hot pepper sauce, like Tabasco sauce

2 tablespoons chili powder

1 tablespoon cayenne pepper

1 tablespoon fresh lemon juice

¾ teaspoon freshly ground pepper

¼ teaspoon salt

⅓ cup cider vinegar

1. To prepare the dry mop: Combine dry mop ingredients. Rub all over brisket. Set aside.

2. To prepare the wet mop: Combine wet mop ingredients, except butter, in a small saucepan. Bring it to a boil. Lower heat and simmer for 20 minutes. Remove from heat and whisk in butter; set aside.

3. Grill brisket slowly for 2 hours, basting every 30 minutes with wet mop.

4. Meanwhile, make the barbecue sauce. Combine onion puree and olive oil in a saucepan. Sauté until translucent, about 5 minutes. Add remaining ingredients, except vinegar, bring to a boil, lower heat and simmer for 20 minutes. Remove from heat, and stir in vinegar.

5. Cut the brisket into thin slices, and serve with barbecue sauce.

May 31, 1992: "Food: A Good Grilling," by MOLLY O'NEILL;
recipe adapted from EILEEN D. WEINBERG,
Good and Plenty to Go, New York City

Burgers Without Borders

Time: Summer evening, the present.

Scene: Backyard barbecue, somewhere in America.

Enter: Grown woman, lurking by the kids' table.

I admit it, I'm not above stealing burgers and hot dogs from children. At cookouts, I admire the grilled soft-shell crabs, pencil-thin asparagus and other adult fare, then check out what the toddlers are getting.

Burgers and sausages—any ground meat on the grill—have always been my favorites, for eating and for cooking. And for those (like me) whose grilling skills are still in development, they are relatively foolproof.

On Memorial Day, a char-grilled American beef burger can bring patriotic tears to the eye. But by the Fourth of July, the pleasure of plain meat may pale, even for me. That's when mixtures that are highly seasoned but still simple come into play. They are the far-flung ancestors of burgers, sometimes shaped into balls or around skewers, but bearing unmistakable family traits of tenderness, juice and spice. In the grilling traditions of countries like Pakistan, Turkey and Indonesia, ground meat, spices and aromatics bloom together over hot coals.

Ground meat, though it doesn't have the mighty heft of a steak in American culture, is an art form in others. In the Middle East, from Lebanon all the way to Afghanistan and Iran, generations of cooks have used every scrap of meat and transformed it into elegant, subtly spiced dishes.

For Lisa Ades, a New York filmmaker whose family has deep roots in Aleppo, Syria, a savory combination of ground beef, onion and allspice was a primary childhood food. (Allspice is the signature flavor of Syrian cooking.) "We would have it on top of pizza, as dinner, mixed with eggs and fried, but never in the summer," she said, "So this summer I put it on a skewer and called it a kebab. I always hated those other kebabs anyway—those chewy chunks of lamb with the hot cherry tomato falling off the skewer."

Ms. Ades is currently doing her grilling at a 1950's house in Amherst, Massachusetts, whose garden has kept its original Asian-Polynesian theme, including a pagoda fitted with a gas grill, tiki masks and a lamp made of whole blowfish. "When you are only cooking one thing, suddenly dinner is so much easier," said Ms. Ades, who serves the crusty meat stuffed into warmed pita bread with a crisp, lemony cucumber salad and black olives. "You can eat them standing up, just like burgers, but they taste amazing."

Ms. Ades's recipe can be used to make burgers or kebabs, shaped around metal skewers. Burgers are easier to form, but the kebabs cook faster and more evenly, eliminating the challenge of figuring out when they are done, my least favorite part of grilling. When they are done on the outside, they are done all the way through to the metal. When choosing skewers, look for wide, flat ones—you want the meat to turn with the skewer, not to stay still on the grill while the skewer spins around uselessly inside it.

The sausage shape I've adopted is not traditional in Turkey, where the kebab is king, and where a single, unbroken tube of meat is the ideal.

"There is only one way to make this kebab, there is only one way to cook it and there is only one way to eat it," said Orhan Yegen, a noted purist on the subject of Turkish cuisine. Mr. Yegen is the chef at Sip Sak, a Turkish restaurant in Midtown. He was born in Istanbul but raised in the eastern city of Adana, famous throughout Turkey for its dark red, succulent ground-lamb kebabs.

The meat is mixed with onions, juicy red bell peppers and *kirmizi biber*—dried hot and sweet peppers rubbed together and roasted in olive oil into flakes of deep reddish black. Mr. Yegen lightly slapped the few ingredients together, not compressing the mixture in his hand, which could make the end result tough.

"You need fat to cook anything on the grill," Mr. Yegen said as he molded the finished mixture around traditional flat metal skewers that were almost an inch wide and two feet long—swordlike compared to the spindly ones used by most Americans, and much better for searing kebabs. "Lean ground meat is a terrible thing," he added. When buying meat for these (or any recipes for ground meat on the grill), make sure to use cuts like lamb shoulder, beef chuck and chicken thighs. If ground versions of these cuts aren't available, it's the work of a minute to grind the meat yourself by pulsing it in batches in a food processor.

Jackson Heights, Queens, is the center for New York's huge Desi community. Loosely interpreted, the term includes almost anyone with recent roots in South Asia. It's also the site of dueling Pakistani kebab empires: Kabab King, the incumbent, and Kababish, the upstart, which recently opened up right across the street. Kababish grills its kebabs over charcoal, giving it an edge on flavor; but Kabab King boasts lacier, crispier nan bread, a delicious necessity for wrapping juicy kebabs. "Kebabs are part of the daily life, but also every party in Pakistan," said Tahir Kamil, an owner of Kababish. "And a large variety of kebabs is a sign of luxury and festivity."

Urdu has as many modifiers for kebabs as Starbucks has for coffee. In Pakistani tradition, *chapli* kebabs—the word refers to the sole of a shoe—are flat, thin patties of minced meat or chicken; they're a popular snack at the delis that serve New York's taxi drivers.

Seekh or *sheekh* kebabs are savory mixtures of minced meat or chicken, onion, cilantro and spices, bound together with egg. *Gola* kebabs solve the binding problem more literally: the ground meat is attached to skewers with a single long thread, wrapped around the meat. The gola kebab slides off the skewer in one piece; when you lift the thread out of the tender meat, it slices the kebab into chunks.

And *reshmi* kebabs—the word is sometimes rendered as "reshami" or "shami," are considered the finest: the word means silky or smooth, and the meat is ground with rich pistachios and cashew nuts, then marinated in yogurt for at least a day.

Smooth meat is traditionally valued in Middle Eastern cooking—wealthy households might devote a servant's entire day to pounding meat in a stone mortar—but that texture is not to modern American taste, and coarsely ground meat works best in these recipes.

Syrian Beef Kebabs

Time: 30 minutes, plus 1 hour for chilling   **Yield:** 4 to 6 servings (8 skewers)

2 pounds fatty ground beef, like chuck

¼ cup tomato paste

⅔ cup minced onion

2 teaspoons salt

Juice of 1 lemon

½ teaspoon ground cinnamon

2 dashes cayenne pepper

1 tablespoon ground allspice

⅓ cup pine nuts

Oil to brush on grill rack

Lemon wedges and pita bread for
    serving

Lemony Cucumber Salad for serving
    (recipe follows)

1.   Combine all ingredients but oil, lemon wedges, pita and salad in a bowl, and knead very well into a paste.

2.   Hold a flat metal skewer—not nonstick, and at least 12 inches long—point up in one hand. Dip other hand in a bowl of water, take a handful of meat mixture and form it around base of skewer in a small sausage shape with pointed ends. Repeat, working your way up the skewer. Each skewer should hold three or four kebabs. (You can also just form meat into eight patties.)

3.   Lay finished skewers on a sheet pan, and smooth kebabs with fingers, making sure they are fairly smooth and secured on skewers. Refrigerate at least 1 hour.

4.   Prepare charcoal grill, or turn gas grill to medium-low. Spray or brush oil on clean grill rack, and set within a few inches of the fire. Fire should not be too hot, and rack should be at least several inches from heat source.

5.   When rack is heated through, gently squeeze kebabs to be sure they are secure on skewers, and place skewers on grill. The meat should start sizzling gently; it should not spit and turn black. Cook undisturbed until deep brown, at least 7 minutes. When meat lifts easily from grill, slide a spatula under kebabs and turn over. Continue grilling until browned on both sides and juicy, but cooked through, 10 to 15 minutes total. Serve hot with lemon wedges and pita that has been warmed on grill. Put a few spoonfuls of salad in each pita with meat.

Lemony Cucumber Salad

Time: 5 minutes   **Yield:** 4 to 6 servings

6 cups romaine lettuce (about 2 hearts)

1 long seedless cucumber or 3 Kirbys,
   peeled, halved lengthwise and sliced
   crosswise ¼ inch thick

3 tablespoons olive oil

2 teaspoons fresh lemon juice

Salt and black pepper to taste

Toss all ingredients. Serve chilled.

June 29, 2005: JULIA MOSKIN;
kebabs recipe adapted from LISA ADES

Beef Brochettes with
Red Peppers and Coriander

Barbecuing a slab of steak requires constant vigilance, carving and serving. An alternative is brochettes of beef with vegetables.

Brochettes not only cook much faster, they also are more forgiving to a backyard chef who wanders from the fire. It's O.K. to overcook a brochette or two, but not the entire steak.

This recipe calls for a marinade of lemon juice, coriander seed, fresh garlic, red pepper flakes, cumin, thyme, red wine, honey and cilantro. Since the meat is lean beef fillet or sirloin, both tender cuts, marination need be only 15 minutes. Any longer, and the meat could begin to break down in the acidic liquid. Reserve the marinade for basting during the cooking.

Brochettes are filled with meat, onions and red pepper chunks. If you do not have a barbecue grill, this recipe works fine under a broiler at 500 degrees. In both cases about four minutes' cooking should leave them rare.

A simple, tasty side dish is rice with peas and parsley. I add a bit of Tabasco sauce to liven things up, but that is optional. This recipe has many variations, especially in summer when so much fresh produce is available. To the rice, you could add okra, cubed beets, green beans, zucchini, sweet peppers, artichokes, tomatoes, fava beans, broccoli and more.

Yield: 4 servings

1½ pounds lean beef, like fillet or sirloin	½ teaspoon ground cumin
2 red onions (about ½ pound)	4 sprigs fresh thyme, or 1 teaspoon dried
2 medium-size red bell peppers	¼ cup dry red wine
2 tablespoons fresh lemon juice	2 tablespoons honey
2 tablespoons coriander seeds	2 tablespoons olive oil
1 teaspoon chopped garlic	¼ cup coarsely chopped fresh cilantro
¼ teaspoon red pepper flakes	Salt and freshly ground pepper to taste

1. Preheat a charcoal grill to high. If wooden skewers are used, soak them in cold water until ready to use.

2. Cut beef into 1-inch cubes. There should be 24 cubes.

3. Peel and cut onions into 24 (1-inch) cubes. Reserve remaining onion for another use. Set cubes aside until ready to cook.

4. Cut away and discard the pepper cores, veins and seeds. Cut peppers into 24 equal-size pieces and set aside until ready to cook.

5. Combine meat and remaining ingredients in a mixing bowl. Blend well and marinate 15 minutes.

6. Drain meat and arrange equal portions of meat, onions and peppers on skewers. Reserve marinade for basting.

7. Place brochettes on grill and cook 4 minutes for rare, basting often with reserved marinade while turning. (For safety, do not baste during last 5 minutes of grilling and discard marinade.)

July 31, 1991: "60-Minute Gourmet,"
by PIERRE FRANEY

Scouts Make a Camp Stew in Foil;
Bacon and Eggs on Can Top

Tradition has it that Boy Scouts, scorning matches, rub two sticks together to start a fire. Yesterday in a camping cookery exhibit at the Skywalk Café of the Astor Hotel the Scouts used not only matches but highly modern aluminum foil to produce a good variation on campers' stew.

The aluminum foil cookery made a dish called "Treasure Oak Special" (after an area at the Scouts' Alpine Camp in New Jersey). Apparently susceptible to numerous variations, Treasure Oak Special yesterday consisted of hamburger, bacon, snap beans, potatoes, tomatoes and onions cooked together in a foil package laid directly on glowing charcoal.

Robert Smith, assistant director of field and education for the Greater New York Councils, Boy Scouts of America, said Scouts often packaged meals in homemade aluminum foil envelopes before outings, marked the package "Sunday lunch" or "Saturday dinner," put them into a cooling unit and when in camp simply popped them on the fire.

Treasure Oak Special

A formal recipe for Treasure Oak Special, arranged in slightly different form from the Scout original by *The New York Times*' home economist, Ruth P. Casa-Emellos, follows.

Yield: One serving for a hungry boy

1 (18-inch) piece heavy-duty foil	1 medium-size carrot
⅔ pound hamburger steak	6 snap beans
2 slices bacon	½ teaspoon salt
1 small potato	Pepper to taste

1. Fold aluminum foil in half. Put hamburger steak between slices of bacon and place in center of foil.

2. Add potato sliced into ¼-inch slices, the carrot frenched and cut in half, snap beans cut in half, salt and pepper.

3. Fold foil over food and seal airtight by folding three times on each edge.

4. Place package on hot coals and turn after 6 to 7 minutes. Cook 15 minutes longer, remove from fire, tear along folded edges and eat right from aluminum foil.

June 16, 1954

Veal Chops with Summer Savory

Yield: 4 servings

4 rib veal chops, about 1 inch thick
Juice half a lemon
3 cloves garlic
Coarse salt

¼ cup fresh summer savory leaves, plus
    more for garnish
½ to ¾ cup olive oil
Freshly ground pepper

1. Wipe veal chops dry with paper towels. Squeeze lemon juice over meat, and set chops aside in shallow dish.

2. Peel garlic cloves, and place in mortar. Sprinkle with salt, and grind up paste with a pestle. Work in summer savory leaves, and gradually add olive oil until thoroughly blended. Season to taste with pepper.

3. Pour marinade onto chops, and toss to coat them thoroughly. Let them marinate for at least 2 hours and up to 1 day in your refrigerator.

4. Remove chops from marinade (discard marinade) and pat dry to remove excess oil. Grill for 4 to 5 minutes on each side, or until done to taste. Sprinkle with summer savory leaves before serving.

NOTE: Hickory or apple wood is especially good for this recipe.

June 30, 1985: "Food: Home Barbecue: Enhanced Possibilities," by MOIRA HODGSON

Grilled Medallion of Veal
with Mustard and Chive Sauce

Yield: 4 to 6 servings

2¼ pounds tenderloin of veal, cut into
    4 pieces
¾ cup buttermilk, approximately
Oil for brushing the grill

Mustard and Chive Sauce (recipe follows)
1 tablespoon finely chopped fresh chives
    for garnish

1.   Put meat in a mixing bowl and add buttermilk barely to cover it. Cover bowl and refrigerate for at least 2 hours.

2.   Preheat a well-scrubbed outdoor gas grill to high, or fire coals of a charcoal grill to white hot. Brush grill lightly with oil.

3.   Using fingers, take out each piece of meat and wipe away buttermilk. Place pieces on preheated grill and cook about 4 minutes or until meat lifts off easily. Turn pieces and cook on second side about 4 minutes. Continue grilling, turning the meat, until it is not resilient to touch, about 7 to 8 minutes longer. (The exact cooking time will vary, depending on thickness of meat.)

4.   Cut meat on bias into ¼-inch-thick slices. Keep slices close together. Spoon mustard and chive sauce over meat and sprinkle with chives.

Mustard and Chive Sauce

Yield: About 1 cup

10 tablespoons butter
1 tablespoon finely chopped shallots
1 cup dry white vermouth
¼ cup white wine vinegar

1 tablespoon Dijon-style mustard
1 tablespoon Pommery-style (grainy)
    mustard
1 tablespoon finely chopped fresh chives

1.   Heat 1 teaspoon of butter in a saucepan and add shallots. Cook, stirring, about 1 minute without browning.

2.   Add vermouth and bring to a boil. Add vinegar and cook over high heat until liquid is reduced to about 2 tablespoons, about 5 to 7 minutes.

3. Immediately start adding remaining butter, a tablespoon at a time, beating rapidly with a wire whisk.

4. Add Dijon and Pommery-style mustards plus any liquid that has accumulated around grilled medallions of veal. At last minute, add chives to sauce.

July 6, 1986: "Food: Grilling as Art,"
by CRAIG CLAIBORNE with PIERRE FRANEY;
recipes from LAURA THORNE and JEFF TRUJILLO,
formerly of Coast Grill, Southampton, New York

CHAPTER FOUR

Pork

Recent years have seen a growing fascination with pork among chefs and home cooks alike. This comes as no surprise to Southerners, who have always cooked pork in every possible way and with every cut from nose to tail. Pork is in many ways a perfect meat for grilling and smoking. It picks up all the nuances of flavor in the acorns, grains and grasses hogs eat. Bottom line, delicious fat, succulent meat, big, big flavor. Fatty 'Cue Spare Ribs (page 137) absolutely crush it. Garlic Roasted Pork Shoulder (page 145) via the Cuban community of South Florida is a celebration of flavor and family. And don't miss Sam Sifton's essay on the ingenious Caja China, a foolproof way to cook a whole pig on the first try (page 148).

Judge samples barbecue at the fifth Annual Taylor (Texas) International Championship Barbecue Cook-off, 1982.

Table to Farm

It's one thing to visit the farm where your salad was grown. It's another to stand on the killing floor where that evening's braised pork originated. But to interview the Missouri chef Jonathan Justus means starting at the beginning of the dish.

So after spending the morning with his butter maker and chicken and egg suppliers, we skipped to the main course and visited Paradise Locker Meats, a small-production slaughterhouse and meat-processing plant that works with Heritage Foods U.S.A. to supply top restaurants with meat from heirloom breeds.

As we parked in the muddy lot, visions of Upton Sinclair and immigration abuses flitted through my formerly vegetarian mind. But Paradise was spotless and calm, save for the man with a band saw bisecting a cow. The only other hints of the previous day's slaughter—conducted, however oxymoronically, according to humane guidelines—were a cart brimming with pigs' heads and boxes marked for Chez Panisse, Lupa, Bar Boulud and Fatted Calf. A few of those boxes would have a much shorter trip to the plate that day.

"What's being served at Momofuku and Spotted Pig is what I'm serving," he said of Justus Drugstore: A Restaurant, located 11 miles away in Smithville. "I'm just here at the source."

Paradise had five employees in 2003, including the owner, Mario Fantasma, his wife and his son. Today they employ 25, with plans to expand to meet demand. The plant, it turns out, has created more than jobs in the community. "One of the reasons we decided we could do a restaurant is because of what Mario's doing here," said Justus, an intense, articulate man who mentions his O.C.D. personality and low self-esteem in fast-paced rotation, making him seem much younger than his 43 years. When his mother and sister approached him about opening a restaurant in the family drugstore—"the anti-plan," as he saw it—the first thing that he looked at was agri-infrastructure. Fortunately, in the decades since he last lived back home, between stints as a bike messenger and butcher in San Francisco and a cook in the South of France, the farm had moved closer to the table. Now he could realize his goal to connect the region's tables to its farms. "This is a big piece of the puzzle," he said of Paradise. "It allows me to do a nose-to-tail menu."

Fantasma beamed as Justus launched into a lecture on the genius of Paradise's four-rib-bone country cut, which he serves both braised and smoked in one dish, topped with bacon-powder-flecked apple chantilly and tag-teamed with a corn flan, bacon-studded cabbage and apple sticks.

"This guy kills me," Fantasma said, elbowing Justus. "He scares me."

When he opened the restaurant two years ago, Justus probably scared many of his 5,000 neighbors, and not just because he's a Democrat. Missouri is more about barbecue than ginger-brined pork with apple foam. Living out their 15-year dream of opening a restaurant, he and his wife, Camille Eklof, transformed his family's 1950's drugstore into a bit of the big city, albeit on "a microbudget." The old soda fountain became the bar, where a local botanist and an environmental scientist were set to work concocting bitters, vermouth and infused liquors.

Locals can now drop by for a Manhattan made with date-infused bourbon and a bar snack of turkey fries (a k a testicles) with a morel-cream sauce. Instead of making the 20-minute drive to Kansas City for rib tips, they now stick around for Akaushi brisket from Paradise braised in homemade root-beer. (Justus uses the G.P.S. on his iPhone to forage for sassafras and other native plants.) Or maybe freshwater striper bass rendered baroque with egg-white gratin, persimmon paint, maple-sherry-ginger foam and caramel-mint dust.

Justus said the food is his version of Midwestern country cooking, "created in a vacuum." Pride, and economic necessity, dictate that many things be made from scratch, like charcuterie, bacon and ham; bread is baked by Eklof, who waits on tables and works as the general manager; fish and meat are butchered in-house. Justus is always bargaining with purveyors for "off cuts" of meat. "All our cuts are off cuts," he said with a laugh.

They live by their food politics, but Justus and Eklof don't proselytize at the table. They let the menu do the talking: on the cover, a quote from Thomas Keller stating that good food takes time lets diners know they won't make the 8 o'clock movie; the back lists 25 local purveyors, intended to open people's eyes to the links a restaurant can have to its area—links that Justus wants to weave into an infrastructure for farmers, breeders, aquaculturists and food artisans that could eventually slow development as farmers reclaim land to meet demand from revolutionary restaurants like his.

While it took the couple a while to come around to coming home, Smithville seems to suit their goals. Justus recalled Eklof's urging him to consider it: "She said: 'Look, we can live in San Francisco forever, and we're never going to change anyone's mind because we're going to be in our insular community. If we ever want to make any change, we've got to be the monkey wrench from the inside.'"

From the outside, the change is evident. Mark Ladner, the executive chef at Del Posto in New York, dined at Justus Drugstore last summer as part of Heritage Foods' pork tour of the area. He was impressed with the "funky, positive" feel, both on the menu and in the dining room. "It felt like they were doing something important,'" he said.

The satisfaction of building a community around food has been rewarding spiritually, if not yet financially. "This restaurant is completely and totally built on philosophy," Justus said. "'Cause it sure as [expletive] isn't about money. It can't be." They live off of Eklof's tips and are saving to be able to provide health insurance for their 16 employees—part of their plan to redefine what a restaurant can be.

"I hope what we're doing is a forefront of a trend," he said, looking out of the window they built onto Main Street. "I feel like, if we can do this here—really!—why can't this be done anywhere?"

Grilled Pork Porterhouse
with an Apple-Maple-Ginger Sauce

Yield: 6 servings

For the brine

¼ cup maple syrup

5 tablespoons kosher salt

3 tablespoons sliced peeled fresh ginger

3 tablespoons crushed garlic

1 sprig fresh sage

¾ cup onion slices, cut into ¼-inch-thick
    rings

5 bay leaves

2 teaspoons peppercorns

6 (1¼-inch-thick) pork loin chops
    (also known as pork porterhouses),
    preferably Berkshire organic (see note)

For the infused oil

1 tablespoon coriander seeds

1 bay leaf

1 tablespoon peppercorns

2 tablespoons minced shallot

1 teaspoon minced fresh thyme

1 teaspoon minced fresh rosemary

½ cup vegetable oil

For the sauce

2 tablespoons butter

¼ cup minced shallot

1 tablespoon minced garlic

2 cups apple juice

½ cup chicken stock

3 star anise

2 tablespoons minced fresh ginger

½ cup maple syrup

½ vanilla bean, seeds scraped

1 tablespoon agar (see note)

Salt and freshly ground black pepper
    to taste

1. Twenty-four hours before cooking, stir all of brine ingredients except pork into 1 quart water in a large pot and bring to a boil. Let cool to room temperature. Submerge pork chops in brine, cover and refrigerate.

2. Next morning, prepare the infused oil: grind coriander, bay leaf and peppercorns in a spice mill or a clean coffee grinder and combine with remaining ingredients in a medium bowl. Let sit at room temperature.

3. Make the sauce: In a saucepan, melt butter over medium-low heat. Add shallot and sauté until caramelized, about 4 minutes. Add garlic and cook for 1 minute. Add apple juice, chicken stock, star anise and ginger. Bring to a boil, lower heat and simmer until reduced by one-quarter. Add maple syrup, vanilla pod and seeds and agar and simmer for 3 minutes. Remove from heat. Discard star anise and vanilla pod. Puree mixture in a blender or food processor, then pass through a fine-mesh sieve into a pan. Season to taste with salt and pepper.

4. Prepare a charcoal or gas grill to medium-high heat. Rinse meat and pat dry with paper towels. Brush chops with infused oil, then sprinkle lightly with salt. Grill to medium doneness, or until internal temperature reads 135 to 140 degrees on a thermometer and middle is light pink, about 6 minutes per side. Let sit for 5 minutes before serving. Drizzle with warm sauce and serve.

NOTE: Berkshire organic pork is available to order through heritagefoodsusa.com. Agar is available at most health-food stores.

March 1, 2009: CHRISTINE MUHLKE;
recipe adapted from JONATHAN JUSTUS and
JEFFREY SCOTT, Justus Drugstore, Smithville, Missouri.

Grilled Pork Chops with Fried Sage Leaves

Time: 30 minutes   **Yield:** 4 servings

4 loin pork chops
Juice of 1 lemon
1 clove garlic, minced
2 tablespoons olive oil
Coarse salt and freshly ground pepper
     to taste

About ½ cup vegetable oil (enough for
     ½ inch in pan)
30 fresh sage leaves

1.   Coat pork chops with mixture of lemon juice, garlic and olive oil. Marinate for
30 minutes at room temperature. Season them with salt and pepper and grill, turning
once, over hot coals for about 20 minutes, or until they are cooked through.

2.   Heat vegetable oil and fry sage leaves about 2 minutes, or until they are crisp.
Remove with a slotted spoon and drain on paper towels.

3.   Garnish pork chops with sage leaves and serve.

August 29, 1993: "Food: Trimmer and Seasoned,
Pork Makes a Comeback,"
by MOIRA HODGSON

Time and Smoke, the Soul of Barbecue

Grilling may lie at the heart of the American summer, but barbecue is its soul, for true barbecue possesses a personality and depth of flavor you simply can't achieve with grilling.

True barbecued Texas brisket, for example, or North Carolina pulled pork relies on long, slow, smoky cooking, not just a short sizzle over hot coals or gas flames. The result is the haunting taste of wood smoke and meat so tender that you can pull it apart with your fingers. True barbecue has about as much in common with a grilled burger as prime rib does with minute steak.

Barbecue achieves these virtues by using indirect cooking: the meat is placed near, not directly over, the fire, and the temperature is deliberately kept low. The traditional fuel is wood, since smoke is the very essence of barbecue. Patience is essential, as the larger cuts of meat can take as long as 16 hours to acquire the proper dose of smoke and tenderness.

The good news is that true barbecue can be made on a backyard grill, even one fueled by gas. It's certainly worth the effort, for nothing adds flavor and succulence to meat like this traditional American method.

Originally, barbecue was cooked in or over a pit, and sometimes it still is, particularly in the South. More often, the "pit" is a brick or steel construction above ground, decades old and blackened with drippings and wood smoke. The fire burns at one end, and the food is cooked at the other. Or the fire burns at the bottom of the pit, while the food cooks on racks high above it.

Given the formidable size of a traditional pit and the logs used to fuel it, true barbecue may seem difficult to duplicate on a backyard grill. On the contrary, today's kettle grills and gas grills, with their high lids, make barbecuing a snap.

As with a professional pit, the fire is built on opposite sides of the grill, or on one side, and the food is cooked in the center, or on the opposite side. The grill has to be covered, to seal in the smoke flavor.

How you approach true barbecue depends on your equipment. With a charcoal kettle grill, you begin by lighting charcoal or charwood (lump charcoal) in your chimney starter. When the coals glow red, dump them into two piles at opposite sides of the grill. (Some grills come with side baskets for this purpose.) Place a foil drip pan in the center of the grill, between the mounds of embers. Place the grate on the grill, and barbecue your food in the center, over the drip pan. Toss a handful of wood chips on the coals to generate smoke. Keep the grill covered, adjusting the vents to keep the temperature at 325 to 350 degrees.

When barbecuing large cuts of meat, you'll need to replenish the coals every hour. Add 10 coals to each side, and leave the grill uncovered for a few minutes to allow them to ignite. Charwood ignites faster and more cleanly than briquettes, so I prefer it. It's available at natural-food stores and at many supermarkets.

A gas grill is even simpler to use, for the temperature remains more consistent. If you have one with two burners, light one side (set the burner on high), and cook the food on the other. If you have three burners, light the front and rear burners (or the left and right ones), and cook the food in the center. If you have four burners, light the far left and far right burners, and cook the food in the center.

The challenge of barbecuing with gas lies in generating sufficient wood smoke. Many gas grills have special smoker boxes in which you can add chips, but some work better than others.

Now, here's the tricky part. If a handful of chips in the smoker box fails to produce enough smoke, you may need to add all of the wood chips at once and run your grill on high until you see smoke. If your grill lacks a smoker box (or if the one provided doesn't work well), loosely wrap the chips in heavy-duty foil, poke a few holes in the top with a fork, and place it under the grate, directly over one of the burners.

North Carolina-Style Pulled Pork

In North Carolina, barbecue means pork, in particular a Boston butt (cut from the pork shoulder) that's been smoked to fall-off-the-bone tender and then pulled into shreds or chopped. The traditional condiment is vinegar sauce, which is mixed right in with the meat.

Time: 5 to 7 hours
Yield: 10 to 12 servings

1 bone-in pork shoulder roast (5 to 6
    pounds)
¼ cup Basic Rub for Barbecue
    (page 145)
4 cups hickory chips, soaked in cold
    water for 1 hour and then drained

For the vinegar sauce
1½ cups cider vinegar
2 tablespoons sugar, or to taste
1 tablespoon red pepper flakes
2 teaspoons salt, or to taste
½ teaspoon freshly ground black pepper

1. Preheat grill to 325 degrees, building fire on opposite sides of grill if using charcoal, or on one side or opposite sides if using gas. Season pork with rub.

2. If using charcoal, every hour for first 4 hours add fresh coals and toss ½ cup wood chips on each mound of coals. If using gas, place wood chips in smoker box, and preheat until you see smoke (depending on model of gas grill, use all 4 cups at once or 1 cup every hour for first 4 hours).

3. Place pork fat side up on grill over drip pan, away from fire. Barbecue until nicely browned and cooked through, for 4 to 6 hours, or until internal temperature is 195 degrees, so that meat will shred properly.

4. Meanwhile, combine ingredients for vinegar sauce in a bowl with ¾ cup water, and whisk to mix. Add additional salt or sugar to taste, if desired.

5. Transfer cooked pork to cutting board, cover with foil and let it rest until cool enough to handle, about 15 minutes. Pull meat into pieces, and discard any skin, bones or fat. With fingertips or a fork, pull each piece of pork into shreds about 2 inches long and ¼ inch wide. (Or finely chop meat with a cleaver.) Transfer to metal or foil pan, and stir in 1 cup vinegar sauce, or enough to keep meat moist and flavorful. Cover with foil, and place on grill to keep warm until serving. Serve on hamburger buns with cole slaw and remaining sauce on side.

May 26, 1999: STEVEN RAICHLEN

Vietnamese Pork Kebabs

Southeast Asia, with its lively tradition of street foods, has a popular kebab tradition. "They should spring back at you, with a little chew and spice," says Corinne Trang, an American chef who specializes in Vietnamese classics like *nem nuong*, grilled pork meatballs. Nem nuong, she said, are popular as a street snack all over Vietnam, cooked to order on jury-rigged grills that might consist of just a handful of charcoal and four bricks set up on a street corner. The pork is studded with shallots and lemon grass, spiked with fish sauce and sugar, grilled to a golden crustiness, and then wrapped, hot, in cool lettuce leaves and fresh herbs and given a light bath in hot, sour, salty and sweet dipping sauce. The result is flavorful, to say the least.

Time: 30 minutes, plus 1 hour chilling
Yield: 4 to 6 servings (8 skewers)

2 pounds fatty ground pork, like shoulder

3 stalks lemon grass, tender white and pale green parts only, minced

4 shallots, minced

2 cloves garlic, minced

1 tablespoon fish sauce

2 teaspoons sugar

1 teaspoon turmeric

1 teaspoon ground black pepper

Oil to brush on grill rack

Whole lettuce leaves, fresh mint and cilantro sprigs for serving

Nuoc Cham for serving (recipe follows)

1. Combine pork, lemon grass, shallots, garlic, fish sauce, sugar, turmeric and pepper in a bowl, and knead very well into a paste.

2. Hold a flat metal skewer (not nonstick, and at least 12 inches long) point up in one hand. Dip other hand in a bowl of water, take a handful of meat mixture and form it around base of skewer in a small sausage shape with pointed ends. Repeat, working your way up the skewer. Each skewer should hold 3 or 4 kebabs. (You can also just form meat into 8 patties.)

3. Lay finished skewers on a sheet pan, and smooth kebabs with fingers, making sure they are fairly smooth and secured on skewers. Refrigerate at least 1 hour.

4. Prepare charcoal grill, or turn gas grill to medium-low. Spray or brush oil on clean grill rack, and set within a few inches of fire. Fire should not be too hot, and rack should be at least several inches from heat source.

5. When rack is heated through, gently squeeze kebabs to be sure they are secure on skewers, and place skewers on grill. Meat should start sizzling gently; it should not spit and turn black. Cook undisturbed until deep brown, at least 7 minutes. When meat lifts easily from grill, slide a spatula under kebabs and turn over. Continue grilling until browned on both sides and juicy, but cooked through, 10 to 15 minutes total.

6. To serve, wrap a kebab in a lettuce leaf with herbs, then dip in nuoc cham.

Nuoc Cham

Time: 15 minutes   **Yield:** 4 to 6 servings

1 serrano chili, thinly sliced

1 clove garlic, thinly sliced

3 tablespoons sugar

1 tablespoon fresh lime juice

1 tablespoon rice vinegar

5 tablespoons fish sauce

Chop chili, garlic and sugar together until fine. Transfer to a bowl. Add ⅔ cup warm water and remaining ingredients. Set aside for 10 minutes before serving.

June 29, 2005: "The Summer Cook: Burgers Without Borders,"
by JULIA MOSKIN; recipe adapted from CORINNE TRANG

Wine Salt: Easier to Make Than to Imagine

It used to be that whenever I wanted to marinate a piece of meat, I'd douse it in wine mixed with garlic, black pepper and bay leaves and let it bathe overnight in the liquid. The cooked meat was tasty, but the exterior was never as crisp-edged as I wanted it, even when I wiped the surface dry before cooking.

Then a few years ago I switched my default to dry brining. I would coat the meat in a mixture of salt, spices and the occasional aromatic (garlic, ginger, scallion) and let it sit uncovered in the refrigerator overnight. This makes the meat flavorful and gives it a nice crust when I sear it.

The only thing missing was the fruity tang of the wine. But liquid has no place in a dry brine, so I didn't dwell on the loss.

Then recently I heard about a wine salt that John Eisenhart, the executive chef of Pazzo in Portland, Oregon, was slathering all over pork, chicken, fish, even squash.

To make it, he simmered wine until it was syrupy and added coarse salt, sugar and seasonings. Next, he dried out the mixture in a low oven (or you can leave it out on the counter overnight), and used it to marinate things before cooking.

His earliest wine-salt experiments involved leftover open bottles of pinot noir. He eventually switched to gewürztraminer for aesthetic reasons (the red wine turned everything purple, he said, which was just unappetizing on a piece of sturgeon).

Making wine salt is a clever idea, and not at all hard to do.

Mr. Eisenhart sent me the recipe, and I made it immediately, rubbing it onto a nice fat-covered pork loin that I grilled slowly over indirect heat. The sugar helped the meat caramelize, while the salt, lemon and thyme permeated the flesh. I'll make it in the winter, too, slowly roasting the meat in a 325-degree oven, then broiling it at the end if it needs color.

It was so good that I already have plans to try the rub on lamb chops with crushed coriander seeds mixed in, and on swordfish that I'll roast with peppers. It's also nice as a finishing salt, sprinkled on sliced tomatoes, radishes with butter or sliced cucumbers. And I'll bet it does wonders for salting eggplant, zucchini and cabbage.

Mr. Eisenhart said that the wine salt would keep for weeks in the refrigerator. But in my house, I think days is more likely. Next time I'm making a double batch.

Grilled Pork Loin with Wine-Salt Rub

Time: 2½ hours, plus marinating time
Yield: 8 to 10 servings

2 cups fruity white wine, such as riesling
    or gewürztraminer
¾ cup coarse sea salt
8 sprigs fresh thyme, leaves stripped
    (about 2 tablespoons leaves)

2 strips lemon zest, finely chopped
1 cup sugar
1 (3½-pound) center-cut boneless pork
    loin, patted dry

1. In a medium heavy-bottomed saucepan over medium heat, simmer wine until it is reduced by half, 20 to 30 minutes; adjust heat to low and continue to cook down to 2 tablespoons. Cool completely.

2. In a food processor, combine salt, thyme leaves, lemon zest and wine reduction. Pulse 2 or 3 times. Add sugar and pulse again until mixture has consistency of damp sand. If your mixture is moister, spread it evenly on a sheet pan and leave it out on the counter for several hours or overnight.

3. Place pork in a baking pan. Spread about ½ cup of salt rub all over pork (reserve remaining rub for another use; it will keep for a month, refrigerated). Cover tightly with plastic wrap and refrigerate for at least 3 hours or overnight.

4. Light grill for high-heat indirect cooking, piling charcoal on one side of grill and leaving other side unlighted. (For gas grills, turn on heat on one side of grill only.) Spread a piece of foil or place a disposable metal roasting pan underneath grill on unlighted side to catch any drips. Place pork on grill over foil. Cover grill and cook, turning every half hour until meat reaches 140 degrees in center, from 1 hour to 90 minutes. Transfer to a cutting board and let rest 10 minutes before carving.

August 31, 2012: MELISSA CLARK;
recipe adapted from JOHN EISENHART,
Pazzo, Portland, Oregon

Grilled Marinated Pork Loin

For thick cuts of meat, like pork loin, that require longer cooking times, a grill with a dome lid is recommended; it allows a more controlled, slow, even cooking. This recipe illustrates the technique, but differs from the usual method as the pork is cooked to only 110 degrees, then is sliced and returned to the grill, uncovered, for another 8 to 10 minutes. It is marinated in a Thai-style sauce, tinged with chili peppers, lime juice and cilantro.

Yield: 4 servings

1 (1½-pound) boneless rolled pork loin roast, tied

6 fresh green chilies, seeded and finely chopped

9 tablespoons peanut oil

6 tablespoons fresh lime juice

3 tablespoons finely minced fresh cilantro

1 tablespoon finely minced garlic

1 tablespoon sugar

1. Place pork roast in a glass bowl. Combine remaining ingredients and pour over roast to coat thoroughly. Cover and refrigerate at least 12 hours.

2. Forty-five minutes before cooking, light charcoal fire.

3. When coals are medium-hot, remove roast from marinade (reserve marinade), dry with paper towels and grill, turning frequently, for 10 minutes. Cover grill with its hood or a makeshift lid of foil and roast for 20 minutes, basting frequently, or until a thermometer inserted into thickest part of loin reads 110 degrees. (Discard marinade.)

4. Remove roast from grill. Cut into 1-inch-thick slices. Grill slices, uncovered, 4 to 5 minutes on each side, until cooked but still juicy. Serve immediately.

May 15, 1988: "Summer Pastimes: For the Adventurous Griller,"
by NANCY HARMON JENKINS;
grilling instructions adapted from Grill Book,
by KELLY MCCUNE (Harper & Row, 1986)

Grilled Pork and Peaches

Here is a simple, intense late-summer dinner you could cook on a pancake griddle set on the grate above a fire pit in someone's backyard, as if performing a magic trick. The result is a plate of thick, luscious pork with a deep, burnished crust, redolent of garlic and rosemary, and a sunset of soft, smoky peaches nutty with brown butter. Those with powerful venting systems in their kitchens might try to cook the dish indoors, but the threat of the smoke alarm will loom. There is little poetry to that. For this recipe, endeavor to cook outside, under the sky.

The technique is what Francis Mallmann, the aristocratic Latin American chef who is its most refined and stylish practitioner, calls "the uncertain edge of burnt." It requires patience and keen observation. What you are looking for on the edges of the meat and fruit is color: a deep, dark brown that is almost black—a black without bitter, a burn that is not burned.

Peter Kaminsky, who wrote a tremendous cookbook with Mallmann, *Seven Fires: Grilling the Argentine Way*, calls this style of cooking Maillardian, for the early-twentieth-century chemist Louis-Camille Maillard, who first described the chemical reaction created as the sugars and amino acids on the surface of food combine in the presence of high heat. The reaction creates all sorts of new and delicious flavor profiles that were not previously present. (Science! It is why we prefer charred steak to boiled.) Mallmann's burned food, Kaminsky says, simply takes the Maillard reaction further than most and creates a welcome dissonance between the crust of the meat and the peaches and their soft, gentle interiors. If Mallmann's cooking were music, it would be very loud.

It is not grilling, not really. Mallmann cooks this dish on an Argentine *chapa*, a piece of cast iron on legs set above an open fire. A *chapa* allows for quick-cooking a thin steak or a smashed-down lamb chop without drying out the meat or scorching it in the direct flames of a roaring fire. Juices are retained. Fats are not lost. You don't need to find and buy a chapa, of course. Similar results can be achieved with cast-iron pans set above the heat, one for the meat, another for the fruit.

Simple. And yet nervous-making, no? Make like a restaurant cook and practice. We all have much to learn from professionals in the kitchen, and this above all: You don't want your first attempt at a new cooking technique to be in front of a crowd. The Flying Wallendas don't walk on wires over the falls without taking a few practice turns. Mallmann suggests cutting a small piece of pork and sacrificing half a peach for a 15-minute test run in advance of the main event. Put these on your improvised chapa and watch closely, observing their progress from raw to cooked, seeing what he means by the uncertain edge and learning your craft.

"There is no recipe or explanation that can teach more than that," Mallmann wrote in an e-mail. "This tiny, silly test will help you make better decisions when you are cooking the real thing."

To the market, then. You will want a thick cut of pork butt, shoulder meat run through with fat. You will butterfly this, cutting it open like a book, then trim it and pound out the flesh to an even thickness of ¾ of an inch, which will allow for even cooking and maximum crust. Also: peaches, now coming off the trees as fat little flavor bombs, bursting with sugar and a zip of acidity. These you will cut in half and pit, directly before cooking. Good olive oil and sweet butter, garlic and rosemary, that's it. Maybe a loaf of good bread, some greens you can slick down with dressing as a side dish, some ice cream for dessert. Bottles of Argentine malbec. Looking good.

To cook, take what will be a strange-looking rectangle of meat (pork butt is a constellation of muscles that, pounded out, resembles an amoeba), and season it aggressively with kosher salt and freshly ground pepper. Make a paste of olive oil and a great deal of minced garlic and minced rosemary needles, then apply this to the two sides of the meat, mashing it onto the flesh with your hands or the side of a knife.

Out at the fire, carefully add a tablespoon of olive oil to the griddle or one of the pans, and spread it around with a spatula. Is it hot enough in there? If a drop of water sizzles on the cooking surface, it is. Lay the pork into the pan and allow it to cook, undisturbed, as you learned in the practice round, for roughly 10 minutes or so. You know what you're looking for here from the crust: the deep, dark brown of Maillardian excellence.

Meanwhile, cook the peaches: same deal, though with the addition of dots of butter along the way, to make a kind of sauce. These will cook somewhat more quickly than the meat and should be removed at their point of doneness to a warm platter tented below some foil, to rest.

Turn the pork, and repeat on the other side. Mallmann again:

"Patience is the most important thing when you cook with fires, and probably the most reliable of all senses is sight." You will know when it is finished. To butcher Borges: It is a fire that consumes you, but you are the fire.

Yield: 4 servings

1 boneless pork butt (about 2 pounds), butterflied and trimmed

8 to 10 cloves garlic, minced

2 tablespoons minced fresh rosemary

8 tablespoons extra virgin olive oil

Kosher salt and freshly ground black pepper to taste

6 fresh peaches, skin on, cut in half and pitted

4 tablespoons (½ stick) unsalted butter, cut into dice

1. Light a fire in a fire pit with a grill, or in a charcoal grill, or set a gas grill to high. Place a large cast-iron pan or two-burner griddle over the heat and allow it to get hot. At this point you can let the fire die slightly with no ill effect. If using a gas grill or stove, turn heat to medium.

2. Meanwhile, put pork on a work surface and, using a meat mallet, pound to an even thickness of approximately ¾ inch.

3. Combine garlic, rosemary and 6 tablespoons of olive oil in a small bowl, mixing to make a rough paste. Season pork aggressively on both sides with salt and pepper, then spread half the garlic mixture over one side and half on other side.

4. Brush pan or griddle with remaining 2 tablespoons olive oil, allow it to heat until it shimmers and is almost smoking, then place meat on hot surface and cook, without touching, until it forms a good crust, approximately 10 minutes.

5. While meat cooks, surround it with peaches, cut side down, and dot fruit with butter. (If you're using two cast-iron skillets, place peaches in their own oiled pan.) Let them cook for approximately 5 minutes, or until they are soft and slightly charred. Transfer to a platter and tent with foil to keep warm.

6. When meat is well browned on first side, use tongs to turn it over, and cook in remaining butter for another 5 to 7 minutes. Remove meat to a carving board and allow it to rest below a tent of foil for approximately 5 minutes. Slice meat and serve with peaches.

August 16, 2012: "Eat: How to Burn Dinner," by SAM SIFTON;
recipe adapted from Seven Fires: Grilling the Argentine Way,
by FRANCIS MALLMANN with PETER KAMINSKY (Artisan, 2009)

The Art of Barbecue

"Six Miles of Roast Pig"

Cooking and eating outdoors have been an American way of celebrating since the colonists adapted the custom from the Indians. "Six miles of roast pig!" wrote a British visitor to New York on the Fourth of July in 1837. "And that in the city alone; and roast pig in every other city, town, hamlet and village in the union." Today millions of Americans have backyard barbecue equipment. In the South and parts of the Middle West, cooks use deep pits containing beds of coal to roast pork shoulders, tenderloins and spareribs, as well as other meat. Here are instructions for building a charcoal fire and recipes for barbecuing pork to help make good use of some of those outdoor grills.

Charcoal Fires for Pork Barbecue

Pork requires cooking for a long time over low heat; therefore, the fire may be started as long as two hours in advance of serving, depending upon the day's temperature and the cook's skill.

1. It is most important to have an even temperature, spread to two inches or more beyond the dimensions of the meat. Use twists of newspaper in place of kindling, laying them side by side. On top of them build a pyramid of charcoal briquettes. Set twists afire and let burn while edges of briquettes begin to turn gray.

2. In 10 to 15 minutes, begin to flatten the pyramid, keeping it a close unit so that the burning briquettes ignite others.

3. Spread the ashen briquettes to cover an area large enough to extend outside the edges of the meat. Add more briquettes as necessary to fill any gaps.

4. Position the grill about four to five inches above the coals. Hold hand flat as close to grill as possible—at same distance that food will be while cooking. Count slowly: "And one, and two, and three," etc., removing hand when too hot. "And one" means you have very high heat. "And five" means low heat, suitable for pork.

5. The bed of coals should look gray when ready to barbecue pork. Add new briquettes sparingly, one or two at a time, just enough to keep heat at a steady low temperature.

Barbecued Pork Tenderloin

Yield: 4 to 6 servings

4 cloves garlic, minced

2 cups chopped onions

½ cup fresh lemon juice

½ cup soy sauce

½ cup corn oil

¼ cup sugar

3 to 4 tablespoons ground coriander

Tabasco sauce

6 pork tenderloins (about ¾ pound each)

1. In a large bowl, combine garlic, onions, lemon juice, soy sauce, oil, sugar, coriander and Tabasco sauce, stirring well. (Tabasco sauce should be added to taste—¼ to ½ teaspoon, depending upon tolerance.)

2. Put whole tenderloins in marinade, spooning to cover all surfaces, and set aside for 5 to 6 hours in refrigerator; turn meat occasionally.

3. When charcoal has burned down and is spread evenly, set wire grill above heat, allowing 4 to 5 inches (see fire instructions above).

4. Remove meat from marinade, scraping off vegetable bits and sauce; put marinade in cooking pan and simmer while meat cooks.

5. Lay tenderloins on grill, allowing space between pieces for turning. After about 20 minutes, turn pieces and spoon marinade over seared surface; repeat to sear each side. Barbecue 1 hour or more.

6. When serving, spread cooked marinade over each tenderloin.

Barbecued Spareribs

Yield: 4 servings

1 (1-pound) can imported peeled tomatoes, or about 1¼ pounds fresh tomatoes, peeled and chopped

1 large onion, finely chopped

2 cloves garlic, minced

3 tablespoons maple syrup or brown sugar

¼ teaspoon Worcestershire sauce

½ cup fresh lemon juice

1 teaspoon salt

Freshly ground pepper to taste

Dash Tabasco sauce

¼ teaspoon dry mustard

½ teaspoon ground ginger

¼ teaspoon ground allspice

2 to 3 pounds spareribs

1. Use a sharp knife to chop tomatoes in can and pour with juice into a saucepan. Stir in all remaining ingredients except spareribs, and bring to a boil. Simmer about 45 minutes.

2. Pour sauce over ribs and set aside for 2 or 3 hours in refrigerator, spooning sauce over meat at intervals.

3. When charcoal has burned down and is spread evenly, put grill in place above heat, allowing 4 to 5 inches (see fire instructions above).

4. Barbecue ribs at least 1 hour, watching closely to prevent burning. Turn at intervals and add marinade carefully so that as little as possible drips onto coals. (Do not baste meat with marinade during last 5 minutes of grilling and discard marinade.)

July 6, 1975: EVAN JONES

Fatty 'Cue Spare Ribs

Zakary Pelaccio, the chef and restaurateur, was in Malaysia recently, continuing his research on the flavors that have brought him relative fame in the food world of New York City, what he called in an e-mail message the appeal of "strong cocktails, chili, palm sugar and smoky fat."

In March 2010, Pelaccio opened Fatty 'Cue, a restaurant in Brooklyn that embraced those very elements. I wrote about the place a couple of months later, in my job as restaurant critic for *The Times*, and I continued to think about it after the review was published. Pelaccio and I corresponded about this during his trip. I was fishing for a recipe.

I wanted to make the restaurant's barbecued pork ribs. They are lacquered in a mixture of palm syrup and fish sauce and are vaguely Malay in aspect and flavor, sweet and fatty with a lingering pong of fishiness, a salty thrum below their caramelized crust.

There are precious few reasons to pity the lot of the restaurant critic. (Though as the joke goes, he has nothing but reservations himself.) But here, perhaps, is one: He cannot be a regular at any restaurant. This is not simply because he dines anonymously, under cloak and toupee. It's also because once he has finished writing about a restaurant, at least until such time as he feels the need to return to check up on it, he has finished writing about it. Other dining rooms beckon. Deadlines loom.

Still, I managed to squeeze in another visit to Fatty 'Cue—after another meal in another borough—for some ribs. I ate at the bar, alone, quickly. I felt a bit like one of those pilgrims that *Gourmet* used to feature, who would drive 75 miles out of the way to eat the apricot scones at a particular bed and breakfast in Somewheresville, Ohio. I sucked at my fingers and thought. Then I wrote to Pelaccio. And so here we are, setting off on a weekend adventure, a project recipe to thrill family and guests. You do have Indonesian long pepper in your larder, yes? And Three Crabs brand fish sauce? (Not Two Crabs, please!) You have a smoker that can hold at 220 degrees for five hours? You've got some palm sugar? We're set, then. You may proceed to the recipe below.

If, however, Indonesian long pepper is not something stocked at your local Kroger or Buehler's Buy-Low, do not despair. You can always head online, where things like long pepper and fish sauce and dependable smokers are generally available at big outfits like Amazon and Cabela's and at little ones like Kalustyan's and *AmazingRibs.com*.

And of course you can cheat, cut corners, make do. Except for the fish sauce, much about Pelaccio's recipe is open to home-cook interpretation.

Start with the brine. At Fatty 'Cue, Pelaccio cooks alongside the pitmaster Robbie Richter, who generally does his magic with oak smoke and dry rubs. Here, however, before smoking he plumps and scents the pork with a mixture of sugar and fish sauce, the Southeast Asian condiment made from fermented anchovies.

Pelaccio and Richter recommend a base of Three Crabs, a Thai sauce processed in Hong Kong. It has a beautiful label and a strong, salty umami punch. But I made the brine with two other brands and could not detect an appreciable difference. Go with what you can get.

Then obtain a couple of racks of pork spareribs, trimmed and clean. Submerge these in the brine, cover well and refrigerate overnight.

On the matter of smokers, you can use a gas grill with wood chips soaked and placed into an improvised bag of aluminum foil pierced with a fork. I rigged up a kettle grill with a low charcoal fire on one side and the ribs on the other, which ran a little hot, and then a little cool, but generally was low and slow enough to make the meat collapse in the braise of the smoke, and to impart the telltale sign of real American barbecue, whatever its accent: a dark red smoke ring around the edges of the meat. (In a pinch, you could even use a low oven and a dash of Liquid Smoke.)

Pelaccio and Richter recommend dusting the meat with freshly ground toasted Indonesian long pepper before cooking. Long pepper, the fruit of a flowering vine, is a hotter, more pungent cousin of black pepper, and a spice with a rich history. The Greeks and the Romans loved the stuff; it was their black pepper.

To use it, if you can find it, you will need a spice grinder. My effort to pack a standard pepper mill with the elongated nubs was an unmitigated failure.

Far less unsuccessful was my attempt to use plain round black peppercorns instead. The loss of heat was not terribly significant, particularly if I increased the dusting of pepper to what you'd see on a classic steak au poivre.

A final cheat came in making the sauce, which you paint on at the end of the process, giving the ribs a sticky-sweet sheen of remarkable flavor.

Pelaccio makes a simple syrup of water and palm sugar, then mixes this with fish sauce. Palm sugar, made from the sap of palm trees, is a common ingredient in Southeast Asia. It generally comes in molded cakes, with a flavor that's somewhere between molasses and brown sugar.

But if it doesn't come at all, or if your desire to make these ribs outstrips even a rush order from an online outfit, feel free to make a mixture of—yes—brown sugar and molasses to approximate it. Chefs and restaurants love to put unfamiliar adjectives in front of common nouns. It helps menus sell. But at home you can cheat. "We're American," Pelaccio had written me. "So we have our own filter."

Yield: 4 to 6 servings

2 cups fish sauce (preferably Three
  Crabs brand; see note)
6 cloves garlic, smashed and peeled
1 medium shallot, sliced
1 tablespoon freshly ground black pepper
½ cup granulated sugar

2 racks pork spare ribs
2 tablespoons toasted and ground
  Indonesian long pepper, or to taste
  (see note)
6 ounces palm sugar (see note)
White toast for serving

1. Combine 1½ cups of fish sauce with garlic, shallot, black pepper and granulated sugar in a large pot. Add at least a gallon of water, then cover and bring to a boil over high heat. Reduce heat and simmer for 30 minutes. Remove from heat, place in a nonreactive container and chill. Place ribs in brine for at least 6 hours and no longer than 12.

2. Remove ribs from brine and dust lightly with ground Indonesian long pepper.

3. In a grill with a cover, build a small fire to one side, making sure all the wood or charcoal becomes engulfed in flame. When flames begin to die down, leaving flickering coals, place ribs on grill on side without fire. Do not let flames touch meat at any time.

4. Cover grill, vent slightly and cook, checking fire every 30 minutes or so and adding a bit more fuel as necessary, for about 5 hours at around 220 degrees, until meat recedes from bone and its internal temperature is at least 170 degrees but no more than 180 degrees.

5. Meanwhile, make a glaze. Combine palm sugar and ¾ cup water in a small pot over a medium flame, and heat until sugar melts. Combine that simple syrup with remaining ½ cup fish sauce.

6. When ribs are ready, glaze heavily and serve, with white toast on side.

NOTE: Three Crabs fish sauce, long pepper and palm sugar can be found at Amazon.com or Kalustyans.com.

July 7, 2010: "Food: Restaurant-Style Spareribs in Your Backyard,"
by SAM SIFTON; recipe adapted from ZAKARY PELACCIO
and ROBBIE RICHTER, Fatty 'Cue, Brooklyn, New York

Braised and Grilled Pork Ribs

This is a story about hedging bets, about taking advantage of some old-fashioned barbecue techniques, and about the heartbreak of Memorial Day.

It grows out of my permanent desire to see our national end-of-May holiday as a start-of-grilling-season holiday, despite the weather in my part of the country at the end of May, which is typically in the 50s and drizzly. It also grows out of my understanding of the links between barbecue and braising.

The barbecued ribs I like best are cooked all the way through, using moist, relatively low heat, then finished over a high flame for a final browning. And you can nicely, if imperfectly, replicate this process by braising the ribs and then finishing them over the grill.

What I did for the ribs in the recipe here was brown them, then slowly braise them in the oven (the top of the stove would work as well).

Though the ribs remain my favorite use of this method, I've tried it on half a dozen types of meat, from short ribs to pork shoulder to beef cheeks, with similar results. It also mitigates the bane of chicken grilling (or, for that matter, broiling), the roaring flame-up. By braising the chicken first, you effectively remove just about all the surface fat, practically eliminating the risk of setting the pieces on fire. This same treatment would work nicely with fatty lamb, like chunks of shoulder or even shanks, which without the initial braising would be just about impossible to grill.

Then there is brisket which, unlike chicken and pork, simply cannot be grilled over direct heat no matter how careful you are; it absolutely requires long, slow cooking. In fact, it's difficult to grill (or broil) without some form of precooking, whether in aluminum foil (a venerable trick that makes sense) or in a barbecue pit.

I'm not hoping for rain on Memorial Day. But at least this year I feel prepared.

Time: About 2 hours   **Yield:** 4 to 8 servings

3 to 4 pounds spare ribs

Salt and freshly ground black pepper

2 tablespoons vegetable oil

10 allspice berries

2 or 3 (3-inch) cinnamon sticks

10 nickel-size slices unpeeled fresh
    ginger, or 1 tablespoon ground ginger

5 dried red chilies, or 1 teaspoon
    cayenne pepper

5 cloves garlic, lightly smashed and
    peeled

1 bottle dark beer, like Guinness or
    any porter

1. Preheat oven to 300 degrees. Cut meat into two racks if necessary; season with salt and pepper. Put oil in a large, deep ovenproof skillet or casserole that can later be covered. Turn heat to medium-high and, when oil shimmers, sear meat on both sides until nicely browned, turning as necessary.

2. Add allspice, cinnamon, ginger, chilies and garlic and stir; add beer. Bring to a boil; cover pan and adjust heat so mixture simmers steadily. Put in oven and cook until meat is tender, 1 hour or more. (You can prepare meat up to a day or two ahead; if you are not going to grill or broil immediately, put whole pan in refrigerator after it cools a bit.)

3. Light a charcoal or gas grill; rack should be about 4 inches away from heat source. Drain meat and sprinkle it with salt and pepper. Grill on both sides until brown and crisp, just a few minutes. Meanwhile, skim cooking liquid of fat, bring to a boil, and use as sauce.

May 21, 2008: "The Minimalist:
Oven Adds Flavor When the Grill Can't,"
by MARK BITTMAN

Pork Barbecue

Darlington, South Carolina, is a normally peaceful town of white-frame houses with big porches on the front and azalea bushes in the yards. But every Labor Day, about 80,000 people show up on the outskirts to observe a Southern ritual called stock-car racing. I travel to Darlington several times a year myself, though no longer on Labor Day. I went to the race once, and I'll never forget it. I couldn't hear a thing for weeks.

No, I go to see my parents, who live there, and to participate in another Southern ritual: eating pork barbecue. Like the race track, the barbecue places tend to be on the outskirts of town. There's Cain's on Pamplico Road near Florence and Country Cousin's on the way to Kingstree. Our favorite is Skeet's, off Highway 34, seven miles north of Darlington. Turn left at the blinking light and pull into the parking lot just the other side of the convenience store. Then shut off the engine and prepare for some serious eating. The exterior of Skeet's is your basic cinder-block cube, painted dark red. Inside, the tables are the long, picnic variety that can take care of a big group without much fuss. Skeet himself serves as both maitre d' and cashier, greeting customers from behind the register as they come in and later collecting their money. He also takes phone orders. With a line of hungry people stretching out the door, a kitchen staff bustling around behind him carrying enormous steaming containers of food and the television right next to the register blaring away, this is not as easy as it sounds. But ambience is hardly the lure here. People come for the barbecued chicken, the ribs, the chicken bog (a peppery mixture of rice and chicken), the red-eye gravy, the cole slaw and, most of all, for the pork barbecue. If there's any room left, and there usually is, they'll take the caramel cake too. All of this is washed down with presweetened ice tea, served by the pitcher.

The pork barbecue at Skeet's is a type indigenous to the Eastern, low-country regions of the Carolinas. The meat is slow-cooked, mixed with a pungent, vinegar-based sauce and then finely chopped. A lot of people use the soft white-bread rolls that are a staple in these places to turn it into a sandwich, sometimes putting a little cole slaw in there as well.

Recipes for this style of barbecue aren't complicated; they usually involve plain white or cider vinegar, ketchup, mustard and a fair amount of pepper. But getting it just right can be tricky. So before our most recent trip South, I called Skeet and asked if he might consider imparting his secrets. He agreed, but there was reluctance in his voice. Sure enough, when we showed up at his cash register a few nights later, he explained that on consideration he had decided not to. He was apologetic but firm; his college-age son was about to join him in the business, he said, and this was no time to be giving away the goods. After my father bought us dinner that night, we had to console ourselves with the several pounds of carryout we'd freeze and take back to New York.

Fortunately, in Darlington, one is never far from a good pork barbecue lead. A woman we know had a friend over in Bishopville who used to cook at Skeet's, but we couldn't reach her. A second cousin of ours, John James, who once owned one of the largest hog farms in the area, said the best barbecue he had ever tasted was cooked by a Mr. C. M. Camlin of Florence. C. M. retired some years ago, John said, and he wasn't sure if the old gentleman was still alive. He suggested we contact one of his sons, Harold L. Camlin, who used to run a local butcher shop.

Reached by phone, Harold said that his father had passed away last year but that the recipe remained in the family. This was beginning to sound familiar. When I inquired whether he would be willing to divulge it, he said to give him a week to think it over and consult with the rest of the Camlins. I didn't ask if his son was about to take over, but I wasn't filled with hope. When I called back, Harold gave me the answer I was afraid of—sorry, but no deal.

In New York, we canvassed a few southern friends, including one couple who has had parties catered long-distance by a barbecue restaurant in Spartanburg, South Carolina, and a woman who fondly recalls the guests at her wedding deserting the catered reception in 100-degree weather to eat barbecue outside. One is never far from a pork barbecue lead in the Big City either.

Finally someone steered us to a recipe by—who else, but Craig Claiborne—that she has sworn by for years.

For the pork
1 (3½- to 4-pound) pork roast
Salt and freshly ground pepper to taste

For the sauce
1½ cups distilled white vinegar
6 tablespoons ketchup

Salt and freshly ground black pepper
   to taste
½ teaspoon cayenne pepper
1 tablespoon sugar
½ cup water

1. Prepare a charcoal fire.

2. Rub pork with salt and pepper.

3. Place pork on grill and sear, turning several times for about 10 minutes.

4. Cook meat near, but not directly over, a slow fire for about 3 to 4 hours, or until an instant meat thermometer reads 185 degrees.

5. Shred meat with a fork and set aside.

6. Make the sauce by combining all ingredients in a small saucepan and bring to a simmer. Cook, stirring, until sugar dissolves. Cool. It makes about 3 cups.

7. Combine with meat and serve.

July 29, 1990: "Food: Ode to Skeet's," by ALEX WARD;
recipe adapted from CRAIG CLAIBORNE

Brochette de Porc au Romarin
(Brochettes of Pork with Rosemary)

Yield: 6 to 8 servings

2¼ pounds lean, boneless pork

1 cup dry white wine

1 tablespoon finely minced garlic

1 tablespoon dried rosemary leaves

2 tablespoons finely chopped fresh
   parsley

1 teaspoon grated lemon zest

Salt and freshly ground pepper to taste

2 tablespoons olive oil

2 tablespoons white wine vinegar

Melted butter

1. Cut pork into 1½-inch cubes and put meat in a mixing bowl.

2. Add wine, garlic, rosemary, parsley, lemon zest, salt and pepper to taste, olive oil and vinegar. Blend well and set aside to marinate for 2 to 4 hours.

3. Drain meat. Arrange equal portions of meat on each of 6 to 8 skewers.

4. Preheat a charcoal grill.

5. Place brochettes on grill and cook, turning skewers often, 15 to 20 minutes or until pork is thoroughly cooked but not dry.

6. Serve with melted butter poured over.

May 25, 1980: "Food: Ready for the Grill,"
by CRAIG CLAIBORNE with PIERRE FRANEY

Garlic Roasted Pork Shoulder

Every year, on the day before Christmas, the sky here is filled with smoke from countless backyard barbecues. This is not just any smoke: it's the aroma of *lechon asado*, pork that has been soaked in a garlicky marinade, wrapped in banana leaves and pit-roasted. It's the fragrance of La Noche Buena, the traditional Cuban Christmas Eve feast.

At no other time are Cuban roots in Miami more visible or more festive. Butcher shops advertise fresh young pigs; bakeries are crowded with customers buying syrup-soaked fritters called buñuelos and nougat-like turron, the Spanish candy of Christmas.

For Latin Americans, and particularly Cubans, Christmas Eve is one of the most festive nights of the year. A traditional Cuban Noche Buena begins with a late-night feast accompanied by drinking, dancing and socializing and followed by midnight Mass. In Miami it combines the belt-loosening largess of Thanksgiving with the conviviality of a Fourth of July barbecue.

I got a preview of La Noche Buena from a friend, Efrain Veiga Sr., 79, who was a butcher in Havana before immigrating to Miami in 1959; he continued to work in the meat industry here. (In the late 1980's, his son Efrain opened what may have been the nation's first nuevo Latino restaurant, Yuca, and he recently opened Mayya, an upscale Mexican place in Miami Beach.)

As Mr. Veiga demonstrated, the first step of La Noche Buena is buying the pig: alive. At a blue cinder-block slaughterhouse called Cabrera's on the outskirts of Miami, in Hialeah Gardens, we waited in line to pick out a 49-pound *macho* (male) that looked appropriately plump and lively. And then waited in another line while he was slaughtered. On a slow day, the ranch kills 300 pigs to order; two days before Christmas, the number jumps to 1,200.

At the bay-front home of Mr. Veiga's son in Miami Beach, we soaked the pig in a tangy marinade called adobo that pits the pungency of lots of fresh garlic against the fragrance of cumin and oregano, with a greenish fruit called *naranja agria*, or sour orange, providing a snappy acidity. The fruit is sold in supermarkets here, but a mixture of three parts fresh lime juice to one-part orange juice is a worthy substitute.

Adobo takes its name from the medieval term "adobar," literally "to ennoble." (The term survives in the English expression "to dub," as in to dub someone a knight.) And what's being ennobled here is the pork.

At the end of the driveway, we dug a pit a foot deep, three feet wide and four feet long and lined it with a sheet of galvanized steel, then poured in and ignited a couple of bags of charcoal. As the coals blazed down to embers, Mr. Veiga raked them into an area in the pit roughly the size and shape of the pig, with extra coals stacked to cover and cook the shoulders and hams more quickly. We then placed the splayed pig, skin side down, on a grate fashioned from steel poles and chicken wire. We splashed on additional adobo and covered the pig with banana leaves to hold in the moisture and smoke while imparting a distinctive flavor.

In the house, Mr. Veiga's wife, Esther, worked on the classic Cuban side dishes: *moros y cristianos*, which means Moors and Christians, for the colors of the soupy black beans and the white rice; *yuca con mojo*; and fried ripe plantains. Yuca is Cuban comfort food, a bland starchy white tuber that tastes vaguely buttery, and mojo is an explosively flavorful sauce made with fried garlic, cumin and lime juice. The mojo will also be slathered over the cooked pork.

As for the plantains, Mrs. Veiga uses the softest, blackest, ripest ones, which are as candy-sweet as ripe bananas. They don't often turn up in supermarkets that black but can be ripened at room temperature.

Like all great barbecue, *lechon asado* requires bursts of intense activity followed by lots of sitting around watching the pig roast. As we sipped beer, Mr. Veiga recalled his last Noche Buena in Cuba. He and his friends strung an enormous pig between two palm trees like a hammock and swung it back and forth over the fire until the skin was as crisp as a potato chip.

By nightfall, the Miami pig was as shiny and dark as mahogany and the meat tender enough to pull apart with your fingers, which is what we did. We filled plates with black beans, rice, yuca and plantains, and splashed garlicky mojo over the pork and licked our fingers. At the end, Mrs. Veiga brought out a shimmering flan delicately flavored with lemon and cinnamon.

Cooking a whole pig can be challenging, so Mr. Veiga suggested an alternative: making lechon asado with a pork shoulder. Like the pig, the roast is marinated in garlicky adobo; for extra flavor, poke holes in the meat to increase the penetration of the marinade.

Time: 3 to 4 hours, plus 12 to 24 hours' marinating
Yield: 8 to 10 servings

1 pork shoulder (7 to 8 pounds), washed and blotted dry

1 head garlic, broken into cloves, finely chopped

1 tablespoon salt, plus more for seasoning

2 teaspoons ground cumin

2 teaspoons oregano

Freshly ground black pepper to taste

2 cups sour orange juice, or 1½ cups fresh lime juice and ½ cup fresh orange juice

1 tablespoon olive oil

2 cups Mojo (recipe follows)

1. Stab roast all over with chef's knife, making ½-inch-deep holes, 2 inches apart. Place roast in baking dish.

2.   Place garlic and 1 tablespoon salt in a mortar and pestle, and pound to a paste. Pound in remaining ingredients except mojo. (Or mix ingredients in a blender.) Pour over pork, forcing marinade into holes. Marinate roast in refrigerator 12 to 24 hours, turning several times. Keep roast covered with plastic wrap.

3.   Set up a grill for indirect grilling and preheat to 350 degrees. Heavily season roast on all sides with salt and pepper, and place, fat side up, on grill away from heat source. Cover grill and cook until roast is nicely browned and cooked through, 3 to 4 hours. Add fresh coals every hour if using charcoal. If meat starts to brown too much, let heat drop to 325 degrees and cover roast with foil.

4.   Transfer roast to a cutting board, and let rest for 10 minutes. Slice, and serve with mojo on top.

Mojo (Cuban Citrus Garlic Sauce)

Time: 10 minutes   **Yield:** 3 cups

1 cup olive oil

12 cloves garlic, thinly sliced crosswise

1⅓ cups fresh sour orange juice, or
    1 cup fresh lime juice and ⅓ cup fresh
    orange juice

2 teaspoons ground cumin

1 teaspoon oregano

2 teaspoons salt, or to taste

1 teaspoon freshly ground black pepper

½ cup chopped fresh cilantro

1.   Heat oil in a deep saucepan over medium heat. Add garlic, and cook until fragrant and pale golden brown, 2 to 3 minutes.

2.   Stir in sour orange juice, ⅔ cup water, cumin, oregano, salt and pepper (sauce may spatter). Bring to a rolling boil. Adjust seasoning. Cool to room temperature, then stir in cilantro. Stir well before serving.

December 22, 1999: "In Miami, Christmas Eve Means Roast Pig,"
by STEVEN RAICHLEN

Roasting a Pig Inside an Enigma

The note came from a friend. It was brief and irresistible. "Have you heard about this item?" it asked. "It can roast a 50-pound pig in four hours."

There are a number of ways to cook a whole pig. One method is to place the carcass on a rotisserie above a heat source and spin it slowly into the night. Greeks do a similar thing with lamb. Another technique is to dig a shallow trench in the ground, line it with rocks, build a fire to heat the rocks and place a pig above them, then cover the whole with wet canvas and sand, the way New Englanders do for clambakes on the beach. Southern barbecue cooks will slide a butterflied pig onto a covered grill, and cook it slowly in a smoky braise. This method takes an extremely large grill and, really, if you want to do it properly, you need to wear overalls.

None of these methods take less than eight or nine hours. None work well during a Northeastern winter.

The message, which had come via e-mail, had a link to a Web site run by a Cuban-American named Roberto Guerra, www.lacajachina.com. The item described on Mr. Guerra's site was called La Caja China—a Chinese roasting box. This turned out to be a rectangular plywood wheelbarrow lined with marine-grade aluminum, with a steel top upon which you could build a fire and under which you could cook a pig, or a great number of chickens. There were three sizes available, with the largest priced at $250.

I wanted it immediately, the way a child would a model airplane, or a trip to the moon. I bookmarked the site and came back to it nearly hourly for the next few days, daydreaming about roast pig.

I also began to shoot off e-mail notes and to make phone calls, inquiring about La Caja China in particular and so-called Chinese roasting boxes in general. That they are Cuban seemed self-evident. They are made by Cubans. But what makes them Chinese?

Mr. Guerra, who was born in Cuba and who lives and works in Miami, related a story about how the Chinese Army tortured its prisoners with heat, and how somehow this had led Cubans to develop a sort of cooking that in turn resulted in the invention of the box, by his father, in the early 1980's. This yarn seemed apocryphal at best. Mr. Guerra and I were talking on the phone, but it did not seem impossible that he shrugged his shoulders in agreement.

John Willoughby, the executive editor of *Gourmet* magazine, also had no answers. But he was ecstatic about what the box could accomplish. He'd had, he said, some pig cooked in one that very weekend, prepared by a fellow named Jesus Lima, of the Jamaica Plain neighborhood in Boston. "It was like pig candy," he said. Mr. Lima, he said, had called the device "a chinee box."

I called Mr. Lima. His box, which he built 12 years ago after seeing similar versions in South Florida, is stainless steel, with a plywood exterior and a stainless-steel top on which he places coals. He has cooked more than 80 pigs in it, he said, and has always called it a chinee box. I asked him why. "That's its name," he said.

Bobby Flay, the television personality and former Joe Allen dishwasher who is the chef and an owner of Bolo and Mesa Grill in Manhattan, said he had tried pig from one of the devices in Miami, cooked by the chef Douglas Rodriguez. "The coolest," he declared, adding that he had purchased a small version, La Cajita China, for his weekend home on Long Island. "It is just awesome," he said.

And Jeffrey Steingarten, the courtly and obsessive gastronomic enthusiast who writes about food for *Vogue*, was intrigued by La Caja China to the point of distraction, sending what seemed like daily e-mail messages on the subject. "Semper Pigatus" was the heading on one of his messages. (Mr. Steingarten ended up buying the largest box and engaging Paul Bertolli, the chef at Oliveto in Oakland, California, to have a pig from the Napa Valley Lamb Company slaughtered for him to cook in it. "The pig was actually eviscerated in Yuba City," Mr. Steingarten added in what he said was the interest of full accuracy.) But he had no idea, at least at that juncture, why the boxes, whether sold commercially or made at home, were called Chinese.

Sidney Mintz, the great food anthropologist at Johns Hopkins University and author of *Tasting Food, Tasting Freedom*, was similarly stymied at first. But in a later e-mail message, casting about for ideas, he told me that 150,000 male Chinese contract laborers were brought to Cuba in the 1850's. They came alone, he said, without family or wives. "As should be clear to all," he added, "without women, culture is mostly not perpetuated." Chinese Cubans who later left the island and opened restaurants in America cooked Cuban food, or Chinese food, or both. But, he said, there was no real mixing of the cuisines—no plantain fried rice, no Shanghai clams in Cuban black bean soup—and to his knowledge there was no real basis in fact for saying that the Chinese roasting box, of Cuban origin, was of Chinese descent.

That said, Mr. Mintz added, "My Caribbean experience tells me that calling something 'chino' or 'China' is a way, perhaps especially in the Hispanophone places, of saying it is clever, exotic, a contrivance, desirable. I could hazard only a bum guess why."

This last echoed something I had heard from a Cuban chef of some standing, Maricel Presilla, of the restaurant Zafra in Hoboken, New Jersey. "Cubans like to call anything that is unusual or clever Chinese," she said. "And this is true all over the Caribbean. Pretty much any culture there, whether Cuban or Puerto Rican or Dominican, they have somewhere some kind of thing like this—a caja China."

As it turns out, it is not just in the Caribbean that pig roasting boxes abound. John Laudun, a folklorist and assistant professor of English at the University of Louisiana at Lafayette, had a great deal to say about cooking pigs in boxes. Cajun microwaves, he called the ovens, and said they were greatly varied in design and size.

"There is more ingenuity in the sheet-metal shops of South Louisiana," Mr. Laudun said, "than in all the fashion houses in New York City."

The Cajun microwave, he continued, was but one example of this creativity. "Some of these things are very high-tech affairs," he explained, with elaborate winch systems for moving the pig in and out of the heat.

But the basic technique was the same as with La Caja China: place a pig in a closed environment beneath rather than on top of a heat source.

I bought La Caja China for just over $300 including shipping, and had it sent to my home. It came in two heavy boxes and took an hour to assemble. When it was complete I gave it a pat and headed off to the supermarket for practice materials.

In Miami, Mr. Guerra had told me, whole pigs are readily available at grocery chains like Publix. In and around New York City, this is not the case. I settled for two picnic hams weighing 15 pounds apiece and ordered a whole pig for a following weekend. "You want that heavy?" asked the butcher at the IGA. Both Mr. Lima and Ms. Presilla had said that a 70-pound pig was ideal for a family roast. I asked for a pig of that weight. "That's a little pig," the butcher said. "You'll have fun with that."

An afternoon of largely unattended cooking followed. There is a kind of rack within the roasting box into which you can load the meat and, in fact, strap it into place; it keeps the flesh off the bottom of the oven and allows the heat to surround the pork completely. I placed my hams into it, unadorned and skin side down, then put the cover on the oven and unceremoniously dumped a little more than 15 pounds of charcoal onto the top, in accordance with the instructions stenciled on the side of the box. The charcoal rested there in the manner of road salt at a highway department depot. It was a large pile. I divided it into two piles at either end of the grate, again in accordance with Mr. Guerra's instructions, and lighted them with a huge whoosh of accelerant. No smoke would ever touch these hams, so the chemical tang of the burning lighter fluid would bother no one but my neighbors.

A quarter-hour later, when the fires were raging, I used a garden rake to spread the coals across the top of La Caja China. They smoldered malevolently but looked a little lonely. I added another 10 pounds of charcoal, then went inside the house and sat on the couch.

When I awoke an hour later, I added more charcoal to the pile, and an hour and a half after that I moved the top of the oven to a resting place on the long arms affixed to the front of La Caja China. The hams inside the box were golden and sweating and soft, and smelled divine. I turned them over, replaced the top, added some charcoal, and returned to the couch.

And so it went, both with the hams and, a few weeks later with the whole animal, which the butcher sold for $130 and carried to the trunk of my car for no charge: periods of rest, punctuated by periods of fire making. When I cooked the whole pig, I burned through 40 pounds of Kingsford charcoal in about four hours, then moved to oak logs, which burned bright in the gathering gloom of a thunderstorm. (It took about five and a half hours to cook the animal; it was cold outside, and this dissipated some of the heat. There was also some rain.) In both cases, the results were splendid, particularly in the case of the whole pig, whose skin caramelized beautifully in the last hour of cooking, after I'd turned it over, under the searing heat of the coals.

Pig candy, Mr. Willoughby of *Gourmet* had said of the result. He was right. Before cooking my whole hog, I used a large veterinarian's needle to inject the animal with a kind of Cuban mojo brine, from a recipe Mr. Guerra thoughtfully sent me when I told him I needed one. The brine was salt, sugar and water, plus lime and orange juice used in place of sour orange, and it left the meat with a delightful top note, a citrus melody above the pork. The meat, served with garlicky black beans and white rice, along with plenty of rum and cold bottles of Coca-Cola, served as a kind of gastronomic vacation—a trip to Cuba on a plate.

That's my New Year's resolution exactly: more Cuba on a plate.

January 7, 2004: SAM SIFTON

Bacon Explosion

For a nation seeking unity, a recipe has swept the Internet that seems to unite conservatives and liberals, gun owners and foodies, carnivores and . . . well, not vegetarians and health fanatics. Certainly not the vegetarians and health fanatics.

This recipe is the Bacon Explosion, modestly called by its inventors "the BBQ Sausage Recipe of all Recipes." The instructions for constructing this massive torpedo-shaped amalgamation of two pounds of bacon woven through and around two pounds of sausage and slathered in barbecue sauce first appeared last month on the Web site of a team of Kansas City competition barbecuers. They say a diverse collection of well over 16,000 Web sites have linked to the recipe, celebrating, or sometimes scolding, its excessiveness.

Where once homegrown recipes were disseminated in Ann Landers columns or Junior League cookbooks, new media have changed—and greatly accelerated—the path to popularity. Few recipes have cruised down this path as fast or as far as the Bacon Explosion, and this turns out to be no accident. One of its inventors works as an Internet marketer and had a sophisticated understanding of how the latest tools of promotion could be applied to a four-pound roll of pork.

The Bacon Explosion was born shortly before Christmas in Roeland Park, Kansas, in Jason Day's kitchen. He and Aaron Chronister, who anchor a barbecue team called Burnt Finger BBQ, were discussing a challenge from a bacon lover they received on Twitter: What could the barbecuers do with bacon? Mr. Day, a systems administrator who has been barbecuing since college, suggested doing something with a pile of sausage. "It's a variation of what's called a fattie in the barbecue community," Mr. Day said. "But we took it to the extreme."

He bought about $20 worth of bacon and Italian sausage from a local meat market. As it lay on the counter, he thought of weaving strips of raw bacon into a mat. The two spackled the bacon mat with a layer of sausage, covered that with a crunchy layer of cooked bacon, and rolled it up tight.

They then stuck the roll—containing at least 5,000 calories and 500 grams of fat—in the Good-One Open Range backyard smoker that they use for practice. (In competitions, they use a custom-built smoker designed by the third member of the team, Bryant Gish, who was not present at the creation of the Bacon Explosion.)

The two men posted their adventure on their Web site two days before Christmas. On Christmas Day, traffic on the site spiked to more than 27,000 visitors.

The Bacon Explosion posting has since been viewed about 390,000 times. It first found a following among barbecue fans, but quickly spread to sites run by outdoor enthusiasts, off-roaders and hunters. (Several proposed venison-sausage versions.)

A man from Wooster, Ohio, wrote that friends had served it at a bon voyage party before his 10-day trip to Israel, where he expected bacon to be in short supply. "It wasn't planned as a send-off for me to Israel, but with all of the pork involved it sure seemed like it," he wrote.

About 30 people sent in pictures of their Explosions. One sent a video of the log catching fire on a grill.

Mr. Day said that whether it is cooked in an oven or in a smoker, the rendered fat from the bacon keeps the sausage juicy. But in the smoker, he said, the smoke heightens the flavor of the meats.

Nick Pummell, a barbecue hobbyist in Las Vegas, learned of the recipe from Mr. Chronister's Twittering. He made his first Explosion on Christmas Day, when he and a group of friends also had a more traditional turkey. "This was kind of the dessert part," he said. "You need to call 911 after you are done. It was awesome."

Time: About 3 hours   **Yield:** 10 or more servings

2 pounds thick-cut sliced bacon
3 tablespoons barbecue rub

1½ pounds Italian sausage,
   casings removed
¾ cup barbecue sauce

1. Using 10 slices of bacon, weave a square lattice like that on top of a pie: first, place 5 bacon slices side by side on a large sheet of foil, parallel to one another, sides touching. Place another strip of bacon on one end, perpendicular to the other strips. Fold first, third and fifth bacon strips back over this new strip, then place another strip next to it, parallel to it. Unfold first, third and fifth strips; fold back second and fourth strips. Repeat with remaining bacon until all 10 strips are tightly woven.

2. Light a fire in an outdoor smoker. Place remaining bacon in a frying pan and cook until crisp. As it cooks, sprinkle bacon weave with 1 tablespoon of barbecue rub. Evenly spread sausage on top of bacon lattice, pressing to outer edges.

3. Crumble fried bacon into bite-size pieces. Sprinkle on top of sausage. Drizzle with ½ cup of barbecue sauce and sprinkle with another tablespoon of barbecue rub.

4. Very carefully separate front edge of sausage layer from bacon weave and begin rolling sausage away from you. Bacon weave should stay where it was, flat. Press sausage roll to remove any air pockets and pinch together seams and ends.

5. Roll sausage toward you, this time with bacon weave, until it is completely wrapped. Turn it so seam faces down. Roll should be about 2 to 3 inches thick. Sprinkle with remaining 1 tablespoon barbecue rub.

6. Place roll in smoker. Cook until internal temperature reaches 165 degrees on a meat thermometer, about 1 hour for each inch of thickness. When done, glaze roll with more sauce. To serve, slice into ¼- to- ½-inch-thick rounds.

January 28, 2009: "Take Bacon. Add Sausage. Blog," by DAMON DARLIN;
recipe adapted from JASON DAY and AARON CHRONISTER

CHAPTER FIVE

Lamb

If you were to take a survey of the general public on their preferred barbecue meats, lamb probably would come in fourth, behind beef, pork and poultry, but that shouldn't be taken to mean that it doesn't have its adherents. Among the peoples of North Africa and the Eastern Mediterranean, it is probably the favorite. Since Jews and Muslims eschew pork, and cattle aren't well suited to most of those countries, a tradition of lamb grilling has grown up. Spit roasted or made into kebabs, lamb can be the most succulent of meats, as in the whole roasted lamb that Florence Fabricant discovered in 1974 (see page 176). Butterflied and grilled leg of lamb is cheaper than the same amount of strip steak or ribeye, but as Moira Hodgson shows in her recipe for it on page 160, it develops the same crusty char and juicy, rosy pink interior as beef and plays just as well with full-flavored sauces, in this case, one prepared with fresh sorrel. Yes, lamb often has a strong, distinctive taste, but barbecue is about robust flavor, and by that measure, lamb fits the bill.

Evan and Judith Jones demonstrate their method for grilling a leg of lamb on a spit on the terrace of their New York City apartment, 1961.

Adana Kebabs

Time: 30 minutes, plus 1 hour for chilling
Yield: 4 to 6 servings (8 skewers)

2 pounds ground lamb

1 onion, minced

½ cup minced fresh parsley

¼ cup minced red bell pepper

1 teaspoon paprika

2 teaspoons Aleppo pepper, or
   1 teaspoon red pepper flakes

2 cloves garlic, minced

1 tablespoon coriander seeds, lightly
   crushed

2 teaspoons salt

Cucumber Yogurt Mint Salad for serving
   (recipe follows)

Lemon wedges and pita bread for serving

1. Combine all ingredients but cucumber salad, lemon wedges and pita in a bowl, and knead very well into a paste.

2. Hold a flat metal skewer—not nonstick, and at least 12 inches long—point up in one hand. Dip other hand in a bowl of water, take a handful of meat mixture and form it around base of skewer in a small sausage shape with pointed ends. Repeat, working your way up the skewer. Each skewer should hold 3 or 4 kebabs. (You can also just form meat into 8 patties.)

3. Lay finished skewers on a sheet pan, and smooth kebabs with fingers, making sure they are fairly smooth and secured on skewers. Refrigerate at least 1 hour.

4. Prepare charcoal grill, or turn gas grill to medium-low. Fire should not be too hot, and rack should be at least several inches from heat source.

5. When rack is heated through, gently squeeze kebabs to be sure they are secure on the skewers, and place skewers on grill. The meat should start sizzling gently; it should not spit and turn black. Cook undisturbed until deep brown, at least 7 minutes. When meat lifts easily from grill, slide a spatula under kebabs and turn over. Continue grilling until browned on both sides and juicy, but cooked through, 10 to 15 minutes total.

6. Serve with cucumber salad, lemon wedges and pita that has been warmed on the grill just before serving.

Cucumber Yogurt Mint Salad

Time: 5 minutes   **Yield:** 4 to 6 servings

2 cups plain whole-milk yogurt

1 teaspoon minced garlic

2 tablespoons olive oil

½ teaspoon salt

1 long seedless cucumber, peeled, halved
lengthwise and sliced crosswise
¼ inch thick

12 fresh mint leaves, cut in thin ribbons,
plus extra whole leaves for garnish.

In a bowl, mix yogurt, garlic, oil and salt together until smooth. Chill until ready to serve. Just before serving, mix in cucumber and sliced mint. Add salt to taste if necessary, garnish with mint leaves and serve.

June 29, 2005: "The Summer Cook: Burgers without Borders,"
by JULIA MOSKIN; recipe adapted from Classical Turkish Cooking,
by AYLA ALGAR (HarperCollins, 1991)

Grilled Lamb and Figs on Rosemary Skewers

Lamb on rosemary skewers has to be one of the oldest recipes in the world. In ancient times, the meat could just as easily have been goat, or something wilder, and fish was no doubt also a candidate. The idea of cutting branches of rosemary for skewers must certainly have occurred to humans soon after they figured out how to build fires.

Rosemary grows wild as a large, hardy shrub throughout the Mediterranean and places with similar climates, like California, Chile, South Africa and parts of Australia. Figs grow in these same climates by the zillions. And it didn't take Escoffier to figure this one out: figs are good—no, fabulous—when grilled. The combination with another ancient food, olive oil, is amazing.

I can't improve on what our ancestors did, but here are some points to consider. Use lamb shoulder when possible; it's fattier and grills better than chunks of leg. Grill the lamb and the figs—nice and ripe, left whole—separately, since the lamb will take a little longer to cook than the figs. The heat can be about the same for both, moderately hot. Also, You might throw together a little basting sauce of lemon, garlic and a little more rosemary. I do, but I know that the skewers are just fine without it, and have been for thousands of years.

Time: 20 minutes, plus time to heat grill   **Yield:** 4 to 6 servings

2 pounds boneless lamb shoulder, cut into chunks	Salt and freshly ground black pepper to taste
10 to 20 fresh figs	½ cup fresh lemon juice
Fresh rosemary branches	2 cloves garlic, roughly chopped
¼ cup extra virgin olive oil, more or less	1 tablespoon minced fresh rosemary

1. Start a charcoal or wood fire or heat a gas grill; fire should be moderately hot. Thread lamb and figs onto rosemary branches, three or four chunks or figs per skewer. Do not mix meat and figs on same skewer.

2. Brush lightly with olive oil and season with salt and pepper. Mix together lemon juice, garlic and minced rosemary and brush a little of this mixture on lamb and figs.

3. Grill, turning skewers as each side browns and taking care to avoid flare-ups; total cooking time should be from 6 to 10 minutes for medium-rare meat, and 4 or 5 minutes for figs. Meat will become slightly more done after you remove it from grill, so take this into account.

July 16, 2008: "The Minimalist: The Tasty Twig, a Barbecue Tradition," by MARK BITTMAN

Brochettes d'Agneau à l'Estragon
(Lamb Brochettes with Tarragon)

Yield: 6 to 8 servings

½ leg of lamb (about 3½ to 4 pounds)

1 cup dry red wine

Salt and freshly ground pepper

1 tablespoon dried tarragon

2 tablespoons red wine vinegar

2 tablespoons olive oil

2 teaspoons finely minced garlic

12 to 16 mushroom caps

Melted butter

Fresh lemon juice

1. Bone leg of lamb or have it boned. Have all fat and skin removed. Cut meat into 1½-inch cubes. There should be about 2¼ pounds of meat. Put meat in a mixing bowl.

2. Add wine, salt and pepper to taste, tarragon, vinegar, oil and garlic. Stir. Let stand 4 hours. Drain.

3. Arrange one mushroom cap on each of 6 or 8 skewers. Arrange equal portions of meat on each of skewers. Add one more mushroom cap to each skewer.

4. Preheat a charcoal grill.

5. Place brochettes on grill and cook, turning often, about 10 minutes. Serve with melted butter and a squeeze of lemon juice sprinkled over.

May 25, 1980: "Food: Ready for the Grill,"
by CRAIG CLAIBORNE with PIERRE FRANEY

Butterflied Leg of Lamb with Sorrel Sauce

Time: 45 minutes, plus overnight for marinating   **Yield:** 8 to 10 servings

1 leg of lamb (about 6 pounds), boned so
   it lies flat
1 cup plain yogurt
1 tablespoon Dijon mustard
1 tablespoon dark soy sauce
½ cup extra-virgin olive oil
Juice of 1 lemon
3 cloves garlic, crushed and chopped
2 teaspoons fresh rosemary leaves

Freshly ground pepper to taste
For the sorrel puree
2 large shallots, sliced
4 tablespoons (½ stick) unsalted butter
¾ pound fresh sorrel leaves
2 cups chicken stock, preferably
   homemade
Coarse salt and freshly ground pepper
   to taste

1.   Wipe lamb dry with paper towels and remove any large pieces of fat. Mix together yogurt, mustard, soy sauce, oil and lemon juice. Add garlic, rosemary and pepper and spread mixture over lamb. Refrigerate overnight.

2.   On day of serving, make sauce. Soften shallots in butter in a large heavy saucepan. Remove stems from sorrel and add leaves to pan. Cook until wilted.

3.   Add chicken stock and bring to a boil. Remove from heat and puree in a blender or food processor. Return sauce to pan. Season to taste with salt and pepper, and allow to simmer gently until thickened. If it gets too thick, cover and keep warm. It can be thinned with more chicken stock.

4.   Preheat coals for cooking lamb. Place lamb on a rack and cook for 7 to 8 minutes. Do not be alarmed by flames flaring up; this is the lamb fat pouring off. The flames will soon die down. Cook for 7 to 8 minutes on other side. The meat should now be ready if you like your lamb rare. If you like it more well done, cook it longer. It is at its best browned on the outside but pink in the middle.

May 24, 1992: "Food: Barbecuing Returns, with Twists,"
by MOIRA HODGSON

Evening in Central Park

During the summer in Cincinnati, people flock to a post-modern, Michael Graves-designed outdoor amphitheater next to the Ohio River to listen to classical music concerts. In Los Angeles, the Hollywood Bowl draws untold thousands to exchange cars for starlit evenings of culture. San Franciscans go to Golden Gate Park, Boston hosts the Boston Pops and the Boston Ballet by the banks of the Charles. In New York, there are concerts or opera or Shakespeare in the city's parks all summer long. Many of these avid music lovers, theatergoers, dance aficionados and opera buffs have more than culture in common, however. Call it a vice or call it a virtue—they are gourmets on the go.

They are all, to a greater or lesser degree, devotees of the city picnic. Whether pre-Shakespeare or pre-symphony, they know to leave hot dogs and hamburgers behind. They have an occasion to rise to—the presentation of a meal in keeping not only with their surroundings but with the more elegant spirit of the cultural event they have come to enjoy.

The menu should be suited to warm weather but should not depend on food that has to be served chilled or piping hot. The best meals are those that can be prepared earlier the same day or even the day before and are attractive yet simple to carry and serve.

A simple meat or poultry dish served at "room temperature," as it were, is preferable, with condiments and salads whose sturdy vinaigrette dressings and forceful seasonings will whet appetites wilted by the heat. Such recipes can often be improvised from various ethnic cuisines. The meal can be finished off with either hot or cold espresso, stored in a thermos and requiring neither milk nor cream.

The best city picnics are more than a few cuts above casual; formal tableware is a given. With Central Park as the dining room, the view of the Art Deco skyline of Central Park West's towers can serve as the cue for the accessories: sleek silver, fine porcelain, elegant stemware and snowy linens.

After the hamper they have traveled in has been unloaded, the plastic containers used for transporting the food can be tucked away there.

A most successful outing last summer was an intimate dinner for two. Dinner began with poached shrimps in a garlic and saffron mayonnaise. The main dish was a whole, boned rack of lamb. Rubbed with olive oil, freshly ground pepper and salt, it was grilled until medium-rare. It is best to not refrigerate it and to slice it just before leaving home, wrapping the slices tightly in heavy-duty foil for their trip.

Accompanying the lamb was a tomato onion chutney (see page 163), which takes advantage of summer's harvest. Both the chutney and a salad of black-eyed peas and scallions dressed with vinegar and olive oil were made a day or two in advance. The bibb lettuce and arugula leaves of a more traditional salad, however, were rinsed, dried, torn and placed in a plastic bag at the last possible minute. A mustardy walnut-oil vinaigrette dressing was carried in a tight-lidded jar so that it could be given a good final shake. A crusty French bread and crottins, or tiny goat cheeses, went with the salads.

Dessert consisted of raspberry chocolate mousse cakes (see page 314 for recipe). They remained undamaged because they were transported in their baking dishes and unmolded just before serving, floating in little puddles of raspberry puree sprinkled with fresh raspberries.

This menu was devised so that it would eliminate the possibility of leftovers, which on a sultry night would get soggy and would have to be carted home afterward. A bag for trash is a good idea, as is a bottle of mineral water, not only for drinking but for giving the tableware a quick rinse.

Don't forget the corkscrew. Then sit back and enjoy the show.

Grilled Lamb Fillet

Yield: 2 servings

1 rack of lamb (about 2 pounds), boned
  and in a solid piece
½ tablespoon extra virgin olive oil
Pinch kosher salt

½ teaspoon coarsely ground black
  pepper
Tomato Onion Chutney (recipe follows)

1.   Preheat barbecue grill.

2.   Rub both sides of meat with olive oil. Sprinkle with salt and pepper.

3.   Grill lamb to desired degree of doneness. About 5 minutes on each side should be medium-rare.

4.   Set lamb aside to cool to room temperature before slicing. Cut meat into slices no more than ½ inch thick. When ready to serve, arrange slices in a fanlike pattern on individual plates and serve with chutney.

Tomato Onion Chutney

Yield: ⅓ cup

½ tablespoon extra virgin olive oil

¼ teaspoon cumin seeds

1 small onion, minced

2 medium, ripe tomatoes (about
   ½ pound), seeded, peeled and
   finely chopped

Salt and freshly ground pepper to taste

1 teaspoon fresh lemon juice

1. Heat olive oil in a small saucepan over high heat. Add cumin seeds, and when they start to sizzle, stir in onion. Sauté over medium heat until onion is tender, about 4 minutes.
2. Add tomatoes and cook over high heat for about 5 minutes, or until mixture thickens. Season with salt and pepper, stir in lemon juice and allow to cool to room temperature.

May 4, 1986: FLORENCE FABRICANT

Grilled Spring Lamb Chops
with Cabernet-and-Caper Butter

In spring, chef Alfred Portale of Gotham Bar and Grill prepares supernal young lamb chops with a red-wine-and-caper butter. "Cabernet and lamb are wonderful together," he says. "You use one glass of wine to prepare the butter, and serve the rest of the bottle with the meal."

Yield: 4 servings

8 loin lamb chops, about 10 ounces each
    (a total weight of 5½ pounds)
4 cloves garlic, thinly sliced
3 to 5 sprigs fresh rosemary
Salt to taste, if desired
Freshly ground pepper to taste
3 sprigs fresh thyme, coarsely chopped

4 shallots (about ¼ pound), thinly sliced
3 tablespoons olive oil
2 tablespoons fresh lemon juice
⅔ cup Cabernet-and-Caper Butter
    (recipe follows)
1 bunch watercress

1. Neatly trim off and discard most of triangle of fat at inner point where the tail flap joins main part of the chops. Do not sever flap from main part.

2. Arrange 3 garlic slices over each flap. Break each rosemary sprig into ½-inch lengths. Arrange 3 or 4 rosemary pieces over each tail flap. Roll up each flap and secure with a toothpick.

3. Sprinkle each chop with salt and pepper. Scatter thyme and shallots over lamb chops, and sprinkle with oil and lemon juice. Let stand at least 15 minutes.

4. Meanwhile, preheat an outdoor grill to high.

5. Put chops on grill and cook 5 minutes. Rotate them to give a grilled pattern to bottom of chops. Turn and rotate chops on second side to give a grilled pattern. Cook to desired degree of doneness, about 5 to 7 minutes longer, for a total cooking time of 13 to 15 minutes. Spoon Cabernet-and-Caper Butter over chops and garnish with watercress.

Cabernet-and-Caper Butter

Yield: About 9 tablespoons

¾ cup full-bodied dry red wine,
preferably cabernet sauvignon
3 tablespoons finely chopped shallots
¼ pound (1 stick) unsalted butter, at
room temperature
2 tablespoons drained capers

2 tablespoons finely chopped fresh
parsley
Salt to taste, if desired
Freshly ground pepper to taste

1.   Combine wine and shallots in a saucepan, and cook until wine is almost completely evaporated, 10 to 15 minutes. Do not let shallots become dry or burned. Set aside until thoroughly cooled.

2.   Put butter in saucepan and start beating with a wire whisk while adding capers, parsley and salt and pepper to taste.

March 20, 1988: "Food: The Fires of Spring,"
by CRAIG CLAIBORNE with PIERRE FRANEY,
adapted from ALFRED PORTALE,
Gotham Bar and Grill, New York City

Hold the Mayo! First Up, Rouille

I consider myself a competent cook. I've baked ethereal soufflés, wrapped lamb legs in suet and even mastered puff pastry. But making mayonnaise in the blender? It brings me to my knees.

It should be easy. Julia Child wrote that it's so simple that "no culinary skill whatsoever enters into its preparation."

Yet every time I've tried it, the sauce implodes into a curdled mess.

A less obsessed person would give up on homemade mayo. But I love the stuff, which, when properly made by other people, turns canned tuna into ambrosia. The jarred fluff just can't compare.

And then there are mayonnaise's kissing cousins: aioli (garlic mayonnaise) and rouille (spicy saffron mayonnaise). It's one thing for me to make do with Hellmann's on a turkey club, but quite another to forsake aioli and rouille, neither of which is easily bought even in the swankiest market.

It was a desire for rouille (pronounced roo-EE) that made me summon my courage. I was reminiscing with my mother about trips to Southern France. I loved when she would order a thick, rich fish soup that was served with croutons, grated cheese and a bowl of garlic-imbued rouille. She sipped the soup while I dunked the croutons in rouille and cheese. There was no better lunch when I was eight.

If I could figure how to make rouille without breaking it, I knew I would slather it on everything from grilled fish to grilled cheese. I found several recipes calling for ingredients ranging from fish livers to potato. But none sounded like the silky rouilles I remembered.

Finally, I opened my *Larousse Gastronomique* and there it was: a mix of egg yolks, saffron, garlic, cayenne and olive oil. The instructions were terse. Mash the garlic, then whisk in the yolks and, gradually, the oil. Grinding garlic to a paste in my blender was impossible, so I lugged out my mortar and pestle and smashed the garlic to a pulp. I was about to transfer it to the blender to test fate when I had another idea: finish the sauce with the mortar and pestle. Maybe unplugged was the way to go.

I tried it, pounding the yolks with the seasonings and adding the oil in driblets. Three minutes later, with no culinary skill employed, I had a thick, glossy mound. Unlike a wimpier mayonnaise, the rouille packed a pungent wallop with a musky saffron kick.

I put it in the fridge while debating what to smear it on. Chicken thighs? Zucchini frittata? In the end, I defrosted the tender little lamb chops I'd been hoarding in the freezer for a special occasion. A successful rouille seemed like as good an excuse as any.

So I rubbed the rouille all over the chops, then plopped them on the grill.

The rouille helped the chops char while they absorbed all that garlicky-saffron flavor, which was underscored by a dollop of sauce on the side and a garnish of sweet cherry tomatoes.

Now that I've mastered rouille, maybe it's time to revisit mayonnaise—made with a mortar and pestle, of course.

Grilled Lamb Chops
with Rouille and Cherry Tomatoes

Yield: 2 to 3 servings

Large pinch saffron threads

2 cloves garlic, minced

⅛ teaspoon kosher salt, plus more to taste

Large pinch cayenne pepper, or to taste

1 large egg yolk

½ cup extra virgin olive oil, plus more for serving

1 teaspoon tomato paste

6 lamb loin chops, 2 inches thick (4 to 6 ounces each)

Freshly ground black pepper

1 pint cherry tomatoes

1 tablespoon chopped fresh celery leaves or chives

½ teaspoon sherry vinegar or red wine vinegar

Thick slices of crusty bread for serving

1. For the rouille: Using a mortar and pestle or food processor, pound or pulse saffron until bruised and fragrant. Mix in ½ teaspoon boiling water and let sit for 5 minutes. Add garlic, salt and cayenne pepper and pound or pulse until a paste forms.

2. Mix in egg yolk until thoroughly combined. While pounding and stirring constantly (or with food processor on), slowly drizzle in olive oil. When oil is fully emulsified, stir in tomato paste. Add more salt and cayenne if necessary.

3. Light grill. Season lamb chops with salt and pepper, and coat with rouille. Allow lamb to rest at room temperature while grill heats up.

4. Halve cherry tomatoes and sprinkle with salt. Toss with celery leaves or chives and vinegar.

5. Grill lamb chops to taste, about 2 to 3 minutes per side for medium rare. Brush bread slices with oil and grill until toasted, about 30 seconds per side. Serve lamb with more rouille drizzled on top, and grilled bread and tomatoes on the side.

September 2, 2009: MELISSA CLARK

Glazed Lamb Ribs

On the docket for today: a weekend dinner of glazed lamb ribs, hot and sticky off the grill.

You could accompany the meat with rice or salad and certainly with beer or cold tea. The dish has the power to transform any porch or garden, roof or chalky concrete side yard into Southampton in high summer.

This recipe is based loosely on one for a snack that used to be served at DBGB, Daniel Boulud's giddy sausage-and-beer restaurant on the Bowery in Manhattan: crunchy little nuggets of small-boned breast meat and fat served with a pale yogurt sauce with a mild pepper kick under a zing of lemon zest. You sat in the restaurant's bar room eating these things with a cold I.P.A. to drink, and it was like discovering a new room off your apartment or a secret entrance to an empty highway out of town.

Because: lamb ribs? Holy cats. Similar in shape and size to pork baby-back ribs, and to veal breast for tenderness, they come from the breast plate of a sheep, sweet and succulent.

You do not see lamb ribs often in the supermarket, at least not in packages marked "lamb ribs." Chops and legs predominate there. But any butcher—even the sullen man in the back of the local I.G.A. or the grumpy fellow down at the Sweetbay near the Beach Road—can get a lamb breast and cut it for you, often with only a day or two's notice.

This is a transaction worth commencing immediately.

For the ribs at DBGB, Jim Leiken, the restaurant's chef, cured the meat for a day in thyme and rosemary, salt and garlic and bay. Then he submerged the racks in olive oil and cooked the result slowly for hours, making a kind of lamb confit. After slicing the racks into individual ribs, he deep-fried them and bathed the result in a honeyed glaze made piquant with vinegar. A final shower of toasted cracked coriander seeds and mild Aleppo pepper, with lemon zest, salt and parsley for crunch and contrast, and the dish went out in pieces to the bar.

It tasted incredible, of course. Leiken could probably follow the same process with a remaindered novel or a worn-out moccasin and almost achieve the same effect.

But his ability to layer flavors on top of flavors, succulence beneath tender crust, is just one marker of what differentiates restaurant chefs from home cooks. Another is the volume and scale of restaurant cooking, which dwarfs that of the home. And for those who cook for families and not hordes, for pleasure more than paychecks, the process of confitting lamb ribs, then deep-frying them, may simply be too time- and equipment-intensive even for the project-mad.

On a summer Sunday, then, it may be better to slow-roast the meat in a low oven, allowing the fat on the ribs to braise the meat. Then, rather than deep-frying the end result, the finished ribs—cut into individual slices, along the bone and straight through the chine—can be grilled and basted again, using Leiken's honey-and-vinegar glaze.

The dish does more than hint at the crispness of the original—charred and glistening, with bits of herb and a few flashes of yellow brightness from the zest—it pays real homage. It tastes of the best parts of summer in Manhattan, sophisticated and cool: Debbie Harry swinging soft and punky down the Bowery from a show at CBGB in 1977, say, past empty lots where someday restaurants would rise.

Yield: 4 main-course servings

For the lamb

2 racks lamb ribs

2 tablespoons kosher salt

6 cloves garlic, finely diced

6 sprigs fresh thyme

3 sprigs fresh rosemary

2 bay leaves

For the glaze

1 cup sherry vinegar

1 cup honey

1 tablespoon fennel seeds, cracked

1 tablespoon coriander seeds, cracked

1 tablespoon freshly ground black pepper

1 tablespoon Aleppo pepper

2 tablespoons unsalted butter, cold

For the sprinkle

2 tablespoons coriander seeds, toasted and cracked, or 1 tablespoon ground coriander

2 teaspoons Aleppo pepper

2 teaspoons kosher salt, or to taste

Grated zest of 1 lemon

1 tablespoon finely chopped fresh parsley

1. Preheat oven to 275 degrees. Trim most of fat from surface of lamb racks and place them in a large roasting pan. Combine salt, garlic and herbs and rub over lamb. Place in oven and roast for 2 hours. Remove pan from oven and turn ribs, then return to oven for 30 to 60 minutes longer, or until lamb is just tender and starting to pull away from bone. Remove pan from oven and set aside.

2. Meanwhile, make the glaze. Combine vinegar and honey in a small saucepan placed over moderate heat. Add fennel, coriander, black pepper and Aleppo pepper and bring to a slight simmer. Lower heat and allow mixture to reduce by half. Remove from heat and whisk in cold butter.

3. Light a fire in grill or preheat broiler in oven. Combine coriander, Aleppo pepper, salt, lemon zest and parsley in a small bowl and set aside. Slice ribs into individual pieces, cutting between each bone. When coals are covered with gray ash and fire is hot, put chops on grill directly over coals. Using a pastry brush, coat lamb lightly with glaze and continue to cook, turning occasionally, until meat begins to turn golden and crisp, approximately 5 to 7 minutes. Remove to a platter and sprinkle with topping.

June 22, 2011: "Eat: Aye, There's the Rib," by SAM SIFTON

Variations on the Barbecue

B arbecues are distinguished from both grilled and spit-turned foods and, although associated with this country, are, in fact, international. In certain sections of this country, the word barbecue is used to imply almost any meat, poultry, game or fish that is cooked over charcoal or on a spit.

For what it is worth, in my view, foods that are cooked on a spit without basting should be referred to as spit-turned foods, while foods that are cooked on a grill without a basting sauce are properly referred to as grilled foods. This is true whether or not they are coated or served after cooking with a barbecue sauce.

A genuine, unadulterated barbecue is food that has cooked over a period of time, while being basted with a sauce, the numbers, kinds and flavors of which are countless.

It saddens me to think that the word barbecue is one of the most abused and misused words in the United States. The finest barbecues are to be found in the South (the famed and fabled foods of the late Arthur Bryant's Barbecue in Kansas City, Missouri, notwithstanding), and barbecues were a focal point of my early nourishment. In the days of my earliest youth, hundreds of guests would arrive on special occasions for barbecues that consisted of long trenches specially dug on my father's property. Wire was laid over these trenches to hold hundreds of pounds of chicken and ribs of pork, which were then basted for hours until the meat shredded at a touch. That was more than half a century ago in the Mississippi Delta.

Although I care a great deal about semantics where food names are concerned, I had never been notably interested in the origins of the word *barbecue* until it occurred to me to see if, by any chance, such a thoroughly American word existed in the *Oxford English Dictionary*. To my utter amazement, it does. The first definition notes that a barbecue is "a rude wooden framework, used in America for sleeping on, and for supporting above a fire, meat that is to be smoked or dried." Sleeping on? The Oxford adds that the name derives from the Spanish *barbacoa*, adopted from the Haitian *barbacoa*—"a framework of sticks set upon posts." The dictionary firmly denies that widely circulated fiction that the name was originally from the French *barbe a queue*, which literally means beard to tail.

But, generally speaking, in this country the sauce used in a barbecue will vary from region to region, and the base may be predominately of ketchup, predominately of vinegar or, rarely, predominately of dried or prepared mustard. Or, it may be a combination of the three.

A friend of mine in North Carolina declared that the best-known formula there is made with vinegar, red pepper and black pepper. The principal meat used is pork shoulder, and beef is all but unheard of. The pork is slow-cooked over wood coals.

An acquaintance in Dallas told me that the traditional Texas barbecue sauce has a vinegar base for basting and that a barbecue sauce—generally containing ketchup—is served on the side. "Not," she said, "the sweet sauce you're likely to find in Georgia."

When I spoke to Martha Nesbit, a friend of longstanding and food editor of the *Savannah Morning News*, she offered one of the most knowledgeable replies as to what, specifically, is a regional barbecue sauce of Georgia.

"These sauces vary from place to place even in the same town," she said. "The best-known sauce here in Savannah is made by Johnny Harris. It is a basting sauce that is heavy on the mustard." In Vidalia (which is known, by the way, as the sweet-onion capital of the world), the sauce is extremely thin and based on vinegar. But, to my mind, the finest, most typical Georgia barbecue sauce is that of Betty Talmadge, which she includes in her book *How to Cook a Pig* (Simon and Schuster, 1977). It's sort of a synthesis of all the best barbecue sauces in the state. The recipe is made predominately with ketchup, but with a pronounced amount of vinegar, a touch of dry mustard and a cup of brown sugar.

"Brown sugar," Nesbit said, "is absolutely essential to give the proper sweet-and-sour balance to Georgia barbecue sauces." I might add that this recipe is almost identical to the one used by my family when I was a child in Mississippi. When it comes to barbecuing as a form of cookery, it is undoubtedly the least exact part of the science. So much depends on the intensity of the heat that is derived from the burning or merely smoldering coals and the position of the foods in relation to those coals. Some cooks place the foods directly over the coals; others insist that the foods be placed a short distance from the coals and not directly over them so that the foods will cook from reflected heat. Much may have to do, as well, with the conditions of the day—to choose two examples, whether there is or is not a breeze, or whether the day is cold or hot.

There is one point on which most fine barbecue cooks seem to agree. If one wants to barbecue well, one must have patience and cook the foods for a long period, basting as often as necessary, over moderate to slow heat, preferably the latter. Much depends on slow cooking. The fire must be tended, and more coals or wood added as necessary—a little at a time—to maintain a heat as constant as possible, start to finish. The foods should be turned with great attention on a spit or on the grill to prevent burning. Some cooks recommend dousing a little water on the coals if the fire becomes too hot. Others recommend the use of flavored woods such as hickory or ash, either in the form of cubes or sawdust, toward the end of the cooking time, to add a special taste.

Over the years I have presumed—chauvinistically, I suppose—that to be a good barbecue cook one had of necessity to be Southernborn. But I have learned in recent months that this is not quite true.

Ron Scher, an advertising executive, is a native of Manhattan and an excellent cook who says he has been fascinated with the theory and practice of barbecuing all his life.

His barbecue begins with a "rub," which is sprinkled onto the foods in advance of cooking and continues throughout, while basting with a special long-cooked sauce made with beef bones, vinegar, Worcestershire sauce, oil and spices. The result ranks with the best I have tasted, whether commercial, home-style or otherwise.

Once the barbecue is done, Scher serves as an accompaniment what I consider a notably authentic barbecue sauce for dipping or coating, and this does have a ketchup and vinegar base, precisely as it may be found in Texas. He uses one "rub" that is on the sweet side for spareribs and other pork, and another that is peppery for chicken and scampi.

Barbecues are, of course, international. A short while ago, a group of cooks and chefs came to my home for an entertainment and each was asked to contribute one dish for the occasion that would serve 30 or more guests. It produced two fantastic barbecues: A Brazilian *churrasco*, or barbecue of beef ribs (see page 99), prepared by Dorothea Elman, a graphic- and industrial-design consultant in Manhattan, and a whole baby lamb cooked on a spit by Edward Giobbi, the artist and cookbook author. The last resulted in a marvelously Italianate, spit-roasted animal flavored with rosemary and garlic. When cooked to a turn, the meat was served with an inspired dipping sauce made with pine nuts and basil, similar to a pesto, but also flavored with mint.

Elman's menu included not only the meat and ribs, which had cooked over a charcoal-filled pit with low heat for several hours while it was brushed with a brine known as *salmoura*, but also a splendid onion sauce essential for the dish and farofa, the tempting native cereal made with manioc flour, and onions and bananas cooked in butter.

A great deal depends on the quality of the wood or charcoal that is used in a barbecue. If wood is used, it will add a desirable flavor if it is a nut or fruit wood such as walnut, pecan, cherry or apple. Within the last few years, mesquite, long a favorite wood of the Southwest, has begun to be marketed on the East Coast and it is excellent from the standpoint of both heat and flavor. Pine should never be used; it will make the food taste of turpentine. Similarly, the fire should not be lighted with gasoline or kerosene. This will impart a highly undesirable off-odor to the food.

Ed Giobbi's Whole-Lamb Barbecue

1 whole lamb, dressed, about 25 pounds
Salt to taste, if desired
Freshly ground black pepper to taste
20 cloves garlic, crushed and peeled

½ cup chopped fresh or dried rosemary
Basting Sauce (recipe follows)
Ed Giobbi's Dipping Sauce (page 174)

1. Rub lamb inside and out with salt, if desired, freshly ground black pepper, garlic and rosemary.

2. Dig a pit 14 inches deep and 3 feet long. Pit should be about 14 inches wide or slightly wider.

3. Surround pit with four metal upright fence posts. Situate posts in a rectangular pattern, surrounding pit. Let rectangle measure about 3½ feet long and 16 inches wide. Pound posts firmly into earth.

4. Run a sturdy and firm but not-too-thick metal or wooden skewer (Giobbi prefers a long solid hickory stick) through body of lamb, including head and tail. The skewer must be long enough so that each end protrudes enough to lie flat on metal or wooden crosspieces.

5. There should be two of these crosspieces for each pair of posts. Place them horizontally on posts at each end of pit. The bottom crosspiece should be about 17 inches from top of pit on each side; the other, about 14 inches above that. Fasten securely with wire.

6. Cook lamb on bottom crosspiece, but, if at any point you find that the heat is too intense and lamb is cooking too rapidly or starting to burn, you may raise lamb to upper horizontal crosspiece. You may also douse a little water on coals to cool them as desired.

7. Start a fire inside pit using paper, kindling and a non-oily hardwood such as oak or hickory. Do not use pine. It will impart the flavor of turpentine to the meat. Let this fire burn until wood develops a white ash. At this point, start adding charcoal, preferably genuine lump charcoal rather than briquettes. Let charcoal burn, offering moderate but steady heat, as lamb roasts. Total roasting time will be from 5 to 6 hours.

8. As lamb roasts, baste it fairly often all over with basting sauce.

9. Cut up and carve lamb while it is still hot and serve it with dipping sauce spooned over.

Basting Sauce

Yield: About 4¼ cups

4 cups red wine vinegar
¼ cup coarsely chopped garlic
¼ cup chopped fresh or dried rosemary
    leaves

1 teaspoon freshly ground black pepper

1. Put 3 cups of vinegar, garlic, rosemary and pepper in a food processor or blender. Blend well.

2. Add remaining 1 cup vinegar and blend as thoroughly as possible.

Ed Giobbi's Dipping Sauce

Yield: About 4 cups

1 cup olive oil

¼ cup safflower oil

¼ cup coarsely chopped garlic

½ cup pine nuts

12 cups loosely packed fresh basil leaves

3 cups loosely packed fresh mint leaves

1½ teaspoons freshly ground black
    pepper

Salt to taste, if desired

1. Combine ¾ cup of olive, oil, safflower oil, garlic and pine nuts in a food processor or blender. Blend well.

2. Add basil, mint, pepper and salt. Blend well.

3. Pour mixture into 1-quart jar and pour remaining ¼ cup olive oil on top. This keeps well in refrigerator.

May 1, 1983: CRAIG CLAIBORNE with PIERRE FRANEY;
recipes from ED GIOBBI

Loin Lamb Steaks with Rosemary

I attended an outdoor barbecue at a neighbor's home the other day and was fascinated to find the host grilling loin lamb steaks, a cut of meat that is little used in American homes but a cut that I often served years ago when I was chef at Le Pavillon Restaurant. They are commonly called lamb steaks or "double" chops and are made by cutting through the center bone of a loin of lamb to produce a single piece of meat—two matching chops joined together by that single bone. The virtue of the lamb steak is the ease of cooking and the appearance, which is very appealing.

A short while after the barbecue I persuaded my butcher to produce enough lamb steaks to serve a party of six. (Incidentally, if you can't buy the steaks, you can achieve similar results by buying 12 individual chops, each cut about 1 inch thick.) This is a very easy and tasty recipe. Prepare a vinaigrette sauce with lemon juice and olive oil and add crumbled dried rosemary to this marinade. Grill the chops with mushrooms (preferably large, whole mushrooms), which are also coated with the sauce.

Yield: 6 servings

6 (1-inch-thick) loin lamb steaks (about ½ pound each), or 12 single lamb chops, each 1 inch thick, about ¼ pound each
Salt to taste if desired

Freshly ground pepper to taste
12 large fresh mushrooms (about 1 pound)
3 tablespoons fresh lemon juice
3 tablespoons olive oil
1 tablespoon dried rosemary leaves

1. Preheat an outdoor charcoal or gas grill to high.

2. Sprinkle steaks on both sides with salt and pepper and place them in one layer in a flat dish.

3. Cut off and discard stems of mushrooms to make flat caps.

4. Put lemon juice in a small bowl and add salt and pepper to taste. Beat juice while adding olive oil. Crumble rosemary and add it to sauce.

5. Arrange mushroom caps over lamb steaks and spoon sauce over all. Turn mushroom caps so they are coated with sauce.

6. Arrange steaks on grill and arrange mushrooms cap side down. Cook 4 minutes on one side and turn meat and mushrooms. Cook 3 to 4 minutes on other side.

August 6, 1986: "60-Minute Gourmet,"
by PIERRE FRANEY

A Whole Lamb Done to a Turn in the Greek Tradition

While not the typical backyard summer barbecue, for Nicocle Michas, his wife, Jill Barber, and their friends, a whole lamb turning slowly on a spit and glazing to a rich mahogany has become an increasingly frequent occurrence.

"It's a Greek tradition," explained Mr. Michas, who was born in Greece.

"We thought we would do it once a year," said Ms. Barber, "but it has gotten so popular that we probably will do three this year. All our friends with houses are now thinking of digging pits in their backyards."

The first attempt, an admittedly unprofessional affair, took place about two years ago. The barbecue pit, dug in the sandy soil behind the Michas home on a quiet wooded street, had been filled with charcoal and wood, which were ignited and then allowed to burn to embers. The whole lamb, clamped and wired to a five-foot-long hand-forged spit, was supported on a pair of heavy notched uprights.

"Then our troubles began," said Mr. Michas with a laugh. "As the lamb cooks, it shrinks, so we had to keep securing it on the spit. Even so, it kept slipping because we hadn't wired it enough. And then the key, with which the clamps are tightened, fell into the fire. Luckily, we found it on the first pass. I think the lamb fell into the fire at some point, too. And, of course, it rained. But you know, it tasted so good, despite all the disasters, that we didn't give up."

A bright sun in a brilliant blue sky smiled on the most recent Michas lambfest. The lamb, a meaty 35-pound carcass, had been brought from New York packed in ice on the previous evening.

Oregano and Garlic

Treated with a liberal rubbing of lemon juice, oregano, salt and pepper and about 40 slivers of garlic inserted into the flesh, the lamb had spent the night, still packed in ice, in the cool of the Michas's cellar.

At about 2:30 in the afternoon, when the embers were nicely glowing, Mr. Michas measured the distance he would need between the uprights to clear the lamb. He hammered the iron supports into the ground on either side of the pit and he and his wife set the spitted lamb upon them. The barbecue pit had recently been improved by a border of brick paving.

To insure against the lamb slipping as it cooked, the entire spine had been carefully wired to the spit at each vertebrae. The legs were tightly wired to it as well. "We have it down to a science now," commented Mr. Michas.

In addition to being hand-forged, the spit is hand-turned. Guests spell each other at the handle. "The one trouble with having a beautiful day like this for a change is that everyone wants to run to the beach," Ms. Barber remarked. The 30 or so guests relieved each other, in turn, for the three hours required to cook the meat while rendering the outside as crisp and brown as autumn leaves.

The lamb must be turned continually or the fire will flare up and char it. Periodically, Mr. Michas brushed it with more lemon juice and oregano and tossed the squeezed lemons right into the fire. During the final half hour, areas around the legs and shoulders were pierced to allow the fat to drain out.

By 5:30 P.M., the lamb looked perfect. The aroma perfumed the neighborhood. Guests, returned from the beach, began to move closer to the pit. At that point, Patrick Savin, a friend and associate of Mr. Michas's who had been actively involved in the lamb ventures from their inception and who supervised a pig on the Michas spit in June, entered into a delicate negotiation with the host. Should they remove the lamb at this point?

Although most of it seemed to be cooked Greek style, medium well done, the legs still complied with Mr. Savin's preference for French lamb, medium rare. There was discussion, a knife was fetched, a few preliminary slivers sampled, more considered evaluations made.

Finally, the long-awaited tour de force was removed from the spit and set on a table, along with such side dishes as rice with yogurt, salad, bread and cheese. From the initial gusto with which it was attacked, it might have been feared that the delicious feast would be completely consumed in minutes.

By eight o'clock that evening, when the sated crowd of children and adults began to leave, succulent chunks could still be cut from the shoulder area although every riblet had been picked clean and all the wonderfully crispy pieces had been eaten.

July 28, 1974: FLORENCE FABRICANT

Poultry

Poultry is simple, but getting it right when grilling can be a challenge. Overdo it and it's dry as Kleenex, but undercooking is even worse. However when grilled to just the right moment, chicken is crispy on the outside, juicy and flavorful on the inside. Mark Bittman gives some critical advice on creating different heat zones on the grill to coax out the perfect combination of doneness and crispness. Poultry accepts as many flavors as you can throw at it. Molly O'Neill goes shopping for ingredients at an Asian market and comes up with a killer lemongrass paste to slather on her Cambodian Barbecued Chicken (page 189), while Julia Moskin reveals the secrets of Jamaican jerk (page 192). Bryan Miller reminds us that the world of barbecueable poultry includes some other birds (quail, squab, duck) that are often overlooked but real winners on the grill.

Smokeless outdoor cookery is easy with electrical equipment. Sarrett Rudley, a script writer, prepares elaborate al fresco meals on her terrace, in 1958. One menu includes duck, wild rice, salad, and ginger soufflé.

Chicken Breasts Marinated in Basil Oil
with Tomato-and-Red-Onion Salad

Food that is completely cooked is a done deal. Food gently handled and embossed with something like a full-flavored oil is food in suspended animation; ripening is slowed but not completely quelled. More important, food that has been treated with infused oil takes on a new life when it is heated, or brought to room temperature, or just put into a warm mouth.

To me, simply made oils, like basil oil, encompass the lustiness of the season while allowing the cook the sort of restraint that brings a slower and more sustained satisfaction.

Yield: 4 servings

4 boneless, skinless chicken breast
    halves
4 teaspoons Basil Oil (recipe follows)
2 large tomatoes, thinly sliced
1 red onion, very thinly sliced

Salt and freshly ground pepper to taste
12 fresh basil leaves, cut across into thin
    strips

1. Using a brush, coat chicken breasts with 1 teaspoon of basil oil. Let stand for 30 minutes. Preheat a grill. Grill chicken until cooked through, about 4 minutes per side. Slice chicken on diagonal and brush slices with 1 teaspoon of oil.

2. Arrange half of tomato slices in center of each of 4 plates. Top with half of onion. Drizzle each one with ¼ teaspoon of basil oil and sprinkle with salt and pepper. Repeat layers. Fan chicken slices around salad. Scatter basil strips over salad and chicken. Can be served cold or at room temperature.

Basil Oil

Use to dress pasta, rice or potato salads; chicken, lobster or fish. It can be the basis of avinaigrette for young greens or slaw, for ripe tomatoes or vegetables that have been briefly blanched.

Yield: About 1½ cups

2 bunches fresh basil, stems on

2 cups plus 7 tablespoons extra virgin olive oil

1. Bring a large pot of water to a boil. Add basil and blanch for 30 seconds. Drain and rinse under cold running water until cool. Drain and dry basil well. Place in a food processor with 5 tablespoons of olive oil. Process until a thick puree forms, stopping several times to scrape down sides of bowl. Scrape into a clean glass jar and pour in 2 cups of olive oil. Shake well and store in a cool place for 1 to 2 days.

2. Strain oil through a fine mesh sieve. Pour remaining 2 tablespoons olive oil through a coffee filter to dampen filter. Fit filter inside rim of clean glass jar. Pour some of basil oil into filter and let drip into jar. Continue pouring and letting oil drip until all has passed through filter. Stored in refrigerator, oil will keep up to a month.

May 30, 1993: "Food: A Summer Drizzle,"
by MOLLY O'NEILL

Grilled Chicken Breast Salad with Curry Dressing

Most people think of salads as cold, but it's not necessarily so. I have been experimenting; warm salads are excellent appetizers or main courses any time of year.

Warm or room-temperature food has more flavor and tenderness than the same ingredients cold. Room-temperature pasta can be appealing. Many restaurants serve warm salads, with shrimp, scallops, lobster, duck, chicken, quail and much more.

The recipe here is ideal for barbecue grills. The curry dressing can be made in advance. Mix mustard, curry powder, balsamic vinegar, chopped scallions, olive oil, salt, pepper and herbs of your choice. Two whole chicken breasts, boned and skinned to leave four fillets, should cook on a grill in six to seven minutes. While the chicken is cooking, warm the curry dressing over a low flame. When the chicken is ready, lay it over greens and pour on the dressing.

The curry wants an equally assertive side dish. Indian-style turmeric rice was a hit at my house.

Yield: 4 servings

4 skinless, boneless chicken breast
　　halves (about 1¼ pounds)
2 teaspoons olive oil
2 tablespoons fresh lemon juice
2 tablespoons chopped fresh rosemary,
　　or 1 teaspoon dried
2 teaspoons finely chopped garlic
Salt and freshly ground pepper to taste

1 head radicchio (about ¼ pound), core
　　removed, rinsed and dried
2 heads bibb lettuce, core removed,
　　rinsed and dried
¼ pound arugula, cut into manageable
　　pieces, rinsed and dried
Warm Curry Dressing (recipe follows)
¼ cup coarsely chopped fresh basil or
　　chervil

1. If chicken breasts are connected, separate halves and cut away membrane or fat. Place oil in a mixing bowl with lemon juice, rosemary, garlic, salt and pepper. Stir well. Add chicken pieces and turn them in marinade to coat well. Cover and set aside until ready to cook. (If marinating for a long period, refrigerate them.)

2. Preheat a charcoal grill.

3. Put chicken pieces on grill. Cover grill. Cook 2 to 3 minutes, turning pieces. Continue cooking until done, about 3 to 5 minutes.

4. Remove pieces. Slice each breast on the bias about ¼ inch thick.

5. In a large mixing bowl, add radicchio, bibb lettuce and arugula. Toss well. Add half the warm dressing, and toss again. Place sliced chicken over salad and sprinkle with remaining dressing and basil.

Warm Curry Dressing

Yield: About 1 cup

2 teaspoons Dijon-style mustard

1 teaspoon curry powder

2 tablespoons balsamic vinegar

¼ cup chopped scallions

⅓ cup olive or vegetable oil

Salt and freshly ground pepper to taste

¼ cup coarsely chopped fresh basil or
    chervil

Place mustard, curry powder, vinegar and scallions in a saucepan. Blend well over low heat with a wire whisk. Add oil, blending well. Remove from heat and add salt, pepper and basil. Keep warm.

August 8, 1990: "60-Minute Gourmet,"
by PIERRE FRANEY

For Perfectly Cooked Chicken, Use Both Sides of the Grill

It took me years to learn how to grill chicken, and I pretty much had to invent my own technique. Standard advice from standard grilling sources too often left me with badly charred chicken or its equally unpleasant underdone cousin.

My technique is not original, I'm sure, but it isn't intuitive either. I assure you it will result in grilled chicken at its best: smoky, crispy and moist, good right off the grill or the day after.

We're talking about chicken with its skin on, preferably thighs, wings or drumsticks, which are far more likely to retain their moist tenderness than breasts.

Skinless chicken is fine cut up for kebabs, but I think that to routinely remove the skin from chicken is to rob it of its flavor, and much of the reason to grill it in the first place. If you want something low in fat, grill zucchini, or halibut.

The key to grilling chicken with its skin on is to allow the solid fat (plenty of that in and under the skin) to render without falling onto coals, wood, metal grates or flames so hot that the fat flares up and sets the chicken on fire.

Therefore, it's essential to begin grilling over rather low heat. A gas grill with one side set on low (or even off) and the other on medium or high works well, as does a charcoal or wood fire built so that one side of the grill remains relatively cool. In either case, you need a cover to keep the heat in and allow it to circulate.

You can create indirect heat with wood, charcoal, briquettes or gas. It doesn't matter much which you use, though if you want a good smoky, woody flavor your best choices are either wood (which can be tricky; you've got to be precise about timing) or hardwood charcoal (which, because it burns hot and fast, may need replenishment).

Gas is all right, too, especially if you sprinkle soaked hardwood chips either on the grates over the hottest part of the fire—the opposite side from where you're grilling—or in a foil tray right above the fire.

I don't like briquettes in general, but they're especially undesirable in a situation where you're covering the grill, because their smoke can flavor the food in an unappetizing fashion.

Put the chicken on the grill skin side up on the cool side and, after some of the fat has been rendered, turn it; if flames flare up, move the chicken to an even cooler part of the fire (this is where gas is handy; it's so easily adjusted). Or turn it so the skin side is up again—remember to keep the fat away from the flame.

When the skin has lost its raw look and most of the fat has been rendered, usually after 20 minutes or so of cooking, it's safe to move the chicken to the hot side of the grill. By then the meat will be mostly cooked through; what you do now is brown it nicely on both sides.

Bingo. If you have any doubts about the meat's doneness, cut into it alongside the bone. It will not make for the most attractive presentation, but it's more attractive than bloody chicken. With experience, you will be able to judge doneness by appearance and feel alone. This technique not only frees you from fear, at least in this little universe, but gives you dozens of options for flavoring.

Grilled Chicken with Chipotle Sauce

This nicely demonstrates that you can grill chicken with virtually no flavorings at all, serving it with a dipping or other sauce, or just lemon wedges for that matter.

Time: 45 minutes   **Yield:** 4 servings

2 tablespoons lard or neutral oil, like corn
    or canola, plus more for brushing
    chicken
1 medium-size white onion, chopped
2 dried chipotle chilies, or to taste
2 cups cored and chopped tomatoes

Salt and pepper to taste
8 chicken thighs, drumsticks or whole
    legs
2 cloves garlic, cut in half
Chopped fresh cilantro leaves for garnish
Lime wedges for garnish

1.   Start a charcoal or wood fire or preheat a gas grill; fire should be moderately hot, part of grill should be cooler than the rest and rack should be 4 to 6 inches from heat source.

2.   Put lard or oil in a medium saucepan or skillet and turn heat to medium. When hot, add onion and cook, stirring occasionally, until it begins to brown, 5 to 10 minutes. Add chilies, tomatoes and ½ cup water. Adjust heat so mixture simmers steadily but not violently. Cook about 15 minutes, stirring occasionally, until chilies are soft and tomatoes break up. Taste and add salt and pepper if necessary. When chipotle sauce is ready, cool for a few minutes, then remove stems from chipotles, put mixture in a blender and puree. (The sauce may be made up to a couple of days in advance.)

3.   Meanwhile, rub chicken with cut side of garlic cloves, brush on oil and season to taste with salt and pepper.

4.   Place chicken skin side up on coolest area of grill. When fat has rendered a bit, turn chicken over. After 20 minutes or so, move chicken to hottest part of grill. When chicken is just about done, brush it with chipotle sauce on both sides, and cook just another minute or two. Serve, garnished with cilantro and lime wedges.

Grilled Chicken with Mediterranean Flavors

To me, this is the model for grilled chicken recipes, a dish that seems perfect for outdoor eating.

Time: 45 minutes   **Yield:** 4 servings

Salt and freshly ground black pepper

1 teaspoon fresh thyme leaves

1 teaspoon chopped fresh rosemary
   leaves

½ teaspoon chopped fresh lavender
   leaves (optional)

¼ cup roughly chopped fresh parsley

Extra virgin olive oil as needed

8 chicken thighs or drumsticks, or
   a combination

8 bay leaves

2 lemons, cut into quarters

1.   Start a charcoal or wood fire or heat a gas grill. Fire should be only moderately hot, part of grill should be kept cooler than the rest and rack should be 4 to 6 inches from heat source.

2.   In a small bowl, combine salt, pepper, thyme, rosemary, lavender and parsley. Add enough olive oil to make a paste. Loosen skin of chicken and slide a bay leaf between skin and meat, then insert a portion of herb mixture. Push skin back onto meat and sprinkle with salt and pepper.

3.   Place chicken skin side up on coolest area of grill. When fat has rendered a bit, turn chicken over. After 20 minutes or so, move chicken to hottest part of grill, brush with a bit of olive oil and cook until meat is done and skin is nicely browned. Serve with lemon wedges. (Bay leaf is not edible.)

September 13, 2006: MARK BITTMAN

Twice-Cooked Mock Tandoori Chicken

This is similar in technique to tandoori but a world apart in flavor. It also mitigates the bane of chicken grilling (or, for that matter, broiling), the roaring flame-up. By braising the chicken first, you effectively remove just about all the surface fat, practically eliminating the risk of setting the pieces on fire.

Time: About 2 hours   **Yield:** 4 to 8 servings

8 chicken thighs, or thighs and
    drumsticks
2 tablespoons peanut or vegetable oil
1 medium-size onion, chopped
Salt and freshly ground black pepper
4 or 5 cloves garlic, smashed and peeled
1 (2-inch piece) fresh ginger, peeled and
    chopped, or 2 teaspoons dried ginger

1 tablespoon ground coriander
1 teaspoon ground cardamom
1 tablespoon paprika
1 teaspoon ground cumin
Cayenne or chopped fresh chilies or red
    pepper flakes to taste (optional)
3 cups plain yogurt

1. Preheat oven to 300 degrees. Put chicken in a deep roasting pan.

2. Put oil in a large skillet over medium-high heat. Add onion, sprinkle with salt and pepper and cook, stirring occasionally, until it softens and begins to color, about 2 minutes. Add garlic and ginger; cook and stir 2 minutes more. Stir in ground spices, and cook until just fragrant, no more than a minute. Stir in yogurt, then spread mixture over chicken. Cover and put in oven; bake until chicken is just cooked through, about 1½ hours. (You can prepare chicken up to a day ahead; if you are not going to grill immediately, put whole pan in refrigerator after it cools down a bit.)

3. Light a charcoal or gas grill; rack should be about 4 inches away from heat source. Remove chicken from yogurt sauce, scraping away any excess.

4. Grill over direct heat, turning once or twice, until skin is crisp and charred and meat dries out a bit, about 15 minutes total. Serve hot or at room temperature.

*May 21, 2008: "The Minimalist: Oven
Adds Flavor When the Grill Can't,"
by MARK BITTMAN*

Spendor in the Lemongrass

The grass is not always greener on the other side, but sometimes it is more aromatic. Take lemongrass. As common in Thailand, Cambodia and Vietnam as front lawns are in America, lemongrass smells like citrus tinged with ginger. But unlike, say, Kentucky bluegrass, lemongrass is edible, occupying a hallowed place in the cooking of Southeast Asia.

Fortunately for America, you can now find lemongrass in most well-stocked supermarkets. However, even the most traveled cook lacks a natural instinct for buying and handling, storing and cooking these fragrant stalks.

In fact, by the time lemongrass arrives here, its tender, grassy blades have been clipped, and what remains—a long spear with a bulbous tip—is tough and fibrous, requiring a sharp knife and plenty of patience to access its perfume.

Obviously, the bulb has the most flavor, but even the upper stalk is aromatic enough to make a powerful oil or to lend a lemony presence to a custard or a sweet souffle. (Since this part of the stalk is too tough to eat, you must mince it first; add it to the oil or milk; boil it and then let it macerate, anywhere from three to six hours, depending on how fresh the lemongrass is.)

To get the most out of lemongrass, you need to smash the bulb with the backside of a heavy knife. Such rough treatment—pulverization, followed by a long, determined maceration—is the opposite of what you can expect when you finally get to taste it.

Tempered as it is with spice and hints of mint, lemongrass is as subtle as a spring sunrise. It is clean and bright and, in its own way, bold. But it is more sheer than incandescent, more, in the end, about the nose than the acid receptors on the tongue.

I have yet to find a soup, a marinade, a stir-fry or a dipping sauce that suffered because I had used too much. Lemongrass has a marvelous capacity to both intensify flavors and disperse them.

But no matter how you cook it or what you cook it with (lemongrass has a natural affinity for chicken, shellfish and firm-fleshed fish like tuna), remember to mince it in the tiniest particles possible. Otherwise, the struggle to eat it politely—read: without dental floss—is simply too great.

Cambodian Barbecued Chicken

Yield: 4 servings

6 chicken legs, thighs and drumsticks
separated
1 teaspoon kosher salt

½ teaspoon freshly ground pepper
½ cup Lemongrass Barbecue Paste
(recipe follows)

1.   Prepare a barbecue for cooking. Place chicken on a baking sheet and season with salt and pepper. Slice log of barbecue paste into disks and dot chicken with them.

2.   When coals are hot, place chicken, with pasted side facing up, on a grill. Cover and cook for 20 to 30 minutes, depending on your grill, until juices run clear. Don't turn. Carefully scrape paste off chicken and discard. Serve with rice.

Lemongrass Barbecue Paste

This paste can be used to enliven chicken, veal or fish like tuna, swordfish or Chilean sea bass before grilling, broiling or baking. It will keep for about a month in the freezer.

Yield: ¼ cup

2 stalks fresh lemongrass
1 (1-inch) piece fresh frozen turmeric (see note)
1 (1-inch) piece frozen galangal (see note)

1 shallot, peeled
1 fresh frozen lemon leaf (see note)
1 clove garlic, peeled
2 tablespoons cold butter

1.   Pulverize lemongrass in a food processor. Add rest of ingredients except butter and process to a fine paste. Take a tiny taste to make sure that mash is fine enough. It will taste terrible. If any fibrous pieces remain, process until they are gone. Add butter and process just to combine.

2.   Remove paste from bowl and shape into a log about 1 inch in diameter. Wrap in plastic wrap. Freeze.

NOTE: Turmeric, galangal and lemon leaf are available in Asian markets.

June 15, 1997: MOLLY O'NEILL

Grilled Tabasco Chicken

Even though I enjoy grilled food year round, barbecuing is primarily a summer activity for us. I grill many types of food on the barbecue grill behind my house, but one of the tastiest and least expensive is chicken.

I use chicken legs for the main dish here, although a whole cut-up chicken, if priced more attractively, can be prepared this way. But use legs, if possible, taking advantage of sales offering large packages of legs at low prices. Chicken legs can withstand higher heat and longer cooking than breasts, without drying out. I partly split the legs at the joint that connects the drumstick and thigh; this is the thickest part of the leg, and cutting halfway through it makes cooking easier.

To reduce calories and lower cholesterol, many chicken recipes advise removing the skin before cooking the chicken, but I don't suggest it for this recipe. When chicken is cooked over intense heat, much of the fat in the skin melts. Flavored with the marinade, the skin is delectably crisp, one of the best parts of the dish. You can remove it before eating the chicken, if you prefer.

The marinade is a simple mixture of a tablespoon each of soy sauce, ketchup, cider vinegar and Tabasco sauce. A tablespoon may seem like a lot of Tabasco, but by the time it is exposed to direct heat, much of the hotness disappears, and you are left with the sauce's great flavor. Ketchup lends a little sweetness and helps the chicken brown beautifully.

Always grill the chicken skin side down to start, turning it after a nice crusty exterior has formed. Most of the marinade should cling to the chicken; any left in the container can be brushed onto the chicken, but for safety, do not continue to baste during the last 5 minutes of grilling and discard marinade at that point. The chicken can be grilled ahead and kept in a warm oven or on the corner of the grill. It is good served hot or at room temperature.

I would pair the chicken with a green salad. For dessert, I suggest whatever well-ripened seasonal fruit is most economical. A well-chilled fruity gamay wine from California would go well with the chicken.

Time: 40 minutes   **Yield:** 6 servings

6 chicken legs (about 3½ pounds)	1 tablespoon cider vinegar
1 tablespoon soy sauce	1 tablespoon Tabasco sauce
1 tablespoon ketchup	

1. Trim off tips of drumsticks and cut halfway through joint that connects thigh and drumstick of each leg.

2. Mix soy sauce, ketchup, vinegar and Tabasco together in a tray and roll chicken legs in marinade.

3. Place legs skin side down on rack of a hot grill about 10 inches from heat, and cook for about 10 minutes. Turn legs over, and cook for about 10 minutes on other side. Turn them again, and cook them skin side down for 10 minutes more.

4. Take legs off the heat to rest for 5 minutes before serving.

July 15, 1992: "The Purposeful Cook:
Tangy Barbecued Chicken: Crispy Skin,
Split Legs and All," by JACQUES PEPIN

Sweet Heat: For Jamaicans, It's About Jerk

On most summer Sundays, Brooklyn is burning.

Smoke rises from grills, many of them charcoal-fueled, illegal and loaded with jerk chicken—the spiced, smoky favorite of the borough's large Jamaican community.

Jerk is Jamaica to the bone, aromatic and smoky, sweet but insistently hot. All of its traditional ingredients grow in the island's lush green interior: fresh ginger, thyme and scallions; Scotch bonnet peppers; and the sweet wood of the allspice tree, which burns to a fragrant smoke.

"It's not a sauce, it's a procedure," Jerome Williams, a Jamaican-born Brooklyn resident, said one Sunday in Prospect Park, where families arrive as early as 6 a.m. for lakeside grilling spots, a few of which are actually authorized by the parks department. "It has to be hot, but it cannot only be hot, or you get no joy from it."

Done right, jerk is one of the great barbecue traditions of the world, up there with Texas brisket and Chinese char siu. Its components are a thick brown paste flecked with chilies, meat (usually pork or chicken, occasionally goat or fish) and smoke, from a tightly covered charcoal grill, that slowly soaks into the food.

"Making jerk is like spending time with a kid," said Oneil Reid, the chef and owner of the shiny Jamaican Dutchy food truck that parks daily on West 51st Street in Manhattan. "You have to watch it every second." His care pays off: the Dutchy's jerk chicken with two sides is one of the best truck lunches in the city.

"I don't change what I do," Mr. Reid said. "I give them the straight-up Jamaican thing, and they eat it up."

Some of jerk's special qualities often get lost in translation to the United States, where the sticky-sweet chicken salads and gas-grilled wings sold as jerk have little to do with the real thing and its particular balance of flavors.

"You have to taste that scallion, taste that fresh herb, taste that Scotch bonnet," said Marilyn Reid, an owner of Islands restaurant in Prospect Heights, Brooklyn, who is not related to Oneil Reid. "It has to absorb all those flavors," she added, punctuating each item with an emphatic nod. "You can't just throw some sauce on grilled chicken and call it jerk."

Jerk began with the Taino Indians, who lived on Jamaica and used the sweet wood of the allspice tree to cook the meat of local wild pigs. As Europeans planted the island with sugar cane, bananas and coffee, the Taino retreated to the safety of the vast inland forests.

The particular genius of jerk—the play of sweet and smoke, green and wood, spicy and herbal—is credited to the Maroons, Africans who taught the Taino their method of smoking food in pits dug into the earth. The Maroons were brought to Jamaica as slaves, but began escaping in the 1650's, joined the Taino in the forests, and fought British and Spanish dominion over the island. (The words jerk and jerky come from *charqui*, the Spanish version of the Quechua word *charki*, meaning dried meat.)

The American writer and anthropologist Zora Neale Hurston chronicled an overnight boar hunt with the Maroons in 1939. "Towards morning we ate our fill of jerk pork," she wrote. "It is better than our American barbecue. It is hard to imagine anything better than pork the way the Maroons jerk it."

The legend of the Maroons' daring and resourcefulness lives on in the islanders' pride in jerk. "This is a dish that is ours, not coming from England like the patty, or from India like the roti," said Winston Currie, owner of the Best Jerk Center in St. Ann, Jamaica. "Real Jamaicans can eat jerk every day; we never get tired of it." Employees from a nearby bauxite mine, their work boots coated with red dust, line up daily for Mr. Currie's dry-rubbed jerk.

Although the seasonings of jerk do not change much around the island, some cooks use more liquid—usually soy sauce or vinegar—to transform the rub into a kind of marinade. A dry rub makes for crustier jerk; a wet rub produces juicier meat. Boston Bay, on Jamaica's east coast, has become the island's most famous destination for jerk. The beach is lined with stalls selling jerk, and the sweet and starchy foods that go well with it: "rice and peas," rice cooked in coconut milk with small red beans; sweet potatoes roasted in charcoal; and "festival," a missile of sweet fried dough that resembles an oversize hush puppy.

"People drive all the way from Kingston for Boston jerk," Mr. Williams said. That's a four-hour journey of hairpin turns over the Blue Mountains, where allspice trees grow wild.

Purists say allspice smoke is a defining element of jerk. The entire tree, which Jamaicans call pimento, is used: the crushed berries are rubbed into the skin; the wood burns hot and slow; the green leaves are tossed on the fire, releasing a sweet smoke that flavors the meat with a warm, woody pepperiness.

In 2007, because of the efforts of Gary Feblowitz, a jerk-obsessed cinematographer for television documentaries, pimento wood for grilling became available in the United States. It took him five years to clear red tape in the United States and Jamaica.

"We are very careful about taking trees," said Mr. Feblowitz, who works with several pimento farmers in Jamaica to ensure a steady supply without any deforestation. "The trees have about a seven-year fruiting period, and after that the farmers cut them down and sell or burn them anyway."

After I acquired a supply of pimento wood, dried leaves and berries—the box alone made the lobby of my apartment building reek of allspice—the only remaining challenge was the rub.

Jerk is so ingrained in Jamaican cooks that the notion of getting a recipe is entertaining, something like asking a Midwesterner for a hamburger recipe.

"Go around the corner to the cellphone store, the music store—you will always find someone to tell you how to do it," Mr. Williams said, gesturing toward Flatbush Avenue, the main artery of West Indian Brooklyn.

Ms. Reid, of Islands restaurant, bakes her jerk, as her mother did before her. "I think men like messing around with hot coals," she said, proving that some gender-culinary stereotypes transcend geography. "Women just want to get a good dinner on the table."

In the end, I tried many methods as I jerk-cooked eight chickens, and they all worked, just as my Jamaican sources had so casually promised. Pimento wood is an expensive novelty, and none of the jerk makers I found in Brooklyn are using it. But the smell and taste of pimento-grilled jerk is highly satisfying.

Refusing to fuss with pans of water and smoker boxes as some grill experts demand, I just dumped in one chimney of hot coals, added the pimento wood, put the chicken on the grill, covered it tightly and left it alone for half an hour. This produced the best jerk I've had outside Jamaica.

The jerk I made with plain hardwood charcoal, showered during the cooking with handfuls of allspice berries, was excellent, and even the batch I baked in the oven wasn't bad. But once you've had the smoke, it's hard to give it up.

To find good jerk in New York, one place to look is near hospitals (serving the many Jamaicans who work in health care), busy subway stops or, better yet, both.

"Jamaicans and Trinidadians like heat," said Tamika Macintosh, a nurse's assistant. "The other West Indians can't take it."

Alternatively, follow the smoke. Some fancy West Indian restaurants make very good jerk rubs, but they are too mindful of the law to put a charcoal grill out on the sidewalk. You have to seek out the renegades.

"If the smoke is so thick outside on the sidewalk that you can't see to put the quarter in the parking meter, that's a good sign," Mr. Williams said.

"We get tickets, sure," said Desmond Mailer, the manager of McKenzie's on Utica Avenue in Flatbush, where smoke billows from blackened oil drums 16 hours a day. "But you know, cops like jerk, too."

Jerk Chicken

Time: About 1½ hours, plus at least 12 hours' marinating   **Yield:** 8 servings

2 (3½- to 4-pound) chickens, quartered,
 or 8 whole legs, or 5 to 6 pounds
 bone-in, skin-on thighs

1 large bunch scallions (about 8),
 including white and green parts

2 shallots, halved

4 to 6 Scotch bonnet chilies, stems
 removed, or habaneros

1 (2-inch) piece fresh ginger, peeled and
 coarsely chopped

6 cloves garlic, peeled

¼ cup fresh thyme leaves,
 or 1 tablespoon dried

2 tablespoons ground allspice, plus more
 for sprinkling

2 tablespoons soy sauce

2 tablespoons dark brown sugar

1 tablespoon salt, plus more for sprinkling

1 tablespoon black pepper

½ cup vegetable oil

1 tablespoon white or cider vinegar

Juice of 2 limes

1.   At least 1 day before cooking, pat chicken dry with paper towels. Combine remaining ingredients in a blender or food processor and grind to a coarse paste. Slather all over chicken, including under skin. Refrigerate 12 to 36 hours. Bring to room temperature before cooking and lightly sprinkle with more salt and ground allspice.

2.   Prepare a charcoal grill: Clean and oil grates, and preheat to medium heat using one chimney of charcoal. The temperature can start as high as 300 degrees and go as low as 250 degrees. For best results, coals should be at least 12 inches away from chicken. If necessary, push coals to one side of grill to create indirect heat. Add two large handfuls of soaked pimento (allspice) wood sticks and chips (www.pimentowood.com) or other aromatic wood chips to coals, then close grill. When thick white smoke billows from grill, place chicken on grate, skin side up, and cover. Let cook undisturbed for 30 to 35 minutes.

3.   Uncover grill. Chicken will be golden and mahogany in places. Chicken thighs may already be cooked through. For other cuts, turn chicken over and add more wood chips, and charcoal if needed. Cover and continue cooking, checking and turning every 10 minutes. Jerk chicken is done when skin is burnished brown and chicken juices are completely clear, with no pink near the bone. For large pieces, this can take up to an hour. Serve hot or warm, with rice and beans.

VARIATIONS: Jerk rub can be used on a boneless leg of lamb or pork roast, to be cooked on a medium-hot grill.

July 2, 2008: JULIA MOSKIN

Poulet Grille au Gingembre
(Grilled Chicken with Ginger)

Yield: 2 servings

1 (2½- to 3-pound) chicken, split in half

1 tablespoon finely chopped fresh ginger

1 teaspoon finely minced garlic

¼ cup fresh lemon juice

2 tablespoons olive oil

1 bay leaf, broken into small pieces

½ teaspoon dried thyme

Salt and freshly ground pepper to taste

Melted butter

1.   Put chicken in a dish.

2.   Blend ginger, garlic, lemon, oil, bay, thyme and salt and pepper to taste in a small mixing bowl.

3.   Pour marinade over chicken and let stand 2 to 4 hours in refrigerator.

4.   Preheat a charcoal grill.

5.   Place chicken skin side down on grill. Cook until nicely browned on skin and turn. Continue cooking, turning chicken every 25 minutes or until chicken is cooked. Serve with a little melted butter poured over.

May 25, 1980: "Food: Ready for the Grill,"
by CRAIG CLAIBORNE with PIERRE FRANEY

Gaylord's Tandoori Chicken

Yield: 4 to 8 servings

2 (2½-pound) chickens

2 cups plain yogurt

½ teaspoon ground cumin

½ teaspoon freshly ground black pepper

¼ teaspoon freshly grated nutmeg

¼ teaspoon ground cloves

½ teaspoon ground coriander

1 teaspoon grated fresh ginger, or
    ½ teaspoon dried ginger

1 clove garlic, minced

⅛ to ¼ teaspoon cayenne pepper

Salt to taste

½ teaspoon ground cardamom

½ cup chopped white onion

2 tablespoons milk

½ teaspoon loosely packed saffron
    threads, or ¼ teaspoon powdered
    saffron

1. Cut off and discard small wing tips of each chicken. Using fingers, pull off and discard skin of chickens.

2. Using a sharp knife, make brief gashes across grain on both sides of chicken breasts and legs.

3. Combine in food processor yogurt, cumin, black pepper, nutmeg, cloves, coriander, ginger, garlic, cayenne pepper, salt to taste, cardamom and onion. Process to a fine liquid.

4. Pour mixture into a mixing bowl and add chickens. Turn chickens to coat all over. Cover and refrigerate for at least 24 hours.

5. Remove chickens from yogurt mixture at least 1 hour before cooking.

6. Preheat oven to 500 degrees. Heat a charcoal grill.

7. Heat milk in a small saucepan and add saffron. Remove from heat and let stand 10 minutes.

8. Spoon saffron mixture evenly over chickens.

9. Line a baking sheet with heavy-duty foil. Place the chickens on it breast side up.

10. Place chickens in the oven and bake 20 minutes.

11. Cut chickens into serving pieces. Put them on grill and cook briefly on both sides.

NOTE: These chickens can be cooked entirely on a charcoal grill. To grill them, split the chickens. After marinating, place on the grill breast side down. Grill on one side. Turn and continue grilling on the second side until the chickens are thoroughly cooked.

May 25, 1980: "Ready for the Grill,"
by CRAIG CLAIBORNE with PIERRE FRANEY;
adapted from Gaylord's India Restaurant, New York City

Volunteer Firemen's Picnic

Old volunteer firemen's daughters and young firemen's sweethearts were thick as hops in Broomer's Union Park at One Hundred and Thirty-third-street and Union-avenue yesterday. They were enjoying the fifth annual picnic and barbecue of the Volunteer Firemen's Association in aid of the charitable fund. Just as soon as they reached the pavilion they began to dance, and they kept it up until away late at night, only stopping for a little while in the afternoon to look at the games and eat some of the half-dozen roasted oxen, and for a little while in the evening to say "Ah!" and "Oh, my!" when the fireworks were set off. There was much interest shown in the playing contest between the old Jefferson Engine No. 26 of New York and Protection Engine No. 5 of Morrisania. They were manned by the old fire boys. Engine No. 26 won the prize, which was a handsome silver trumpet. The half-mile race for members of the Volunteer Firemen's Association over fifty-five years of age was won by Charley Hadden of Hose Company No. 43. John Goodman won the ten-dollar prize in the mile race for members.

September 3, 1889

Jalapeño-Stuffed Game Hens

Yield: 4 servings

2 Cornish game hens (about 1½ pounds each)

Salt and freshly ground pepper to taste

4 jalapeños, halved and seeded

6 slices bacon

1. Heat a grill until hot.

2. Season hens with salt and pepper. Place 4 jalapeño halves in cavity of each hen. Wrap 3 slices of bacon over breast on each hen, securing bacon with toothpicks that have been soaked in water.

3. Place hens on grill and cook until well browned on all sides, about 10 minutes.

4. Cover grill and cook until hens are cooked through, about 40 minutes, turning once.

5. Remove toothpicks, split hens in half lengthwise, divide among 4 plates and serve immediately.

July 4, 1993: "Food: The Texas Three-Step," by MOLLY O'NEILL; adapted from The New Texas Cuisine, *by STEPHAN PYLES (Broadway, 1993)*

Pakistani Seekh Kebabs

Time: 30 minutes, plus 1 hour for chilling   **Yield:** 4 to 6 servings (8 skewers).

2 pounds ground chicken thighs

1 egg yolk

1 onion, minced

¼ cup minced fresh ginger

4 cloves garlic, minced

2 tablespoons tomato paste

1 teaspoon cumin seeds

1 teaspoon ground black pepper

1 teaspoon garam masala

1 teaspoon turmeric

¼ cup minced fresh cilantro, leaves and
   stems

⅛ teaspoon cayenne pepper

2 teaspoons salt

Cilantro Mint Chutney for serving
   (recipe follows)

Lemon wedges and pita bread for serving

1.   Combine all ingredients but chutney, lemon wedges and pita in a bowl, and knead very well into a paste.

2.   Hold a flat metal skewer—not nonstick, and at least 12 inches long—point up in one hand. Dip other hand in a bowl of water, take a handful of chicken mixture and form it around base of skewer in a small sausage shape with pointed ends. Repeat, working your way up the skewer. Each skewer should hold three or four kebabs. (You can also just form mixture into eight patties.)

3.   Lay finished skewers on a sheet pan, and smooth kebabs with fingers, making sure they are fairly smooth and secured on skewers. Refrigerate at least 1 hour.

4.   Prepare charcoal grill, or turn gas grill to medium-low. Fire should not be too hot, and grill rack should be at least several inches from heat source.

5.   When rack is heated through, gently squeeze the kebabs to be sure they are secure on skewers, and place skewers on grill. Meat should start sizzling gently; it should not spit and turn black. Cook undisturbed until deep brown, at least 7 minutes. When meat lifts easily from grill, slide a spatula under kebabs and turn over. Continue grilling until browned on both sides and juicy, but cooked through, 10 to 15 minutes total.

6.   Serve with cilantro mint chutney and lemon wedges and pita warmed on the grill just before serving.

Cilantro Mint Chutney

Time: 5 minutes   **Yield:** 4 to 6 servings

6 tablespoons plain yogurt

2 tablespoons fresh mint leaves

¼ cup fresh cilantro leaves and stems

1 tablespoon fresh lemon juice

½ teaspoon sugar

2 dashes cayenne pepper, or more to taste

¼ teaspoon salt, or more to taste

Combine ingredients in a blender or a small food processor and process until smooth, scraping down sides of bowl once or twice. Taste for salt and cayenne, adding more as needed. Refrigerate up to 2 days. Taste for salt and cayenne before serving.

June 29, 2005: "The Summer Cook: Burgers Without Borders,"
by JULIA MOSKIN; recipe adapted from MADHUR JAFFREY

Barbecued Cornish Hens

The number of barbecue sauces on the market is growing at an astonishing rate. Each claims to have a magic blend of herbs and spices that enhance foods cooked over open fire, but while some are fairly good, most others are humdrum and loaded with sugar.

It is clear from looking at the ingredient lists that the sauces are simple—and much cheaper—to make at home. First think of the flavor you want to achieve: Spicy? Herby? Fiery? Sweet? Then pick the appropriate ingredients.

For these barbecued Cornish hens, I wanted a sauce with a complex flavor from spices and a hint of sweetness. The spices were chili powder, coriander, red pepper flakes, Tabasco, cumin, oregano, bay leaves, thyme and black pepper. With all the heat coming from the peppers and Tabasco, I knew I needed a counterbalance. Honey served well.

The sauce takes 30 minutes to cook. It lasts indefinitely if covered tightly and refrigerated.

Cornish hen is ideal for barbecuing. Its flesh is firmer and moister than that of chicken. The hens generally weigh one to two pounds, convenient for single-serving portions. Cornish hens are a cross between an American fowl, the Plymouth Rock hen, and the Cornish or Bantam rooster. Originally, they were marketed as Rock Cornish game hens, but actually they lack a gamy flavor. Gamy or not, they can be delicious. I find that the birds barbecue more evenly if the backbone is removed and an incision is made where the leg meets the thigh. This allows them to lie flat on the grill.

Yield: 4 servings

4 (1-pound) Cornish hens

2 tablespoons vegetable oil

1 teaspoon paprika

Salt to taste

1 teaspoon freshly ground pepper

1½ cups Barbecue Sauce with Honey
(recipe follows)

1. Preheat a charcoal grill to high.

2. For more efficient grilling, have backbone removed from hens. Turn hens skin side down on a flat surface. Using a sharp knife, carefully split joint halfway down where leg and thigh bone meet. Do not split it all the way through.

3. Rub hen halves with oil, paprika, salt and pepper. Put them skin side down in a shallow baking dish. Arrange necks, livers and gizzards between hen halves. Let stand 10 minutes.

4. Drain hens and put them skin side down on grill. When skin is nicely browned, turn hens and cook on other side. Baste with barbecue sauce, and continue turning and basting every 5 minutes for about 15 minutes more, or until done. Serve with more barbecue sauce if needed.

Barbecue Sauce with Honey

This sauce is good for any barbecued meat and keeps very well refrigerated.

Yield: 5 cups

2 tablespoons olive oil
1½ cups finely chopped onions
2 tablespoons finely chopped garlic
1 (28-ounce) can crushed tomatoes
1 (6-ounce) can tomato paste
½ cup red wine vinegar
¼ cup Worcestershire sauce
1 tablespoon chili powder
1 tablespoon ground coriander
3 tablespoons fresh lemon juice

¼ teaspoon red pepper flakes
1 tablespoon Tabasco sauce, or to taste
2 tablespoons chopped fresh oregano,
 or 1 tablespoon dried
2 teaspoons ground cumin
2 bay leaves
4 sprigs fresh thyme, or 1 teaspoon dried
1 teaspoon freshly ground black pepper
¼ cup honey
Salt to taste

1. Heat oil in a saucepan and add onions. Cook, stirring, until wilted. Add garlic, cook briefly and add remaining ingredients. Bring to a simmer and cook, stirring often, about 30 minutes.

2. Let sauce cool and use for basting.

August 7, 1991: "60-Minute Gourmet,"
by PIERRE FRANEY

Cooks Move Beyond Humble Hot Dog

Inspired by California-style grill restaurants that have swept across the country like a brush fire, grill cooks now consider anything that can be held down without falling through the grates suitable for charcoal cooking—tiny quails, leeks, fennel bulbs, radicchio, lobsters, clams, mussels, wild mushrooms.

Some of the most delectable results can be achieved with game birds—squabs, quails and guinea hens in particular. Once luxury foods available only in season, these succulent birds have now become available year-round in many supermarkets and butcher shops in the area. Large-scale commercial breeding farms in the United States and Canada have expanded the market from the restaurant trade to the home consumer.

Squabs, quails and guinea hens are diverting alternatives to barbecued chicken. They have distinctive flavors and textures ideal for grilling, without being too gamy. Squabs, which weigh about a pound each, are the mildest tasting, somewhere between chicken and pheasant, with dark meaty breasts and legs that withstand open-fire cooking better than chickens, which can dry out quickly. Quails have pinkish meat that absorbs smoky nuances from charcoal more than that of other game birds. The most assertive meat is guinea hen, which is dark, rich and moist, with just a hint of gaminess in the aftertaste.

All three birds can be delectable crowd pleasers for Fourth of July celebrations and all the summer parties to come. While they are less vulnerable to dryness than commercially raised chickens, care must still be exercised in their preparation. Judicious use of marinades and basting sauces can yield spectacular results.

Another trick when grilling small game birds, or any small poultry such as poussins (baby chickens) and Cornish game hens, is to split them down the middle and pound them slightly so that they lie flat on the grill. The French call this technique *crapaudine* from the word *crapaud,* or toad, because a halved and flattened squab or quail is toad-shaped. The technique is the same for all birds and poultry. Split the body down one side of the backbone (or, with very small birds such as quail, directly through the backbone) and pull the body apart. Place it on a flat surface, skin side up, and pound with a heavy cleaver or flat frying pan.

Many barbecue grills come with lids, which, when secured, create an oven that can exceed 450 degrees. This can cut cooking time almost in half. Cooking game birds or chicken this way may not yield as crispy a skin as desired; this can be corrected, however, by removing the lid during the final 10 to 15 minutes of cooking to let cooler air circulate.

Lids are particularly useful on windy days. Some of the better gas barbecue grills come with rotisseries, the preferred method for preparing larger game birds such as guinea hens and pheasants as well as chickens and large ducks. Long roasting on a rotating spit yields a crisp, succulent skin.

Because there are so many variables when it comes to barbecue cooking—the grill's heat output, cool spots in the fire, the foods' thickness and so on—consider suggested grilling times to be rules of thumb. Test the food when you feel it is just approaching rare; you can put something back on the grill to cook further, but desiccated meat or fish is beyond repair.

Grilled Squabs with Thyme

A marinade of white wine, mustard, thyme and lemon permeates and moistens the squab meat, while the tanginess of the mustard and lemon bring out the bird's subtle flavor. In using oil-based marinades, the point is to flavor the meat, not to cause flare-ups that char it.

Yield: 6 servings

For the squabs
6 squabs
Salt and freshly ground pepper to taste
2 tablespoons unsalted butter
¼ cup chopped fresh chervil or parsley
For the marinade
¾ cup white wine

¼ cup Dijon-style mustard
¼ cup fresh lemon juice
4 sprigs fresh thyme, chopped,
   or 1 teaspoon dried
3 tablespoons vegetable oil
Salt and freshly ground pepper to taste

1. Split squabs in half lengthwise along one side of backbone using a heavy chef's knife. Lay each half on a sturdy flat surface and pound gently with side of knife to flatten. Place squabs in a high-sided heat-proof baking dish large enough to hold them in one layer. Salt and pepper generously.

2. Mix marinade ingredients in a bowl. Pour marinade over squabs evenly, covering them. Seal dish with plastic wrap and refrigerate for several hours.

3. Transfer squabs to a platter and pour marinade into a small pan. Add butter and chervil or parsley to marinade and bring to the boil. Remove sauce from heat and cover to keep warm.

4. Lay squabs over barbecue grill, skin side down, and grill for 7 minutes. Flip and grill for 10 minutes more.

5. When squabs are cooked, return them to cleaned baking dish and pour warm sauce over squabs. Serve immediately..

July 2, 1986: BRYAN MILLER

Grilled Spiced Squab

When I think of the Statue of Liberty, I think of New York and all its ethnic variety," says chef Joyce Goldstein. "I grew up in a Russian-Jewish household in New York where everything was cooked to death. It was New York ethnic food that saved me. This is a 'melting pot' recipe, with a combination of Arab-Moroccan spices—I guess I'm a Sephardic throwback."

Yield: 6 servings

6 squab (about 1 pound each)

4 cloves garlic, peeled

1 (2-inch) piece fresh ginger, peeled and sliced

2 tablespoons aniseed, pan-toasted and crushed

½ teaspoon saffron threads, finely chopped

1 tablespoon paprika

1 teaspoon cayenne pepper

½ cup fresh lemon juice

1 small bunch fresh cilantro, chopped, to yield ¼ cup

4 green onions or scallions, chopped, to yield ¼ cup

1½ cups light olive oil

Freshly ground black pepper to taste

Salt to taste

1. Remove heads and feet from squab. Insert a sharp knife through neck cavity and carefully split each bird down the back, keeping breast intact. Remove backbone, then carefully remove breastbone, cartilage and ribs. The bird should look like a butterfly, with only wing and leg bones attached.

2. Place garlic cloves and ginger in a food processor, and blend to a paste. Add aniseed, saffron, paprika, cayenne pepper and lemon juice, and blend about 30 seconds to combine. Transfer blended ingredients to a mixing bowl, add cilantro and green onions and whisk in olive oil. Add black pepper to taste.

3. Place squab in a shallow ceramic or enameled dish, add spice marinade and turn to coat well. Cover and refrigerate overnight. Bring to room temperature before grilling.

4. Preheat outdoor grill to highest temperature. Sprinkle squab with salt. Grill squab (discard marinade), skin side up, for 4 minutes, and then turn to grill 3 minutes, skin side down. Test for doneness: squab are best served rare. Suggested times are for a very hot fire.

5. Serve with couscous, rice or a combination of bulgur wheat and rice, sprinkled with minced green onions and accompanied by a lemon wedge.

June 25, 1986: "For Liberty's 100th, Fireworks from 12 Top Chefs,"
by NANCY HARMON JENKINS; recipe by JOYCE GOLDSTEIN

Ed Gorman's Grilled Quails with Ginger and Sherry

This recipe was devised by Edward Gorman, a former retail business executive and longtime resident of East Hampton, Long Island. The tiny quails—a portion of two weighs slightly less than a pound—are combined with dry sherry, fresh ginger and soy sauce in a Chinese-inspired marinade that adds vibrancy to the meat.

Too long a time marinating can be as detrimental as too short a time. In testing this recipe, half the quails were cooked after marinating less than two hours; they were excellent—crisp-skinned, firm and perfumed with ginger. Five hours later, the remaining quails were cooked; they were disappointingly soft and mealy.

Yield: 6 servings

For the quail

12 fresh quails

Salt and freshly ground pepper

¼ cup hoisin sauce

2 tablespoons chopped fresh cilantro

2 tablespoons unsalted butter

For the marinade

½ cup dry sherry

2 tablespoons grated fresh ginger

2 tablespoons dark soy sauce

2 tablespoons sesame oil

½ teaspoon freshly ground black pepper

1 teaspoon sugar

1. Split quails in half lengthwise through backbone, using a heavy chef's knife. Lay each half on a sturdy flat surface and pound gently with side of knife to flatten. Place quails in a high-sided heat-proof baking dish large enough to hold them in one layer. Season with salt and pepper.

2. Mix together marinade ingredients in a bowl. Pour marinade over quails evenly, covering them. Seal dish with plastic wrap and refrigerate for 1 to 2 hours.

3. Transfer quails to a platter and pour marinade into a small saucepan. Add hoisin sauce, cilantro, and butter to marinade and bring to a boil. Remove from heat and cover to keep sauce warm.

4. Lay quails over grill, skin side down, and grill for 5 minutes. Flip and grill for 5 minutes more.

5. When quails are cooked, transfer them to a cleaned baking dish and pour sauce over them to coat. Serve immediately.

July 2, 1986: "Cooks Move Beyond Humble Hot Dog,"
by BRYAN MILLER

Magret of Duck Gascon Style

Yield: 6 to 8 servings

6 boneless breasts of fatted moulard
ducks (about ½ pound each),
trimmed of excess fat
Salt and freshly ground black pepper to
taste
4 cloves garlic, sliced

2 bay leaves, crushed
8 sprigs fresh thyme, or 2 teaspoons
dried
2 tablespoons vegetable oil
2 tablespoons unsalted butter

1. Put duck breasts in a high-sided baking dish large enough to hold them in one layer. Salt and pepper them. Sprinkle with garlic, bay leaves and thyme. Pour oil over them and rub herbs in evenly on both sides. Cover with plastic wrap and refrigerate overnight.

2. Lay duck breasts over grill, skin side down, and cook for 8 minutes. If fire flares up as fat drips, move breasts around grill and douse flares with a little water. Flip duck and grill for another 6 minutes. (Duck breasts should be cooked no more than medium-rare, about 140 degrees internal temperature).

3. Place duck breasts in cleaned baking dish along with butter. Put dish on grill to melt butter and brush butter over duck. Serve immediately.

July 2, 1986: "Cooks Move Beyond Humble Hot Dog,"
by BRYAN MILLER

Grilled Turkey Breast with Chive Butter

The all-American turkey is most often thought of in the fall around holiday time, but it makes a fine centerpiece for summer meals as well, especially for barbecues. Turkey meat has been cooked over flames as far back as the Aztecs and the Indians of the Southwest, who domesticated the bird as a dietary staple. Farther east, they were part of the diet of the Plains Indians and tribes throughout New England.

So I felt a strong link with North American history when I fired up my barbecue grill and cooked turkey breast steaks for dinner. Turkey can be found in supermarkets year round, and the boneless steaks are ideally suited to quick cooking.

In the recipe here, I pound the turkey steaks to about ¼-inch thickness. This allows them to cook faster and more evenly. Season well and grill them over hot coals for about two minutes on each side. A simple chive butter sauce is all they need before serving. Because turkey breast is so lean, some sort of sauce is usually necessary.

A side dish of buttered carrots with parsley would add color and a touch of sweetness, not to mention lots of vitamins. Serve with sautéed potatoes.

Yield: 4 servings

4 turkey breast steaks (about 1½ pounds)

Salt and freshly ground pepper to taste

2 tablespoons olive oil

2 tablespoons chopped fresh sage or
    2 teaspoons dried

4 tablespoons (½ stick) butter

1 tablespoon fresh lemon juice

¼ teaspoon ground cumin

1 teaspoon Worcestershire sauce

¼ cup finely chopped fresh chives

1. Preheat a charcoal grill until quite hot. Coals should be placed quite close to grill because meat will only be seared.

2. Place each turkey steak between sheets of clear plastic wrap. Pound lightly and evenly with a flat mallet or meat pounder to make slices about ¼ inch thick.

3. Season turkey with salt and pepper. Brush both sides with olive oil and sprinkle both sides with sage.

4. Heat butter until melted. Add lemon juice, cumin, Worcestershire sauce, salt, pepper and chives. Blend well. Keep warm.

5. Place steaks on grill and cook on both sides for about 2 minutes to a side or until done. Do not overcook. Transfer steaks to a serving dish. Pour chive butter over them and serve.

June 12, 1991: "60-Minute Gourmet,"
by PIERRE FRANEY

CHAPTER SEVEN

Fish and Shellfish

The plain truth is that many people are afraid of grilling fish. Most everyone reading this book has probably had a fillet fall apart as you attempted to lift it off the grill. Likewise, with whole fish, getting a beautiful char and then leaving it behind because the skin sticks to the grill is a common misstep. It doesn't have to be this way. You will be hard pressed to find two more sensible primers on grilling fish than Florence Fabricant's "The Tricks for Perfect Fish on the Grill" (page 212) and longtime Outdoors columnist Nelson Bryant's "A Lesson on Cooking Fish" (page 228). Among the recipes you'll find is Grilled Whole Porgy with Lime Butter (page 226), which treats an often overlooked fish with new-found respect. The grilled salmon with pinot noir sauce (page 242) from Ray's Boathouse in Seattle is a reliable go-to recipe when Copper River and king salmon come into season.

Joe Lewis butters baking shad at Ross Dock in Palisades State Park, New Jersey, in 1959. Shad is covered with two strips of bacon and nailed to hickory planks before baking.

The Tricks for Perfect Fish on the Grill

A perfect charred edge, burnished skin crisply seared, an alluring hint of smoke in the flavor—ah, the pleasures of grilling. But when fish is involved, most home cooks stop before they start, fearing that an ingredient costing $12 a pound or more will fall apart, stick or overcook on the grill.

But grilling fish is not daunting when you master a few details, like selecting the right type of fish, keeping your grill clean and—the moment of truth—knowing how to turn.

Over the years I have picked up some tricks from experience and from chefs, some of whom have come up with novel ways to prevent fish from sticking when it's turned or lifted off the grill. Fort Lauderdale–based chef Mark Militello wraps a whole fish like a yellowtail snapper in fennel fronds before grilling: the oiled herbs facilitate turning. Taking this cue, I have grilled whole bluefish on a bed of sturdy rosemary branches, and also on big bunches of dill. At Parea, a Greek restaurant in the Flatiron district of New York City, whole fish are roasted wrapped in grape leaves, and that works when grilling, too.

These are clever ways to make a fish flavorful—and make it behave. But the very best advice I can give you is this: buy two of the largest spatulas you can find. I prefer metal spatulas because they are sturdier. The business end should be broad, at least eight inches across, and the blade should taper to a sharp edge. If possible, buy spatulas with long handles; more than 12 inches is good.

Some other suggestions: once you have seasoned your fish, whether with a dry rub, a marinade or herbs, brush it with oil. The grill should be hot and oiled, too (more on this later). Using direct heat will give the fish handsome grill marks.

Most fish cooks quickly, so watch closely. Fish on the bone is more tolerant, requiring at least 10 minutes on each side for a whole two-pounder. Thick fillets or steaks should be turned after five minutes.

Often, the fish will tell you when it's ready to be turned. Like almost anything you grill, once moisture has evaporated from the underside, the food is easier to lift off the grates.

For fish steaks or compact fillets, gently place one spatula on top of the fish to secure it. Firmly but gently ease the second spatula under the fish to separate it from the grilling surface. Turn the steak or fillet sandwiched between the two, then gently slide them out. You cannot use tongs with fish the way you might with a pork chop.

An easy way to turn a large fillet is to cover it with a double thickness of heavy-duty foil, slide a spatula under the fish, turn it over onto the foil, then lift the fillet a bit to slide the foil out.

A whole fish can simply be rolled over: make sure you have room on the grill to achieve this. For a very large fish, like a seven-pound wild striped bass, you will need to shovel two spatulas under it, then roll it.

But even the cook with the best fish-flipping skills will have trouble if the fish itself is wrong. Thick steaks and slabs, preferably with skin, and many kinds of whole fish, gutted and cleaned but not boned, are best for grilling. Delicate flounder, sole and small fluke fillets are not suitable. Cod is another fish to avoid because it flakes and falls apart too easily.

Small whole fish, like sardines, red mullet, butterfish or the seasonal baby bluefish that the fishermen on eastern Long Island call snappers are all excellent candidates. Mackerel, bluefish, porgies, weakfish and striped bass are all winners on the grill.

Many grilled fish recipes call for fairly dense and meaty fish like tuna and swordfish. They can be cut thick so that the fish acquires its burnish before it overcooks. Except for salmon and tuna, which are often left rare or medium-rare, most fish with bones are ready to serve when the flesh separates easily from the bone when poked with a skewer or a paring knife.

The first step, before you even light the grill, is to clean it. (Thick, cast-iron grates conduct heat best; if at all possible, try to equip your grill with them.) Scrub the grates with a wire brush. Then, once they are hot, brush them with oil. I hold a thick wad of paper towel dipped in grapeseed oil with long-handled tongs. Avoid using a long-handled basting brush for this job because the bristles might melt from the heat. Silicone brushes can melt at temperatures over about 650 degrees, and the grates can—and should—get hotter than that.

As far as other equipment goes, metal fish-shaped baskets are effective, but they usually will not accommodate a whole fish bigger than 2½ pounds. The flat, two-sided baskets that can be used for burgers are also useful for cooking small fish like sardines. A large, flat perforated metal sheet is good if your grill does not have cast-iron grates and cannot be fitted with them. (Lodge makes an excellent cast-iron one.) Most measure about 12 by 16 inches. Once again, oil it before you use it. There is nonstick grilling equipment, but keep in mind that health concerns have been raised about its safety when used at high heat.

For kebabs, buy flat skewers, or thread the fish onto two skewers so that the chunks cannot spin around as the skewers are lifted for turning.

Cooking a fish on a soaked wooden plank makes grilling fillets easy but you sacrifice direct char for smoky taste. The same goes for wrapping a whole fish in heavy-duty foil.

After cooking, cover the grill to retain the heat from the dying coals, which will help burn off debris on the grates. Then you can scrape the grates clean. If you are using a gas grill, relight it briefly so the grates are warm, making them easier to clean.

Once the grates are clean, oil them again, liberally, and you will be all set for your next round of fish on the grill, now with newfound confidence.

A pair of whole Arctic char at the same time? A slab of glistening fresh mahi-mahi glossed with wasabi oil? Piece of . . . fish!

Halibut with Indian Rub and Corn Salsa

Time: 25 minutes, plus three hours' marinating   **Yield:** 4 servings

2 teaspoons ground cumin

1½ teaspoons turmeric

1 teaspoon ground coriander

½ teaspoon ground fennel seeds

Salt and freshly ground black pepper

4 halibut steaks (Pacific salmon, wild
   striped bass, hake steaks or fillets of
   these fish can be substituted), 1 inch
   thick (2 to 2½ pounds total)

2 lemons

4 tablespoons ghee (sold in Indian stores
   and specialty food shops) or clarified
   butter; vegetable oil can be substituted

1 tablespoon minced fresh ginger

½ cup finely chopped onion

1 cup cooked fresh corn kernels (about
   1 ear of corn)

Oil for grill

1 tablespoon chopped fresh cilantro
   leaves

1.   Combine cumin, turmeric, coriander, fennel, ½ teaspoon black pepper and
½ teaspoon salt or to taste. Rub fish steaks on both sides with juice of ½ lemon, then
rub with all but 2 teaspoons of spice mixture. Refrigerate 3 hours.

2.   While fish marinates, heat 2 tablespoons of ghee in a skillet, add ginger and onion
and sauté until onion just starts to brown. Stir in remaining spice mixture and sauté,
stirring, until spices smell toasty, then add corn and juice of ½ lemon. Cook briefly and set
aside.

3.   Remove fish from refrigerator and brush on both sides with remaining 2 tablespoons
ghee or butter. Heat grill and oil grates. When hot, place fish on grill over medium-hot
coals or gas fire and cook about 5 minutes. Use a spatula to turn fish and grill 3 to
4 minutes, until a little liquid just begins to pool on surface of fish and a paring knife
inserted just at the bone can move flesh away from it easily. Salmon should be cooked
about 3 minutes on each side. Remove fish to a warm platter or individual plates.

4.   Reheat corn mixture, adding cilantro and a couple tablespoons water to moisten it.
Spoon corn on fish, garnish with wedges cut from remaining lemon and serve.

Charred Striped Bass Niçoise

Time: 30 minutes   **Yield:** 4 servings

3 tablespoons extra virgin olive oil, plus
  more for grill
2 cloves garlic, sliced
1 (2-pound) skin-on wild striped bass
  fillet (Pacific salmon, mahi-mahi or
  barramundi may be substituted)
Juice of ½ lemon
Salt and freshly ground black pepper

2 medium-size ripe tomatoes, cut in
  ¼-inch-thick slices
12 pitted oil-cured black olives, coarsely
  chopped
1 tablespoon finely slivered fresh basil
  leaves
Aioli (optional)

1.   Heat oil in a small pan, add garlic and cook over medium heat until golden. Remove from heat, drain garlic and chop it.

2.   Brush fish with half the oil on both sides. Brush flesh side with lemon juice and season with salt and pepper. You will need two large spatulas to turn fish; if you do not have them, cut fillet in half or in 4 portions. Brush tomato slices with remaining oil.

3.   Heat grill to very hot and oil grates. Briefly sear tomato slices, turning once. Remove to a platter and tent with foil to keep warm. Use edge of spatula to scrape grates clean. Re-oil. Place fish, skin side up, on grill. Cook about 5 minutes. Use spatulas to turn. Cook 3 to 4 minutes on skin side, until skewer inserted horizontally in middle feels just warm. (Salmon needs less time.)

4.   Transfer fish to a warm platter and pave flesh side with overlapping tomato slices. Scatter with olives, chopped garlic and basil and serve, with aioli on the side, if desired.

August 23, 2006: "Turn, Turn, Turn:
The Tricks for Perfect Fish on the Grill,"
by FLORENCE FABRICANT

Charcoal-Grilled Striped Bass

Yield: 4 to 8 servings

1 (3- to 4-pound) striped bass, gutted

Salt and freshly ground black pepper

1 clove garlic, peeled

1 large sprig fresh rosemary

1 bay leaf

Oil

¼ pound (1 stick) butter, melted and kept hot

¼ cup chopped fresh parsley

Lemon wedges

1. Prepare a charcoal fire. When white ash forms on top of coals, they are ready.

2. Meanwhile, prepare fish. Rub it inside and out with salt and pepper. Cut garlic clove into slivers. Using a sharp paring knife, make a few small incisions along backbone of fish. Insert slivers of garlic.

3. Place rosemary sprig and bay leaf in cavity of fish. Tie fish in two or three places with string to secure cavity. Rub fish generously all over with oil. Place fish on hot grill and cook 10 to 15 minutes on one side, brushing occasionally with butter. Using a pancake turner or spatula or both, loosen fish from grill and turn it to other side. Cook 10 to 15 minutes on that side, or until fish is done and flesh flakes easily when tested with a fork. Cooking time will depend on size of fish, intensity of heat and how close fish is to coals.

4. Transfer fish to a hot platter and pour remaining butter over it. Sprinkle with parsley and garnish with lemon wedges.

August 23, 2006: "It's the Fourth of July,
and That's an Occasion for a Barbecue,"
by CRAIG CLAIBORNE

Greek-Style Fish with Marinated Tomatoes

You've probably eaten fish baked in tomato sauce, a dish on the menu of most Greek restaurants in the United States. There are dozens of versions—with bread crumbs, or red bell peppers, or loads of aromatic vegetables—but at this time of year, all seem needlessly complicated. In summer I want a dish that tampers with the tomato-fish formula as little as possible. So instead of cooking the tomatoes, I marinate them, and instead of braising the fish, I grill it. Neither fish nor tomatoes need much help.

Bass, rockfish and even trout are good options here—you want a medium-size fish (or two), preferably local and obviously fresh. If you have good fishmongers, ask them to clean, butterfly and fillet it. If not, just clean and gut it.

Time: 45 minutes   **Yield:** 4 servings

2 cups cherry tomatoes, preferably
  Sun Gold, halved
4 tablespoons olive oil, or more as
  needed
2 tablespoons white wine vinegar
1 tablespoon minced fresh hot chili, like
  jalapeño, or more to taste
1 tablespoon chopped fresh oregano,
  or 1 teaspoon dried

4 cloves garlic, sliced, or more to taste
Salt and freshly ground black pepper
1 large whole fish or 2 smaller ones
  (2 to 3 pounds total), like striped bass,
  rockfish or trout; preferably butterflied and boned, or simply gutted
1 lemon, sliced
4 to 6 sprigs fresh thyme

1. Prepare grill; heat should be medium-high and rack about 4 inches from fire. Combine tomatoes, 2 tablespoons of olive oil, vinegar, chili, oregano, a few slices of garlic and a sprinkle of salt and pepper in a bowl; let sit at room temperature for 30 minutes.
2. Meanwhile, using a sharp knife, make three or four diagonal, parallel slashes on each side of fish, just about down to the bone. Sprinkle inside of fish with salt and pepper, then stuff with remaining garlic, a layer of lemon slices and thyme sprigs. Rub outside of fish with remaining 2 tablespoons oil and sprinkle with salt and pepper.
3. Grill until firm enough to turn, 5 to 8 minutes. Turn and cook second side for 5 to 8 minutes. Fish is done when exterior is crisp and a knife passes easily through the flesh.
4. Taste tomato mixture and adjust seasoning, adding more oil if needed. Serve fish topped with tomatoes and their liquid.

July 2, 2010:"The Minimalist: Simplify Greek Fish for Summer,"
by MARK BITTMAN

Seafood of the Desert

The southwestern region of the United States is vividly beautiful, spare, parched. So parched, it seems as though a strong wind would easily rearrange its sunset-hued desert landscape.

Such incomparable geography must clear the senses to provide fertile ground for creativity. For it inspires food that is as far from parched as can be imagined. Sparked with heady salsas, sauces redolent of cilantro and tinged with lime, and boisterous relishes of peppers and fruit, the cuisine emerging in the Southwest is neither Mexican nor Texan, though it has elements of both. As Robert Del Grande, chef and owner of Cafe Annie and Cafe Express, both in Houston, says, "It's definitely not Chinese and it looks a little American, so I guess you'd call it Southwestern."

By whatever label, it hardly spawns images of seafood cookery. Yet the American seafood revolution is established there, galloping apace with the rest of the country. As unorthodox a complement as it sounds to Southwest desert food with its staples of beans, corn and chilies, seafood isn't all that unusual a tradition, according to Mark Miller, chef and owner of the Coyote Cafe in Santa Fe, New Mexico. "I stuff poblano chilies with shrimp," he says, "an idea that's based on jalapeño chilies stuffed with tuna, a classic dish from Mexico."

The Southwest claims coastline along the Gulf of Mexico, so grouper, snapper and redfish, oysters and pompano aren't surprising there. And dried salt cod brought to New Mexico by the Spaniards was probably incorporated into early foods of the inland Southwest, though it has since disappeared. But salmon or mussels? "There are new wrinkles in regional cuisine," says Mr. Del Grande. "With air transportation, salmon can almost be considered a regional seafood anywhere. All I have to do is get on the phone and the next day I have whatever seafood I want from anywhere in the world."

Shrinking regional boundaries aside, salmon on a Southwest menu still sounds like a tulip on the stem of a rose. But in Mr. Del Grande's hands it makes perfect regional sense. He grills salmon steak over a low-temperature mesquite fire. (Mr. Del Grande, who has a doctorate in biochemistry, doesn't believe in searing anything, whether it be meat or seafood.) He then sets it on a spicy sauce of roasted tomatoes, garlic, shallots and peppers and drizzles a seductive garlic cream sauce over the salmon.

Cafe Annie's signature seafood dish is equally appropriate, despite the main ingredient of mussels, which come from the East Coast. Take one taste of the creamy, beguiling green mussel soup that looks as demure as creme de cresson, and you know you're in Southwest territory as fire from serrano chilies sparks at the back of your throat.

Stephan Pyles, chef and owner of the Routh St. Cafe and the Baby Routh bistro in Dallas, is a musician by training, but he learned cooking at his family's West Texas truckstop. "Everything we served there was Southern and fried, like catfish and hush puppies," he says. A visit to France and subsequent cooking experience with French chefs has taken him well beyond that realm, though his menus are anchored by strong Southern influence.

He gives a soft nuttiness to sweet Southern catfish by dusting it with blue cornmeal before frying; then he serves it with a tangy pecan butter sauce. He makes a brilliant sauce of smoked tomatoes blended with peppers and plenty of cilantro, and offers it with grilled red snapper and a snappy relish of black-eyed peas, peppers and melon.

Mr. Miller, formerly of the Fourth Street Grill in Berkeley, California, is a cultural anthropologist by training, and he travels extensively in southern Mexico, where he gets much of his culinary inspiration. "They do a tremendous amount of seafood there, using native ingredients which are similar here," he says. "I take local ingredients, which also match other cuisines in the world, including Asian and Indian, where they use a lot of seafood, and I make seafood dishes that are as authentic as possible to the Southwestern taste esthetic." His manila clams in a subtle red chili pesto sauce with bits of toasted pine nuts are a fragrant, pleasing example.

Southwestern cuisine is taking an adventuresome turn in the hands of these chefs, as they slip seafood into foods of the desert.

Stephan Pyles's Grilled Redfish with Smoked Tomato Salsa and Black-Eyed Peas–Jicama Relish

Yield: 4 servings

For the black-eyed pea–jicama relish

6 tablespoons dried black-eyed peas

1½ cups fish or chicken stock

2 ounces jicama, peeled and cut into small, ¼-inch pieces

1 tablespoon each diced red and yellow bell pepper

1 tablespoon diced sweet onion

1 small serrano chili, seeded and minced

2 tablespoons diced cucumber

3 tablespoons diced mango, papaya or cantaloupe

1 teaspoon finely chopped fresh spearmint

Salt to taste

For the smoked tomato salsa

4 small (about 1 pound) very ripe tomatoes

1 tablespoon extra virgin olive oil

2 tablespoons each diced green, red and yellow bell pepper

3 medium-size scallions, including white and green parts, diced

3 small serrano chilies, seeded and diced

½ cup fresh cilantro leaves, finely chopped

Salt and freshly ground black pepper to taste

4 (6-ounce) redfish fillets (you may substitute any snapper or grouper)

2 tablespoons tasteless vegetable oil or clarified butter

Salt and freshly ground black pepper to taste

1. Make the black-eyed pea relish 1 hour before serving: Soak black-eyed peas in warm water until they are somewhat soft and have increased slightly in size, about 20 to 30 minutes. Bring them to a boil in fish or chicken stock and cook until they are soft but still crisp, about 20 minutes. Combine peas with remaining relish ingredients in a medium-size bowl. Season to taste with salt and mix thoroughly.

2. To smoke the tomatoes: Build and light a fire in a barbecue, with hardwood charcoal briquettes if possible. Soak 6 to 8 chunks of aromatic wood, or 4 cups of wood chips, in warm water for 20 minutes.

3. When briquettes are glowing but slightly gray (after about 20 minutes), add soaked wood chunks and let them burn for 5 minutes.

4. Place tomatoes on grill. Close barbecue and smoke tomatoes for 10 minutes, then remove them from barbecue. Peel, seed and dice tomatoes, then set aside.

5. Add enough charcoal to barbecue to maintain a hot fire with plenty of red coals.

6.   To make the smoked tomato sauce, heat olive oil in a large skillet over medium-high heat. Add peppers, scallions and serrano chilies and cook them until they are slightly soft, about 3 minutes. Add smoked tomatoes and cilantro and stir, then season to taste with salt and pepper. Remove from heat and keep warm.

7.   To grill the snapper, rub fillets on each side with oil and grill them on barbecue until they are opaque but still give slightly, not too soft or overly tough, about 4 minutes on each side. Season with salt and freshly ground pepper.

8.   To serve, evenly divide smoked tomato sauce among 4 warmed dinner plates. Place a snapper fillet on top of sauce and spoon relish, in a diagonal line, over fillet. Serve immediately.

August 30, 1987: SUSAN HERRMANN LOOMIS;
recipe by STEPHAN PYLES, Dallas, Texas

White-Fish Fillets with Grilled Cabbage

Whether Copenhagen's Noma is the world's best restaurant doesn't matter: Rene Redzepi, its chef, has responded to his well-deserved recognition with the kind of inspiration and energy that guarantee he'll be around for a while. Redzepi is also a sweet guy running an oddly nonhierarchical kitchen, and talented people from all over the world are flocking to Denmark to work for him.

Meanwhile, well-heeled people from all over the world are flocking to Noma to get a sample of the restaurant's "new Nordic cuisine." ("Noma" is a conflation of the Danish words for "Nordic" and "food.") Much of the food is actually Nordic, though not exclusively so.

Mostly the cuisine is intelligent and delicious, a welcome, contemporary, well-grounded departure from so-called molecular cuisine. Redzepi is a true hybrid—the son of a Danish mother and an Albanian father who lived in Macedonia when it was still part of Yugoslavia—and he displays the expected vigor. He grew up primarily in Copenhagen ("with many long bus rides to Macedonia"), began cooking when he was 15 and has worked all over the world. Not surprisingly, there is some indefinable talent present as well.

As a result, Noma has become—as El Bulli, Ferran Adrià's restaurant on the Spanish coast of the Mediterranean, was in its heyday—a laboratory of young, smart, adventuresome chefs who have a guarantee of a welcoming and appreciative audience. It has made Copenhagen a destination on the culinary world tour.

Much of the success relies on Redzepi's judgment, which is superior: he has scores if not hundreds of dishes to choose from for the menu, with new ones being developed all the time, and his batting average (says me, after two visits) is around .800, meaning only one in five dishes isn't terrific. (I usually think a restaurant is pretty good if one in three dishes is exciting.)

This fish-in-cabbage recipe is an adaptation of the restaurant's more complicated version. If you do nothing other than make the sauce and use it as a dip for celery sticks, you'll be one happy eater. My only advice on grilling the cabbage leaf is to have a few other things ready to grill afterward, because you do need a quite-hot fire to char that moist leaf while barely steaming the fish inside of it, and it would be a shame to waste those coals.

Time: About 45 minutes   **Yield:** 2 to 4 servings

Salt

4 savoy cabbage leaves

8 ounces skinless white-fish fillets (like black sea bass, cod or halibut), cut into 4 small pieces

4 teaspoons chopped fresh dill

Salt and black pepper

Olive oil as needed

1 tablespoon neutral oil (like grapeseed or corn)

2 tablespoons butter

Several sprigs fresh thyme

1 meaty skeleton from a small white fish, like sea bass, chopped

2 cups dry white wine

Microgreens or flowers for garnish

1. Heat a grill with rack very close to flame and heat quite hot.

2. Bring a large pot of water to a boil and salt it. Remove thickest part of central vein of each cabbage leaf without cutting leaf in half. Blanch cabbage leaves in boiling water until just tender, about 30 seconds; drain on paper towels. Put a piece of fish on one side of each leaf and top with 1 teaspoon dill, a sprinkle of salt and pepper and a drizzle of olive oil. Fold other half of leaf over the fish and trim edges with a big cookie cutter or a knife to form an oval. Rub outside with a little bit of olive oil.

3. Put neutral oil and 1 tablespoon of butter in a skillet large enough to hold fish bones in one layer over medium-high heat; when butter melts, add thyme and fish bones and cook, stirring occasionally, until very well browned, about 5 minutes. Add remaining 1 tablespoon butter and wine and cook until creamy and reduced in volume, about 10 minutes. Strain and discard fish bones. Season sauce with salt and pepper and keep it over very low heat while you grill fish.

4. Grill fish packages for 30 seconds per side; cabbage should brown and fish should steam but just barely. (You can tell whether fish is done by poking a toothpick into it. If it meets a little resistance, it's ready; if it's very rubbery, it's not.)

5. Whisk sauce or use an immersion blender to foam it up a bit. Drizzle cabbage and fish with sauce, garnish with microgreens or flowers and serve.

November 3, 2011: "Eat: Prince of Denmark," by MARK BITTMAN; adapted from Noma: Time and Place in Nordic Cuisine, *by RENE REDZEPI (Phaidon Press, 2010)*

Grilled Fish with Aromatics

This recipe works with just about any fish. At La Cagouille in Paris, white fish are prepared this way, but it is an equally wonderful preparation for salmon or mackerel.

Yield: 4 servings

4 (1-pound) saltwater perch, rock cod or
snapper or 1 (4- to 5-pound) salmon,
cleaned, heads on
Vegetable oil for oiling the grill, spatula
and baking dishes
6 tablespoons extra virgin olive oil

20 cloves garlic, peeled
12 sprigs fresh thyme
12 sprigs fresh rosemary
2 bay leaves
Kosher or coarse sea salt and freshly
ground black pepper to taste

1. Rinse fish and pat dry. Make 3 or 4 shallow cuts just through skin of fish, so it can expand during cooking. Refrigerate until ready to cook.

2. Build and light a fire in an outdoor grill.

3. Preheat oven to 300 degrees.

4. When coals are bright red and evenly dusted with ash, place grill over fire and let it heat up for 2 to 3 minutes. Thoroughly oil grill, using vegetable oil and paper toweling, being careful not to use so much oil that it will drip on coals and cause them to flame up.

5. Place fish on grill so rungs are vertical under it. Cook just until there are golden grill marks on fish, about 3 minutes per side. Using a metal spatula that is lightly brushed with vegetable oil, transfer fish to one or two oiled baking dishes, depending on how many fish you are preparing. Place them in oven and bake until they are opaque throughout—this will be approximately 12 minutes for smaller fish, 20 to 25 minutes for larger fish.

6. About 10 minutes before fish is done, pour 6 tablespoons olive oil into an oven-proof dish or ramekin and place it in oven to heat gently. Bring 2 cups water to a boil in bottom of a steamer over high heat. Place garlic cloves in steamer, cover and steam until they are nearly soft throughout, about 8 minutes. Add remaining herbs to steamer in an even layer, cover and continue steaming for 3 minutes.

7. To serve, pour equal amounts of olive oil in center of warmed dinner plates. If using small fish, place them whole on top of oil. If you are using a large fish, such as a salmon, remove the fillets and place equal-sized pieces of fillet on oil. Season to taste with coarse salt and pepper. Arrange steamed herbs and garlic on one side of plate and serve immediately.

April 17, 1988: "Food: As Catch Can,"
by SUSAN HERRMANN LOOMIS;
recipe by GERARD ALLEMANDOU, La Cagouille, Paris

Grilled Snapper with Cumin

Gerard Allemandou serves sea bream this way at his restaurant La Cagouille in Paris. Just about any small, white-meated sea fish can be used. One trick to this is to finish cooking the fish in the oven, so it has a lovely grilled flavor and all its natural moisture.

Yield: 4 servings

4 (9- to 12-ounce) rosethorn snappers (from Alaska) or 2 (1- to 2-pound) Alaska red snappers or redfish, cleaned, heads on

Vegetable oil
½ teaspoon cumin seeds
4 tablespoons plus 2 teaspoons olive oil
Kosher or coarse sea salt to taste

1. Rinse fish and pat them dry. Refrigerate until ready to use.
2. Build and light a fire in an outdoor barbecue.
3. Preheat oven to 300 degrees.
4. When coals are bright red and evenly dusted with ash, thoroughly oil grill, using vegetable oil and paper toweling.
5. While the fire is burning, cut four ⅛-inch-deep cuts in each side of each fish, working a very sharp knife blade under scales of the fish to make cuts. Press equal amounts of cumin seed (15 seeds is desired amount) firmly into cuts.
6. Rub each fish all over with 2 teaspoons of olive oil. Place fish on grill, so rungs are vertical under body of fish. Cook just until fish has golden grill marks on it, no longer than 3 minutes per side for a small fish, 4 to 5 minutes for a large fish.
7. Using a lightly oiled metal spatula, transfer fish to an oven-proof dish or baking sheet covered with foil and continue cooking in oven until fish is opaque throughout, 8 to 10 minutes for a small fish, 15 to 20 minutes for a larger fish. To test for doneness, stick point of a sharp knife into meat just behind head of fish and pull back. The meat should be opaque.
8. About 5 minutes before fish is done, place remaining 4 tablespoons olive oil in a heat-proof dish or a ramekin and place it in oven to heat gently.
9. To serve, place each fish in center of a dinner plate. Pour 1 tablespoon of warm olive oil on one side of fish and pour a narrow strip of coarse salt on other side of plate. If you are using larger fish, remove fillets and place equal-sized pieces of fillet on each plate, garnishing with salt and oil. Serve immediately.

April 17, 1988: "Food: As Catch Can,"
by SUSAN HERRMANN LOOMIS;
recipe by GERARD ALLEMANDOU, La Cagouille, Paris

Grilled Whole Porgy with Lime Butter

July is barbecue season across America. To me, it has a special appeal in New York's Hamptons, on the south shore of Long Island. There are few pleasures in life that can equal the aroma of freshly grilled fish mingling with the clear saltiness of a sea breeze.

Thus it seems a perfect occasion to demolish the age-old shibboleths surrounding the art of summer grilling. For example, barbecuing does not require charring food beyond recognition; barbecuing is not just "Dad's job"; and a good barbecue does not require mesquite or hickory chips.

Most important of all, a barbecue for family or friends need not imply oversauced chicken and hamburgers. Outdoor grilling can be as elegant as the finest restaurant cuisine.

That, at least, is the word from two talented chefs, Laura Thorne and Jeff Trujillo.

"The trouble with most people who grill foods," Laura told me, "is their tendency to char whatever they are cooking. That gives a burnt flavor and destroys the natural taste of the foods. If you cook a flat piece of fish like this swordfish," she said, pointing with a spatula to the swordfish steak she was cooking, "let it cook briefly until a grill-pattern just starts to form, then give it a quarter-turn to prevent overcooking and burning." (Later, she served the swordfish, which had been marinated for several hours in red wine, orange juice and walnut oil, with a delicious relish of tomato, orange and onion. See the recipe on page 232.)

An important technique for high-quality grilling is to "feel" whether the food is done. Fish they remove from the grill while it remains a trifle resilient to the touch. One surprise, for the home chef accustomed to cooking only fish fillets on the grill, is that both chefs prefer to cook most fish—including the whole porgies with lime butter they prepared for me—with the bone in; that way, it remains moist and retains more flavor. Yet another surprise, for those who look at barbecuing as an opportunity to overseason food, is that, when grilling, they do not use pepper or salt. "We like the natural flavors of foods," explained Laura. "We use fresh herbs and spices, fine oils and vinegars to give flavor to foods."

Yield: 4 servings

4 whole, cleaned porgies (about 1 pound each)

¼ cup olive oil

1 large lime

10 tablespoons butter

1 tablespoon finely chopped shallots

1 cup dry white vermouth

¼ cup fresh lime juice

¼ teaspoon finely grated or chopped lime zest

1 tablespoon finely chopped fresh chives

1. Preheat a well-scrubbed outdoor gas grill to high, or fire coals of a charcoal grill until they are white hot.

2. Hold a heavy kitchen knife at an angle and score both sides of each porgy, slicing down to bone at three equidistant spots.

3. Brush grill lightly with oil. Brush fish on both sides with oil and place them on grill. Squeeze a little juice from lime on top of each fish. Grill fish on one side for about 6 minutes or until they can be lifted from grill without sticking. (Cooking time will vary, depending on size of fish.) Turn and cook about 6 minutes longer.

4. Meanwhile, heat 1 tablespoon of butter in a skillet and add shallots. Cook, stirring, about 1 minute. Add vermouth, lime juice and zest and cook over high heat until liquid is almost but not quite evaporated.

5. Add remaining 9 tablespoons butter, stirring rapidly with a wire whisk. Cook until butter is melted and very hot. Remove from heat.

6. Arrange fish on a platter and pour hot lime-butter sauce over them. Sprinkle with chives and serve immediately.

July 6, 1986: CRAIG CLAIBORNE with PIERRE FRANEY;
recipe by LAURA THORNE and JEFF TRUJILLO,
formerly of Coast Grill, Southampton, New York

A Lesson on Cooking Fish

The greatest sin in preparing fish for the table, which no sauces or spices will mitigate, is overcooking. Many recipes specify a certain number of minutes for a fish of a certain weight, or a fish steak of a certain thickness, but the only sure test—long before the suggested time is up—is to prod them with a fork. They are done when the meat readily flakes apart under gentle pressure.

Broiling fish over an open fire is tricky because the heat is inconsistent. There is also the problem of turning the fillet, which isn't required when it is broiled in an oven, without its falling apart. An easy way around this is to put the fish in a separate, hinged grill. Separate grill or not, fish cooked over coals must be constantly attended.

Fish steaks lend themselves to outdoor barbecue cooking, but if you use fillets leave the skin on them; this helps keep the meat in one piece.

If you are ever moved to cook fish for a large group at lakeside or seashore over an open wood fire, you can arrange the fish—which should be split or in steaks or fillets—on a grill measuring about 2 by 3 feet. Wire another grill of similar size over the fish and fasten 6-foot (total length) loops of chain or wire to each of the grill's long ends. These loops will enable two of your helpers to suspend the fish at varying distances above the fire. Fish broiled in this manner, and over a barbecue as well, should be brushed with melted butter, or vegetable oil, seasoned with salt and pepper, and basted often during cooking.

Many years ago during an all-night shore fishing trip for striped bass on which I had ventured without eating supper, I was beset by hunger pangs shortly before dawn. I had brought no food with me, but I did have two medium-size bass on the beach. I dug a shallow hole in the sand, lined it with round rocks the size of oranges, cut a one-pound steak from one of the fish, wrapped it in a thick layer of rockweed, and, when the fire died down, placed it on the coals and hot rocks.

I piled additional rockweed on top and less than an hour later—my table a boulder—reveled in what at the time seemed the sweetest fish I had ever enjoyed. The setting—a crisp, early October dawn, the murmur of small waves on a wild and rocky shore—and the simplicity of my repast undoubtedly contributed to my pleasure, but the steaming rockweed had imparted a marvelously delicate flavor to the bass. It was as if I had seasoned the fish with a gentle sea breeze.

August 16, 1987: NELSON BRYANT

Grilled Sardines

If you've only had sardines from a can, you may turn up your nose at them. Fresh ones will change your mind. Brush them with olive oil, toss a few sprigs of rosemary onto a hot grill, and grill them. Sardines take two to three minutes to grill and about that long to eat. They're a rare treat and a great nutritional package, containing omega-3 fats, selenium, vitamin B12, calcium, niacin and phosphorus.

Yield: 4 servings

24 medium or large sardines, cleaned
2 tablespoons extra virgin olive oil
Salt and freshly ground pepper

A handful of sprigs fresh rosemary
Lemon wedges

1.   Prepare a hot grill, making sure grill is oiled. Rinse sardines, and dry with paper towels. Toss with olive oil, and season with salt and pepper.

2.   When grill is ready, toss rosemary sprigs directly on fire. Wait for flames to die down, then place sardines directly over heat, in batches if necessary. Grill for a minute or two on each side, depending on size. Transfer from grill to a platter using tongs or a wide metal spatula, and serve with lemon wedges.

ADVANCE PREPARATION: This is a last-minute preparation, but you can rinse and dry the fish hours ahead. Keep in the refrigerator.

May 11, 2009: "Recipes for Health: The Seafood Conundrum,"
by MARTHA ROSE SHULMAN

Marinated Grilled Swordfish

Summer is fresh swordfish season. The warm months are also the best time to cook this distinctively meaty fish. Giant swordfish often weighing over 200 pounds yield thick steaks that are particularly delicious when grilled over charcoal.

Swordfish has virtually no waste since the heavy center bone is removed before it is sliced into steaks and weighed. Its richness makes it possible for one pound to serve two to three persons.

Its texture is dense and somewhat dry, and while there is a concentration of fat in the dark areas of the flesh, there is not enough fat throughout to keep the meat succulent. Marinating swordfish before cooking is a good idea, and basting it with seasoned oils or butters in cooking or just before serving enhances the flavor.

It is difficult to assess the freshness of a swordfish steak, but it should be virtually odorless and there should be no signs of dark dryness around the edges. The flesh should be firm, not watery or spongy (signs of fish that has been frozen). Although swordfish does not deteriorate as rapidly as some of the smaller, more delicate fish, it is one species that is best purchased from a market in which you have confidence.

Swordfish steaks are best when grilled or broiled. Have them cut at least one inch thick so they will not dry out in cooking.

Yield: 4 servings

2 swordfish steaks (about 1 pound each)

½ cup olive oil

Juice of 2 lemons

1 clove garlic, minced

2 sprigs fresh or 1 teaspoon dried thyme

Salt and freshly ground black pepper

6 tablespoons unsalted butter

1½ teaspoons crushed black peppercorns

1 tablespoon minced fresh parsley

1. Trim skin from swordfish and cut each steak in half. Place in a shallow glass dish.

2. Mix oil, juice of 1½ lemons, garlic and thyme together. Season marinade with salt and pepper and spoon over fish. Set aside for 2 hours.

3. Preheat barbecue grill. Grill swordfish, basting frequently with marinade, for about 8 minutes on one side. Turn and grill another 5 minutes or so. Cooking time is likely to vary, depending on heat of grill, but be sure not to overcook. Fish is done when it begins to flake easily.

4. While fish is grilling, melt butter in a saucepan. Add remaining lemon juice, crushed peppercorns and parsley. Spoon this sauce over fish just before serving.

July 20, 1980: "It's Swordfish Time," by FLORENCE FABRICANT

Grilled Swordfish Steaks
with Orange Thyme Sauce

Time: 30 minutes   **Yield:** 4 servings

2 swordfish steaks (about 2 to
   2½ pounds in all)
3 tablespoons olive oil
2 tablespoons unsalted butter
1 shallot, minced
1 clove garlic, minced
2 medium-ripe tomatoes, peeled, seeded
   and chopped

¼ cup fresh thyme leaves
⅔ cup fresh orange juice
¼ to ½ cup dry white wine
Coarse salt and freshly ground pepper
   to taste

1. Wipe swordfish steaks dry with paper towels. Coat on both sides with 2 tablespoons of olive oil. Set aside.

2. Heat remaining 1 tablespoon olive oil in a skillet with 1 tablespoon of butter. Add shallot and garlic and cook until soft. Add tomatoes and thyme and cook for 3 minutes.

3. Add orange juice and white wine and reduce slightly, cooking for 5 more minutes. Season with salt and pepper and set aside until fish is about to be grilled.

4. Preheat coals for grilling. Cook fish about 5 minutes on each side, depending on thickness of steaks. Meanwhile, bring sauce to a boil. Off heat, stir in remaining 1 tablespoon butter. Pour sauce over steaks and serve.

May 24, 1992: "Food: Barbecuing Returns, with Twists,"
by MOIRA HODGSON

Grilled Swordfish
with Tomato and Onion Relish

Yield: 4 servings

The fish in marinade

1 tablespoon finely chopped shallots

¼ cup dry red wine

¼ cup fresh orange juice

½ cup oil, preferably walnut oil, plus oil
    for brushing grill

2¼ pounds fresh, boneless swordfish
    fillet, cut into 4 pieces, each about 1
    inch thick

The relish

2 tablespoons dark brown sugar

1 cup fresh orange juice

½ cup wine vinegar, preferably rosé wine
    vinegar

Zest of 1 orange, cut into thin strips

2 cups peeled, seeded and cubed
    tomatoes

1 cup peeled, seeded, sectioned and
    cubed oranges

½ cup finely chopped red onion

1–2 dashes hot sauce, or to taste

1. At least 2 hours before you are ready to grill swordfish, put shallots, red wine, orange juice and oil in a mixing bowl and blend well. Add swordfish pieces and coat well with marinade. Cover and refrigerate.

2. Preheat a well-scrubbed outdoor gas grill, or fire coals of a charcoal grill to white hot.

3. To prepare relish, put brown sugar in a skillet and add orange juice, vinegar and strips of orange zest. Cook about 10 minutes, or until sauce is reduced to about ½ cup. Set aside. In a sieve, combine cubed tomatoes and oranges and onion. Drain thoroughly. Pour mixture into a mixing bowl and add orange sauce and hot sauce. Stir to blend.

4. Brush grill lightly with oil. Place swordfish pieces on grill (discard marinade) and cook about 2 minutes. Lift up each piece of fish with a spatula and give it a quarter-turn, forming a grill pattern. Continue cooking about 1½ to 2 minutes, and turn fish over. Cook about 2 minutes and give pieces a quarter-turn. Cook about 1 minute longer. Serve with relish.

July 6, 1986: "Food: Grilling As Art,"
by CRAIG CLAIBORNE with PIERRE FRANEY;
recipe by LAURA THORNE and JEFF TRUJILLO

Marinated Broiled Tuna Steaks with Sauce Niçoise

Tuna can be marinated with all kinds of fresh herbs, and it usually needs about 30 minutes to pick up the flavors. Many cooks make the error of marinating tuna and other fish too long, which breaks down the outer muscle tissue and leaves the fish with a mushy texture. This reminder is especially important if you plan to barbecue tuna steaks, for overmarinated fish will steam rather than char on the grill.

The recipe here is a twist on tuna niçoise. Fresh fennel and lemon rind give the vegetable melange a refreshing lift; the olives, garlic and tomato provide the Provençal accent.

Yield: 4 servings

4 (6-ounce) center-cut tuna steaks, about
    1 inch thick
Salt and freshly ground pepper to taste
6 tablespoons olive oil
4 sprigs fresh thyme, or 2 teaspoons dried
2 crumbled bay leaves
4 small sprigs fresh rosemary, or 2
    teaspoons dried
⅛ teaspoon red pepper flakes

4 ripe plum tomatoes
½ cup sliced fennel
½ cup sliced red onions
2 teaspoons coarsely chopped garlic
4 pitted black olives
2 teaspoons grated lemon zest
2 tablespoons red wine vinegar
4 tablespoons coarsely chopped fresh
    basil or parsley

1. Preheat outdoor grill.

2. Place tuna in a dish and sprinkle both sides with salt and pepper. Brush both sides with 2 tablespoons of olive oil. Add thyme, bay leaves, rosemary and pepper flakes. Cover with plastic wrap and let it stand for 20 minutes.

3. Place tomatoes in boiling water for about 9 seconds. Drain and pull away skins. Cut and discard cores and chop tomatoes coarsely.

4. Place remaining 4 tablespoons olive oil in a small saucepan over medium-high heat. When it's hot, add fennel, onions and garlic. Cook briefly until wilted. Add the tomatoes, olives, lemon zest, vinegar, salt and pepper to taste. Cover and simmer for 5 minutes.

5. Transfer mixture into a blender or food processor. Add 3 tablespoons of basil, then blend for 5 to 7 seconds, taking care that it remain coarse. Transfer sauce to a saucepan, check for seasoning, reheat briefly. Keep warm.

6. Place steaks on a hot grill and cover. Cook for 4 minutes. Turn fish, cover grill and continue cooking for about 3 minutes. Serve with prepared sauce around the fish and sprinkle with remaining 1 tablespoon basil.

August 4, 1993: "60-Minute Gourmet," by PIERRE FRANEY

Broiled Tuna Couscous Salad

The firm, rich flesh of fresh tuna is well suited to barbecuing and broiling, and the quick recipe here makes a delicious main course that can be prepared slightly ahead of time and held if you are entertaining.

I combine cubed tuna steaks with a light and flavorful couscous salad brightened with onion, garlic and cumin, all tossed in a mildly spicy oil and vinegar dressing. I have one confession about this dish: if there is no time to run to the fish market, I sometimes use canned tuna, packed in oil. It is delicious.

A pleasantly tart arugula salad with a garlic vinaigrette makes a fine side dish with this summer meal.

Yield: 4 servings

For the tuna

1 (1¼-pound) skinless and boneless tuna
    steak, about 1 inch thick

Salt and freshly ground pepper to taste

1 tablespoon olive oil

2 sprigs fresh thyme, or 1 teaspoon dried

For the couscous

1 tablespoon olive oil

4 tablespoons finely chopped onion

1 teaspoon finely chopped garlic

1 teaspoon ground cumin

Salt and freshly ground pepper to taste

1 cup couscous

For the salad dressing

4 tablespoons red wine vinegar

6 tablespoons olive oil

2 tablespoons light soy sauce

½ teaspoon finely chopped jalapeño, or
    to taste

¼ teaspoon Tabasco sauce

1 cup finely diced celery

1½ cups peeled, seeded and diced
    tomatoes

2 teaspoons finely minced garlic

½ cup coarsely chopped fresh basil,
    cilantro, chervil or parsley

2 tablespoons fresh lemon juice

2 teaspoons grated orange zest

Salt and freshly ground pepper to taste

1. Preheat outdoor grill.

2. To prepare the tuna, put it on a plate and sprinkle both sides with salt and pepper and brush with a mixture of oil and thyme. Cover closely with plastic wrap and let stand until ready to grill.

3. Put steak on hot grill and cover. Cook 4 minutes. Turn fish, cover grill and cook about 4 minutes more. Remove fish; let cool.

4. To prepare the couscous, heat oil in a small saucepan. Add onion, garlic and cumin and cook, stirring, until vegetables are wilted. Add 1 cup water, salt and pepper. Bring to a boil and add couscous, stirring. Cover closely. Remove from heat and let stand 5 minutes. Put in a bowl to cool.

5. Meanwhile, combine all ingredients for salad dressing in a large bowl. Blend well with a wire whisk. Check for seasoning.

6. Cut tuna into bite-size pieces and add to couscous in bowl. Pour dressing over all and toss well. Serve immediately.

July 13, 1988: "60-Minute Gourmet,"
by PIERRE FRANEY

Grilled Salmon with Herb-Butter Sauce and Tomatoes

July may mark the official beginning of barbecuing season, but those with a passion for grilled foods gladly overlook such formalities. In deep winter, these people can be found scraping the snow from their grills; in spring, they huddle under umbrellas as they cook.

"I can remember driving my mother crazy," says Alfred Portale, the chef at Manhattan's Gotham Bar and Grill, who grew up in Buffalo. "I'd shovel a path out to the backyard barbecue to grill steaks, then track snow back into the house."

Portale is especially partial to grilling in the spring. This, he says, not only requires raincoats and heavy sweaters; it also demands certain foods. "Spring is a time for what I call 'tentative' grilling," says Portale. "It's a time for dusting off the grill, a time when you may cook out of doors but it's still too chilly to eat out there. It's also the beginning of the season for cooking things more simply. Salmon, spring lamb, asparagus and leeks should all be celebrated. I think of spring foods as the youngest and freshest foods. One ought to preserve their delicate flavors."

To that end, Portale prefers grilling these spring foods over charcoal and fruitwood to, for instance, an oak fire. "Grilling over oak chips tends to throw a heavy smoke, which may overwhelm the food," he says. "Fruitwood has a much lighter smoke and a more delicate flavor." Portale believes that a wood or charcoal fire gives more flavor to food than a gas flame does. "It's kind of silly to grill things like onions and fennel over a gas grill," he says. "They don't take on the same smoky taste."

To grill salmon, Portale simply brushes the fish on both sides with olive oil. He then paints a little oil on the clean gratings of the grill and places the fillet on top. After about a minute, he gives the fillet a quarter turn to create an attractive crosshatch pattern.

Yield: 4 servings

For the sauce

1 tablespoon olive oil

2½ tablespoons finely chopped shallots

¾ teaspoon finely minced garlic

1 cup peeled, seeded tomatoes cut into
    ¼-inch cubes

Salt to taste, if desired

Freshly ground pepper to taste

4 sprigs fresh parsley

2 sprigs fresh tarragon

¾ cup rich chicken broth

¼ cup heavy cream

½ pound (2 sticks) butter, cut into
    16 pieces

1 teaspoon dried thyme

2 tablespoons dry white wine

**For the salmon and final preparation
of sauce**

1 slab skinless, boneless salmon fillet
  (about 1¼ pounds)
Olive oil
Salt to taste, if desired

Freshly ground pepper to taste
1 tablespoon finely chopped fresh parsley
1 tablespoon finely chopped fresh chives
1 tablespoon finely chopped fresh tarragon
4 oven-baked, sun-dried tomatoes
  (optional)

1.   Preheat an outdoor grill to high.

2.   For the sauce, heat olive oil in a heavy saucepan and add shallots and ½ teaspoon of garlic. Cook over gentle heat without browning for 7 or 8 minutes.

3.   Add tomatoes and salt and pepper to taste. Tie sprigs of parsley and tarragon into a bundle and add it. Add chicken broth and bring to a boil. Cook about 30 seconds, then remove from heat. Line a saucepan with a sieve and pour tomato sauce into it. Let it drain. Discard parsley-and-tarragon bundle. There should be about ½ cup of tomato pulp. Set this aside. There should be about ⅔ cup of liquid. Bring liquid to a boil in a saucepan and add cream. When mixture returns to a boil, let it cook over moderately high heat, stirring constantly with a wire whisk, about 3 minutes.

4.   Add butter fairly rapidly, two or three pieces at a time, stirring constantly with whisk. Cook only until butter is melted and sauce is smooth. Add reserved tomato pulp, remaining ¼ teaspoon minced garlic, dried thyme and white wine. Bring to a simmer, stirring, and remove sauce from heat.

5.   Cut salmon crosswise into 4 pieces of equal size. Brush each piece lightly on both sides with olive oil and sprinkle on both sides with salt and pepper. Brush surface of a clean grill with olive oil and add pieces of salmon. Cook, with grill lid open, about 1 minute. Lift up pieces, one at a time, and give each a quarter-turn laterally (this will leave a crosshatch pattern on one side); continue cooking about 1 minute. Turn pieces to second side and repeat cooking procedure. Cook on second side 3 to 4 minutes longer, depending on whether you want fish medium-rare or fully cooked.

6.   Reheat sauce gently and add chopped parsley, chives and tarragon. Bring sauce just to a simmer, stirring.

7.   To serve, spoon equal portions of sauce onto 4 heated dinner plates. Place one piece of salmon in center of sauce on each plate. Garnish each serving, if desired, with one sun-dried tomato, and serve.

*March 20, 1988: "Food: The Fires of Spring,"
by CRAIG CLAIBORNE with PIERRE FRANEY;
recipe from ALFRED PORTALE,
Gotham Bar and Grill, New York City*

Wild Alaskan Salmon: The Glory Days Are Here

The Gulf of Alaska was tossing up waves of 20 feet or more and the winds roared to 40 miles an hour, but the storm did not deter the fleet in pursuit of what is arguably the world's best-tasting fish—Copper River salmon—on their first run of the season.

In Seattle, New York, Tokyo and Los Angeles on May 15, anxious chefs clicked on to Web sites and called fishermen on cell phones. Forget the weather. The chefs wanted to know how the fish looked. Then, "Bulletin! Bulletin! Six kings landed!" flashed on computer screens.

Rick Cavanaugh, a seafood buyer for the Thriftway supermarket chain in Seattle, had the salmon hoisted directly from the boat into a rented helicopter to take it to a waiting jet in the Alaskan port of Cordova. Then, he airlifted it 1,500 miles south to Seattle. Looking as if he had just won the Powerball lottery, he displayed his 500 pounds of Copper River king salmon to reporters at 5 A.M.—10 hours after they were yanked from the Alaskan seas. Mr. Cavanaugh's catch was sold out by mid-morning.

Why all the fuss? After all, the world is full of farm-raised Atlantic salmon, available year-round. And there is certainly no shortage of Alaskan wild salmon: from now until October, about 150 million salmon will be harvested from the Last Frontier State.

But Copper River fish are different. A string of restaurants and fish vendors from Puget Sound to Long Island Sound, from Miami to Los Angeles, swear that there is no other fish that gets people quite like this first wild salmon of the season. In the Pacific Northwest, grilling the first Copper River fillets on the barbecue is a seasonal ritual, like roasting spring lamb. For the restaurants and grocery stores that compete to bring home the first fish, by a matter of minutes, it is an obsession.

Most of the Copper River's bounty will be available until August. But the best-tasting of these fish, connoisseurs say, are the early-running ones, which are available until mid-June. Fishermen harvest the salmon for 24 hours at a time about twice a week on average, according to the dictates of Alaskan state fish managers.

Copper River salmon are rich in oil, firm in flesh, almost nutty in taste. They are high in omega-3 fatty acids, which have been shown to have certain health benefits. They are hardy, having bulked up for the river journey of nearly 300 miles to icy headwaters in the Wrangell Mountains. And they are smart, which gives fishermen more respect for them and gives diners something to brag about. The flesh, especially of the king variety, is so red and rich that most people prefer to drink red wine—typically an Oregon pinot noir—as an accompaniment.

Still, none of this quite explains the fever that builds at this time every year, when Copper River salmon start to mass outside the mouth of their spawning stream, about 200 miles southeast of Anchorage.

Taste and see, the disciples say.

"I go nuts over this fish," said Rick Moonen, the executive chef at Oceana in Manhattan.

Barely 24 hours after the season opened, Mr. Moonen had Copper River salmon on plates at his restaurant. Soon after, he was going from table to table, talking about the salmon's journey, their sex lives and the setting in which they come to spawn and die. "I get people so psyched about it that they end up talking about the sex life," he said.

As fish sex lives go, that of Copper River salmon is noble but prosaic: after a few years at sea, they dodge ice chunks and sharp-eyed eagles and fight the gravitational torrent of the river to find a little home in the gravel hundreds of miles upstream, near the very place of their birth. Then, they spawn and die. Fishermen catch them just before they head for the sex-and-death grounds.

Just 15 years ago, barely anyone except fishermen and people who look closely at canning labels had any idea what Copper River salmon was all about. Most of the fish caught in the waters near the mouth of the river were canned, some even sold as pet food. In tough years, fishermen would be lucky to sell a few extra fish to a handful of Alaskan restaurants.

The legend of how a fish became a phenomenon is usually traced to Jon Rowley, a Seattle broker of salmon, oysters and other briny commodities.

His story, as with most Alaska fish narratives, begins in a bar.

Mr. Rowley and a few of his Alaskan fishing buddies were sitting in a bar in Seattle, in 1982. "I was aware of the superiority of the fish," he said. How? "By tasting it."

He asked his fishermen friends if they would be willing to try to bring the salmon into harbor in good shape, to be sold fresh. At the time, he said, most of these fish were caught quickly, pressed into holds of boats, mixed with bilge water and then sloshed around at sea. The flesh was mush when the boats came into port, he said.

"I said I could handle the marketing if they just learned how to treat the fish right once they got them on board," he said. The fish, caught in long volleyball-like gill nets, had to be bled immediately upon landing, and then iced.

The key to preserving flavor and texture, Mr. Rowley explained, in perhaps more detail than most people want to hear, "is to get them on ice just before they go into rigor mortis, and then to eat them just as they are coming out of rigor."

The first year, 1983, Mr. Rowley marketed 300 pounds of fish. It was sold in a handful of Seattle restaurants. "It was clear, immediately, that we had something world class," he said. "There was so much excitement, there was energy. People were talking about this salmon like nothing they had ever tasted before."

The next year, more fishermen tried selling fresh Copper River salmon. By the 1990's, virtually the entire Cordova fleet—more than 500 fishing boats—was following the bleeding and icing techniques in order to sell to the fresh market. It required much more than a change in attitude: boats had to be overhauled, costing thousands of dollars, and deckhands had to be taught to treat the fish with respect. But it had its rewards. Fish that brought a boat owner barely 30 cents a pound from canneries were drawing six times that amount, if handled properly.

Mr. Rowley "carried the gospel" of Copper River from city to city, he said, adding that he has never made much money from it. Other West Coast cities picked up on the competition. It was like trying to be the one to bring the first Beaujolais nouveau into town. Supermarket chains, including giants like Safeway, got into the frenzy. Now, chains in the Midwest, long known as a seafood desert, run advertisements proclaiming their first-of-the-season Alaskan salmon, just a few days removed from the sea.

"I just got off the phone to Julia Child," Mr. Rowley said between fish-brokering chores in his office in Seattle. "She's going to take a 10-inch-long chunk of Copper River king and roast it."

In Seattle, restaurants like Ray's Boathouse—one of the first restaurants to offer the salmon, in the 1980's—will usually grill the fish over alder wood, or sear it and then bake it to serve with a pinot noir sauce (see recipe on page 242). Mr. Rowley prefers to put a touch of olive oil on both sides of a fillet and sear it in a hot pan. Then, he bakes it for about 20 minutes at 280 degrees. The process, not unlike cooking a steak, preserves the juices inside. As side dishes, he prefers wild Northwest morels and Yakima Valley asparagus. And he favors the obligatory Oregon pinot noir for the accompanying wine.

"It's like shuffling cards," he said. "The pinot has all the flavors of Oregon fruit, the mushrooms have all the taste of the wild forest, the salmon are the essence of the cold waters of the Copper River—all mixing together."

In New York, Mr. Moonen of Oceana says the handling of the fish makes all the difference. "I can get fresh salmon from the Fulton fish market, but it's generally abused," he said. "Now, I have the kings sent directly from Cordova to me in New York. I don't take any chances."

The farm fish purveyors have not taken this run of the wild kings lying down. The farmers say they have struggled to improve the flavor and texture of Atlantic salmon raised in pens. Last year, for the first time, there were more farm-raised salmon sold worldwide— better than 825,000 tons—than fresh wild salmon, the overwhelming majority of which comes from Alaska. And the farm-raised fish cost a bit less, about $11 a pound, compared with about $14 a pound for the wild variety.

But fish from pens and cement ponds are salmon without a story, the Alaskans say. Consider the Copper River Delta. At 700,000 acres, it is the largest wetlands on the Pacific coast of North America. More than 235 species of birds—from trumpeter swans to bald eagles to horned puffins—nest in the delta. The marine waters are home to killer whales, Steller sea lions, sea otters. On shore, moose, grizzly bears and wolves are abundant.

And then there are the salmon. Five species of wild Pacific salmon—the small pinks, the bigger sockeyes or reds, the medium-size coho or silver, the late-running chums, and the majestic kings or chinook—are caught off Alaska's shore. The two prized Copper River fish are the reds and the kings.

The State of Alaska estimates that this year fishermen will net about 50,000 Copper River kings and nearly two million reds. The kings, which can reach 45 pounds, are the thickest, and tend to be the richest. They are marbled with layers of fat and oil, the better to protect them on the long journey to the spawning grounds.

Cordova, the home port of most Copper River fishermen, is on Prince William Sound, not far from the oil port of Valdez. When the Exxon Valdez hit a reef in 1989, spilling 11 million gallons of crude oil into the sound, the Cordova fishermen were among the most angry, and the most diligent in putting up floating barriers that kept the oil from coming their way. The Copper River salmon runs were untouched by the spill, but the market for Alaskan fresh salmon was badly hurt, as people associated the state with one of the worst environmental catastrophes of all time.

Now, Alaska fresh salmon are sold around the world, though none have quite obtained the snob appeal of Copper River. Yukon River kings, Bristol Bay sockeyes and coho from southeast Alaska are all quite good—when fresh and well handled—and are abundant throughout the summer.

Fishermen have tried to protect their catch by insisting on labels, much as wine growers did more than a century ago in France and Italy. But substitutes and fakes—advertised as Copper River fish—still find their way to market, the fishermen say.

"You pretty much have to trust the restaurant and the fish vendor," said Cheri Shaw, the director of Cordova District Fishermen United, which promotes Copper River fish for about 250 boats. They are leading the effort to try to trademark the fish. "Early in the season, it's easy to tell you're getting the real thing, because no fresh fish has been caught yet," she said. "Later in the season, you just have to ask."

Ms. Shaw, who lives in a town that is to salmon what Haut-Medoc is to wine, prefers her Copper River fish cooked on the grill, with garlic, salt and pepper. And she drinks French Bordeaux with her fish—another indication, perhaps, of how well the Cordova fishing fleet is doing these days.

Mr. Rowley is justly proud of the journey Copper River fish have taken from barroom dream to high cuisine. He sees the Copper River banners flapping in the wind outside supermarkets up and down the West Coast. He chuckles over the way restaurants in humid Houston can tout fish that is two days removed from swimming next to a glacier. He enjoys the helicopter rentals and general frenzy of the competition. But nothing beats the simple pleasure, he said, of indulging in a taste of the Alaskan spring.

"That's all it is," he said. "It's a taste of the season."

Grilled Copper River King Salmon Fillet

Time: 15 minutes   **Yield:** 6 servings

6 (6-ounce) Copper River king salmon
    fillets

Olive oil
Pinot Noir Sauce (recipe follows)

1.   Prepare a grill using mesquite or charcoal coals. When coals are hot, brush flesh side of fillets with olive oil and place flesh side down on grill. Allow bars of grill to sear fish (it will take only a few seconds), then use spatulas to give fillets a quarter turn; this sears crisscross lines on flesh.

2.   Brush skin side of fillets with olive oil. Turn fillets, and grill just until center of fish begins to look less transparent, about 6 to 8 minutes, depending on thickness of fish. Serve with pinot noir sauce.

Pinot Noir Sauce

Time: 20 minutes   **Yield:** 1¼ cups

1 head garlic
Olive oil
1 cup pinot noir
1 cup fish stock or bottled clam juice
4 teaspoons chopped shallots
2 sprigs fresh thyme leaves

¼ cup heavy cream
¼ pound (1 stick) salted butter, cut into
    1-inch pieces
¼ pound (1 stick) unsalted butter, cut
    into 1-inch pieces

1.   To roast the garlic, preheat oven to 350 degrees. Brush garlic with oil, and wrap in foil. Roast until cloves are soft when pierced, about 45 minutes. Cool. Puree two cloves, and set aside. Reserve rest of garlic for another use.

2.   In a heavy saucepan, combine pinot noir, fish stock, shallots and thyme stems. Place over high heat, and reduce until just more than a glaze, 7 to 10 minutes. Add cream, and reduce by half. Reduce heat to low, and whisk in salted and unsalted butter, one piece at a time, until thoroughly incorporated. Do not boil, or sauce will separate.

3.   Immediately pour sauce through a mesh strainer or cheesecloth; discard solids. Add 1½ teaspoons thyme leaves and pureed cloves of roasted garlic. Mix well, and keep warm.

June 3, 1998: TIMOTHY EGAN;
adapted from RAY'S BOATHOUSE, Seattle, Washington

Smoked Redfish Louviere

" I like to think that something new can happen in America each day," Michel Patout says. "We can invent new things, the way I invented this recipe for smoked redfish, because here we have the opportunity." Mr. Patout is a chef and one of five siblings who operate restaurants in New Iberia, New Orleans and Los Angeles. The Patouts will gather on the Fourth of July at Cytremort Point near New Iberia, Louisiana, where, Mr. Patout says, "We'll sing, parade with flags, get into the water and eat masses of food."

Yield: 4 servings

4 (10- to 12-ounce) fillets redfish or other
    fresh, firm saltwater fish
1 tablespoon salt
1 teaspoon ground red pepper
1 teaspoon ground black pepper
1 teaspoon ground white pepper
3 cloves garlic, finely chopped
¼ pound (1 stick) butter

Juice of 2 lemons
1 tablespoon Worcestershire sauce
2 teaspoons dry vermouth
1 pound lump crab meat
1 pound fresh medium shrimp, peeled
½ cup finely chopped green onions
¼ cup finely chopped fresh parsley

1. Pat fillets dry.
2. In a small bowl, mix together salt, peppers and garlic. Rub mixture all over fish.
3. Place fillets in a smoker and smoke for 5 hours at low heat.
4. Just before fish is done, melt butter in a small saucepan over medium-high heat. Add lemon juice, Worcestershire sauce, vermouth, crab meat and shrimp. Sauté, stirring, for 3 minutes. Add green onions and parsley and mix well.
5. Pour sauce over fish portions and serve immediately, accompanied by rice, if you wish.

ADVANCE PREP: Fish may be smoked in advance and refrigerated, covered. When ready to serve, preheat broiler to 400 degrees. Place fillets on a cookie sheet or in a large, flat pan. Prepare butter sauce as above and pour over it. Place pan under broiler just long enough to heat fish through, 3 to 4 minutes.

June 25, 1986: "For Liberty's 100th, Fireworks from 12 Top Chefs,"
by NANCY HARMON JENKINS; recipe by MICHEL PATOUT

Dry-Cured Smoked Salmon

Since mankind has been cooking food over glowing embers at least since Prometheus, the technique, by all rights, should be at a very high level. But there is one major impediment to achieving this degree of skill—that typically American failing, lack of patience.

Patience is the principal requisite for mastery of the grill—patience to wait for the coals to catch, for the flames to die down, for the slow roasting that will ensure aromatic, succulent, tasty, properly cooked food that is imbued with the rich, smoky flavors only grilling over coals can impart.

Fish can be tricky, since it is so easily overcooked. Steaks or skewered chunks of meaty fish like swordfish, halibut, mako shark and tuna seem to work best. Bluefish fillets and whole gutted tinker mackerel or fresh herring are also magnificent. More difficult are the delicately flavored fish, such as fillets of Norwegian salmon or catfish, or whole baby trout, but they are delicious "roasted" with a little oil or butter, lemon juice and fresh herbs in an envelope of aluminum foil.

Better yet, these kinds of fish respond well to the gentle touch of mild wood smoke, and if they are cured first, they will retain more of the smoky flavor. The recipe here for salmon fillets is an example of a dry-cured smoked fish, and requires a smoker, or a covered grill that can achieve the same effect (see note following the recipe).

Yield: 4 servings as a main course, 8 servings as an appetizer

For the dry cure
½ cup kosher salt
½ cup brown sugar
1½ teaspoons dried lemon zest
1½ teaspoons dried basil
¼ teaspoon freshly ground white pepper
For the smoked salmon
2 pieces salmon fillet (about 1 pound each)

About 2 handfuls soaked mesquite, apple or hickory chips
6 tablespoons olive oil
2 tablespoons fresh lemon juice
Freshly ground pepper to taste
4 cups mixed greens (arugula, watercress, radicchio or other spicy bitter greens), optional

1. To make the dry cure, combine all ingredients. This will make about 1 cup. Mixture may be kept, covered, for 6 months or more. For this recipe, you will need 4 tablespoons.

2. Rub each salmon fillet on both sides with 2 tablespoons of dry cure and place in a glass baking dish. Refrigerate for 6 hours, or overnight.

3. Remove fillets from dish and rinse quickly under running water, just to remove excess cure. Place fillets on a raised grid surface to allow air to circulate around them. Leave to dry for 3 hours, or until surface is dry and shiny.

4.   Forty-five minutes before cooking, light a charcoal fire.

5.   When ready to cook, throw a handful of soaked wood chips on coals. Add hot water to water pan of smoker, or an improvised smoker (see note). Place fillets on grid over water pan. Cover with lid and leave fish for at least 45 minutes, depending on thickness of fish. Check periodically and replenish fuel or chips if necessary. Smoker temperature should not exceed 190 degrees (use an oven thermometer). Fish is done when flesh is firm to touch.

6.   In a mixing bowl, whisk olive oil, lemon juice and pepper to blend. Remove fish from grill and cut crosswise into serving pieces. Serve fish immediately on its own with vinaigrette, or on a bed of greens dressed with vinaigrette.

NOTE: A smoker may be improvised using a hooded grill and a metal bowl half filled with hot water. Follow the first four steps of the recipe. When ready to cook, throw on the chips and place the bowl in the center of the coals, rearranging the coals around the bowl. Put the fish on the grill and replace the hood. Continue with the recipe.

May 15, 1988: "Summer Pastimes: For the Adventurous Griller,"
by NANCY HARMON JENKINS

Grilled Shellfish with "Barbecue Sauce"

Clams, mussels and oysters offer the lazy summer cook an advantage: they're enclosed in perfectly sealed pots, Mother Nature's very own pressure cooker. With a bit of heat from the grill, shellfish literally steam themselves and then pop open, ready for consumption, with virtually no effort required on the part of the griller.

I've been eating grilled shellfish for years, and I occasionally take the unorthodox (for me) step of serving them with a "barbecue" sauce rather than my old standby of lemon juice and sometimes salt. This sauce, which barely qualifies as a recipe, can be made on the grill while the shellfish cook. Also, it can usually be pulled together without a trip to the grocery store, since all it contains is half a stick of butter, a few chopped garlic cloves, some Worcestershire sauce and as much fresh lemon juice as you like. I make it in a small, old cast iron saucepan, perfect for outdoor use. (Don't use anything with a wooden or plastic handle, obviously, since it's going right over the flame.)

To serve, just drizzle a bit of sauce into each shell and dig in. The buttery sauce combines with the mollusks' natural brine to form a liquid that's pretty heavenly. Not bad for a grilled dish that doesn't even require a spatula.

Time: About 15 minutes   **Yield:** 4 to 6 servings

30 to 40 clams or mussels or 24 oysters, well scrubbed
4 tablespoons (½ stick) butter
1 tablespoon minced garlic

¼ teaspoon Worcestershire sauce, or more to taste
Fresh lemon juice to taste

1. Prepare grill; heat should be medium-high and rack about 4 inches from fire. When grill is hot, put shellfish directly on grill, or put them in a basket and put basket on grill.

2. Melt butter in a small saucepan on part of grill not exposed to direct heat (a shelf works well here if your grill has one); add garlic, Worcestershire sauce and lemon juice, and let the mixture warm for a couple of minutes.

3. As clams open—some will take a minute or two; others will take longer—transfer them to a platter, and move the more stubborn ones to hotter parts of fire. Try to keep liquid in shells of those that open, but don't worry if you lose some. When they're all cooked, drizzle "barbecue" sauce over them and serve immediately.

June 24, 2011: "The Minimalist:
Grilled Shellfish with 'Barbecue Sauce,'"
by MARK BITTMAN

Paella à la Giner

Spanish cooks argue about the kind and quantities of ingredients needed for authentic paella (the traditional rice, chicken and fish dish) but no more vigorously than Sebastian and Peter Giner (pronounced hee-NER) debate the amounts of spices and seasonings to add to the paella their mother taught them to make. The homes of the Giner brothers are on the same six-acre hilltop estate with sweeping views of the Westchester woodlands.

American born, of Spanish parents, the brothers run Tano, Inc., a concern founded by their father that imports leather handbags from Spain. The business takes the Giners to Spain at least four times a year.

The Giner brothers and their sister, Teresa, a frequent visitor to the Giner compound, agree on one thing: that a paella (pronounced pie-AY-yah) must be made out of doors.

With this in mind, a stone and brick fireplace with an opening to hold the traditional shallow, black-bottomed paella pan was an integral part of their terrace building plan. Experience proved, however, that the old Spanish way of sticking three metal poles into the ground, balancing the pan on top and building a fire of twigs underneath worked better.

Little blackened areas among the big boulders bordering the tree-shaded terrace attest to the popularity of this method. With seven Giner children (five belonging to Sebastian), there is no lack of stick gatherers.

"We know when the pan is level," Sebastian's wife, Diana, explained as she poured Spanish olive oil into the pan atop the poles. "The oil spreads all over evenly."

"The barbecue taste from the smoke is important," Mrs. Giner said, and her husband showed how simply a twig fire could be controlled as he scattered the burning pieces.

In Alicante, south of Valencia, where the Giner family home is, it is not unusual for families and friends to decide on a paella party on the spur of the moment and tote poles, pans, ingredients and wooden spoons out into the country. The women gather the ingredients, cut the meat and have everything ready, but the men do the actual cooking.

"It is the same here," said slim, dark-haired South American-born Mrs. Peter (Marie) Giner.

In Alicante when the group is large and two paellas are needed, the men sit around one and eat wedge shaped sections directly from the pan with wooden spoons. The women and children serve themselves from the second, eating from pottery bowls.

During the ritual of the paella cooking on the Giner terrace, which takes about an hour from start to finish, sangria was served in small green tumblers.

"A small amount of cognac makes the difference," one Giner brother insisted.

"We make it with white wine, too, but then the garnish must be slices of apple and pear only," Marie Giner said.

"The meat [usually chicken and lean pork] must be cut up small with the cleaver and browned very well," a Giner cook said as the flames were fanned by a breeze and the oil sizzled around the meat.

Paella in Valencia and Alicante is drier than the same dish prepared in Barcelona or Catalonia, the Giners explained, and a true paella à la Valenciana is made with chicken, snails and green beans with no seafood or peas. In Alicante a paella is likely to have chicken, lean pork, shrimp and clams.

As the Giner brothers tended the paella pan, adding the ingredients in sequence, the women talked of other family food favorites. Burnt onion rings, they agreed, were an acquired taste but delicious and easily cooked on a cast-iron griddle with no oil or salt until very dark brown. The onions are then dressed with oil, wine vinegar and salt.

Miss Giner described a simple sauce of pressed garlic (with the skins left on), lemon juice, oil, salt and parsley that they use on broiled lamb chops and on swordfish.

Thin slices of ham and olives were passed as the rice melange bubbled, releasing heady aromas. A tossed green salad was the only accompaniment to the paella. Dessert was wedges of melon. Sangria was served throughout the meal.

Following is the Giner method for preparing paella adapted from the recipes of Sebastian and Peter Giner.

Yield: 10 servings

¾ cup Spanish olive oil

1 (2½- to 3 -pound) frying chicken, cut
    into 2-inch pieces

1 pound lean pork, cubed

1 teaspoon paprika

1 onion, finely chopped

3 cloves garlic, peeled

½ teaspoon saffron threads

1 quart hearty homemade chicken broth,
    warmed

2 cups long-grain rice

2 teaspoons salt

2 tablespoons finely chopped fresh parsley

1 cup lima beans (see note)

1 pound shrimp, shells left on

1 large tomato, cut into wedges

1 green bell pepper, seeded and cubed

1 quart clams, scrubbed

1. Pour oil into a paella pan set over a fire of twigs, and check that pan is level. Add chicken and pork pieces and allow to cook slowly until well browned, 20 to 25 minutes, stirring occasionally with a wooden spoon.

2. Sprinkle meat with paprika and stir. Add onion and cook 5 minutes longer.

3. Crush garlic cloves with a pestle and mortar until well mashed. Add saffron and crush. Stir in 1 tablespoon of broth. Add to cooked meat in pan along with rice. Stir to coat rice with oil.

4. Slowly add remaining broth, salt, parsley and lima beans. Bring to a boil. Simmer slowly, stirring occasionally, until rice is barely tender, about 15 minutes.

5. Add remaining ingredients and cook until rice and shrimp are cooked and clams open, 8 to 10 minutes. If mixture appears to be getting too dry at any point during cooking, extra chicken broth may be added.

NOTE: If frozen lima beans are used, they will require less cooking time and may be added with the shrimp.

June 23, 1966: "Campfire Paella Turns into a Family's Labor,"
by JEAN HEWITT

Politics and Clams

It must puzzle the inhabitants of other continents who take any interest in our institutions to account for the apparently intimate relationship between politics and clams. Not that we would have the foreign reader infer that all politics are immediately connected with that shell-fish. There are localities where this is impossible. The prairies of the boundless West, as the dwellers of the region euphemistically term a certain section of our country, are destitute of the clam-bed and, necessarily, of the political clam-feast. The provender consumed at party gatherings in the West and South-west, unless furnished by the casual inn-keeper, is generically known as barbecue. A barbecue includes an infinite variety of victual, but the main part, of course, is the carcasses of sheep, pigs, or even oxen, roasted whole. Hence the name "barbecue." A Southern barbecue is no mean occasion; and at one of these feasts the generous Southern hospitality finds expression in masses of savory and toothsome viands that might tempt the palate of an anchorite. The Kentuckian may tickle his epicurean fancy with barbecued hog, or the Illinoisan regale himself with oxen roasted whole and decorated with the flag of our country, while toasts and politics go round; but there are no clams for them. This strange feast, a relic of aboriginal days, is reserved for the people who live on the border of the North Atlantic.

There are two distinct varieties of politic clam-feeding—the chowder and the clam-bake. The first of these has, of late years, been given up to the cities; the other is a more truly rural festival. In New York, the political clam-chowder excursion has partly succeeded the old-time "target shoot," with which it was once combined. The Dennis O'Dennis Association, for example, keenly alive to the necessity of electing to some office the gentleman whose name is borne upon their social banners, hire several of those ancient omnibuses which look now so very queer when seen on the streets. These venerable stages are covered with signs bearing the proud title of the Dennis O'Dennis Assocation; they are decorated with Chinese lanterns, drawn by spanking eight-horse teams, and filled with enthusiastic connoisseurs of politics and clams. The vehicles, musical with sleigh-bells and brass bands, parade the streets, and convey the association to some point whence they reach the scene of chowder-making. When there, Dennis O'Dennis, duly filled with pride, clams, and other good things, makes a speech. His friends and supporters, to whom he stands as a sort of political godfather, cheer and ask for more. Then certain gentlemen of the Dennis O'Dennis ward—whatever that may be—make other speeches. When mellow with chowder and enthusiasm, the association go home merrily, making the streets of New York very musical as they wind back and are lost in the dim recesses of Mackerelville or Cow Bay. Nor does it detract from the enjoyment of the festive company to know that the total cost of the entertainment is charged to the account of Mr. O'Dennis' campaign expenses.

Very different from this is the political clam-bake of New England. Not that the chowder, by itself, is to be despised. So great a statesman as Daniel Webster did not think it beneath his dignity to give instructions in the art of chowder-making, and his recipe for concocting that noble dish is, we venture to say, quite as well known in Massachusetts as his famous speech on Bunker Hill. But the political gatherings on the shores of Rhode Island, Connecticut, Maine, and Massachusetts, at which the clam is baked and eaten, is broader, freer, and more generous than the petty club-feasts of New York Democratic politicians. Speakers and voters, with wives and children, are gathered in from great distances. The superheated stones on the sea beach, after due preparation, are heaped with layers of green corn, sweet potatoes, chickens, suckling pigs, and various other products of farm and garden; but the solid substratum of all is the clam—hard-shelled, blue in color, indigestible, and meditative as to his nativity and ultimate destiny. Over this mass is spread damp seaweed to produce steam, and over all is fixed a canvas cover. When the heap is cooked and disinterred, the orgies begin. And when hunger is more than appeased, and everybody is full, the band begins to play. After that the orators make speeches; and as it was for this that the clam-bake was invented, all that has gone before is but a mere overture.

It is thought that the feast of clams is especially necessary to a Summer political campaign. In New England, people travel many miles to get at the sea and a political clam-bake. In New Hampshire, where the want of an outlet was severely felt, special provision was made for this very purpose by allowing the Granite State a narrow passage to the sea between Maine and Massachusetts. A glance at the map will show that this curious concession was made for the purpose that the institution for which every son of WEBSTER'S State is ready to die—the clam-bake of domestic politics. A comic poet has remarked of the clam that its case is exceeding hard. Torn from its silent bed to disturb the stomach of a noisy politician, there seems to be some mysterious law of compensation by which such extremes are brought together. Noise and silence, activity and calm—never were more diverse qualities combined than when the politician swallows the clam. But hard as is the case of this much-sought-for bivalve, the problem of its real relation to American politics is still harder of solution. How far nations and races are affected by their diet we are just beginning to learn. How far the clam enters into questions of protective tariff, contraction, and human liberty, we may in time discover.

September 16, 1875

Shrimps Wilder

Anyone who would disparage the country cooking of America simply doesn't know what good is. Much of the finest food in Florida comes from the kitchens of non-urban areas where they beat a little love into biscuits and say grace before meals.

The residents of the agrarian community of Pahokee do not boast that they are 40 miles from the gold coast of Palm Beach, but they say with pride that they are 10 miles from Belle Glade, said to be the largest shipping point for vegetables in the world.

It seems that almost everyone cooks for pleasure in Pahokee, and a knowledgeable exponent of local cuisine is a planter named Edgar Wilder. When he is not tending his 5,000 acres of sugar cane, he is often tending the fires of a charcoal grill.

To judge from a recent visit, it appears that every meal in the Wilder home is a feast. But it is feasting without gluttony.

Florida is very proud of its native shrimp, which the Wilders often cook on their outdoor grill.

Yield: 4 to 6 servings

2 pounds shrimp

2 cloves garlic, finely minced

½ cup peanut or olive oil

¼ cup soy sauce

½ cup fresh lime or lemon juice

3 tablespoons finely chopped fresh parsley

2 tablespoons finely minced scallions, including green part

Salt and freshly ground black pepper to taste

1. Shell and devein shrimp but leave on last tail segment. Dry and place in a shallow dish.

2. Combine remaining ingredients and pour over shrimp. Let stand 3 to 4 hours in refrigerator.

3. Thread shrimp on skewers (discard marinade) and place them on a grill over hot coals. Coals should be approximately 3 inches from shrimp. Cook quickly, about 3 minutes on one side. Turn and cook 3 to 5 minutes longer. Serve with lime or lemon wedges.

March 1, 1985: "Food News: Florida Country Cooking,"
by CRAIG CLAIBORNE

Grilled Soft-Shell Crabs with Scallions, Ginger and Deep-Fried Capers

"I was born on the Fourth of July," Alfred Portale says. "I guess that explains my passion for fireworks. When I was working on this dish, I kept thinking of fireworks, of explosive flavors and colors.

Yield: 4 servings

8 jumbo soft-shell crabs, cleaned

3 tablespoons minced shallots

3 tablespoons fresh lemon juice

6 tablespoons white Port

6 tablespoons heavy cream

1 (2-inch) slice fresh ginger, peeled and finely grated

1 stick unsalted butter, broken into pieces

Salt and cayenne pepper to taste

¾ cup peanut oil for deep-frying

¼ cup large capers, drained

2 tablespoons olive oil

Salt and freshly ground white pepper to taste

1 large scallion, finely sliced

1. Clean crabs if necessary: remove eyes, then turn each crab on its back and remove apron. Turn over again, lift up flaps at each end and pull out spongy gill tissue. Pat dry and refrigerate until ready to grill.

2. Place shallots in saucepan with lemon juice and white Port, and reduce over medium heat until about 2 tablespoons of sauce remain, 5 to 7 minutes. Add cream and ginger. Bring to a boil, and reduce by a third, to about 3 tablespoons.

3. Reduce heat to very low, and whisk in butter, one piece at a time, whisking constantly. Season with salt and a pinch of cayenne pepper; strain sauce through a fine-mesh strainer. Adding a few drops of lemon juice if necessary. Set sauce aside and keep warm.

4. In a heavy-bottom saucepan, heat peanut oil to 325 degrees. Carefully drop in drained capers and deep-fry until buds open fully and are crisp, about 2 to 3 minutes. Remove with a slotted spoon, and drain on paper. Set aside and keep warm.

5. Preheat outdoor grill until medium-hot. Brush crabs with olive oil, and season with salt and white pepper. Grill approximately 3 to 4 minutes on each side, until nicely crisp.

6. Arrange crabs on a serving plate, drizzle sauce over them, and sprinkle with scallions and deep-fried capers. Serve with summer vegetables and a dry white wine.

June 25, 1986: "For Liberty's 100th, Fireworks from 12 Top Chefs,"
by NANCY HARMON JENKINS; recipe from ALFRED PORTALE,
Gotham Bar and Grill, New York City

Grilled Lobster

Throughout the world, lobster is commonly considered the height of elegance: it's often the priciest thing on the menu in restaurants, served on fancy platters with lots of fanfare. But in many parts of the Northeast, lobster is a casual favorite, no fancier than steamed mussels or fried clams. Steamed or boiled or mixed with mayonnaise for lobster rolls, there is nothing elegant about it.

Yet grilled lobster falls somewhere in the middle of this spectrum, and that's only because the grilling itself presents challenges. Grilling lobster is not like grilling a steak, because the animal is alive in your kitchen. And this freaks many people out.

If it doesn't bother you, put the critter on a table and cut it in half lengthwise. Then start grilling. But there is an easier way: boil the lobster for two minutes, just until it turns red (for four or five minutes if it weighs more than a pound and a half). The point here is to kill the lobster. Afterward, plunge it in ice water, then keep it cool until you're ready to cook. If you really don't want to put a live creature into a pot, many fishmongers or supermarkets will do this for you.

When the lobster has gone through the first stage of cooking, cut it in half: Start at the head, right between the eyes, and make one long cut until you can split the lobster in half and separate it. There's no need to remove any organs; just put the lobster, cut side up to start, on a hot grill for a few minutes. Turn it and continue cooking until the meat is opaque and firm to the touch: that's it.

Time: About 20 minutes   **Yield:** 4 servings

Salt

4 live lobsters (about 1½ pounds each)

Ground black pepper

Lemon wedges or melted butter, or both

1.   Bring a large pot of water to a boil, and salt it. Using tongs, put lobsters in pot, one by one. Cover pot. Cook just until bright red, about 2 minutes each (longer if lobsters weigh more). Remove lobsters from pot with tongs; plunge into a bowl, sink or bucket of ice water; then continue cooking, or refrigerate for up to a day.

2.   Prepare grill; heat should be medium-high and rack about 4 inches from fire. Cut lobsters in half along back, then grill for 3 to 5 minutes on each side, starting with cut side up, sprinkling with salt and pepper before turning. Lobster is done when meat is firm and opaque. Serve with lemon wedges or melted butter, or both.

August 6, 2010: "The Minimalist: Grilled Lobster with a Head Start,"
by MARK BITTMAN

Alice Waters's Charcoal Grilled Lobster

Yield: 6 servings

¾ cup coarse salt

6 (1- to 1½-pound) lobsters

½ pound (2 sticks) unsalted butter

Reserved coral (if any) from lobsters

Coarse salt and pepper to taste

Fresh lemon juice to taste (optional)

3 to 4 tablespoons heavy cream

1. To prepare the lobsters for grill, bring 10 to 12 quarts of water with coarse sea salt to a rapid boil. Water should be very salty. One by one plunge lobsters into boiling water for 1 minute.

2. Prepare a low wood charcoal fire and put lobsters on it. Cook them for 10 to 12 minutes, turning frequently.

3. To serve lobsters, cut them in half lengthwise through center of head and tail and remove stomach sack and coral. Reserve coral for sauce and remove lobsters to a warm serving platter.

4. Gently melt butter and whisk reserved coral into it. Season with salt and pepper. Add lemon juice to taste and cream to sauce. Serve sauce in small dishes.

June 30, 1985: "Food: Home Barbecue: Enhanced Possibilities,"
by MOIRA HODGSON;
recipe from The Grilling Book, *by A. Cort Sinnes,*
with recipes by JAY HARLOW (Aris Books, 1985)

CHAPTER EIGHT

Vegetables and Sides

Barbecue is not the place for shy, demure vegetables. Since the main dish is often so brawny with flavor, the sides that accompany it need to be able to stand up for themselves. A good barbecue side also needs to provide some contrast in texture, traditionally provided by the crunchiness of slaw or the smooth creaminess of beans, both of which are well represented here. But more and more in recent years, other vegetables have made their way onto barbecue menus. Early on, Alice Waters offered Grilled Ratatouille (page 263), which is re-markable in its simplicity and clean flavors, as are Molly O'Neill's Tuscan Grilled Summer Vegetables (page 258). Corn on the cob is a long-time favorite at summer barbecues, and no wonder—it's crunchy and sweet, and you can eat it with your hands. Martha Rose Shulman dresses hers with a smoky, creamy, spicy chipotle mayon-naise that elevates this cook-out stalwart to unexpected gastronomic heights (page 270).

Five famous French chefs—(l-r): Pierre Franey, Jacques Pepin, Roger Fessaguet, Jean Vergnes, and Rene Verdon—are gathered for a gourmet picnic on Gardiner's Island, New York, in 1965.

Tuscan Grilled Summer Vegetables

Yield: 4 to 6 servings

1 eggplant (1 pound), sliced into 2-inch-thick rounds

1 white eggplant (½ pound), sliced into 2-inch-thick rounds

2 zucchini, cut into 2-inch-thick slices lengthwise

2 summer squash, cut into 2-inch-thick slices lengthwise

2 patty pan squash, cut into 2-inch-thick slices

1 tablespoon kosher salt

3 large, ripe tomatoes, cut into 2-inch-thick slices

1 yellow bell pepper, seeded and cut into 2-inch-wide slices lengthwise

1 red bell pepper, seeded and cut into 2-inch-wide slices lengthwise

1 medium red onion, cut into ½-inch-thick slices

1 cup coarsely chopped fresh basil

2 cups Tuscan Marinade (recipe follows)

1. Put eggplant, zucchini and squash in a colander. Add salt. Toss and set aside to drain for 30 minutes.

2. Rinse, pat dry and place in a large, shallow glass or ceramic dish. Add remaining vegetables and basil. Cover with marinade. Refrigerate for 8 hours, turning once.

3. Grill over hot coals until tender, about 5 to 10 minutes per side.

Tuscan Marinade

Yield: 1 cup

⅓ cup red wine

⅓ cup olive oil

2 cloves garlic, minced

1 tablespoon grated orange zest

½ cup minced fresh sage leaves

¼ cup minced fresh rosemary leaves

1 tablespoon black peppercorns, crushed

Combine all ingredients in a glass or ceramic bowl. Refrigerate in an airtight container for up to 3 days.

May 31, 1992: "Food: A Good Grilling,"
by MOLLY O'NEILL

Salada de Legumes (Brazilian Vegetable Salad)

Yield: 12 to 16 servings

3 potatoes (about 1¼ pounds)

Salt to taste

1½ pounds broccoli

¾ pound green beans

¾ pound small zucchini

1 head cauliflower (about ¾ pound)

¾ pound carrots

3 pounds fresh peas in the pod, or two
10-ounce packages frozen peas

2 cans hearts of palm, drained

2 cups chopped celery

1½ cups chopped scallions

3 cups mayonnaise, preferably homemade

1 tablespoon imported mustard

1 teaspoon Worcestershire sauce

Fresh lemon juice to taste

Tabasco sauce to taste

1. Put potatoes in a saucepan and add cold water to cover and salt to taste. Bring to a boil. Let simmer, partly covered, about 20 minutes or until tender. Drain and let cool.

2. Prepare remaining vegetables. Cut broccoli head into bite-size "flowerettes."

3. Trim off ends of green beans. Cut beans into half-inch lengths.

4. Trim off ends of zucchini. Cut into ½-inch-thick slices. Cut slices into ½-inch strips. Cut strips into ½-inch cubes.

5. Break off or cut cauliflower into small, bite-size "flowerettes."

6. Trim carrots. Cut them into ¼-inch or slightly larger cubes.

7. Shell peas. There should be about 2 cups.

8. Put broccoli, green beans, zucchini, cauliflower, carrots, and peas into individual saucepans (the same saucepan may be used as each vegetable is cooked). Add cold water to cover and salt to taste. Bring to a boil and simmer until each vegetable is crisp tender. The broccoli and cauliflower should each require about 8 to 10 minutes; green beans and zucchini, 2 to 3 minutes each; the carrots, about 1 to 2 minutes. As each vegetable is ready, empty it into a colander or sieve and run cold water over it to chill quickly. Drain each vegetable.

9. Peel potatoes. Cut into ½-inch-thick slices. Cut each slice into ½-inch strips. Cut each strip into ½-inch cubes.

10. Combine all the cooked, well-drained vegetables in a mixing bowl.

11. Quarter hearts of palm lengthwise. Cut quarters into ½-inch lengths. Add to bowl.

12. Add celery and scallions. Add mayonnaise and remaining ingredients and blend well. Taste salad and add more seasonings as desired.

September 7, 1977: "In the Style of the Gauchos: A Brazilian Barbecue,"
by CRAIG CLAIBORNE; recipe from DOROTHEA ELMAN

Throw Another Melon on the Barbie

The grill, as everyone knows, is the best place to cook a steak, but that doesn't mean you have to cook a steak every time you fire up the grill. Putting aside the philosophical reasons to avoid beef, let's discuss the practicality and appeal of those foods that take on a delicious, chewy, steaklike texture when grilled—for example, vegetables.

I don't mean your basic Tuscan-style grilled vegetables. This is about thicker, meatier "cuts" that may not remind you of a real steak but that might mean you don't miss your steak either.

The most famously meaty vegetable is actually a fungus. Longtime vegetarians may groan at the prospect of eating anything resembling a portobello-mushroom burger—which remains the only meatless option on many casual-dining restaurant menus—but everyone else should give them a try. Brushed with an intense marinade flavored with fish sauce (and loads of black pepper) or soy sauce and charred over an open flame, portobello mushrooms expertly mimic the darkly savory flavor and chewy texture of steak.

There are unexpected vegetables that can fill in for steaks as well. Take sweet potatoes and jicama. Each is naturally starchy, not meaty, but when you cut them into planks and sear them just until tender inside, they develop a fabulously smoky crust. Eggplant slices can also be grilled until tender without losing a certain rugged chew. And thick hunks of cabbage can be nearly as much fun to tear into as a porterhouse.

Vietnamese-Style Portobello Mushrooms

Time: 20 minutes   **Yield:** 4 servings

¼ cup peanut oil

¼ cup fresh lime juice

2 tablespoons chopped fresh mint, plus
more for garnish

1 fresh hot red chili (like Thai), seeded
and minced

1 tablespoon fish sauce

½ teaspoon sugar

Salt and lots of black pepper

4 large portobello mushrooms, stems
removed

1.   Heat a charcoal or gas grill until quite hot and put rack about 4 inches from flame. Mix together oil, lime juice, mint, chili, fish sauce and sugar and sprinkle with salt and pepper. Brush mushrooms all over with about half of this mixture.

2.   Grill mushrooms with tops of their caps away from heat until they begin to brown, 5 to 8 minutes. Brush with remaining marinade and turn. Grill until tender and nicely browned all over, 5 to 10 minutes more. Garnish with more mint and serve hot, warm or at room temperature.

Chili-Rubbed Jicama Steaks with Queso Fresco

Time: 20 minutes

1 tablespoon neutral oil, like grapeseed
or corn

1 teaspoon chili powder

Salt and black pepper

1 pound jicama, peeled and cut into
½-inch-thick slices

4 ounces queso fresco cheese, crumbled

Lime wedges for serving

1. Heat a charcoal or gas grill to moderately high heat and put rack about 4 inches from flame. Combine oil, chili powder and a sprinkle of salt and pepper in a large bowl. Add jicama and toss until well coated.

2. Put jicama on grill and cook until golden brown, about 2 minutes. Turn slices and sprinkle with queso fresco; continue to grill for another 2 to 3 minutes. Serve hot or at room temperature with lime wedges.

Teriyaki Cabbage Steaks

Time: 1 hour   **Yield:** 4 to 6 servings

½ cup soy sauce

½ cup mirin (or ¼ cup honey mixed with
¼ cup water)

1 tablespoon minced fresh ginger

1 teaspoon minced garlic

2 tablespoons chopped scallions

1 small cabbage, cored and
cut crosswise into 1½-inch-thick slices

2 tablespoons neutral oil, like grapeseed
or corn

Salt and black pepper

Lemon wedges for serving

1. Heat a charcoal or gas grill to moderately high heat, keeping part of grill cool for indirect grilling, and put rack about 4 inches from flame. Combine soy sauce and mirin in a small saucepan over medium-low heat and cook until mixture begins to bubble, 2 to 3 minutes. Remove pan from heat and add ginger, garlic and scallions.

2. Brush cabbage slices with oil and sprinkle with salt and pepper. Put cabbage on cool part of grill and close grill cover. Cook, checking and turning occasionally, until you can pierce leaves easily with a sharp knife, 40 to 45 minutes. When cabbage is tender, brush it liberally with teriyaki mixture and move it to hotter part of grill. Cook, turning once or twice and brushing with more of the sauce, until it's browned, 3 to 5 minutes.

3. Drizzle cabbage with any remaining teriyaki sauce, and serve hot or warm with lemon wedges.

Curry-Rubbed Sweet-Potato Planks

Time: 40 to 45 minutes   **Yield:** 4 servings

2 teaspoons curry powder

1 teaspoon ground cumin

1 teaspoon ground coriander

Salt and black pepper

2 pounds sweet potatoes, peeled and cut lengthwise into ½-inch-thick slices

2 tablespoons neutral oil, like grapeseed

Lime wedges for serving

1. Heat a charcoal or gas grill to moderately high heat, keeping part of grill cool for indirect grilling, and put rack about 4 inches from flame. Combine curry powder, cumin, coriander and a good sprinkle of salt and pepper in a small bowl. Brush sweet-potato slices with oil and rub all over with spice mixture.

2. Put sweet-potato planks on cool part of grill and close grill cover. Cook, checking and turning occasionally, until flesh is very tender all the way through, 20 to 25 minutes. Move planks to hotter part of grill and cook, turning once or twice, until golden brown on both sides, 3 to 5 minutes. Serve hot, warm or at room temperature with lime wedges.

Miso-Glazed Eggplant Slices

Time: 30 minutes, plus optional time for salting   **Yield:** 4 servings

1 large eggplant, cut into ½-inch-thick slices

3 tablespoons neutral oil, like grapeseed

1 tablespoon sesame oil

Salt and black pepper

½ cup miso

¼ cup honey

1. If time allows, sprinkle eggplant liberally with salt, put it in a colander in sink and let it sit for 20 to 30 minutes; rinse and pat dry with paper towels. Heat a charcoal or gas grill to medium-high heat and put rack about 4 inches from flame.

2. Combine neutral and sesame oils and brush eggplant on both sides with oil mixture. Sprinkle with salt (if you salted the eggplant, hold off) and pepper, then brush with more oil. Grill until browned on both sides, about 10 minutes total, turning once or twice and brushing with more oil if it looks dry.

3. When eggplant is almost done, whisk together miso, honey and ¼ cup hot water and generously brush eggplant with this mixture. Continue to grill for another minute or two, then serve hot, warm or at room temperature, drizzled with any remaining miso sauce.

July 10, 2011: MARK BITTMAN

Grilled Ratatouille

For a main dish serving, this may be served tossed with pasta. This recipe prepares enough vegetables for one pound dried pasta.

Yield: 6 servings

3 small Japanese eggplants

2 large red bell peppers

1 large yellow bell pepper

4 canned anchovy fillets

3 cloves garlic, peeled

1 cup extra virgin olive oil

2 medium red onions, quartered

1 zucchini, halved lengthwise

3 ripe, firm tomatoes, cut in half

Salt and freshly ground pepper to taste

2 tablespoons fresh basil, cut into thin strips

1 tablespoon capers

1.   At least an hour before cooking, light charcoal fire.

2.   Cut away stems of eggplants but do not peel. Quarter and slice them into 3-inch sticks. Place eggplant on skewers. Set aside.

3.   Roast peppers on grill until skins are blackened and loose. Remove from grill, place in a paper bag and set aside for 10 minutes. Then peel under running water, discarding stems, seeds and ribs. Slice lengthwise into strips about ¼- to ½-inch wide. Place pepper strips in a serving bowl.

4.   Chop anchovies and garlic together to make a coarse mixture. Mix in olive oil. Add ¼ cup of this mixture to pepper strips and stir. Place eggplant in remaining marinade while preparing rest of vegetables.

5.   Place onion quarters on skewers, brush with a little of marinade and grill until they are browned, almost black. Remove from skewers, chop roughly and toss with peppers.

6.   Brush zucchini with a little of marinade and grill. When browned on both sides, remove them and cut into ¼ - to ½-inch pieces. Add to other vegetables.

7.   Brush tomatoes with marinade. Grill them, cut side up, until skins are loose. Remove and cut each half into thirds. Add them, with their juice, to other vegetables.

8.   Grill eggplant sticks until they are well browned on both sides. Add to vegetables. Mix well.

9.   Add any remaining marinade to vegetables. Mix well and season with salt and pepper to taste. Garnish with basil and capers. The dish may be served immediately or set aside, but should be served at room temperature.

May 15, 1988: "Summer Pastimes: For the Adventurous Griller,"
by NANCY HARMON JENKINS; based on a recipe from
Chez Panisse Pizza, Pasta, and Calzone, *by ALICE WATERS*
(Random House, 1984)

Roasted Eggplant in Yogurt

Mrs. Mahbubeh Stave, a native of Tehran, uses an excellent and time-honored method for roasting eggplant over charcoal. The whole vegetable is turned occasionally until thoroughly tender, when the inside pulp is scooped out and mixed with yogurt and garlic.

Yield: 6 servings

2 small eggplants
1 clove garlic, very finely chopped
1 cup plain yogurt

Salt and freshly ground black pepper
to taste

1. Place eggplants on a charcoal grill and turn them frequently until they are tender, about 15 minutes (outside of eggplants may become somewhat charred and smoke-flavored).

2. Cool eggplants briefly, then, using fingers, peel off eggplant skins and discard.

3. Place eggplant pulp on a hot platter and chop it into small pieces with a knife and fork. Add remaining ingredients and mix thoroughly. Serve as a side dish with kebabs.

July 23, 1961: "From a Persian Grill,"
by CRAIG CLAIBORNE;
recipe from MAHBUBEH STAVE

Radicchio Grilled with Olive Paste and Anchovies

Time: 60 to 90 minutes, plus preparation of grill
Yield: 4 servings

4 Treviso radicchio or 2 to 4 small round radicchio, halved lengthwise, or 1 large round one, quartered

¼ cup extra virgin olive oil, plus more as needed

2 tablespoons balsamic vinegar, plus more as needed

Coarse sea salt and black pepper to taste

2 anchovy fillets (or to taste), drained

2 tablespoons olive paste or tapenade

1. Arrange radicchio cut side up in a baking dish. Drizzle with ¼ cup olive oil and 2 tablespoons vinegar. Season with salt and pepper. Marinate for 30 to 60 minutes.

2. Prepare a grill for direct grilling over medium heat. Brush and oil grate. Place anchovies in a small bowl and mash with a fork. Add olive paste or tapenade and mix.

3. Arrange radicchio on grill cut side down slightly on diagonal to bars of grill grate. Grill until lightly browned, 6 to 10 minutes, rotating each radicchio a little halfway through to create a crosshatch of grill marks. Baste with some of marinade.

4. Turn radicchio over. Spread each with a little anchovy and olive paste. Continue grilling and basting until a skewer or knife pierces radicchio easily, about 3 minutes more.

5. Transfer to plates. Drizzle with a little olive oil and vinegar.

June 28, 2011: "For These Chefs, Even Fire Can Be Improved,"
by STEVEN RAICHLEN; adapted from Le Louis XV, Monaco

Grilled Leeks
with White Beans and Blue Cheese

Yield: 4 servings

4 leeks (about 1¼ pounds)

Salt to taste, if desired

2 tablespoons olive oil

Freshly ground pepper to taste

4 cups loosely packed assorted salad
    greens, such as radicchio, chicory and
    romaine

2 ¾ cups, approximately, Blue-Cheese
    Dressing (recipe follows)

2 cups cooked white beans (page 267)

4 teaspoons chopped hard-cooked eggs

2 teaspoons finely chopped fresh chives

1. Trim off ends of leeks. Trim off all but an inch of green parts. Split lengths almost, but not quite, down to trimmed-off base. Rinse thoroughly between leaves.

2. Bring 12 cups (3 quarts) water to a boil in a saucepan and add salt to taste. Add leeks and cook 12 to 15 minutes or until tender. Remove leeks to a flat surface and cut each leek lengthwise in half. Spoon 1 tablespoon of oil over split leeks. Sprinkle with salt and pepper.

3. Meanwhile, preheat an outdoor grill to high. Put leeks on grill, cut side down, and cook about 7 minutes, turning once.

4. Remove leeks to a platter and spoon remaining 1 tablespoon oil evenly over all.

5. Cut each length of leek in half crosswise. This produces 16 pieces.

6. Put salad greens in a bowl and add about 1 tablespoon of blue-cheese dressing. Toss to blend.

7. Put equal portions of beans slightly off center on 4 salad plates. Arrange 4 pieces of leeks next to beans. Arrange equal portions of greens next to leeks. Spoon a small amount of salad dressing over leek pieces and sprinkle with chopped hard-cooked eggs. Sprinkle eggs with chives. Serve any leftover dressing on the side.

Blue-Cheese Dressing

Yield: About ¾ cup

½ cup (about 3 to 4 ounces) crumbled
   blue cheese
2 tablespoons red wine vinegar
¼ cup heavy cream

Salt to taste, if desired
Freshly ground pepper

1. Put cheese in a bowl and mash to a paste with a fork.

2. Add vinegar and beat with a wire whisk until blended. Continue beating with whisk while adding cream. Add salt and pepper to taste.

White Beans

Yield: About 2 cups

⅔ cup dried white beans, such as Great
   Northern, picked over and rinsed

Salt to taste, if desired.

1. If you wish, soak beans overnight to shorten cooking time. Place beans, soaked or otherwise, in a saucepan and add about 4 cups water. Bring to a boil and cook 20 minutes. Add salt to taste.

2. Continue cooking, adding water as necessary, until beans are tender, 45 minutes to an hour, depending on whether beans have been soaked. Drain.

March 20, 1988: "Food: The Fires of Spring,"
by CRAIG CLAIBORNE with PIERRE FRANEY;
recipes from ALFRED PORTALE,
Gotham Bar and Grill, New York City

Great Roasted Peppers:
First, Get a Pile of Wood

If learning how to cook is easy enough for a child to do (and it is), the continuing-education portion of it lasts a lifetime. I remember the first time I roasted a pepper, 44 years ago. It was a revelation. And I remember when I thought I had it down pat, 15 years ago, around the time I wrote my first Minimalist column.

I didn't have it mastered, of course. And the other day I was reminded just how fantastic good peppers are when roasted nicely, and just how easy they are. If, that is, you have a good fire going. Because roasted peppers are at their best when they're charred peppers, and they're best charred over wood, or at least real charcoal.

They're also at their best when they're the right peppers. (We're talking about sweet peppers here, not chilies, which are a whole other story.) Of this I was reminded about a week ago, when I had lunch at De la Riva, a fine Madrid restaurant with traditional daily menus, the kind of place where a gentleman brings a variety of appetizers and then asks if you'd rather have meat, fish or both.

On the day I visited with some friends, among those appetizers was a plate of gorgeous long, bright-red peppers, perfectly roasted and peeled, sprinkled with salt and drizzled with oil. They looked the way they should, with a few stubborn bits of blackened skin still clinging to the flesh.

Two days later, wandering through the markets of a small town in Greece, I came across those same kinds of peppers, in both red and green. Their name doesn't matter much: what matters is that they're long, tapered and fairly regular, without a lot of wrinkles and twists. And what matters is that they're not bell peppers, which are usually not only weaker in flavor but also more difficult to peel.

I'm not a lifelong fan of green peppers, which are the unripe specimens of whatever color they'll eventually become, but in recent years I've come to appreciate them as not inferior but different. I bought about a dozen of each.

The market was one where you claim space on the counter and load your stuff there. Unnoticed, a fellow shopper's bag of 30 or 40 green peppers joined my pile. So when I got back to the house I was staying in, I had not 25 but something like 60 peppers. This, plus a huge grill with lots of dry wood, gave me a chance to practice my craft; over all, a happy accident.

I make roasted peppers many ways: with a fork over a gas flame, as I did 44 years ago (a silly method, unless maybe you are doing only one); in an oven or gas grill (efficient, but imperfect); in a broiler (better); and over charcoal, which is the best way, unless you have (as I did last week) actual wood.

Nothing smells better, nothing tastes better and nothing works better than blistering, direct heat. Both nights, I roasted the peppers, and some whole eggplant, as the fire began to peak; I grilled the rest of my food as it cooled a bit. The results were, if not optimal (personally, I could have done with a few anchovies), a bit of a revelation.

Charred Peppers

Time: 1 hour or more, largely unattended
Yield: About 6 servings

12 or more long peppers, red, green or both
2 or so tablespoons olive oil
Salt (optional)

Fresh lemon juice, capers or anchovies (optional)

1. Build a hot fire. Wood is ideal, charcoal a good second. The rack shouldn't be more than 3 to 4 inches from fire, and you can start peppers just as flames begin to die down; there will be no flare-up.

2. Put peppers on grill without crowding too much. As they blacken, turn them so they char on all or at least most surfaces. As they finish, transfer to a bowl, where you can pile them up. (There is no need to put them in a paper bag, as you may have read.)

3. Let cool. Peel and seed, using as little water as you can to rinse remaining seeds and skin from peppers. But don't be too compulsive: a few seeds and bits of skin are fine. Also, the closer to whole the peppers remain, the more attractive they are.

4. Serve, dressed with olive oil, and salt if desired. Lemon juice won't hurt; neither will capers or anchovies. These will keep, refrigerated, for at least a week.

May 29, 2012: MARK BITTMAN

Grilled Corn on the Cob with Chipotle Mayonnaise

The spicy dip that I serve with grilled corn (as well as with steamed or boiled corn) is sort of like a Mexican aïoli, pungent with garlic, smoky and spicy with chipotle chilies. You can also serve it as a dip with vegetables or chips, or use it as a flavorful spread for sandwiches and panini. The recipe makes more than you'll need for six ears of corn—if you're having a crowd for a barbecue, you'll have enough.

Yield: Makes 1 cup of dip

6 to 12 ears corn

2 large cloves garlic, cut in half, green shoots removed

¼ teaspoon salt

1 large or 2 small chipotle chilies in adobo, seeded

1 teaspoon adobo sauce from canned chilies

¼ cup mayonnaise, preferably Hellmann's or Best Foods

½ cup thick plain low-fat yogurt

1.   Light a medium-hot grill while you prepare your corn. Remove outer leaves of husk, leaving two layers. Gently pull down remaining leaves, pull off silk and fold husks back up, covering corn. Cut 12 to 24 pieces of butcher's string about 6 inches long, and moisten them with water. Tie cobs at top and midway down with the wet string. Place in a bowl or a sink full of cold water, and soak for 15 to 30 minutes while you prepare chipotle dip.

2.   Place garlic in a mortar and pestle with salt, and mash to a smooth paste. Add chipotle, and mash together with garlic. Stir in adobo sauce, mayonnaise and yogurt, and mix together well.

3.   When coals of your grill are medium-hot, remove corn from water and pat dry. Place on grill, and grill until corn is uniformly charred, turning ears often. This could take anywhere from 10 to 20 minutes, depending on heat. Remove from grill and, holding onto ears with a kitchen towel, cut away strings and remove leaves. Wrap corn in a kitchen towel to keep warm.

4.   Serve with chipotle dip. Place a generous spoonful on a plate, and roll corn in it or spread it on corn with a knife.

ADVANCE PREPARATION: You can prepare the corn for grilling hours ahead. The dip will keep for a day in the refrigerator.

July 9, 2009: "Recipes for Health: Sweet Corn: Getting an Earful in Summer," by MARTHA ROSE SHULMAN

Corn Pudding

"Corn is a wonderful thing for the Fourth of July," says Gene Hovis. Mr. Hovis is a New York cook, consultant and food writer transplanted from North Carolina's Piedmont region. "This recipe falls somewhere between my grandmother's spoonbread, and the way she'd scrape corn off the cob and steam in a pot with bacon fat," Mr. Hovis says. "We were also great barbecue eaters—everybody in North Carolina barbecues for the Fourth of July."

Yield: 8 to 10 servings

2 tablespoons butter, melted

6 to 12 ears fresh corn, enough to make
    4 cups

6 large eggs, at room temperature

2 cups half-and-half

½ cup all-purpose flour

Salt and freshly ground white pepper
    to taste

2 tablespoons sugar

1 teaspoon ground nutmeg

4 tablespoons (½ stick) soft butter

1. Grease a round 10-inch baking dish, 2½ inches deep, with melted butter. Set aside.

2. Remove husks and silks from corn. With a sharp knife, carefully scraping upward, slice corn kernels into a bowl, reserving cobs. With back of knife, carefully scraping downward, scrape remaining part of kernels and milk from cob into the bowl. You should have about 4 cups in all.

3. Preheat oven to 350 degrees.

4. Use steel blade of food processor. Place corn in container with eggs, half-and-half, flour, salt and pepper to taste and sugar and process just 3 to 4 seconds. This can be done in 2 batches if necessary. Pour mixture into prepared baking dish. Sprinkle top with nutmeg and dot with softened butter.

5. Place dish in a larger pan in preheated oven. Add enough hot water so that it comes halfway up sides of baking dish. Bake 1 hour, or until a knife inserted in center comes out clean. Serve immediately.

*June 25, 1986: "For Liberty's 100th, Fireworks from 12 Top Chefs,"
by NANCY HARMON JENKINS; excerpted from
Gene Hovis's Friends and Relations (Little, Brown)*

Corn-Bread Salad

Connoisseurs know corn bread has a shelf life just slightly longer than a soufflé. Hot out of the oven, it reaches perfection in those few heartbeats between the moment you get the butter slathered on and the second it starts to fall apart as you take the first bite.

Once corn bread goes cold on you, it's no longer fit to be bread. It never reheats well; it just dries out and turns to crumbs. And then it starts to get interesting.

Leftover corn bread is one of the great secret ingredients in summer, when it seems there's always corn bread left over, along with the excess coleslaw and barbecued chicken. Even at its most forlorn, hours or a day old, it still has a strong corn flavor and crunchy texture. You just can't eat it by the wedge. You have to crush it into crumbs and make it into a topping for baked fish, break it up and treat it like couscous in a salad or cube it and use it in savory puddings or as a stuffing for baked tomatoes or zucchini.

I started recycling stale corn bread instead of tossing it out many summers ago after interviewing a Texas barbecue impresario who called himself Crazy Sam Higgins. Along with educating me in the finer points of rubs as opposed to sauces and in smoking rather than grilling, he passed along a recipe for a corn-bread salad that he swore was so good, anyone who made it would be tempted to eat the whole bowlful. An ingredient list that started with a full pint of mayonnaise made it easy to understand why.

But it's more than just unflinching richness that makes this salad irresistible. It's the contrast of color and crunch in natural complements for corn: scallions, celery, bell pepper, pimentos, toasted pecans and juicy tomatoes. I bake corn bread just to let it go cold so I can eat this dish.

Time: 10 minutes, plus chilling   **Yield:** 8 servings

About 6 cups stale corn bread (recipe follows), crumbled

1 large green bell pepper, seeded and diced

1 to 2 large ripe tomatoes, diced

2 stalks celery, diced

1 large bunch scallions, trimmed and chopped

1 (2-ounce) jar pimentos, drained and chopped

2 cups mayonnaise

½ cup toasted pecans, chopped

Salt and fresh black pepper to taste

1. Combine all ingredients in a large bowl and mix well.

2. Chill before serving.

Corn Bread

Time: 25 minutes   **Yield:** 8 to 10 servings

1 tablespoon plus ¼ cup peanut or
    corn oil
1 cup coarse yellow cornmeal
½ cup flour
1 teaspoon baking powder

1 teaspoon baking soda
½ teaspoon salt
2 tablespoons sugar or honey
2 eggs
1 cup buttermilk

1. Preheat oven to 425 degrees. Use 1 tablespoon oil to grease 9-inch square or round pan.

2. Combine dry ingredients in one bowl, whisk wet ingredients in another. Combine and stir together just until batter is moistened but not smooth. Spread into pan and bake 15 to 20 minutes, until toothpick inserted in center comes out clean. Cool on rack.

*June 20, 2001: "Encore! Encore! For a Star of Summer,"
by REGINA SCHRAMBLING; adapted from* I'm Glad
I Ate When I Did 'Cause I'm Not Hungry Now,
by SAM HIGGINS (Crazy Sam Enterprises, 1984)

Hobo Pack of New Potatoes, Red Onion and Orange

Hobo packs are foil-wrapped parcels of vegetables or meat that cook directly in the hot coals.

A well-composed hobo pack, with adequate moisture and herbs, braises stout vegetables like potato chunks, broccoli or brussels sprouts thoroughly in about 15 to 25 minutes.

The packs are quick to throw together at home, and they stack nicely in the cooler. We composed our pack to be a warm spin on potato salad, with new potatoes, red onions, oranges, oregano and garlic, tossed in a mustardy vinaigrette.

Time: 35 minutes   **Yield:** 6 servings

1 pound new potatoes (about 14 golf-ball size), trimmed and cut into quarters

2 medium navel oranges (about ¾ pound), peeled and sectioned

4 pieces orange zest, 1 inch long and ½ inch wide

2 medium red onions (about ¾ pound), ends trimmed and each cut into 6 pieces

2 tablespoons tightly packed fresh oregano leaves

1 teaspoon coarse salt

½ teaspoon freshly ground black pepper

2 tablespoons grainy mustard

1 tablespoon balsamic vinegar

2 cloves garlic, minced

3 tablespoons olive oil

1.　In a large bowl, mix potatoes, oranges, orange zest, red onions, oregano, salt and pepper. In a small bowl, whisk mustard, vinegar and garlic, then add olive oil in a thin stream, whisking until emulsified. Pour dressing over potato and orange mixture, and toss gently to combine.

2.　Tear off 6 (12-inch) sheets of heavy-duty foil and stack in two piles (three sheets each). Pour half the potato mixture into center of each top sheet of foil. Shape ingredients on each sheet into a pile 6 inches by 6 inches, and pour any dressing left in bowl over piles. Wrap ingredients in each pile in top sheet of aluminum foil, sealing it tightly, followed by second and third sheets.

3.　Prepare a fire in a grill. When flames have subsided and coals are glowing, carefully remove grill grate, and set hobo packs directly on coals. With tongs, gather a few hot coals around hobo packs. Replace grill grate, and let cook 25 minutes. Remove grill grate, and with kitchen mitt or spatula, remove hobo packs from grill. Cut a vent through top of each pack, and serve.

June 30, 2004: "When the Park Is Your Kitchen,"
by MATT LEE and TED LEE

Potato Fondantes with Oregano

I use medium-size new potatoes for this dish, leaving them unpeeled, cutting them in half lengthwise and placing them cut side down in one layer in a large nonstick skillet. A little oil and butter are added along with the oregano, salt and some water. The potatoes cook in the water awhile and finally absorb most of it, with the remainder evaporating just as the potatoes are nearly cooked through. They start to brown at this point in the oil and butter, becoming crusty on the outside while remaining wonderfully moist and creamy in the center—hence the name *fondantes*, which means "melting" in French. These potatoes are so good that sometimes we eat them for lunch with just a green salad as an accompaniment.

Time: 40 minutes   **Yield:** 6 servings

3 pounds medium potatoes (about 8)

1½ tablespoons unsalted butter

2 tablespoons canola oil

3 tablespoons coarsely chopped fresh oregano

½ teaspoon salt

1.   Do not peel potatoes, but remove any eyes and dark spots. Cut potatoes in half lengthwise and arrange them cut side down in one layer in a large (preferably 10-inch) nonstick skillet.

2.   Add 1½ cups water, butter, oil, oregano and salt. Bring mixture to a boil over high heat, and cover. Reduce heat to medium, and cook for 20 to 25 minutes. (At this point, water should be gone and potatoes should be browning nicely in butter and oil.)

3.   Turn potatoes over and sauté them for 2 to 3 minutes to brown them lightly on other side.

July 15, 1992: "The Purposeful Cook: Tangy Barbecued Chicken: Crispy Skin, Split Legs and All," by JACQUES PEPIN

Smashed Potatoes with Tapenade

Time: 45 minutes   **Yield:** 4 servings

For the tapenade

1 cup Kalamata olives, minced

2 tablespoons capers, rinsed and minced

1 teaspoon grated lemon zest

1 tablespoon fresh lemon juice

1½ teaspoons fresh thyme leaves,
    chopped

½ cup extra virgin olive oil

Freshly ground black pepper

For the potatoes

4 red or white potatoes (about 5 ounces
    each), well scrubbed

2 tablespoons red wine vinegar

1 bay leaf

6 black peppercorns

Salt

1.   In a bowl, combine all ingredients for tapenade. May be refrigerated up to one week in a tightly sealed container.

2.   Put potatoes in a saucepan with vinegar, bay leaf, peppercorns, salt and water to cover. Bring to a boil, then reduce heat and continue to cook for 12 to 15 minutes, until potatoes are soft. Drain. While still warm, place potatoes in a dishtowel and gently crush with flat of your hand on a hard surface.

3.   Heat a seasoned griddle over medium-low grill until a drop of water sizzles on surface. Place potatoes on griddle and cook without moving until golden brown, about 5 minutes. Remove potatoes to a plate with a wide spatula. Top uncooked side with 2 tablespoons tapenade, pressing it into potato. Put potatoes back on griddle, tapenade side down, and cook another 5 minutes. Serve immediately.

May 20, 2009: "Grilling Over Wood as a Sweaty, Smoky Sport,"
by OLIVER SCHWANER-ALBRIGHT;
adapted from Seven Fires: Grilling the Argentine Way,
by FRANCIS MALLMANN with PETER KAMINSKY (Artisan, 2009)

Hot Potato Salad with Herbs

Yield: 6 to 8 servings

2 pounds red-skinned potatoes

Salt to taste

2 tablespoons finely chopped shallots

½ cup finely chopped onion

3 tablespoons chopped fresh parsley

2 tablespoons chopped fresh basil or
    tarragon

1 teaspoon imported mustard, preferably
    Dusseldorf or Dijon

3 tablespoons wine vinegar

Dry white wine

Vegetable or olive oil

Freshly ground pepper to taste

1. Place potatoes in a kettle and add water to cover to a depth of ½ inch above tops of potatoes. Add salt to taste and bring to a boil. Cook 20 minutes or until tender when tested with a sharp knife. Drain immediately.

2. The important thing in preparing this salad is to peel potatoes while still hot. When they are cool enough to handle, peel potatoes and slice them into a bowl.

3. Sprinkle with shallots, onion, parsley and basil.

4. Add mustard and vinegar to an 8-ounce glass measuring cup. Add enough wine to make ⅔ cup. Add enough oil to make 1 cup. Add salt and pepper to taste and pour this over hot potatoes. Toss gently to blend and serve lukewarm.

July 4, 1968: "It's the Fourth of July,
and That's an Occasion for a Barbecue,"
by CRAIG CLAIBORNE

Korean Potato Salad

Korean potato salad is similar to American potato salad in that its dressing is mayonnaise-based, but the Korean version sometimes uses julienned rather than chunked potatoes and also contains carrots, peas, scallions and chives. It's far from conventional and far from bland.

Yield: 4 to 6 servings

1 pound potatoes, julienned or shredded

1 pound carrots, julienned or shredded

½ cup fresh or frozen peas

½ cup mayonnaise

3 tablespoons rice vinegar

½ cup chopped fresh chives, plus more for garnish

¼ cup chopped scallions, plus more for garnish

Salt and pepper to taste

1. Cook potatoes and carrots in salted boiling water until barely tender, about 5 minutes; add peas for last minute of cooking. Drain and rinse with cold water.

2. Whisk together mayonnaise and vinegar; toss with potatoes, carrots, peas, chives and scallions. Garnish with more chopped scallions and chives, season with salt and pepper to taste and serve.

June 1, 2011: "Eat: Backyard Bulgogi,"
by MARK BITTMAN

Sesame Spinach and Tofu

Yield: 4 to 6 servings

1 tablespoon minced garlic

2 tablespoons sesame oil

1 pound fresh spinach, chopped

½ pound extra-firm tofu

1 tablespoon soy sauce

Pinch sugar

1 tablespoon sesame seeds

Cook garlic in sesame oil over medium-high heat for 1 minute; add spinach and cook, stirring occasionally, until it begins to wilt. Crumble in tofu and stir until warmed through. Stir in soy sauce, sugar and sesame seeds. Serve hot or warm.

June 1, 2011: "Eat: Backyard Bulgogi,"
by MARK BITTMAN

Drunken Beans

Yield: 6 to 8 servings

2 slices bacon, diced

1 onion, diced

2 cloves garlic, minced

2 cups dried pinto beans, picked over,
    rinsed, soaked overnight and drained

1 quart chicken broth, homemade or
    low-sodium canned or water

2 cups beer

2 to 4 jalapeños, thinly sliced, with seeds

Salt and freshly ground pepper to taste

2 tablespoons chopped fresh cilantro

1.   Place bacon in a large pot over medium heat until fat is rendered. Remove bacon with a slotted spoon and discard. Add onion and garlic and cook until soft, about 5 minutes. Add beans, broth or water and beer. Bring to a boil, reduce heat to a simmer and cook for 30 minutes.

2.   Stir in jalapeño slices. Cook until beans are tender, about 30 minutes, adding water if necessary to keep beans covered. Season with salt and pepper to taste. Stir in cilantro and serve immediately.

July 4, 1993: "Food: The Texas Three-Step,"
by MOLLY O'NEILL;
adapted from The New Texas Cuisine,
by STEPHAN PYLES (Broadway Books, 1993)

Spicy Baked Beans

Long, slow cooking is ideal for dried beans, which should never be served al dente and which offer an opportunity to push the envelope to delectable lengths on cooking time. Left undisturbed in a slow oven, a crock or casserole of beans becomes richly flavorful.

Time: 9 hours, including 4 hours soaking time for beans
Yield: 6 servings

1 cup dried kidney beans
½ cup dried cannellini beans
½ cup dried Great Northern or navy
  beans, picked over and rinsed
2 sprigs fresh thyme
1 tablespoon cumin seeds
1 tablespoon olive oil
1 large onion, chopped
1 carrot, chopped
½ pound smoked slab bacon, cut into
  ½-by-1-inch nuggets
1 jalapeño, seeded and chopped

2 cloves garlic, chopped
½ cup crushed canned tomatoes
4 ripe plum tomatoes, diced
¼ cup maple syrup
¼ cup light brown sugar
1 bay leaf
Grated zest of 1 orange
½ tablespoon crushed black peppercorns
⅓ cup chopped fresh cilantro leaves
¼ cup cider vinegar, or more, to taste
Salt to taste

1. Place all beans in a bowl, cover with water to a depth of 2 inches, add thyme and soak at least 4 hours.

2. Heat a heavy 3-quart casserole. Add cumin seeds, and cook, stirring, until they dance around and smell toasty. Remove them.

3. Add oil, onion, carrot and bacon to casserole, and sauté over medium heat 10 minutes, until bacon is golden. Stir in jalapeño, garlic and toasted cumin seeds.

4. Preheat oven to 250 degrees.

5. Drain beans, and add them along with canned and fresh tomatoes, maple syrup, brown sugar, bay leaf, orange zest and crushed peppercorns. Stir in all but 1 tablespoon of cilantro, and add 3 cups water. Cover, and bring to a slow simmer. Place in oven, and cook 2 hours.

6. Add vinegar and salt to taste. Return to oven 2½ hours longer, until liquid has been absorbed but beans are still moist. Adjust seasonings, adding more vinegar and salt if needed. Sprinkle with remaining cilantro, and serve.

January 28, 1998: "Giving Dinner a Long, Lazy Day in the Oven,"
by FLORENCE FABRICANT; adapted from
Biba restaurant, Boston, Massachusetts

Ralph R. Olswang, A Manufacturer: Inventor of the Outdoor Grill for Barbecues Dies at 56

Ralph R. Olswang, whose childhood fondness for the outdoor life led to the development of the multimillion-dollar backyard barbecue industry, died Saturday of a heart attack at his summer home in Martha's Vineyard, Mass.

Mr. Olswang, who was 56 years old, held patents on numerous inventions ranging from portable folding grills to electric fire igniters. He lived at 104 Garden Road, Scarsdale, N.Y.

He first perceived a market for inexpensive portable barbecue grills while he was working as a buyer of housewares for the May Company in Baltimore during World War II. At the time most grills were made of cast iron.

Mr. Olswang moved to Scarsdale in 1944 and began to manufacture lightweight grills of his own design. One early grill was made of an aluminum blanket container to which Mr. Olswang added four legs and a container for charcoal.

Later the company of which he was a co-founder, Kamkap, Inc., began to manufacture the grills.

When outdoor barbecues became popular, Mr. Olswang introduced round grills and developed folding ones for easy movement on picnics and outings.

Other Inventions

He himself was an outdoor cooking enthusiast. "We became quite well-known in Baltimore because we used to cook outside during the summer on rude makeshift grills," his wife said yesterday. "Absolute strangers would say, "If I bring the steak, will you show us how to cook it?"

Mr. Olswang also invented a folding backyard clothes drier, many children's toys and a pan lid containing an electronic catalyst to remove cooking odors. This device, which was originally designed for oil refineries, was later modified for use over kitchen ranges.

Mr. Olswang was an avid fisherman who would travel hundreds of miles for a day's fishing when a season opened.

Mr. Olswang was born in New York and was graduated from the Massee Preparatory School in Stamford, Conn., and from the New York University School of Finance and Retailing.

He worked for the May Company from 1930 to 1944, then with Kamkap, Inc., until

1962. At his death he was consultant to the Straightline Manufacturing Company in Cornwells Heights, Pa., producer of barbecue grills; Powrpak, Inc., Bridgeport, Conn., manufacturer of aerosols, and the Rotary Drier Corporation, Hatfield, Pa.

Mr. Olswang is survived by his widow the former Aline De Santos-Saxe, and two daughters, Mrs. Joseph N. Strumer of Briarcliff Manor, N.Y., and Mrs. Robert L. Rosenfeld of Princeton, N.J.

A funeral service will be held at 10 A.M. tomorrow at the Jewish Community Center, White Plains. Burial will be in Mount Pleasant Cemetery, Hawthorne, N.Y.

July 12, 1965

Rooster Baked Beans

Nothing compliments barbecue more than corn on the cob and baked beans. At Red Rooster Harlem, the chef and owner Marcus Samuelsson serves a bowl of beans with a jerk bacon appetizer that's unreal. Taste them yourself, then try reproducing them at home.

1 onion, chopped

4 cloves garlic, minced

4 jalapeños, chopped

6 slices bacon, chopped (optional)

3 tablespoons olive oil

½ cup tomato paste

6 cups vegetable or chicken stock

1 pound dried Great Northern beans, picked over, rinsed and soaked overnight

½ cup molasses

Salt and freshly ground pepper

1. In a pot, sauté onion, garlic, jalapeños and bacon in olive oil until onion is translucent and garlic is lightly golden.

2. Add tomato paste, stock and beans. Stir and bring to a simmer, cover, then let cook for 4 to 5 hours.

3. Add molasses and cook for another 10 minutes. Add salt and pepper to taste. Serve and enjoy!

July 11, 2011: "Food: Now Grilling: Juicy Summer Chicken," by BRIAN NICHOLS; recipe from MARCUS SAMUELSSON, Red Rooster Harlem, New York City

Black Beans and White Rice

Time: About 1 hour, plus 4 hours' soaking   **Yield:** 8 to 10 servings

For the beans

1 pound dried black beans, picked over
   and rinsed
2 bay leaves
1 small onion, cut in half
2 cloves
4 cloves garlic, peeled
½ green bell pepper, seeded
1 teaspoon ground cumin
1 teaspoon oregano

For the sofrito

2 tablespoons olive oil
½ small onion, finely chopped
2 cloves garlic, finely chopped
½ green bell pepper, finely chopped
3 scallions, trimmed and finely chopped
Salt and freshly ground black pepper
6 cups cooked rice

1. Soak beans in cold water to cover by 3 inches for at least 4 hours.

2. Pin bay leaves to onion halves with cloves. Combine beans, soaking liquid, onion halves, garlic, bell pepper, cumin and oregano in a large heavy pot, and bring to a boil. Skim off any foam. Reduce heat, and gently simmer, covered, for 45 minutes, stirring occasionally. Add water as needed to keep beans submerged. Remove onion, garlic, bay leaves and bell pepper, and discard.

3. Prepare the sofrito. Heat oil in skillet. Add onion, garlic, bell pepper and scallions, and cook over medium heat until just beginning to brown, 3 minutes. Stir into beans. Uncover pot, and continue simmering beans until soft and soupy, 15 minutes more. Season with salt and pepper.

4. Ladle beans into deep bowl. Serve rice in separate bowl. Have each guest ladle beans on a portion of rice.

December 22, 1999: "In Miami, Christmas Eve Means Roast Pig,"
by STEVEN RAICHLEN; recipe from ESTHER VEIGA

Jamaican Rice with Coconut and Red Beans

Time: 40 minutes   **Yield:** 8 servings

2 teaspoons vegetable oil

1 clove garlic, minced

1 scallion, including green parts,
  trimmed and thinly sliced

2 cups uncooked white rice

1 (14-ounce) can coconut milk, well
  shaken

1 sprig fresh thyme

1 Scotch bonnet chili (optional)

About 3 cups cooked small red beans
  or pinto beans (start with 1½ cups
  dried beans or use two 15-ounce
  cans, drained)

Pinch salt

Freshly ground black pepper to taste

1.   In a heavy saucepan with a tight-fitting lid, heat oil over medium heat. Add garlic and scallion and cook, stirring, just until softened, about 3 minutes; reduce heat if necessary to prevent browning.

2.   Add rice, coconut milk, 1 cup water, thyme, Scotch bonnet if using, beans and salt. Bring to a boil over high heat, then stir well, reduce heat to very low, cover tightly and cook without disturbing for about 25 minutes, until liquid has been absorbed and rice is very tender. Add black pepper and more salt, if desired. Fluff before serving.

July 2, 2008: "Sweet Heat: For Jamaicans, It's About Jerk,"
by JULIA MOSKIN; adapted from Jerk from Jamaica,
by HELEN WILLINSKY (Ten Speed Press, 2007)

Rice Chello

This dish has one outstanding characteristic. After partial cooking it is steamed with butter until an amber crust forms on the base. This crust, prized at Iranian meals, is served as a garnish with rice.

Yield: 6 servings

½ teaspoon saffron threads

3 cups rice

6 tablespoons butter, melted

1 medium onion, thinly sliced

1 medium potato, peeled and thinly sliced

Salt and pepper to taste

1. Soak saffron in ¼ cup cold water 30 minutes.

2. Add rice gradually to 1 quart boiling salted water. Return to a boil and cook until rice is half done, about 10 minutes. Drain rice in a colander.

3. Add butter to kettle in which rice cooked. Arrange onion and potato slices in a flat layer on bottom. Cook briefly, then spoon rice over vegetables to make a pyramid. Season with salt and pepper.

4. Sprinkle saffron over rice and cover with a damp tea towel. Cover kettle and steam rice over very low heat until done, 30 to 45 minutes. Add more melted butter or water if necessary to prevent burning. Note, however, that vegetables and bottom layer of rice turn the color of amber. This crust is served with the dish.

5. When rice is done, place bottom of kettle in cold water and let stand 3 to 5 minutes. This helps extricate the brown layer from the kettle.

July 23, 1961: "From a Persian Grill," by CRAIG CLAIBORNE; recipe from MAHBUBEH STAVE

Crusty Macaroni and Cheese

The dirty little secret of an honest macaroni and cheese is often American cheese. American cheese is simply cheddar or colby that is ground and emulsified with water, said Bonnie Chlebecek, a test kitchen manager at Land O'Lakes in Arden Hills, Minnesota.

"The process denatures the proteins in the cheese," she said, "which in plain English means that it won't clump or get grainy when you melt it. With natural cheese, it's much harder to get a smooth melt. The cheese industry and the Food and Drug Administration call a cheese "natural" if it has been produced from milk, as cheddar and mozzarella (and virtually all other nonindustrial cheeses) are.

Plain American cheese, labeled pasteurized process cheese, contains the most natural cheese and is the best for cooking.

Time: 1 hour 15 minutes   **Yield:** 8 to 12 servings

3 tablespoons butter

¾ pound extra-sharp cheddar cheese, coarsely grated

¾ pound American cheese or cheddar cheese, coarsely grated

1 pound elbow pasta, boiled in salted water until just tender, drained and rinsed under cold water

⅛ teaspoon cayenne pepper (optional)

Salt to taste

⅔ cup whole milk

1. Preheat oven to 375 degrees. Use 1 tablespoon butter to thickly grease a 9-by-13-inch baking dish. Combine grated cheeses and set aside 2 heaping cups for topping.

2. In a large bowl, toss together pasta, cheeses, cayenne pepper if using and salt to taste. Place in prepared pan and evenly pour milk over surface. Sprinkle reserved cheese on top, dot with remaining 2 tablespoons butter and bake uncovered 45 minutes.

3. Raise heat to 400 degrees and bake 15 to 20 minutes more, until crusty on top and bottom.

January 4, 2006: "The Winter Cook; Macaroni and Lots of Cheese," by JULIA MOSKIN

Jicama Coleslaw

Yield: 6 to 8 servings

2 cups shredded radicchio or
  red cabbage
½ cup grated carrots
1 small onion grated
1 medium jicama, peeled and julienned
1 red bell pepper, seeded and julienned
1 yellow bell pepper, seeded and julienned

1 jalapeño, seeded and minced
½ cup mayonnaise
1 tablespoon honey
1 tablespoon raspberry vinegar
1 tablespoon fresh lemon juice
Salt and freshly ground pepper to taste

1. In a large bowl, combine radicchio or cabbage, carrots, onion, jicama, bell peppers and jalapeño.

2. In a small bowl, whisk together mayonnaise, honey, vinegar, lemon juice, salt and pepper. Add to salad and toss to coat well. Refrigerate until ready to serve.

July 4, 1993: "Food: The Texas Three-Step,"
by MOLLY O'NEILL; adapted from
The New Texas Cuisine,
by STEPHAN PYLES (Broadway Books, 1993)

Onion Slaw

Time: 10 minutes   **Yield:** 8 servings, ½ cup per serving

¼ cup reduced-fat ricotta cheese

½ cup plain nonfat yogurt

2½ tablespoons red wine vinegar

1 teaspoon celery seeds

⅛ teaspoon celery salt

2 teaspoons prepared mustard

3 tablespoons finely grated onion

½ tablespoon minced garlic

1 tablespoon sugar

2 cups finely grated cabbage

1 teaspoon chopped fresh parsley

1. Puree ricotta in a food processor or blender until very smooth. Add yogurt and vinegar, and process thoroughly. Remove from processor, and add celery seeds, celery salt and mustard.

2. Combine onion, garlic, sugar, cabbage and parsley, and fold in dressing.

July 12, 1995: "Eating Well," by MARIAN BURROS;
recipe from JEFFREY BUBEN,
Vidalia restaurant, Washington, D.C.

Zucchini with Basil Oil and Mint

Yield: 4 servings

4 small zucchini, trimmed and cut across
    into ¼-inch-thick slices
2 teaspoons Basil Oil (page 181)
1 teaspoon fresh lime juice

1 tablespoon minced fresh mint
1 teaspoon salt, plus more to taste
Freshly ground black pepper to taste

1. Bring a medium pot of lightly salted water to the boil. Add zucchini and blanch for 45 seconds. Drain and immediately place under cold running water until cool. Drain again and pat dry.

2. Place zucchini in a bowl and toss with basil oil, lime juice, mint, salt and pepper. Taste and adjust seasoning if desired. Can be served cold or at room temperature.

May 30, 1993: "Food: A Summer Drizzle,"
by MOLLY O'NEILL

CHAPTER NINE

Desserts and Breads

Summer fruits, particularly peaches, have a great affinity for smoke. Ligaya Mashan goes beyond mere grilling as she adds an Egyptian savory spice mix and blueberries to her greenmarket-inspired dessert (page 300). In a similarly offbeat dessert, Francis Mallmann combines rosemary with oranges and burnt sugar for a nuanced offering prepared on a griddle set on the grill (page 299). Good as *a la minute*, hot-off-the-grill desserts are, there is a long tradition of bringing covered dishes to a cookout and Susan Spicer's Danish Rice Pudding with Fresh Cherries (page 308) is a fresh new take on an old favorite.

Bread is too often relegated to the task of allowing you to pick up barbecued food without getting your fingers sticky, but artisan bread toasted on the grill, rubbed with garlic and herbs, wakes up the palate in a way that plain old bread doesn't. Steven Raichlen offers a raft of grilled bread recipes from around the globe. Biscuits, too, are a favorite at barbecues, and Janet Bukovinsky's oven-baked Sweet Potato Biscuits (page 325) demonstrate that there are new tricks to be found even in old recipes.

Couple dining out on barbecue in 1985.

A Dessert That Dances on the Grill

Aquick grilled fruit dessert is packed with conceptual allure. Take delivery speed, for instance. Lifted from the grill in minutes flat, the fruit slumps into a puddle of caramel and smoke, revived by a scoop of ice cream. There. It is so dashingly of the moment, so breathlessly outside. But does it work?

Any grill master will tell you that by building a fire properly and using techniques suitable to the food in question, the grill becomes a device over which you can exercise mastery and control. Professionals do this by creating microclimates with hardwood coal set at varying heights and a big time-out zone where they can drag their quarry when it gets in trouble.

In this case, I had my doubts: setting any soft, juicy fruit, cut to reveal its innermost flesh, on a blazing grate, made me wince. Pineapples and bananas, sure; they show stamina under fire. But how does one grill a plum?

I am not, by nature, a cautious cook, and have the scars to prove it. But my impulse with soft fruits was to go gentle: medium-ripe and medium-hot. I called my friend Chris Schlesinger for counsel. Mr. Schlesinger, a chef and co-author of *The Thrill of the Grill* and other books, has not cooked a meal indoors since 1985. "You want ripe fruit, hot fire," he said.

Grill marks? Hokey pokey razzle-dazzle, Mr. Schlesinger said. Refuel your fire after dinner and go for a uniform sear. (The hottest fires come to you by way of hardwood charcoal. It burns hot, dies fast and gets out of town.)

It turns out that grilling pieces of plum, nectarine and mango is not much different from searing any one of them face down in a ripping hot pan. The temperature rages but the pain is brief.

The grill is not intended to scar the fruit or fan its flesh with aromatic smoke. In fact, soft fruits do not really cook at all. Sprayed or brushed with grapeseed oil, they warm, soften and glow. Turn the seared halves carefully with tongs and let their backsides heat up. Paint their faces, toward the end, with a sweet, racy glaze, and they shine.

The sweet glaze is the key, by the way. A nectarine with perfectly civil nibbling properties turns acerbic on the grill.

In the context of that glaze, I wanted to offer each fruit its own flavor wardrobe, a sort of ethnic dress. I saw the plums in sweet soy and sesame, the mangoes with lime and yogurt, the nectarines in spiced honey butter.

Liquid sugars are typically enlisted to baste grilled fruits. But the usual choices were not doing it for me. Maple syrup and honey ran; molasses fought. It must have been a nostalgic impulse—or a faint counter-grilling protest—that prompted me to toss a can of sweetened condensed milk into the grocery cart along with the fruit. I cannot remember ever having cooked with it. Yet its sinewy viscosity flowed with the affection of an old friend.

In fact, the very properties that make sweetened condensed milk cloying and old-fashioned make it peerless for glazing grilled fruit. Loaded with sugar, creamily bland and just about thick enough to chew, the sluggish milk-in-a-can carries flavors forward, then stays where it is placed. It goes straight to caramel on the grill but, lofted with aromatics to suit a particular fruit, becomes a fine sauce to drizzle as well. I kept the can, and canned the yogurt, butter and honey instead.

As I observed the fruits that came fainting off the grill, I thought that they might like a bit of cushion, and that we, the diners, might like an in-lieu-of-crust option. Like fat slices of grilled cinnamon toast for the nectarines, and chubby bolsters of sweet sticky grilled rice for the plums and mangoes.

A confetti shower of seeds or berries, ice or whipped cream, and a piece of fruit gets dressed up fast, so fast, in fact, that it prompts me to wonder: will I bother to bake a fruit pie this summer?

Grilled Mango with Sweet Sticky Rice Cakes and Pistachios

Time: 40 minutes, plus 1 hour's chilling for rice cakes   **Yield:** 4 servings

For the sweet sticky rice cakes

1 cup short-grained rice, rinsed

1 tablespoon sugar

¼ teaspoon fine sea salt

For the sauce

3 tablespoons sweetened condensed milk

2 teaspoons finely grated lime zest

1 teaspoon fresh lime juice

½ teaspoon rose water

Pinch fine sea salt

For the mangoes and garnish

2 large ripe mangoes, cut in two
  lengthwise

Grapeseed spray or oil

1 lime, sliced ¼ inch thick

1 tablespoon finely chopped raw
  pistachios

1.   For the sweet sticky rice cakes: Combine rice and 1 cup water in a 10-cup rice cooker or heavy 2½-quart saucepan. If using rice cooker, cover and cook until light goes on. Let rest 10 minutes. If using pot, cover and bring to a simmer over medium heat. Reduce heat to low, and simmer gently until water is absorbed and rice is tender, about 15 minutes. Turn off heat, wrap lid in a clean kitchen towel, replace lid and let saucepan rest on hot burner for 10 minutes.

2. Turn rice onto a sheet pan and spread to cool. Turn into a bowl, and add sugar and salt. Toss with fingers to combine. Roll rice with wet hands into eight 3-inch balls. Flatten balls into cakes and transfer to plate. Cover and chill at least an hour.

3. For the sauce: In a bowl, combine all ingredients and stir to combine. Set aside.

4. Heat a gas grill to high or make a hot fire in a charcoal grill, raking coals to one side to come within 3 inches of upper grill rack. Make shallow cross-hatch pattern in each mango fillet with a paring knife. Dry this side of the fruit with paper towels, and spray or brush lightly with grapeseed oil. Place fruit slices cut side down on rack, and grill without turning about 1 minute. Turn fruit skin side down, and cook 30 to 45 seconds more. Brush cut surface with sauce. When fruit is warm and soft, turn and grill glaze side down until spotty brown, about 30 seconds. Pull to cool side of grill.

5. Spray or brush rice cakes with grapeseed oil. Place on rack and grill 1 minute per side. Brush each surface with sauce, and grill until spotty brown, about 2 minutes total. Dry lime rounds with paper towels; spray or brush with oil, and grill until edges are burnished, 1 minute.

6. Place rice cakes on plate, top with mango and lime rounds, drizzle with additional sauce and sprinkle with pistachios. Serve.

Grilled Nectarines with Cinnamon Toast and Berries

Time: 20 minutes, plus 1 hour to macerate currants
Yield: 4 servings

For the sauce

1 tablespoon bourbon

1 tablespoon currants

3 tablespoons sweetened condensed milk

2 teaspoons minced candied ginger

¼ teaspoon ground cardamom

Pinch fine sea salt

For the cinnamon toast

2 tablespoons sugar

¼ teaspoon ground cinnamon

2 tablespoons unsalted butter, softened

4 slices slightly stale white bread, ½ inch
    thick

For the fruit and garnish

2 large ripe nectarines

Grapeseed spray or oil

1 cup blueberries, strawberries or
    raspberries (or a combination)

1. For the sauce: Heat bourbon in a small saucepan. Add currants, stir, cover and remove from heat. Set aside at room temperature for at least one hour, and up to four. In a small bowl, combine condensed milk, ginger, cardamom, salt and macerated currants, and stir to combine.

2. For the cinnamon toast: In small bowl, stir sugar and cinnamon together. Add butter, and stir until smooth and incorporated. Spread half the butter on one side of bread slices. Place buttered side on parchment or waxed paper. Spread remaining butter on second side. Set aside.

3. Heat a gas grill to high or make a hot fire in a charcoal grill, raking coals to one side of grill to come within 3 inches of upper rack. Cut nectarines in two, and pit them. Dry cut side of fruit with paper towels, and spray or brush lightly with grapeseed oil. Place fruit halves cut side down on grill, and cook without turning, about 1 minute. Turn fruit skin side down, 30 to 45 seconds more. Brush cut surface with sauce. When fruit is warm and soft, turn and grill glaze side down until spotty brown, about 30 seconds. Pull to cool side of grill.

4. Place toast on grill for 10 seconds. Turn and grill 10 seconds more. Repeat until sugar and butter have melted and toast is brown. Divide grilled nectarines and toast among 4 plates; garnish with berries. Serve.

Grilled Plums with Star Fruit

Time: 15 minutes   **Yield:** 4 servings

For the sauce

1 tablespoon sesame seeds

3 tablespoons sweetened condensed milk

¾ teaspoon soy sauce

½ teaspoon dark toasted sesame oil

1 tablespoon dark brown sugar

¼ teaspoon ground cinnamon

For the plums and star fruit

6 small or 4 medium, ripe black plums

Grapeseed spray or oil

1 star fruit, sliced ¼ inch thick

2 tablespoons powdered sugar

Sweet Sticky Rice Cakes (page 295; optional)

1. For the sauce: Place sesame seeds in a small skillet, and toast over medium heat until golden, about 5 minutes. Remove from heat and set aside. In a small bowl, combine condensed milk, soy sauce, sesame oil, brown sugar and cinnamon; stir to combine. Set aside.

2. Heat a gas grill to high or make a hot fire in a charcoal grill, raking coals to one side of grill to come within 3 inches of upper grill rack. Cut plums in two and pit. Dry cut side of fruit with paper towels, and spray or brush lightly with grapeseed oil. Place fruit halves cut side down on grill, and cook without turning about 1 minute. Turn fruit skin side down, and cook 30 to 45 seconds more. Brush cut surface with sauce. When fruit is warm and soft, turn and grill glaze side down until spotty brown, about 30 seconds. Pull to cool side of grill.

3. Place star fruit on grill for 45 seconds. Holding slices with tongs, dip grilled side in powdered sugar; turn and grill until burnished, 30 seconds more. Divide plums and star fruit among 4 plates and serve, with grilled rice cakes if desired.

July 21, 2004: KAY RENTSCHLER

Burnt Oranges with Rosemary

A gratifying end to a grilled meal.

Time: 15 minutes   **Yield:** 4 servings

4 oranges, halved, peeled and pith
   removed
2 tablespoons fresh rosemary

½ cup sugar
1 cup plain thick Greek yogurt

1.   Place oranges cut side up on a plate and sprinkle rosemary on top, pressing it into oranges so it adheres. Sprinkle with ¼ cup of sugar.

2.   On a grill, put a 12-inch cast iron skillet over medium heat until a drop of water sizzles on surface. Spread remaining ¼ cup sugar in skillet and when it starts to caramelize, place oranges cut side down on sugar. Let cook for 3 to 4 minutes, not moving oranges, so cut side burns nicely and oranges soften.

3.   To serve, place 2 orange halves in a bowl with ¼ cup yogurt, and drizzle with burnt sugar juices from skillet.

May 20, 2009: "Grilling Over Wood as a Sweaty, Smoky Sport,"
by OLIVER SCHWANER-ALBRIGHT;
adapted from Seven Fires: Grilling the Argentine Way,
by FRANCIS MALLMANN WITH PETER KAMINSKY
(Artisan, 2009)

Grilled Peaches with Dukkah and Blueberries

I did not taste a fresh peach until I was 28 years old. In our house in Hawaii, we ate canned peaches, the flesh lurid and spongy, slick with syrup. We stowed them next to the canned litchis and the Spam, a shelf above the powdered milk.

I didn't care for them: too sweet. But my father loved them, especially with cottage cheese. It was a treat he rationed himself carefully, a habit ingrained, perhaps, from his childhood in England during the Second World War. My mother, who survived the Japanese occupation of the Philippines, had a similar faith in food built to last.

I knew what peaches were supposed to look like. I'd seen them in books: *Momotaro* (*Peach Boy*), *James and the Giant Peach*. Later, in high school, there was J. Alfred Prufrock, dithering. Did I dare to eat one?

Not until I moved to New York, where one day, my incredulous boyfriend (now husband) handed me an intact, fuzzy peach, and said, "It's time." I grudgingly took a bite.

Oh, those lost years.

I am making up for it now. I love the velvety skin, how it dimples at the touch when it's ripe. I love the eternal surprise when you break through the skin and the juice trickles down your tongue.

This is a fruit that needs no adornment. Or so I thought until this summer, when I stopped by the Kitchen Porch stall at the farmers' market on Martha's Vineyard. There I discovered dukkah, an Egyptian blend of nuts, seeds and spices that is so good you can eat pinches of it straight, as a snack.

On the night of what would have been my father's 82nd birthday, we daubed some peaches with olive oil, put them on a very hot grill, then sprinkled them with dukkah. The result was like peach pie without the crust: warm and yielding, with just a hint of char.

It was not quite canned peaches and cottage cheese. But, Dad, you would have loved it.

Yield: 4 servings

4 peaches	Whipped cream for serving
Olive oil for brushing	Blueberries for serving
1 tablespoon dukkah (see note; recipe follows)	

1. Prepare grill. Halve and pit peaches, then brush them with oil. Grill peaches cut side down for 5 minutes, without turning.

2. To serve, transfer 2 peach halves to each of 4 plates. Sprinkle with some dukkah, then spoon over some whipped cream and top with blueberries.

NOTE: Dukkah, an Egyptian nut-and-spice blend, can be purchased from kalustyans.com or made using the recipe below.

Dukkah

Sprinkle dukkah on fruit, grilled fish or zucchini.

Yield: About 1 cup

⅓ cup pistachios, lightly toasted

⅓ cup almonds, lightly toasted

1 tablespoon coriander seeds

1 tablespoon cumin seeds

1 tablespoon caraway seeds

1 teaspoon crushed Urfa pepper, or
    substitute Aleppo pepper

3 tablespoons sesame seeds, lightly
    toasted

2 teaspoons fine sea salt

1 teaspoon nigella seeds

1 teaspoon dried mint

1 teaspoon dried lemon zest

½ teaspoon dried marjoram

Roughly chop pistachios and almonds. Grind coriander, cumin and caraway seeds in an electric coffee grinder or spice mill. Combine all ingredients and mix well. Keep in a tightly covered jar.

August 5, 2011: "Last Call for Summer: Grilled Peaches with Dukkah and Blueberries," by LIGAYA MISHAN

Outdoor Cookery: The Inside Story

While his fellows are busy in backyards burning good meat and themselves,
a man here finds the craze 'out,' but not 'in.'

One of the most alarming aspects of these troubled times is not, as one might be led to believe, the rock 'n' roll singer or Khrushchev or even Brigitte Bardot. It is the spread of outdoor cooking and the way people now regard it as an Art.

In backyards from Scarsdale to Sacramento, once-rugged American men are busy with grills and skewers, sending up palls of smoke and, it is suggested, even exchanging recipes in this fashion. Worse, the cook-out, as it is called by the suburban charcoal cult, is threatening the supremacy of the formal dinner and cocktail party.

The craze is even invading Manhattan. Invitations from fashionable city friends with roof terraces or small gardens no longer read "Come to Cocktails." Now one is invited to "Fall-out for a Cook-out!" or told that "You're in—for a Cook-out!" It is even rumored that at one recent cocktail party, where one might normally expect to cram in a bit of dinner between chit-chat, the hostess was so bemused as to replace the usual turkey, ham and deviled eggs with bits of raw meat and twin hibachis—small table grills—and invite the guests to cook on their own.

Someone has come up with the statistic that, before the summer is over, at least half of all American families will fix—and try to eat—their meals outdoors. Further, they are expected to spend more than one hundred million dollars on outdoor cooking equipment this year, compared to the sixteen or eighteen million spent five years ago, and burn up more than 150,000 tons of charcoal (not to mention countless pounds of steak) as against the 60,000 tons they used in 1955. "It is," said one equipment manufacturer over an air-conditioned, soot-free steak, "bigger than Christmas!"

Women's magazines now devote practically whole issues to this way of cooking, with detailed ritual and ever more elaborate recipes that even the chef at Le Pavillon might pale at. Busybody engineers for the grill manufacturers, all too aware of the male weakness for the newest model, turn out increasingly extravagant contraptions. Even the food processors, whether they are in frozen fish or chocolate chip cookies, now insist their products can be relished only if taken with the prevailing breeze.

Cooking outdoors is, of course, as old as man and a couple of dry twigs. With today's ultra-efficient, air-conditioned kitchens, however, it could reasonably be assumed that the practice would be revived only for a community clambake, an occasional private lark or perhaps as a subtle way of informing dinner guests that hereafter they should leave the dog and their children at home.

For such rare occasions one had a simple grill—perhaps a grate salvaged from an old coal stove—a pair of tongs and some worn garden gloves. The children were kept occupied gathering wood for the fire, with the promise of being permitted to roast marshmallows for dessert, while the adults enjoyed leisurely drinks. One stuck to the simple foods, too—frankfurters, hamburgers, perhaps a steak if it were just a family affair. A man could feel he had done pretty well if the hamburgers turned out only a little removed from cinder and only one or two fell through the grill.

All that has changed, now that the old-fashioned barbecue has turned into the cook-out, and become class-conscious as well. True, one can still buy a simple grill at, say, $4.98—a grill, however, that would only bring derisive guffaws from the spit-and-skewer set and might even bring petitions from the neighbors. And hamburgers? "Yeah, come on over for a cook-out. The kids are fixin' hamburgers on the old grill, but the wife wants to know how about some marinated beef on skewers with eggplant fingers, and white bean salad with fish garnitures for a change?" Or "Yeah, it's a Sunday brunch cook-out. I figure on doing that mixed grill à l'Anglaise with béarnaise sauce, Galette potatoes and that snickerdoodle you like so much."

As the cuisine gets more and more haute, the equipment to cook it gets more and more frightening. The newest outdoor grill may come in stainless steel, brass or aluminum, with motorized spits, automatic fire starter, built-in blower, heat indicator and temperature control, counterbalance for even rotation of the meat, warming oven, hood, plastic side table, cutting board, racks for utensils. It may cost anywhere from $200 to $400 or more, without the electric cable needed to run it—unless, of course, one already has five or six electrical outlets conveniently spotted in the backyard.

Then there are the accessories, or what one home magazine refers to as "Barbecuties." These include such exotica as steer-head potholders that tinkle to alert bored guests that the cook is starting to "rustle the grub"; repellent torches to keep bugs from getting in the act; paper plates with tape on the bottom that stick to the table or lap with equal facility, and aprons with humorous sayings like "Danger, Men at Work!" or "Come and Get It." (The men who wear these are surely the same men who like to convulse cocktail parties by putting on women's hats.)

With all this fancy equipment and the involved menus served up, the simple backyard barbecue is a thing of the past. What goes on at a cook-out today may well be divided into three parts—Ritual, Fire Dance and Immolation.

The Ritual begins with the host pouring himself a double jigger as he and his wife start to move most of their household effects outdoors. It continues with the arrival of the first guests, who automatically join in the demolition process. Usually at this point the host sees his next-door neighbor, whom he loathes, puttering pointedly about his yard, and calls out a hollow invitation for him and his wife to join the party but "Don't forget to bring a few chairs."

While the host serves the drinks, pouring himself another double jigger, his wife busily occupies herself arranging things, a job she never completely finishes since there is always something she has forgotten to bring out. Meanwhile the guests make the expected remarks about the host's cooking prowess, debate the various merits of barbecue sauces, and half-heartedly try to shoo the flies off the tables.

Now the host dons chef's hat, stenciled apron and asbestos gloves, spreads the charcoal—hoping no one has noticed the grill is still grimy from last week—and prepares for the Fire Dance.

This is performed by host and guests, accompanied by smoke, the various smells of singed hair, lighting fluids and burning garbage, and the frequent sounds of coughing and minor nausea. It may last anywhere from a half-hour to two hours, depending on (a) the weather; (b) the perversity of the electric fire-starter; or (c) the methods suggested to keep the fire going when the automatic blower fails (the reverse end of a vacuum cleaner does an efficient job); (d) the kind of meat being cooked and (e) the number of drinks consumed by the host. The major part of the dance movement is performed by the guests as they move their chairs constantly to avoid the billowing smoke.

The Immolation that follows is merely the act of sighing rapturously while choking down over or underdone meat, laughing lightly at grease spots on one's best trousers or coat, gracefully helping oneself to a second portion of wilted salad while wondering if that spot you passed on the way out will still be open for dinner on the way home.

If the cook-out menu happens to include shish kebab, the Immolation becomes even more trying. In this event each guest is given half a loaf of French bread sliced through the middle. As the host advances toward the guest with the dripping skewer and the guest gingerly sidesteps to avoid being thrust, he must quickly clamp the bread over the skewer and pull, while simultaneously the host rears back.

The vogue for outdoor cooking has gone to such extremes that inevitably it raises disquieting problems for the sociologists. Why is it that the most indolent, undomesticated men, seeing a grill, some charcoal and a piece of raw meat, turn to it as they would turn to Marilyn Monroe in a bikini? And why is it that these same men, who once snarled at their wives for not serving just plain steak and potatoes, are up to their elbows in white bean salad with fish garnitures, and staying home nights zealously marinating beef? Is it because, as one wife puts it, "The poor idiots have always thought they could cook better than women"? Shrugging mysteriously, she added, "If that's what they want, let 'em." Or is it because, as another wife suggests, men have simply been pushed out of their own homes? "My husband likes broiled foods, but my kitchen is so lovely, I don't want it ruined by smoke," she said.

The theory that women are behind the male obsession with outdoor cooking is corroborated in several ways. For one thing, it is the women's magazines which are largely responsible for turning the old-fashioned barbecue into something chic. "Roughing it with elegance," they call it. And always they picture the man doing the work, as illustration for such diabolically clever articles as "So He Thinks He Can Cook Outdoors" and "Let Him Try These Recipes!" One psychologist says bluntly: "The whole thing is a plot by modern women to achieve further equality with man. And she's doing it by shifting more of the onerous household tasks on her husband."

The experts have other theories, too: that the craze stems from the return to the suburbs and the rediscovery of family life; that modern man is stirred by ancient yearnings and that the man bent over a grill is Man providing for his Brood, albeit with blackened face and burned fingers; that it is the little boy instinct, an attempt to recapture carefree boyhood days, when passing the test in outdoor cooking meant another merit badge.

This last theory is partly corroborated by an executive of a top corporation. At first he said that he liked to cook outdoors because it gave meat a different flavor. He said he used charcoal; when it was pointed out that charcoal gives no flavor—only the smoke from the drippings, if the meat is fat, gives flavor, he broke down and admitted that he was once a Boy Scout counselor.

Enough of theorizing. Curiously, as outdoor cooking becomes more and more fanciful, with equipment beginning to resemble second kitchens and the men spending more and more hours in the kitchen preparing food to cook outdoors, the craze seems well on its way to making a complete cycle, with the cooking once more back indoors where it started and, let us hope, the women doing it. Then, perhaps, we shall have no more of such stories as that of the outdoor cook who saved his potato skins and when he had enough, would cut them into bite-size pieces, put cheese, garlic and salt on them, pop them into the oven and serve them as fresh hors d'oeuvres to unsuspecting cocktail guests.

August 16, 1959: JOHN WILLIG

Skewered Grilled Fruit
with Ginger Syrup

Johnny Earles is a self-trained chef who opened a restaurant 16 years ago because, he said, he thought it would be "a hoot."

His restaurant, Criolla's, is in Grayton Beach, Florida, in the state's northwestern panhandle, an area locals self-mockingly call the Redneck Riviera. When Criolla's opened, it was funky indeed—Mr. Earles's grill was outside, his primary means of cooking was an electric wok and his tastes ran true to his roots—Cajun-Caribbean.

Never mind. Mr. Earles trusted his instincts for flavor combinations. His place has grown to be just about the only restaurant in the area with a national reputation, so he is able to make pronouncements like "What I'm doing now is a kind of international equatorial style of cooking."

But what he is really about is simplicity. "These days, I'm going for clean, direct flavors and combinations that work," he said. "It's not the easiest thing to pull off."

A dish he created that is one of easiest things to pull off is a melange of quickly grilled fruit, brushed with a ginger sauce that itself takes about five minutes to put together. The sauce is a simple sugar syrup—half sugar, half water, boiled together until the sugar melts—and is infused with a lot of ginger. You could use other flavors instead (mint, lemon verbena, thyme, even chili), but ginger seems perfect to me.

The fruit can be varied, but Mr. Earles and I have between us tried just about everything, and we agree that pineapple and bananas are the top choices. Star fruit, also called carambola, is another good choice, although not always easy to find. Many other fruits can be grilled, but pineapple browns so beautifully and banana develops such a luxurious creaminess that it isn't worth looking further.

Mr. Earles recommends gas—or clean wood charcoal—for grilling fruit. "Real wood just overwhelms the fruit with flavor," he said. "And briquettes impart a weird taste." Whatever your fuel, make the fire hot and keep the grilling time short.

Time: 30 minutes   **Yield:** 4 servings

½ cup sugar

¼ cup thinly sliced fresh ginger (don't
   bother to peel it)

4 unpeeled bananas (not overripe)

1 small pineapple

1 star fruit (optional)

1. Heat a gas or charcoal fire; it should be quite hot, with the rack positioned 4 to 6 inches from source of heat.

2. Combine sugar, ginger and ½ cup water in a small saucepan over medium heat.

Bring to a boil, and simmer for 3 minutes. Remove from heat, and let sit while preparing fruit. (Refrigerate if you're not using this right away; it will keep for at least a week.)

3. Cut unpeeled bananas into 2-inch-long chunks, and make a shallow vertical slit in the skin for peeling at table. Peel and core pineapple, then cut it into 2-inch chunks. If you're using starfruit, cut it into slices ½ inch thick.

4. Skewer fruit. Strain syrup, and brush it on fruit lightly. Grill fruit until pineapple is nicely browned, 2 to 4 minutes to a side. While it is grilling, brush it occasionally with syrup.

5. When fruit is done, brush once more with syrup. Serve hot or warm.

*July 22, 1998: "The Minimalist: Grilled Fruit: Fast and Festive,"
by MARK BITTMAN; adapted from JOHNNY EARLES,
formerly of Criolla's, Grayton Beach, Florida*

Danish Rice Pudding with Fresh Cherries

At a produce stand in Amagansett, Long Island, Susan Spicer spotted some ripe summer cherries and decided to modify her dessert recipe to include them. The original rice pudding recipe called for mixed berries.

She prefers basmati rice because it yields a firmer, toothier texture than, say, converted rice. The simple sauce can be made with most favorite summer fruits.

"My mother is Danish, and that's where the inspiration for this recipe comes from," she said while boiling the rice and milk. Thickened with whipped cream and sweetened with a reduced cherry sauce, this is no spa dessert.

"I know the whipped cream adds calories, but I love the rich, thick texture it gives," Ms. Spicer said.

Time: 1 hour   **Yield:** 8 servings

½ cup blanched almond slivers

¾ cup basmati rice

1 quart whole milk

6 tablespoons sherry

½ cup sugar

1½ cups mixed fresh cherries, pitted and sliced

½ cup red currant jelly

1 cup heavy cream

1. Preheat oven to 350 degrees.

2. Place almonds on a baking sheet, and cook in oven for 10 minutes or until they are lightly browned.

3. Combine rice and milk in a heavy saucepan over high heat. Bring to a boil, stirring constantly. Then, reduce heat to simmer and cook for about 30 minutes, stirring frequently, until rice absorbs milk.

4. Remove rice from heat, and stir in sherry, sugar and almonds. Refrigerate.

5. Meanwhile, place cherries and jelly in a saucepan over medium heat. Cook, stirring occasionally, for 5 minutes. With a slotted spoon, remove cherries to a bowl. Refrigerate.

6. Cook remaining fruit liquid over high heat until it is reduced by half. Set aside to cool.

7. Whip heavy cream until it develops firm peaks. Fold whipped cream, one third at a time, into rice pudding.

8. Assemble dessert in large wine goblets, with cherries on bottom, then a layer of rice pudding and then some slivered almonds. Pour reduced fruit liquid over everything.

July 27, 1994: "Great Cooks: Susan Spicer; Bold Flavor for Sultry Days,"
by BRYAN MILLER and PIERRE FRANEY;
recipe from SUSAN SPICER, Bayona, New Orleans, Louisiana

Guava Crème Brûlée

Time: 1 hour   **Yield:** 6 servings

8 large egg yolks

1 cup heavy cream

1 cup frozen guava puree (see note), defrosted

Sugar

1.   Preheat oven to 300 degrees. Place a kettle of water over high heat, to bring to a boil. Put egg yolks in a mixing bowl, and set aside. Place cream in a small saucepan over medium heat, to bring to a simmer.

2.   When cream simmers, remove it from heat. Whisk yolks vigorously, while adding cream in a slow, thin stream. (Do not add cream too quickly or mixture will curdle.)

3.   Pour cream mixture through a fine mesh strainer into a bowl. Add guava puree, and stir until blended. Pour into six ½-cup ramekins, and set in a small baking dish. Carefully add boiling water to come halfway up sides of ramekins. Bake until set, about 45 minutes. Remove ramekins from water, and allow to cool.

4.   Just before serving, cover surface of each ramekin with a thin layer of sugar. Caramelize sugar under a broiler or with a kitchen blowtorch, until light golden brown and crisp. Serve immediately.

NOTE: Frozen guava puree is available at Hispanic markets.

June 16, 2004: From "No Bams, No Tricks, Just Food and a City,"
by JENNIFER STEINHAUER; adapted from FELIBERTO ESTÉVEZ,
Gracie Mansion, New York City

Coriander Ginger Cake

Yield: 6 to 8 servings

1 cup molasses

½ cup sugar

¼ pound (1 stick) unsalted butter, at
 room temperature

2 eggs, beaten

2 tablespoons grated fresh ginger

1 teaspoon ground cloves

1 teaspoon ground cinnamon

1 heaping teaspoon ground coriander

1 teaspoon salt

2½ cups flour

2 teaspoons baking soda

1 cup white raisins

½ cup chopped walnuts

1. Combine molasses, sugar and butter. Add eggs, ginger, spices and salt.

2. Sift flour with baking soda three times. Add to butter mixture a little at a time, alternating with 1 cup hot water. Stir in raisins and nuts.

3. Put mixture in a well-greased mold with a capacity of 5 to 6 cups. Put the mold into a cast-iron Dutch oven with a lid on and cook over hot coals for about 20 minutes. Put hot coals from fire on top of lid and cook for another 20 minutes.

4. Unmold cake on a rack and let cool for 30 minutes before serving.

November 18, 1984: "Food: A Blazing Hearth,"
by MOIRA HODGSON; recipe from BILL and CINDY CLARK,
formerly of Amos Benedict Farm, South Salem, New York

Rose Water Adds a Subtle Kick

Rose water has a long and illustrious culinary history. Made by distilling rose petals with steam, it was created by chemists of the Islamic world in the Middle Ages. It became firmly ensconced in the cooking of the Middle East, North Africa and North India, all cuisines in which the floral and the aromatic are highly prized.

But don't think of it as an exotic ingredient used in far corners of the world. Before 1841, when vanilla became widely available (after a 12-year-old slave figured out how to hand-pollinate the vanilla orchid so that it could be commercially produced outside its native Mexico, but that's another story), rose water was also a primary flavoring in a wide range of desserts and pastries in Europe and even the United States.

It's not hard to figure out why. This relatively inexpensive product allows you, with just a drop or two, to add the alluring fragrance of one of the world's great flowers to your cooking.

In one respect, though, rose water does resemble the cologne that detractors so often compare it to: too much can have the opposite of the intended effect. The idea is that people should notice it, but have to ask you exactly what that subtle flavoring is, not quite able to put a finger on it. Uncooked, rose water has a full, rounded fragrance; heat erases some of its aromatic qualities but still leaves a warm, muted flavor.

If you're looking for clues as to how to use this distinctive flavoring, there are plenty of traditional recipes to turn to, most of them for sweets.

Taking a cue from eighteenth-century bakers, substitute rose water for the vanilla in cupcakes, puddings or scones. Or (a personal favorite) add a teaspoon or so to your next batch of French toast batter. Put a drop or two in a glass of lemonade for a remarkably refreshing summer drink—or make a rose martini in the same manner.

Rose water matches uncannily well with many fruits, drawing out their shy aromas. Try adding a bit to a bowl of strawberries, or sprinkling sliced melon, plums or peaches with rose water mixed with a bit of riesling.

Despite its lack of mainstream popularity, rose water is surprisingly easy to find in this country. Middle Eastern stores carry it, as do most Indian stores and many specialty-food stores. Most brands are fine, though the readily available Cortas, made in Lebanon, seems to me to have particularly clear flavor. Just don't buy rose syrup, which may have added sugar that will throw off your recipes.

Grilled Rose-Water Poundcake

Rose-water poundcake sliced thick and then left over the coals just long enough to get a little toasty and a tiny bit smoky is a fine finish to any summer meal. Draping it with a peach-and-rose-water compote doubles the pleasure.

Time: About 1 hour 45 minutes   **Yield:** 8 to 10 servings

½ pound (2 sticks) plus 4 tablespoons
    unsalted butter, softened
2 cups all-purpose flour
1½ teaspoons baking powder
½ teaspoon salt

1 cup sugar
5 eggs, separated
2 teaspoons rose water
Peach Compote with Rose Water (recipe
    follows)

1.   Preheat oven to 325 degrees. Butter a 9-by-5-inch loaf pan with 1 tablespoon of butter and line bottom with parchment paper.

2.   Mix flour, baking powder and salt in a medium bowl, and set side.

3.   Using an electric mixer, cream 1½ sticks of butter (12 tablespoons) in a large bowl until very smooth. Continuing to beat, slowly add sugar until light and fluffy, about 5 minutes, scraping down side of bowl as necessary. Add egg yolks one at a time, beating after each addition until incorporated. Beat in rose water. Stir in dry ingredients by hand until just incorporated.

4.   Beat egg whites until they form soft peaks, then fold them gently into butter-sugar mixture. (Batter will be quite stiff.)

5.   Transfer batter to prepared pan, smooth surface and bake until a toothpick inserted into center comes out clean, 1 hour to 1 hour 15 minutes. Allow cake to rest for 5 minutes, then invert it onto a baking rack. Turn right side up and allow to cool to room temperature before cutting into ¾-inch-thick slices.

6.   Light a medium fire in a grill. When hot, brush each slice of cake lightly with some of the remaining butter and grill until lightly toasted, about 2 minutes a side. Serve immediately, accompanied by peach compote.

Peach Compote with Rose Water

Yield: About 1½ cups

7 medium peaches

¼ cup sugar

3 teaspoons rose water

Pinch salt

1. Peel and pit peaches and chop them roughly. Combine them in a small heavy-bottomed saucepan with sugar, 2 teaspoons of rose water and salt. Cook over medium-high heat, occasionally stirring and mashing peaches lightly with a wood spoon, until they are very soft, about 10 minutes.

2. Remove from heat, stir in remaining 1 teaspoon rose water and serve over grilled poundcake or ice cream.

August 31, 2010: JOHN WILLOUGHBY

Raspberry Chocolate Mousse Cakes

Yield: 2 servings

2 tablespoons unsalted butter, at room temperature, plus more for greasing molds

1½ ounces unsweetened chocolate

⅓ cup granulated sugar

1 large egg, separated, at room temperature

2 tablespoons seedless raspberry preserves

½ tablespoon eau de vie de framboises

3 tablespoons all-purpose flour

1 cup fresh raspberries

1 tablespoon superfine sugar, or to taste

1. Preheat oven to 325 degrees.

2. Butter two ½-cup ramekins or molds. Line bottoms of molds with circles of wax paper and butter paper.

3. Melt chocolate in top of a double boiler over hot, barely simmering water, making sure not to let pan touch water. Set aside.

4. Cream 2 tablespoons butter and granulated sugar together until smoothly blended. (Although this can be done with a food processor or a mixer, it is better to do it by hand, because quantity is so small.) Beat in egg yolk, and stir in raspberry preserves, eau de vie and melted chocolate. Stir in flour.

5. Beat egg white until it holds a peak but still has a creamy quality. Stir a little of egg white into chocolate mixture to lighten batter, then fold remaining egg white into chocolate mixture.

6. Divide batter between two prepared ramekins. Place ramekins in a baking dish that will accommodate both comfortably, and pour enough boiling water into baking dish to come halfway up sides of ramekins. Place baking dish in oven and bake for 40 minutes.

7. Remove baking dish from oven and allow ramekins to cool in water.

8. Set aside ¼ cup of raspberries. Press rest through a sieve to remove seeds. If desired, sweeten sauce to taste with superfine sugar.

9. When ready to serve, unmold cakes by running a knife around inside of each mold, then inverting cakes onto individual plates. (For a picnic, it is best to transport cakes in their molds.) Peel off wax paper.

10. Surround each cake with a pool of sauce and scatter reserved fresh raspberries in it.

May 4, 1986: "Stylish Picnics: Evening in Central Park,"
by FLORENCE FABRICANT

Maury Rubin's Grilled Chocolate Sandwich

Bread pudding, of course, has long been a favorite of children of all ages. And the French have always paired bread with chocolate; pain au chocolat is now ubiquitous. But the grilled chocolate sandwich is both simpler and more decadent, a primal blast of bread and chocolate in which the two components are evenly matched—and mutually enhancing.

At the City Bakery, the owner and chef Maury Rubin has come up with the simplest and most delicious variation. He uses the finest-grained white bread, lightly buttered, then filled with a ganache and batons of dark chocolate. Grilled and cut on the diagonal, it evokes the joys of that archetypal childhood treat, the peanut-butter-and-jelly sandwich, but it is a far darker, more sophisticated creation. "Most pastry looks great but never tastes quite as good as you think it will," Rubin says. "This is exactly the opposite experience."

Yield: 6 to 8 sandwiches

8 ounces dark (bittersweet) chocolate
½ cup heavy cream
12 to 16 slices plain white bread

Chocolate chips (about ⅓ cup) or handful
    of chocolate batons (½ inch long)
3 to 4 tablespoons soft butter

1.   Chop chocolate fine and set aside in a medium bowl.

2.   Heat cream in a small saucepan until just boiling and pour over chopped chocolate. Let stand 1 minute, then whisk until smooth. Refrigerate until just slightly solid, about 30 minutes.

3.   Spread a layer of chocolate mixture ¼ inch thick (approximately 2 to 3 tablespoons) on half the bread sides to within about ¼ inch of edges. Press about 2 teaspoons of chocolate chips (or 5 or 6 pieces of batons) into center of each filling.

4.   Spread a bit of softened butter over one side of remaining slices. Buttered side up, place slice over each chocolate-spread slice and press lightly around edges to seal. Refrigerate for at least 15 minutes before putting on a grill.

5.   Heat a grill over medium-high heat and add sandwiches. Press on one side only for a minute or two until bread is nicely browned; chocolate should be barely melted and not swimming out the side. Cut in half and finish with a frilled toothpick.

September 7, 2003: "Food: Bread Alert,"
by MICHAEL BOODRO;
adapted from MAURY RUBIN,
City Bakery, New York City

Breads of All Sorts, Grilled to a Turn

Grilled breads are the latest trend in the barbecue frenzy that is sweeping the nation. Gordon Hamersley of Hamersley's Bistro in Boston serves a grilled herb and shallot focaccia. Mark Militello of Max's Place in North Miami, Florida, offers an open-faced sandwich of grilled walnut-olive bread and exotic mushrooms. Robert Rabin of the restaurant Chillingsworth in Brewster, Massachsetts, on Cape Cod, grills tortillas and quesadillas. And grilled pizza is so popular at Lucky's and Al Forno, both in Providence, Rhode Island, that the restaurants serve more than 600 orders a week.

"We discovered grilled pizza through someone else's mistake," said Johanne Killeen, the co-owner with her husband, George Germon, of Al Forno and Lucky's. "We were working with a fish dealer who claimed to have eaten grilled pizza in Italy. We talked it over and decided he had mistaken a wood-burning oven for a grill." Nonetheless, Ms. Killeen and her husband were intrigued enough by the idea to make a batch of pizza dough and stretch it out on their barbecue grill. "Much to our amazement, it didn't fall through the grate," Ms. Killeen said.

They tasted it and uttered "ahas!" that may go down in gastronomic history. Grilled pizza was born.

But grilled breads of other types are neither new nor uniquely American. It is likely that the first breads made by neolithic cooks were grain pastes cooked crisp on the heated stones of campfires. Villagers in Lebanon still use this technique for cooking pita bread. In India chapati, whole-wheat flat bread, is roasted on the side of wood-fired tandoor ovens. In Mexico tortillas are cooked on a metal conveyor belt that passes over open flames. Scouts may remember cooking biscuit dough wrapped around a stick over a campfire.

Now, the possibilities have expanded, and the techniques are relatively simple. The easiest way to grill bread is to use glowing coals as a toaster. This is the origin of Italian bruschetta, a thick slice of grilled bread rubbed with garlic and sprinkled with olive oil.

Bruschetta inspired Mr. Militello's grilled sandwich with walnut-olive bread and exotic mushrooms. "We cut the bread into thick slices to help it hold together during grilling," he said. "The finished toast is crusty on the outside, moist inside and permeated with the scent of smoke."

A second method involves cooking the raw dough itself on a grill. Mr. Hamersley flattens fresh focaccia dough into paper-thin rounds and cooks them over the grill. "We burned a lot of bread when we started," he said.

The chefs are emphatic about using hardwood or hardwood charcoal. Mr. Militello uses North Florida oak. Ms. Killeen swears by Canadian hardwood charcoal.

"Briquettes contain petroleum products," she said, "so your pizza winds up tasting like oil." She also advocates the use of an electric starter or a metal chimney-type starter instead of lighter fluid, which can impart an off taste, she said.

Here are some other tips from the chefs:

- When using a gas grill, a smoky flavor can be obtained by throwing wood chips on lava stones. "Use a light wood, like cherry, apple or alder," Ms. Killeen said. "The bread is very delicate. You don't want to overpower it with mesquite."

- When using wood chips, be sure to soak them in water for a couple of hours beforehand to slow the rate of combustion. Grape-vine trimmings, fennel stalks and fresh or dried herbs can be sprinkled on the coals or stones for additional fragrance.

- When building the fire, the coals should be arranged so there are hot spots and cool spots. Mr. Militello piles up the coals at the back of the grill and spaces them out in front. "We control the heat simply by moving the bread backward and forward," he said.

- "Don't try to get the dough on the coals too soon," Ms. Killeen said. "Cooking over direct flames chars the bread and makes it bitter. The fire is ready when the flames have died down and the coals are completely covered with gray ash."

- There are two ways to flatten the dough: by rolling and by stretching. The easiest tool for rolling is a solid pin with tapered ends. The dough can also be rolled out in a pasta machine.

- The thickness of the dough will determine the final texture of the bread. Thin dough (⅛ inch or less) produces a cracker-crisp flat bread. A thicker dough (¼ inch) will result in a soft, pliable bread, like pita.

- Grilled bread burns easily, so don't leave it unattended. "Take your phone off the hook," said Mr. Hamersley. He added that the breads can be grilled ahead of time and then warmed in an oven. Unbaked flatbreads can be frozen.

- Don't be overambitious. "Keep the flavorings simple," Ms. Killeen said. "You want to taste the smoke and the dough, not the contents of your refrigerator." She arranges the flavorings in little piles, leaving large expanses of crust exposed.

- Useful tools include tongs, a long-handled basting brush and a sturdy spatula with an insulated handle. Mr. Militello recommends using a branch of rosemary for basting, and Mr. Hamersley uses a water pistol for controlling sudden flare-ups of flame.

Grilled Walnut-Olive Bread with Exotic Mushrooms

Time: 20 minutes   **Yield:** 8 servings

1 loaf Walnut-Olive Bread (recipe
    follows), sliced
¼ cup extra virgin olive oil
2 pounds assorted fresh exotic
    mushrooms (chanterelle, shiitake,
    portobello, cremini, oyster or black
    trumpet)

1 small clove garlic, minced
Salt and freshly ground black pepper
    to taste
8 sprigs fresh flat leaf parsley
8 lemon wedges
¼ pound Parmigiano-Reggiano cheese
    for shaving on top

1.   Preheat grill until it is quite hot.

2.   Cut bread into 8 (¾-inch-thick) slices. Lightly brush each slice with olive oil. Wash and trim mushrooms. Thread mushrooms on skewers by size (large ones together on one skewer, small ones on another). Brush mushrooms with oil, and sprinkle with garlic, salt and pepper.

3.   Just before serving, grill mushrooms over high heat for 1 to 2 minutes per side, or until cooked. Grill bread slices for 30 seconds per side, or until toasted. Put bread on warm plates, and top each slice with mushrooms. Garnish with parsley sprigs, lemon wedges and thin shavings of cheese.

Walnut-Olive Bread

Time: 55 minutes, plus 2 hours for rising   **Yield:** 2 loaves

1 cake yeast or 1 envelope active dry
    yeast
2 tablespoons sugar
2 tablespoons extra virgin olive oil, plus
    more for greasing
1½ teaspoons salt
½ cup chopped fresh herbs (basil,
    rosemary, oregano, thyme or parsley)

1 teaspoon minced garlic
1 tablespoon minced shallots
3½ to 4 cups bread flour
⅓ cup chopped walnuts
⅓ cup pitted, chopped black olives
    like Gaeta or nicoise

1.   Combine yeast, sugar and 1 cup warm water in a bowl, and let stand for 5 minutes. When mixture is foamy, stir in remaining ingredients. Knead dough for 8 to 10 minutes in a mixer with a dough hook or by hand until it is smooth, shiny and elastic. (Dough can also be made in a food processor.) Place dough in an oiled bowl, cover with plastic wrap and let rise in a warm place for 1 hour, or until doubled in bulk.

2. Punch dough down, roll it into 2 oblongs (about 8 inches long, 4 inches wide and 3 inches high) and place in oiled loaf pans. Let rise for 30 minutes or until doubled in bulk.

3. Preheat oven to 375 degrees.

4. Bake for 25 to 35 minutes, or until crust is crisp and loaf sounds hollow when tapped. Let cool before slicing.

Hot from the Coals: Grilled Herb Focaccia

Time: 35 minutes, plus 1 hour for rising **Yield:** 8 pieces

1 cake yeast or 1 envelope active dry
  yeast
1½ teaspoons sugar
2 tablespoons olive oil, plus 2 to 3 tablespoons for greasing and brushing
3 to 3¼ cups all-purpose flour

2 to 3 cloves garlic, peeled
¼ cup mixed chopped fresh herbs,
  including basil, marjoram and thyme
1 tablespoon cracked black peppercorns
1 tablespoon kosher salt

1. Combine yeast, 1 cup warm water and sugar in a bowl, and let stand for 5 minutes, or until foamy. Stir in oil and 3 cups of flour. Knead dough by hand for 6 to 8 minutes until smooth and elastic, or use a food processor or a mixer fitted with a dough hook. If necessary, add more flour; dough should be soft and pliable but not sticky.

2. Place dough in an oiled bowl, brush top with oil, cover with plastic wrap and let rise in a warm place for 1 hour or until doubled in bulk.

3. Punch dough down, and form it into a long 2-inch-thick roll. Cut roll into 2-inch pieces. Form each piece into a ball, and keep covered with a damp dish towel. Roll out each ball as thinly as possible to make a flat bread 6 to 8 inches in diameter and ⅛ inch thick. Lightly dust each round with flour, and stack, separated by pieces of wax paper.

4. Heat grill until it is medium-hot. Mince garlic, and combine with herbs in a small bowl. Combine cracked peppercorns and salt in another small bowl. Lightly brush each round with olive oil, sprinkle with herbs and salt mixture and place, oiled side down, on grill. Cook for 30 to 60 seconds, or until slightly puffed and blistered. Lightly brush top with oil, and sprinkle on more herbs and salt mixture. Turn focaccia, and cook another 30 seconds or until lightly browned. Cook all dough the same way.

5. Just before serving, sprinkle each focaccia with a few more herbs and salt mixture.

NOTE: Focaccia can be cooked ahead and reheated in the oven.

July 19, 1989: STEVEN RAICHLEN;
walnut-olive bread recipe adapted from MARK MILITELLO,
formerly of Max's Place, North Miami, Florida;
foccacia recipe adapted from GORDON HAMERSLEY,
Hamersley's Bistro, Boston, Massachusetts

Spider Bread

This cornbread from a 1796 recipe gets its name not from its ingredients but from the three-legged iron pot in which it cooks.

Yield: 4 to 6 servings

1½ cups white cornmeal

1 teaspoon sugar

Salt to taste

1 teaspoon baking soda

2 cups buttermilk

2 eggs, beaten

1½ tablespoons unsalted butter, melted

1. Sift together cornmeal, sugar, salt and baking soda.

2. Combine buttermilk and eggs and stir into cornmeal mixture. Mix until smooth.

3. Grease a 9-inch cast-iron pan with legs and pour in cornmeal mixture. Bake over coals for about 30 minutes.

NOTE: This bread can also be baked in a preheated 400-degree oven for 30 minutes.

November 18, 1984: "Food: A Blazing Hearth,
by MOIRA HODGSON;
recipe from BILL and CINDY CLARK,
formerly of Amos Benedict Farm, South Salem, New York

Grilled Chapati

Although it has become fashionable to grill pizza, there is at least one traditional, mostly whole-grain, unyeasted bread that is tailor-made for the grill. Foolproof and not much work, it is chapati, the Indian flatbread that can be served with almost anything you have going on the fire.

Chapati dough can be made in the food processor in less than a minute; unlike doughs made with yeast, it needs no time to rise, though it does benefit from at least a half hour of resting before cooking.

There are other advantages. Handling the dough is pretty much trouble-free. A bit of surface flour applied when needed instantly deals with stickiness. It can be wrapped and left in the fridge for a full day.

When you're ready to grill, just tear off walnut- to golf-ball-size pieces, roll them out with a little flour (if you have a tortilla press handy, it would speed things up a bit) and toss onto the grill. They'll puff up and brown in a minute; turn and brown the other side and they're done. You can deal with a whole batch, from starting to roll to completing the grilling, in 15 minutes or less.

And because you're starting with a food processor, additions are nearly effortless. I especially like thyme leaves, a little garlic, fresh or dried chilies or chopped onion; this last I'd add by hand, because it's a shame to lose its crunch.

It's also perfectly acceptable to brush the chapatis with a little olive oil or melted butter while they're grilling. Toppings? I suppose, but then you're in pizza territory.

Yield: 8 to 12 chapatis, 4 to 6 servings

2¼ cups whole wheat flour

1 cup all-purpose flour, plus more
  for dusting

1 teaspoon salt

1. Mix flours in food processor; add salt and, with machine running, pour in 1 cup warm water. Process for about 30 seconds, then remove cover. Dough should be in a well-defined, barely sticky, easy-to-handle ball. If it is too dry, add warm water a tablespoon at a time and process for 5 to 10 seconds after each addition. If it is too wet, which is unlikely, add a tablespoon or two of flour and process briefly.

2. With floured hands, shape dough into a ball, cover with plastic and let rest for at least 30 minutes. (At this point, you may wrap dough tightly in plastic and refrigerate it for up to a day; bring to room temperature before proceeding.)

3.   When ready to grill, pinch off a piece of dough and roll as thin as is practical. Dust lightly with flour to keep from sticking, and cover with plastic or a damp cloth while you roll out remaining dough. (It is O.K. to overlap them a bit, but do not stack them.) Or just roll as you grill.

4.   Grill chapatis until they start to blister, char and puff up a bit, about a minute or so. Turn and repeat. Serve immediately.

August 13, 2008: "The Minimalist: Bread Born for the Grill,"
by MARK BITTMAN

Southern Shore Flavors

No sooner had I put my spoon to the she-crab soup than the room went dark. Outside, 40-mile-an-hour winds slammed ashore, bending the shrubby yaupon trees and bringing a dose of rain that formed small lakes around the Ocracoke, North Carolina, Island Inn and Dining Room, where I was having dinner. Eaten blind, as it were, the tangy coral-hued soup—made of female blue crabs and their roe, sherry and a cream of celery base—took on new significance, the flavors lingering pure and vibrant in the mouth. "Don't you panic, anyone," came a woman's low voice. "We'll have you all lit in just a minute."

Wild summer weather is commonplace on the North Carolina barrier islands known as the Outer Banks, of which Ocracoke is one of the most remote. Just two nights earlier, at Bubba's BarBQ on Hatteras Island, north of Ocracoke, I was halfway through chopped barbecue with slaw on a bun when the same thing happened. No big deal. Julie Schauer, also known as Mrs. Bubba, called out to us from the kitchen to pull down the windows, and resumed whacking barbecued pork into chunks with a cleaver in the dark. The storm blew over by the time we were ready for her justly renowned chocolate pie. In the morning, at our campground, the sizable pond around our trustworthy new tent shimmered in the sunlight. For breakfast, along with the sweet Virginia peaches we'd bought on the drive down, I fulfilled a dream of eating as many soft-shell crabs as I wanted—six, in fact, just slapped on the campground grill and squirted with a bit of lime. Then we followed a path through dunes thick with wildflowers to an ocean beach that was virtually deserted. Can you blame me if I recall thinking there was no better place to be on a drowsy day in August?

Ocracoke—pronounced lazily, without the r, by natives—is accessible only by ferry or private boat. Neither chic nor crowded, it offers bliss to the sport fisherman and haven for those who don't ask much more from a vacation retreat than clean, secluded beaches, a decent place to sleep and lots of seafood coupled with a simple culinary sensibility that's undeniably Southern.

Unlike the "discovered" Outer Banks towns—Kitty Hawk, Kill Devil Hills and Hatteras—with their department stores, mesquite-grill restaurants and raucous college students, Ocracoke is rough around the edges. The car ferry from Hatteras anchors 14 miles from the island's single village, a collection of modest houses, motels and a Coast Guard station built around Silver Lake, a harbor. The rest of Ocracoke belongs to the Cape Hatteras National Seashore. Aside from the new two-lane highway, most of the roads are narrow, sandy lanes shaded by huge, gnarled oaks and vines. Because the island is just two miles across at its widest point, the Atlantic Ocean and Pamlico Sound on the other side are rarely more than a short walk away.

Ocracoke is not a place for fancy ingredients. Its restaurants are few and food hobbyists may find that their most diverting experience is exploring the aisles of the local variety stores (where fried pork rinds, fishing tackle and paperback books share space) to see what the 700 or so year-round village residents eat to supplement a steady diet of seafood.

The regional canned goods and packaged groceries—collard greens, figs and beans—remind one that this shimmering sand bar is indeed part of the South. As further proof, a mound of snowy grits (with the essential crater of melted butter), a couple of burnished cornmeal hush puppies or a basket of beaten biscuits—perhaps, if you're lucky, all three—will surely appear at every meal.

The fish in Ocracoke's waters have names both strange and familiar. Flounder, croaker, sea mullet, bluefish, cobia, wahoo, grey trout, Spanish mackerel, pompano and tuna begin the list, though only the standard ones show up on restaurant menus, most often fried.

Some of the more exotic fish, like puppy drum and sheepshead, appear regularly on local tables and in recipe collections, such as *The Ocracoke Cook Book,* published by the local United Methodist Church. In it, Mrs. Dell Scarborough's recipe for "Old Baked Drum" calls for baking a channel bass, or "red drum," liberally doused with rendered salt-pork fat, in a slow oven for two hours. To prepare stewed sea turtle (now a Federally protected animal), Mrs. Eva Williams gives directions beginning: "Pour boiling water over turtle and skin it."

Sweet Potato Biscuits

Yield: 12 to 18 biscuits

2 large sweet potatoes or yams (about ¾ pound)	½ teaspoon salt
	1 to 1½ cups flour
¼ pound (1 stick) unsalted butter, at room temperature	¼ cup sugar
	1½ teaspoons baking powder

1.   Boil sweet potatoes or yams in a pot of salted water to cover until they are tender, about 30 to 40 minutes. Drain, peel and mash potatoes. Stir in butter and salt and let mixture cool.

2.   Preheat oven to 450 degrees. With a wooden spoon, beat 1 cup of flour into sweet potatoes. Stir in sugar and baking powder. If dough seems too sticky, gradually add more flour until it just adheres.

3.   Roll out dough on a lightly floured surface. Cut into 2-inch circles with a cookie cutter or juice glass and transfer dough circles to an ungreased baking sheet.

4.   Bake for 15 to 20 minutes, until biscuits are just crisp on top. They are meant to be flat and will not rise much.

August 3, 1986: JANET BUKOVINSKY

CHAPTER TEN

Marinades, Rubs, and Sauces

Full of powerful flavor, marinades, rubs, and sauces can add so much to food on the grill. The judicious mixing of spices, herbs, and condiments can add flavor in all steps of barbecuing. Marinating before grilling, as Molly O'Neill does in her Spice Island Marinade (page 330), infuses meat with flavor. Spice rubs can add complexity to a crust and are especially effective with the long-cooked ingredients typical of smoking and low-heat grilling. As for sauces, there are basting sauces that help build flavor in the crust during grilling, but for traditional barbecue sauces (like Blondell's Barbecue Sauce on page 339), the best advice is to save them for the last few minutes of grilling or after slicing.

At the fifth Annual Taylor (Texas) International Championship Barbecue Cook-off in 1982, judges sample seventy team offerings. Two tons of barbecue were judged according to exacting local standards.

From "Barbecue Sauce as Individual as Each Creator"

When it comes to barbecue, there are as many opinions as there are cooks. So the question of when and how to apply sauce to meat is sure to result in more arguments than answers. Some swear by rubbing meats with spices before cooking; others prefer to marinate; still others apply sauce only in the last minutes of cooking or do not use sauce at all. Whatever the method, these are some of the most common sauce terms in barbecue cookery:

Dry rub: Dry mixture of spices rubbed directly into the meat before cooking.

Finishing sauce: Sauce (usually containing sugar, ketchup or other sweeteners) applied in the final 15 minutes of cooking. In general, sweet sauces should be applied only in the final stages; otherwise, the sugars in these sauces will burn.

Mopping sauce: Sauce used to baste meat while cooking.

Table sauce: Sauce served after the meat is cooked, usually on the side.

Wet marinade: Sauce in which meat is soaked before cooking.

East North Carolina style: Clear vinegar sauce applied while meat is cooking.

West North Carolina style: Vinegar-based sauce combined with ketchup.

South Carolina style: Vinegar-based sauce combined with ketchup and mustard, usually orange in color.

Memphis style: Hot, sweet, sticky red sauce based on tomatoes or ketchup.

Kansas City style: Sweet, sticky sauce, often thicker than Memphis style.

Texas style: Tomato-based sauce, often hot and spicy and generally thinner than Kansas City and other Midwest varieties.

June 28, 1989: DENA KLEIMAN

Soy Sauce Marinade

Use to baste charcoal-grilled chicken, pork and fish when they are almost done.

Yield: About ¾ cup

½ cup soy sauce

¼ cup dry sherry

1 tablespoon finely chopped fresh ginger

2 teaspoons finely minced garlic

2 teaspoons sugar

¼ teaspoon red pepper flakes

Combine all ingredients in a mixing bowl. Stir until sugar dissolves.

July 2, 1980: "Mastering Marinades Is Simple,"
by CRAIG CLAIBORNE

Lemon Marinade

Use to baste charcoal-grilled chicken, fish, lamb and veal.

Yield: About 1 cup

⅓ cup fresh lemon juice

½ cup olive oil

1 teaspoon finely minced garlic

Salt and freshly ground pepper to taste

1 teaspoon oregano

6 very thin, seeded lemon slices

Put lemon juice in a small mixing bowl. Add oil while stirring vigorously with a whisk. Add remaining ingredients and blend well.

July 2, 1980: "Mastering Marinades Is Simple,"
by CRAIG CLAIBORNE

Tarragon Marinade

Use to baste charcoal-grilled chicken, lamb, fish and veal.

Yield: About ¾ cup

¼ cup red wine vinegar

½ cup peanut, vegetable or corn oil

2 teaspoons chopped fresh tarragon

Salt and freshly ground pepper to taste

Put vinegar in a small mixing bowl and add oil, beating with a wire whisk. Add tarragon and salt and pepper to taste. Blend well.

July 2, 1980: "Mastering Marinades Is Simple,"
by CRAIG CLAIBORNE

Spice Island Marinade

This marinade imparts a pungent Indian flavor to chicken, beef or ribs, but it works particularly well with tuna steaks or fish fillets. For four 6- to 8-ounce tuna steaks, marinate 1½-inch-thick steaks in the refrigerator for 4 hours. Discard marinade and grill over hot coals until rare, about 3 minutes per side.

Yield: 2 cups

1 ripe papaya (3/4 pound), peeled, seeded and diced

½ pound fresh, ripe apricots, pitted and finely chopped

¼ cup fresh lime juice

2 cloves garlic, minced

2 small Thai or jalapeño chilies, seeded, deveined and minced

1 tablespoon grated fresh ginger

1 tablespoon cardamom pods, crushed

2 tablespoons coriander seeds, crushed

Combine all ingredients in a glass or ceramic bowl. Refrigerate in an airtight container for up to 2 days.

May 31, 1992: "Food: A Good Grilling," by MOLLY O'NEILL

Korean Barbecue

This marinade is wonderful with pork chops, flank steak or chicken wings. For pork chops, marinate four 8-ounce chops in the refrigerator overnight. Grill over hot coals until medium-rare, about 5 minutes per side. For London broil or flank steak, marinate one 1½- to 2-pound piece in the refrigerator for at least 8 hours. Grill over hot coals until rare, about 3 to 4 minutes per side.

Yield: 2 cups

1 tablespoon grated fresh ginger
1 medium papaya, peeled, seeded and
   coarsely chopped
1 small pear, peeled, cored and chopped
1 small onion, chopped
1 small clove garlic, minced
1 tablespoon honey
¼ cup soy sauce

⅓ cup pineapple juice
1 tablespoon Korean rice wine or sake
½ teaspoon freshly ground pepper
½ teaspoon sugar
2 tablespoons sesame oil
½ teaspoon sesame seeds
¼ cup minced scallions

Put all ingredients, except sesame seeds and scallions, in a blender. Puree until smooth. Pour marinade into a glass or ceramic bowl. Add sesame seeds and scallions. Refrigerate in an airtight container for up to 3 days.

May 31, 1992: "Food: A Good Grilling," by MOLLY O'NEILL

For the Best Cuts, Here Are the Rubs

Some people believe you can improve on a good grilled steak: the Italians use lemon and olive oil, the French compound butter or even béarnaise.

But with true American chauvinism most of us believe that because our beef is better it needs nothing but salt and pepper. That may be true of the absolute best meat, but if you're going to tinker—and it's a good idea to do so when using subpremium meat—you may want to think about a rub.

A rub is a dry spice or spice and herb mixture used to coat the meat before grilling, adding not only strong flavor but a bit more crunch, especially if you toast, mix and grind the spices yourself.

My favorites are basic: chili powder, with mild chilies; fragrant curry powder; jerk seasoning, which contains fresh garlic and ginger and is quite powerful; and five-spice powder, which, when homemade, is unlike anything you can buy in a store.

Using any of these is straightforward: rub a good teaspoon or more into each side of the steak, then grill over slightly lower heat than you would normally use, so the spices don't burn.

Jerk Seasoning

Time: 5 minutes   **Yield:** About ¼ cup

1 tablespoon allspice berries

¼ teaspoon nutmeg pieces (crack a whole nutmeg with a hammer)

1 teaspoon black peppercorns

2 teaspoons dried thyme

1 teaspoon cayenne pepper, or to taste

1 tablespoon paprika

1 tablespoon sugar

1 tablespoon salt

2 teaspoons minced garlic

2 teaspoons minced fresh ginger, or 2 teaspoons ground ginger

1. Put allspice, nutmeg, peppercorns and thyme in a spice or coffee grinder and grind to a fine powder.

2. Mix in remaining ingredients and use immediately. To use later, omit garlic and ginger and store in a tightly covered container; add garlic and ginger immediately before using.

Five-Spice Powder

Time: 5 minutes   **Yield:** About ¼ cup

1 tablespoon Sichuan peppercorns

6 star anise

1½ teaspoons whole cloves

1 stick cinnamon

2 tablespoons fennel seeds

Put all ingredients in a spice or coffee grinder and grind to a fine powder. Store in a tightly covered opaque container for up to several months.

Warm Curry Powder

Time: 15 minutes   **Yield:** About ¼ cup

10 cardamom pods

1 cinnamon stick

1 teaspoon whole cloves

½ teaspoon nutmeg pieces (crack a
    whole nutmeg with a hammer)

1 tablespoon cumin seeds

1 tablespoon fennel seeds

1.   Crush cardamom pods with side of a knife or bottom of a pot; remove seeds and discard husks. Put all ingredients in a small skillet and turn heat to medium. Toast, occasionally shaking pan, until mixture is fragrant, 3 to 5 minutes.

2.   Grind in a spice or coffee grinder until powdery. Can be stored in a tightly covered container for up to several weeks.

August 22, 2007: MARK BITTMAN

Provençal Spice Rub

This rub from the south of France can be used with lamb or beef, but is particularly delectable with chicken and game. For chicken, marinate two 3-pound chickens, split in half, in the refrigerator for 6 hours. Place the chicken on the grill, skin side down. Cook over hot coals until the skin is charred, about 5 minutes. Turn the chicken and cover the grill. Continue cooking slowly until the meat is opaque at the bone, about 20 to 25 minutes.

For duck breast, marinate two 10- to 12-ounce breasts in the refrigerator for 6 hours. Grill skin side down until charred, about 5 minutes. Turn the breasts and continue grilling until medium-rare, about 3 to 5 additional minutes.

Yield: 1 cup

1 teaspoon juniper berries

1 whole clove

1 teaspoon white peppercorns

1 (¼-inch) cinnamon stick

¼ teaspoon freshly grated nutmeg

2 teaspoons dried savory

1 tablespoon dried thyme

1 red onion, minced

2 cloves garlic, minced

½ cup fresh mint leaves

¼ cup olive oil

1 teaspoon grated orange zest

¼ cup red wine

Grind all dried spices and herbs together in a spice mill or coffee grinder until finely ground. Place spice powder in a large glass or ceramic bowl. Add onion, garlic, mint, olive oil, orange zest, and red wine. Mix well. Refrigerate in an airtight container for up to 2 days.

May 31, 1992: "Food: A Good Grilling,"
by MOLLY O'NEILL

Thrill of the Grill Spice Paste

This paste is wonderful with steaks or chicken. It also adds a husky note to veal chops.

Yield: ¾ cup

2 tablespoons ground cumin

2 tablespoons curry powder

2 tablespoons sweet paprika

2 tablespoons coriander seeds, cracked

2 tablespoons black peppercorns, cracked

1 tablespoon ground cinnamon

1 teaspoon salt

¼ cup olive oil

2 cloves garlic, minced

2 tablespoons minced fresh oregano

¼ cup minced fresh cilantro

1.   Combine all dry spices in a small cast-iron skillet. Dry-roast over medium-low heat until they begin to smoke but not burn, about 3 to 5 minutes.

2.   Transfer roasted spices to a large bowl. Add remaining ingredients. Mix well. Refrigerate in an airtight container for up to 3 days.

3.   To use, rub over chosen meat and refrigerate for 4 to 6 hours before grilling.

May 31, 1992: "Food: A Good Grilling,"
by MOLLY O'NEILL;
adapted from CHRIS SCHLESINGER,
East Coast Grill, Cambridge, Massachusetts

Barbecue Sauce as Individual as Each Creator

As the United States gets ready to celebrate its 213th birthday, there is one substance that seems to have emerged as a symbol of the nation's treasured values of democracy, free expression and tolerance for individual difference. Barbecue sauce. Face it. What other commodity inspires such raw creativity, passionate debate and celebration of regional differences? What else is at once so devoid of pretense, yet is capable of bowling over the most aristocratic gourmet?

As the backyard barbecuing season moves into full swing, people all over the country who may never otherwise cook a meal indoors are in the kitchen, blending secret ingredients with a kind of zeal otherwise reserved for patriots. "What's one man's barbecue sauce is another man's axle grease," observed Sam Higgins of Arlington, Texas, an old barbecue hand and author of the book *I'm Glad I Ate When I Did 'Cause I'm Not Hungry Now*. He said barbecue sauce gave him a new appreciation for American individualism.

When it comes to barbecue sauce, there is no limit to the variety. There are sweet sauces, mild sauces, thick sauces, thin sauces, sauces that burn the tongue. There are orange sauces, red sauces, clear sauces, brown sauces, sauces that are nothing more than vinegar. There are raw sauces, cooked sauces, ketchup-based sauces, mustard-based sauces and sauces made of beer. There are basting sauces, finishing sauces, table sauces, marinades and some who say they do not use sauce at all.

"When you eat a steak do you want it swimming in béarnaise sauce?" asked Robert Pearson, who owns Stick to Your Ribs, a popular Texas-style barbecue restaurant in Stratford, Connecticut. Mr. Pearson is adamant that sauce should be optional, and that, in any case, it should not be applied to meat while cooking, but served on the side.

Barbecue sauce has become a statement of identity. In some areas of the country, stating your sauce is almost as good as giving out your ZIP code. Do you use vinegar? Chances are you are from the coast of North Carolina. Brown sugar? Good odds you are from Kansas. Tabasco? Take bets the chef is from Texas. "There is nothing like going to the South for a pig sandwich," said Carolyn Wells, a barbecue aficionado and cookbook writer who grew up in Nashville. She now lives in Kansas City, Missouri, where, she said, people don't know that a pig sandwich is made of chopped barbecued pork doused in a sticky tomato-based sauce often spiked with whisky.

"Here we use a vinegar-based sauce," said Bobby Prescott, a high-voltage electrician and amateur barbecue chef, who grew up on a ketchup-based sauce in South Carolina but now, as a resident of the North Carolina coast, would never consider using anything else on barbecue except Tabasco and vinegar.

Entrepreneurial-minded sauce makers, inspired by Horatio Alger-like barbecue success stories, dream of making fortunes bringing their recipes to the masses.

Take Dr. Rich Davis. For 25 years, Dr. Davis practiced child psychiatry in a suburb of Kansas City, Missouri. Like so many Americans, he worked the barbecue on weekends, giving his wife a respite from cooking. Then one day he had an idea while at a hamburger restaurant. It occurred to him that one of the most popular condiments nationwide was the combination of mustard and ketchup served at such fast-food establishments. He decided that what this country really needed was to be able to buy this sauce premade, and he went ahead and made plans to bottle it. He called it "mustchep." At the same time, he said he thought he might as well bottle his own barbecue sauce too.

"I brewed up the sauce in my kitchen," Dr. Davis recalled modestly of his barbecue creation, K.C. Masterpiece, which took Kansas City by storm after it was introduced in 1977. Eventually Dr. Davis went nationwide and was grossing $7 million a year when he was bought out in 1986 by the Clorox Corporation of Oakland, California. K.C. Masterpiece is now one of the top-selling barbecue sauces in supermarkets across the country. (Kraft, which has been marketing its barbecue sauce since 1960, is still the No. 1 commercially available sauce.) "Mustchep" never took off.

Dr. Davis's name is now bandied about at barbecue contests and in backyards as thousands of Americans cook up their own special blends of tomato paste, vinegar, herbs and spices in the hopes that they too will be rewarded.

Jim Turner, for example, an insurance claims representative from West Memphis, Arkansas, has been entering his sauce for years in barbecue competitions under the name "Super Swine Sizzlers." His sauce took first place and $5,750 in the "whole hog" competition last month at the annual Memphis in May Championship Barbecue Cooking contest.

But don't ask him for a recipe. He'll hem and haw, like so many barbecue hands like to do, wanting to be polite and appreciating the interest, but taking particular satisfaction in the secrecy of the invention.

"I make my own recipe," Mr. Turner said cryptically when asked about his sauce. He would say only that he cooks 125-pound hogs, that he typically rubs the pig with lemon pepper, ground basil, garlic salt, dry mustard, onion salt, paprika and chili powder and then bastes with a mixture of water and concentrated lemon juice. The sauce he serves it with, he said, includes pineapple, cherries, cloves, brown sugar, ketchup and tomato paste, but he would not say in what proportion.

Jessica Kirk, a special-education elementary-school teacher who lives in a Kans suburb of Kansas City and was the Kansas state barbecue champion in 1984, was forthcoming about her barbecue secrets. To her, who is preparing the sauce and important as what goes into it.

"There is a lot of ego involved in this thing," said Mrs. Kirk, who comp Kansas Barbecue Cookoff last weekend, winning sixth place in the b

Ardie Davis, a 47-year-old administrator in the Missouri De

founder of the Diddy Wa Diddy National Barbecue Sauce Contest, devoted exclusively to barbecue sauce.

Mr. Davis, who describes himself as a food fanatic, grew up in Oklahoma, where, he said, he teethed on rib bones. While dreaming one day of the myriad sauces around the country that he had never been able to taste, he was inspired to write to barbecue restaurants nationwide, asking for samples of their sauces. What began as an informal taste test among neighbors has since grown into a national event, named after a blues song Mr. Davis was listening to when the idea struck.

"It is a good nonsense word," Mr. Davis said. "Taste is so subjective. For me to say this is best may mean nonsense to you. I thought it would be a good name for a tasting contest. Plus, you can't say it without smiling. Part of what I like about barbecue is that it's fun."

Cowtown Cookers' Basic Barbecue Sauce

Time: 2 hours, 40 minutes   **Yield:** 4 cups

1 (32-ounce) bottle ketchup

1 cup dark molasses

1½ tablespoons Tabasco sauce

1½ medium onions, finely chopped

1 large green bell pepper, seeded and
    finely chopped

½ cup lemon juice

1 teaspoon garlic powder

2½ tablespoons dry mustard

3 tablespoons white vinegar

¾ cup packed brown sugar

¼ cup liquid smoke

¼ cup Worcestershire sauce

vy pot.

bottle and swirl around. Pour into pot.

tly. Reduce heat and simmer 2 hours.

OKBOOK

Carolina Basting Sauce

Time: 15 minutes
Yield: 2½ cups, or enough to baste 3 chickens or 5 to 6 pounds of pork or beef

2 cups cider vinegar
½ pound (2 sticks) margarine or butter
1 teaspoon salt

1 tablespoon lemon juice
¼ teaspoon red pepper flakes

In a saucepan, combine vinegar, butter or margarine and salt. Heat slowly until butter or margarine is melted. Add lemon juice and pepper flakes.

Blondell's Barbecue Sauce

Use to baste meats or chicken during the last 15 minutes of cooking.

Time: 30 minutes   **Yield:** 1½ cups

½ cup chopped onions
1 tablespoon bacon drippings or
   vegetable oil
½ cup apple juice
2 tablespoons wine vinegar
¼ cup lemon juice

¼ cup molasses
1 cup chili sauce
1 teaspoon ground pepper
1 teaspoon French-style mustard
¼ cup ketchup

Sauté onions in drippings or oil until brown. Add remaining ingredients and bring to a boil. Reduce heat and simmer for 20 minutes.

June 28, 1989: DENA KLEIMAN; recipe for basic barbecue sauce
adapted from The All-American Barbecue Book,
by RICH DAVIS and SHIFRA STEIN (Vintage Books, 1988);
recipe for basting sauce adapted from Barbecue Ribs and Other Great Feed,
by JEANNE VOLTZ (Alfred A. Knopf, 1985);
recipe for Blondell's barbecue sauce attributed to the late actress
JOAN BLONDELL, in Real Barbecue, *by GREG JOHNSON*
and VINCE STATEN (Harper & Row, 1988)

Mango and Scotch Bonnet Barbecue Sauce

Everyone has a favorite barbecue sauce. Mine is a little different. I use mangoes, Scotch bonnet peppers and tamarind to give the sauce spiciness and a strongly sweet-and-sour accent. But it has what you want from a barbecue sauce: richness, spiciness and sweetness coming together. My sauce has a smokiness, too, which I like—even when you don't use it for grilling, you get some of the wood-fired flavor into your food.

The recipe for all this must go back 20 years. I just made it up one day, playing around in my home kitchen.

I start by smoking sweet peppers and tomatoes. It's not absolutely essential that you smoke them, but if you can—home smoking is not as complicated as you might think—you'll add a nice dimension to the sauce. The simplest home smoker is a closed container that allows you to heat wood chips to the point where they begin to smoke. You can make do with a covered wok on the stove, and tea-smoke your vegetables like the Chinese do chicken. The smokiness helps bring the tart, sweet and spice together.

You'll want your mangoes to be ripe but not soft, and if you can get fresh tamarind puree, you won't be sorry. It has a very lively flavor. (But you can also use tamarind paste.)

I puree the sauce with a hand-held blender right in the pot, but you can also use a food processor. Either way you have to pass it through a sieve.

I use the sauce when I grill meats like steak or hamburgers, and I love it on swordfish. I even spread the stuff on thin slices of chayote squash before throwing them on the grill. You have to be a little careful so the sauce doesn't blacken before your food is cooked, especially when you use it on chicken. There's plenty of sugar in the sauce that will caramelize. And it's not just for grilling. It's a great marinade.

My lunch chef, Francy Deskin, makes the barbecue sauce in the restaurant. It's the sauce that goes on our grilled chicken pizza: a plain pizza crust, spread with the sauce and covered with grilled chicken, roasted chilies, corn kernels, black beans and Monterey Jack cheese. With all of those flavors, you need a sauce you can taste. This mango barbecue sauce has taste power to spare.

Time: 2 hours   **Yield:** 6 cups

2 green bell peppers, halved and seeded

2 red bell peppers, halved and seeded

4 ripe tomatoes, peeled, halved and
   seeded

3 ripe mangoes, peeled, seeded and
   chopped

1 large sweet onion, chopped

2 tablespoons minced garlic

2 Scotch bonnet chilies, halved

¾ cup cider vinegar

1¼ cups packed light brown sugar

¼ cup molasses

¼ cup Dijon mustard

¼ cup tamarind paste

2 tablespoons ground cinnamon

1 tablespoon ground cumin

1 tablespoon fresh thyme leaves

1 tablespoon fresh marjoram leaves

Salt and freshly ground black pepper

1. Light a home smoker, and smoke bell peppers and tomatoes 30 minutes, preferably over oak chips. (Alternatively, a smoker can be made by completely lining the bottom and cover of a wok with foil and placing 2 tablespoons each of rice, brown sugar and black tea leaves in bottom of wok. Place wok, covered, over medium heat. When smoke starts rising, put peppers and tomatoes on a rack in wok, cover, and smoke vegetables 30 minutes.) Chop vegetables and transfer them to a 5-quart saucepan. (Without a smoker, peppers and tomatoes can be chopped and placed in saucepan.)

2. Add remaining ingredients to saucepan with 1 cup water. Bring to a boil, reduce heat and simmer, stirring occasionally, 1 hour. Allow to cool briefly.

3. Puree mixture in a food processor. You may have to do this in two shifts. Pass puree through a medium-mesh strainer. Check seasoning. Refrigerate until ready to use.

June 5, 2002: "The Chef: Mark Militello,"
by MARK MILITELLO

Bourbon Barbecue Sauce

Ketchup-based barbecue sauce is a crowd-pleaser. Bourbon and a bit of Worcestershire sauce cut through the typical sweetness of such concoctions. The whiskey also thins the sauce, making it less sticky and more gravylike. You can make this sauce as far in advance as you like, even the weekend before you plan to serve it; it will reheat well.

Time: 20 minutes   **Yield:** 2 cups, 8 or more servings

2 cups ketchup

½ cup bourbon

¼ cup rice vinegar

1 tablespoon Worcestershire sauce

1 tablespoon chili powder

¼ cup minced onion

1 teaspoon minced garlic

Salt and ground black pepper

1. Combine all ingredients except salt and pepper in a small saucepan over medium-low heat. Cook, stirring occasionally, about 10 minutes.

2. Taste and adjust seasoning. Use immediately or cool, cover and refrigerate for up to a week; reheat before serving.

November 14, 2007: "The Minimalist; More Gravy? It's Nice to Have Options," by MARK BITTMAN

Ketchup Sauce for Barbecues

Use to baste charcoal-grilled chicken, pork and beef when they are almost done.

1 cup ketchup

3 tablespoons fresh lemon juice

2 tablespoons honey

1 tablespoon finely minced garlic

1 tablespoon Worcestershire sauce

Tabasco sauce to taste

4 tablespoons (½ stick) butter

Salt and freshly ground pepper to taste

4 thin, seeded lemon slices

Combine all ingredients in a saucepan and bring to a boil, stirring.

July 2, 1980: "Mastering Marinades Is Simple," by CRAIG CLAIBORNE

Lillian Jackson Duncan's
Superior Barbecue Sauce

A short while back a letter arrived from Phyllis Friedman Perkins offering a friend's recipe for a spicy Texas barbecue sauce. It is credited to Lillian Jackson Duncan and this is an adaptation of that recipe.

Yield: About 4½ cups

1 cup very strong black coffee

2 cups Worcestershire sauce

1¼ cups ketchup

¼ pound (1 stick) butter

1 tablespoon salt

4 teaspoons sugar

1 to 2 tablespoons freshly ground black pepper (the larger amount will make the sauce spicier)

1. Combine all ingredients in a heavy pot or kettle and bring to a boil over low heat.
2. Cook, stirring frequently, at least 30 minutes. Brush on foods as they are grilled.

July 28, 1978: "From Green Chutney to Barbecue Sauce: Four of Craig Claiborne's Favorite Hot Sauces"; adapted from LILLIAN JACKSON DUNCAN

Barbecuing with a World Full of Accents

When it comes to the condiments served at backyard barbecues, America can seem downright provincial. Ketchup, mustard and bottled barbecue sauce are at every cook's fingertips, yet they are the *vin ordinaire*.

Travel the world's barbecue trail, however, and you will find condiments of bolder constitution. Fiery sambals that blast your gullet and soothing chutneys to cool you. Exotic purees of chilies and fruit and pugnacious pastes of garlic and vinegar.

So why grab for a commonplace condiment when it is easy to go global?

French West Indian Sauce Chien

The French West Indies are home to a fiery vinaigrette called sauce chien, literally "dog sauce." There are several theories about how this sauce acquired its name. One chef maintained that *chien* refers to the bite of Scotch bonnet chilies. Others suggested that the preparation is a mongrel among French sauces because it lacks such honorable ingredients as butter, cream or egg yolks. Whatever its origins, sauce chien never fails to electrify grilled chicken, seafood or lamb.

Time: 10 minutes   **Yield:** About 2 cups

3 cloves garlic, peeled

2 medium shallots, quartered

1 Scotch bonnet or habanero chili, seeded and quartered

2 teaspoons chopped fresh ginger

½ cup fresh flat leaf parsley leaves

¼ cup chopped fresh chives or scallion greens

½ teaspoon fresh or dried thyme

1 scant teaspoon salt, or more, to taste

½ teaspoon freshly ground black pepper

Pinch ground allspice

⅓ cup fresh lime juice, or more, to taste

½ cup extra virgin olive oil

Finely chop garlic, shallots, chili, ginger, parsley and chives in a food processor. Add remaining ingredients, and process just to mix. Add ¼ cup boiling water, and process to mix. Run machine in short bursts until you have a coarse puree. If desired, add more salt or lime juice, to taste. The sauce can be served immediately, but it becomes more flavorful if you let it sit for an hour.

Romesco Sauce

Romesco is a traditional condiment for barbecue in Barcelona. Few sauces can rival its earthy complexity, the result of charring the vegetables and nuts under the broiler before combining them in the blender. Romesco isn't pretty to look at—like most Catalan dishes, it's brown—but few sauces pack more punch with grilled seafood, meat or vegetables. Romesco is traditionally served with grilled calcots (large Spanish green onions); try it with grilled green onions (green Vidalias, if you can get them) or scallions. In Spain, romesco would be seasoned with a Spanish dried chili called anorra. Our recipe uses similar-tasting ancho chilies, more readily available here.

Time: 35 minutes   **Yield:** 2 cups

1 dried ancho chili or 3 dried anorra
    chilies, stemmed
2 tablespoons blanched almonds
2 tablespoons hazelnuts
3 ripe tomatoes (about 1¼ pounds), cut
    in half
1 small onion, quartered
½ red bell pepper, seeded
1 jalapeño, halved and seeded
5 cloves garlic, peeled

1 slice country-style white bread
¼ cup finely chopped fresh flat leaf
    parsley
½ cup extra virgin olive oil (preferably
    Spanish)
2 tablespoons red wine vinegar, or more,
    to taste
¼ teaspoon sugar, or more, to taste
Salt and freshly ground black pepper
    to taste

1. Soak dried chili(es) in hot water until soft and pliable, 30 minutes. Drain, reserving soaking liquid, and blot dry.

2. Meanwhile, preheat broiler. Arrange nuts on a foil-lined baking sheet, and broil until toasted and fragrant, 4 to 6 minutes, shaking pan two or three times to insure even browning. Transfer nuts to a plate. When they have cooled a bit, rub hazelnuts between palms of your hands to remove skins. (Don't worry about removing every last bit.)

3. Arrange tomatoes, onion, bell pepper, jalapeño and garlic on baking sheet, and broil until darkly browned, turning to ensure browning is even. This will take 4 to 6 minutes a side: remove vegetables as they are ready. Transfer vegetables to a plate and let cool.

4. Place bread on baking sheet, and toast under the broiler, 2 minutes a side, until dark. Break toast into several pieces.

5. Place nuts and toast in food processor, and grind to a fine powder. Add vegetables and parsley, and puree to a coarse paste. Add oil, vinegar, sugar, salt and pepper, and process to mix. The sauce should be thick but pourable: if it is too thick, add a little soaking liquid from the chili. If desired, add salt, sugar or vinegar to taste.

Georgian Plum Sauce (Tkemali)

In the Caucasus Mountains, the mythical birthplace of fire, barbecue sauce means *tkemali*, a piquant puree of sour plums or rhubarb, with garlic, dill and cilantro. This is not as strange as it may seem: after all, many Americans add apple or pineapple to their barbecue sauces. You don't need to journey as far as the Republic of Georgia, for tkemali turns up at Georgian restaurants in Brighton Beach, Brooklyn. As for the appropriate meat, well, you haven't fully savored grilled lamb, pork, sausage or salmon until you have tasted it with a dab of tkemali.

Time: 20 minutes   **Yield:** 2 cups

1 pound plums (not too ripe)

2 tablespoons fresh lemon juice, or more, to taste

2 tablespoons olive oil

1 teaspoon red wine vinegar, or more, to taste

3 cloves garlic, minced

1 teaspoon ground coriander

½ teaspoon salt, or more, to taste

½ teaspoon red pepper flakes

¼ teaspoon black pepper

¼ teaspoon ground cumin

2 tablespoons finely chopped fresh cilantro

2 tablespoons finely chopped fresh dill

½ teaspoon sugar (optional)

1. Cook plums in boiling water to cover for 30 seconds. Drain in a colander, rinsing with cold water. Pull off skins. Remove stones.

2. Combine plums, 1 cup water, lemon juice, olive oil, vinegar, garlic, coriander, salt, pepper flakes, black pepper and cumin in a saucepan. Simmer until plums are very soft, 5 minutes. Puree mixture in a food processor. Return it to saucepan, and stir in cilantro and dill.

3. Simmer sauce until thick and flavorful, about 5 minutes. If desired, add salt, lemon juice or vinegar to taste. If too tart, add sugar. Serve at room temperature.

Vietnamese Pineapple-Shrimp Sauce

Vietnamese cooks are also no strangers to fruit-based barbecue sauces. What may seem strange to a North American is a barbecue sauce flavored with pineapple, shrimp, and fish or anchovy sauce. But the combination isn't as odd as it sounds, especially when you stop to think that some bottled American steak sauces contain fruit and anchovies. In any case, you would be hard pressed to find a more interesting accompaniment to grilled fish or shellfish.

Time: 20 minutes   **Yield:** 2 cups

2 tablespoons peanut oil

3 cloves garlic, minced

1 shallot, minced

1 serrano chili, seeded and minced

6 ounces shrimp, peeled, deveined and finely chopped

2 cups finely chopped fresh pineapple

1 cup pineapple juice

3 tablespoons Asian fish sauce

1 tablespoon Vietnamese or Thai chili sauce, or more, to taste

2 teaspoons fresh lime juice or rice vinegar

½ teaspoon black pepper

½ teaspoon sugar

3 tablespoons chopped fresh cilantro

Pinch salt (optional)

1. Heat oil in a wok or sauté pan over medium heat. Add garlic, shallot and chili, and stir-fry until they just begin to brown, about 1 minute. Add shrimp, and stir-fry until opaque, 2 minutes. Stir in pineapple and pineapple juice, and bring to a boil.

2. Stir in fish sauce, chili sauce, lime juice, pepper, sugar and cilantro, and bring to a boil. Reduce heat, and simmer until sauce is thick and richly flavored, 3 minutes. If desired, add pinch of salt or dash of chili sauce. Puree sauce in a food processor. Serve at room temperature.

June 2, 1999: STEVEN RAICHLEN

Watermelon Pico de Gallo

Yield: 4 to 6 servings

1½ cups diced (¼-inch) seeded watermelon

¼ cup diced (¼-inch) honeydew melon

¼ cup diced (¼-inch) cantaloupe

¼ cup diced (¼-inch) red onion

1 jalapeño, seeded and chopped

2 tablespoons fresh lime juice

½ cup chopped fresh cilantro

½ teaspoon salt, plus more to taste

Place all ingredients in a bowl and toss gently until well combined. Serve immediately.

July 4, 1993: "Food: The Texas Three-Step," by MOLLY O'NEILL;
adapted from DEAN FEARING, Mansion on Turtle Creek, Dallas, Texas

....

Honey Gremolata

A bright and balanced sauce, this honey-sweetened gremolata adds a note of sophistication.

Time: 10 minutes, plus 30 minutes' to 24 hours' macerating   **Yield:** 1½ cups

1 cup fresh flat leaf parsley leaves, chopped

½ cup fresh oregano leaves, chopped

1 teaspoon minced garlic

¾ teaspoon grated lemon zest

1 tablespoon fresh lemon juice

1 tablespoon honey

1 cup extra virgin olive oil

Salt and freshly ground black pepper

In a bowl, mix together ½ cup of parsley and remaining ingredients. Season to taste. Cover and refrigerate for at least 30 minutes and up to 24 hours. Just before serving, mix in remaining ½ cup parsley.

May 20, 2009: "Grilling Over Wood as a Sweaty, Smoky Sport,"
by OLIVER SCHWANER-ALBRIGHT;
adapted from Seven Fires: Grilling the Argentine Way,
by FRANCIS MALLMANN with PETER KAMINSKY (Artisan, 2009)

....

Madhur Jaffrey's Fresh Green Chutney

This is a spicy yogurt chutney, made with hot green chilies. A relish, it goes well when served on the side with barbecued foods.

Yield: About 1½ cups

1 cup loosely packed chopped fresh
    cilantro leaves
1 fresh hot green chili, trimmed and
    sliced
1 cup plain yogurt

Salt and freshly ground pepper to taste
½ teaspoon ground cumin (preferably
    made from roasted cumin seeds)
1 tablespoon fresh lemon juice

1. Combine cilantro and chili in a food processor or blender. Add 3 tablespoons water, and blend to a smooth paste. As mixture is blended stir down as necessary with a plastic spatula.

2. Spoon and scrape mixture into a mixing bowl. Add remaining ingredients and blend well.

July 28, 1978: "From Green Chutney to Barbecue Sauce:
Four of Craig Claiborne's Favorite Hot Sauces," by CRAIG CLAIBORNE;
adapted from An Invitation to Indian Cooking,
by MADHUR JAFFREY (Knopf, 1973)

Topics of The Times:
The Outdoor Grill and the Ego

Awoman stands over a hot stove to cook one thousand meals a year and 998 of them are not only taken for granted, demanded and grumbled at if late, but also consumed with quite evident smacking lips and an equally nonevident verbal commendation. A man stands ten feet away from a hot charcoal grill in the shade of a tree and cooks twenty meals a year, none of which can be taken for granted, all of which are late; consumes the largest, choicest portions and receives fulsome adulation. A woman has to take corned beef hash and produce an epicurean chef d'oeuvre; a man takes a three-inch slab of prime sirloin Grand Champion 4-H Baby Beef and produces a two-and-a-half-inch gastronomic char. A woman juggles three burners and an oven, cooks potatoes thirty minutes, peas ten minutes, baby's food five minutes and the roast one hundred ninety-five minutes, sets the table, tosses the salad, feeds the baby, answers the phone, settles the children, soothes the husband, and the family enjoys a peaceful meal. A man twirls his barbecue fork, smokes a cigarettes, chats with his neighbor, makes one turn of the steak and forty-nine test cuts to see if it's done and creates domestic bedlam.

What makes all this difference? The difference is simply that of a man and a woman, a husband and a wife, day and night. It has no explanation, unless one wants to delve into the ego, and our purpose here is not to investigate the backyard broil in all its intriguing psychological smoke and fire. No matter how this psychology beckons to be explored, the plain facts of the case are even more beckoning. What should be common knowledge remains an amazing secret. Actually it has nothing to do with the well-known phenomenon that when a woman puts on an apron she feels like a maid, but when a man puts on an apron he feels like a chef (and looks like a maid). The explanation does not lie inward, in the small and rarely developed urge of every man to become the world-famous chef at Maxim's every time he draws a glass of water from the tap with a debonair finesse that draws gasps of admiration.

To watch the full flower of this largely latent talent for culinary histrionics is indeed a pleasure. The first step of the practiced charcoal broiler is a consultation of the Farmer's Almanac to insure the prevailing monsoons will not prevail for many moons soon, for not even Pierre Bouillabaisse can cook with rain. The next is the purchase involving the largest cut worthy of the consummate skill soon to be lavished upon it. The third step is the placement of the grill, derived from wind readings of the meteorological wet-thumb. The fourth step is lighting the fire. Two schools of thought clash in this controversy. One holds that the charcoal lighter fluid impairs the natural taste; the other holds a can of charcoal lighter fluid. If all goes well the steak can generally be placed on the grill for five to six minutes before remembering that the fat around the edges, now quaintly curling the meat away from the flames, should have been cut five or six minutes ago.

The flames also by this time have reached the frightening one-alarm stage. A cauldron of fire engulfing the steak shoots grotesque, flaming arms at the feeble darts of the fork of the aproned fire-fighter in a back-yard dance macabre. This, then, becomes the crucial stage, with a supper riding on the outcome. Either the wife has been standing inconspicuously aside waiting for this development, or she has been standing conspicuously aside. Grabbing the ever-flagging barbecue fork, she fences the flames as only a true helpmate can do. It is in the next step—the seventh or eighth step, though generally there is no doubt about the count whenever the flames reach the height of two or two and a half feet—in which the outdoor chef universally excels. This is the step where he leaves his wife alone with the cauldron, loudly announces his intention to get the salt, then hops, skips, and skulks into the house to apply the soothing balms of an ointment to his singed fingers in just the right proportions.

The steak, when served, is delicious. And that is the secret, the amazing secret. Steaks, no matter how underbroiled, overbroiled, charcoal-broiled, parbroiled, by-whom-broiled, or, in fact, anything but boiled, are always delicious.

August 22, 1956

Fresh Dried Chili Oil

This is more salsa than sauce. Russell Moore, chef and owner of Camino, in Oakland, California, describes it as "a super-rough harissa."

The recipe is really a template—you can use any mild chili, such as chihuacle or mulatto, and any herb—and drizzle it over whatever vegetable looks good that week, from artichokes to new potatoes to escarole to summer chanterelles. "You want all the freshness of the seasons in there, and three strong flavors," Mr. Moore said.

Time: 15 minutes   **Yield:** ¾ cup

2 medium-hot dried chilies, like a New
    Mexican red or other Southwestern
    chili
1 small clove garlic, pounded into a paste
    in a mortar and pestle

¼ cup chopped fresh mint
½ cup extra virgin olive oil
Salt to taste

1. Crush chilies with fingers into pieces no bigger than ¼ inch across. Place in small bowl and add just enough boiling water to cover, about 1 tablespoon; let sit until chilies are hydrated, 10 minutes.

2. Add garlic and mint, and mix while slowly adding olive oil. Taste and season with salt. For best flavor, make several hours before using.

May 20, 2009: "Grilling Over Wood as a Sweaty, Smoky Sport,"
by OLIVER SCHWANER-ALBRIGHT; adapted from
RUSSELL MOORE, Camino, Oakland, California

Sauce Chermella

Ninette Hayot Lukashok was born in Rabat and raised in Casablanca and frequently writes about food. She generously gave us the following recipe for one of her favorite native hot condiments, sauce chermella.

"In Morocco," Mrs. Lukashok said, "this hot tangy sauce is a staple accompaniment for all barbecued foods. It may be used as a 30-minute marinade for fish or meats that are to be grilled, or it can be served as a sauce after the foods have been cooked, and it is a wonderful dipping sauce for fried fish.

"We especially like it with broiled or fried fresh sardines or fried swordfish. It is an essential ingredient in the spicy eggplant puree, Zallouk, that can be used as a dip for strips of pita bread or raw vegetables, or as a salad with roast lamb."

The basis of sauce chermella, as well as many other Moroccan hot sauces, Mrs. Lukashok said, is a blend of cayenne pepper and oil that is kept ready-mixed, in the refrigerator. To make it, combine ⅓ cup cayenne pepper with ⅔ cup light peanut oil. Store in the refrigerator and stir well before using.

Yield: 1 cup

2 cloves garlic, peeled

2 tablespoons fresh cilantro leaves

2 teaspoons salt

⅓ cup water

⅓ cup red wine vinegar

1 tablespoon sweet paprika

1 teaspoon cayenne pepper and oil
   mixture

1 tablespoon ground cumin

½ cup French or Italian olive oil

1. All ingredients should be blended together to form a paste. If you work with a blender or food processor, combine all ingredients and puree until a paste is obtained. If you work with a mortar and pestle, begin by crushing the garlic and cilantro leaves with salt, then mixing in all the ingredients except the olive oil. When you have a thick paste, slowly trickle oil in, stirring constantly, as when making mayonnaise.

2. Place mixture in a small saucepan, bring to a boil for a minute or two, then refrigerate until well chilled.

July 28, 1978: "From Green Chutney to Barbecue
Sauce: Four of Craig Claiborne's Favorite Hot Sauces,"
by CRAIG CLAIBORNE;
recipe from NINETTE HAYOT LUKASHOK

3-Alarm Chili Sauce

It is hard to believe there is a chili buff anywhere who is not aware of Wick Fowler's one-, two- or three-alarm chili seasoning mix, the number of alarms obviously increasing with the amount of fiery cayenne pepper used in the preparation. This mix can also be the basis of a wonderful hot chili-flavored sauce that can be used as a marinade, a glaze or a final topping for barbecued food.

What you get in a package of Wick Fowler's two-alarm chili mix is seven envelopes containing masa (a corn flour thickening agent), paprika, cayenne, chili powder, combined oregano and cumin, salt and a blend of dehydrated garlic and onion. The first thing to do is discard that last packet; substituting fresh ingredients does wonders for the final result. Adjust the seasoning to the alarm rating that suits you by the addition of none, some or all of the cayenne pepper.

If you want to use the three-alarm sauce as a marinade or glaze, do not thicken it with masa. Otherwise this mellow meal is advisable both for binding the sauce and giving it depth of flavor. It is true, of course, that all of the ingredients in the Fowler kit can be purchased separately but somehow the results are never quite the same.

This recipe is delicious on spareribs, grilled chicken and barbecued fish and meat.

Yield: 3 cups

2 tablespoons light Italian oil, or as needed

2 slices fatty bacon, coarsely chopped

1 large onion, finely minced

3 large cloves garlic, finely minced

All Wick Fowler ingredients except masa and dehydrated onion and garlic

1 (8-ounce) can tomato sauce

2 cans water with 2 tablespoons glace de viande (see note), or 2 (8-ounce) cans strong beef stock

3 tablespoons dark brown sugar or dark honey, or to taste

2 to 3 tablespoons white vinegar

⅓ cup ketchup

Masa flour, if using recipe as a sauce

Salt to taste

1.   Heat oil slightly in a very heavy 1- to 1½-quart saucepan. The sauce scorches easily, and only a heavy pan such as enameled cast iron or copper will be really reliable. Add bacon and sauté slowly until all bacon fat is rendered and bits are golden brown. Remove pieces and reserve.

2.   Add onion and garlic to hot fat and sauté slowly, stirring frequently, until soft and yellow. Do not let them brown. Return bacon to pan and add all Wick Fowler ingredients except the masa, dehydrated onion and garlic. Stir spices through the fat, adding just enough additional oil to moisten mix slightly. Sauté over low heat, stirring constantly for 3 to 4 minutes, or until spices lose their scent.

3. Add tomato sauce, then refill can twice with strong beef stock or water. If using water, stir glace de viande into sauce. Add sugar or honey and vinegar and simmer, half covered, for 10 minutes, stirring several times.

4. Stir in ketchup. If you are using this as a sauce, dissolve masa in 3 tablespoons warm water, and stir it in simmering mixture. Simmer, half covered, over low heat, for about 15 minutes, stirring frequently to prevent scorching on bottom of pot. Add salt and adjust other seasonings (especially sugar or vinegar) to taste. Sauce should be about thickness of a hot fudge sauce. The flavor of this sauce is extremely intense and cannot be fully appreciated until it is combined with meat or fish. It improves in flavor if allowed to sit overnight in the refrigerator before being reheated and served. Spoon over hamburgers or any other grilled meats.

NOTE: Glace de viande adds a richer flavor than beef stock.

July 28, 1978: "From Green Chutney to Barbecue
Sauce: Four of Craig Claiborne's Favorite Hot Sauces,"
by CRAIG CLAIBORNE

Menu Ideas

NOTE TO READERS: Most recipes in the book serve 4–6 people, but before embarking on a menu, please check yields on each recipe. Some may need to be halved to serve a smaller group (others may need to be doubled to serve 8–10).

#1: It's Always Five O'Clock Somewhere
Dirty Martini with Grilled Olives (page 9)
Best Grilled Artichokes (page 1)
Barbecued Steak au Poivre (page 80)
Grilled Leeks with White Beans and Blue Cheese (page 266)
Maury Rubin's Grilled Chocolate Sandwiches (page 315)

#2: Intimate Dinner, Bold Flavors
Grilled Clams with Lemon-Cayenne Butter (page 25)
Grilled Pork Loin with Wine-Salt Rub (page 129)
Hobo Pack of New Potatoes, Red Onion and Orange (page 274)
Guava Crème Brûlée (page 309)

#3: The Backyard Is the Place to Be
Smoky Brisket (page 105)
Drunken Beans (page 280)
Onion Slaw (page 290)
Sweet Potato Biscuits (page 325)
Grilled Nectarines with Cinnamon Toast and Berries (page 296)

#4: Rosemary Runs Through It
Grilled Sardines (page 229)
Grilled Lamb and Figs on Rosemary Skewers (page 158)
Radicchio Grilled with Olive Paste and Anchovies (page 265)
Burnt Oranges with Rosemary (page 299)

#5: In a Latin Direction
Ginger and Chili Grilled Shrimp (page 30)
Garlic-Roasted Pork Shoulder (page 145)
Black Beans and White Rice (page 285)
Watermelon Pico de Gallo (page 348)
Grilled Grapefruit (page 9)

#6: In a Middle Eastern Direction
Roasted Eggplant in Yogurt (page 264)
Syrian Beef Kebabs (page 108)
Lemony Cucumber Salad (page 109)
Charred Peppers (page 269)
Grilled Peaches with Dukkah and Blueberries (page 300)

#7: In an Indian Direction
Grilled Corn with Curried Yogurt and Onion (page 2)
Twice-Cooked Mock Tandoori Chicken (page 187)
Cilantro Mint Chutney (page 201)
Rice Chello (page 287)
Grilled Chapati (page 322)
Skewered Grilled Fruit with Ginger Syrup (page 306)

#8: In a Pan-Asian Direction
Chicken Yakitori (page 36)
Bulgogi (page 88)
Miso-Glazed Eggplant Slices (page 262)
Grilled-Scallion Salad (page 13)
Sesame Spinach and Tofu (page 279)
Grilled Plums with Star Fruit (page 298)

#9: Shades of Ginger

Grilled Soft-Shell Crabs with Scallions, Ginger and Deep-Fried Capers (page 253)

Ed Gorman's Grilled Quails with Ginger and Sherry (page 207)

Vietnamese-Style Portobello Mushrooms (page 260)

Grilled Baby Bok Choy (page 2)

Grilled Mango with Sweet Sticky Rice Cakes and Pistachios (page 295)

#10: Simply Mediterranean

Grilled Pizza with Italian Cheeses and Bitter Greens (page 22)

Marinated Grilled Swordfish (page 230)

Grilled Tuscan Summer Vegetables (page 258)

Grilled Figs Stuffed with Goat Cheese (page 3)

#11: Something Special for Family Dinner

Grilled Leeks with Romesco Sauce (page 14)

Grilled Shellfish with "Barbecue" Sauce (page 246)

Corn-Bread Salad (page 272)

Grilled Fruit Salad (page 8)

#12: September Supper

Grilled Tomatoes with Fresh Mozzarella (page 1)

Beef Brochettes with Red Pepper and Coriander (page 110)

Smashed Potatoes with Tapenade (page 276)

Grilled Belgian Endives (page 2)

Peach Compote with Rose Water (page 313)

#13: Familiar Flavors Made Fresh

Grilled-Onion Guacamole (page 12)

Braised and Grilled Pork Ribs (page 140)

Corn Pudding (page 271)

Jicama Coleslaw (page 289)

Grilled Rose-Water Poundcake (page 312)

#14: Herbs and Spices over the Coals

Barbecued Eggplant and Pine Nut Appetizer (page 20)
Butterflied Leg of Lamb with Sorrel Sauce (page 160)
Hot Potato Salad with Herbs (page 277)
Spice-Rubbed Carrots (page 1)
Hot from the Coals Grilled Herb Focaccia (page 320)
Coriander Ginger Cake (page 310)

#15: Sunny Island Flavors, All Year Round

Shrimps Wilder (page 252)
Jerk Chicken (page 195)
Jamaican Rice with Coconut and Red Beans (page 286)
Grilled Mango (page 2)

#16: Easy Enough for a Weeknight

Grilled Clams with Fried Garlic (page 26)
Salmon Burgers (page 60)
Curry-Rubbed Sweet-Potato Planks (page 262)
Grilled Apricots with Bourbon, Sugar and Mint (page 8)

#17: New Old-Fashioned Surf and Turf

Alice Waters's Charcoal Grilled Lobsters (page 255)
Grilled Flank Steak (page 83)
Potato Fondantes with Oregano (page 275)
Charred Iceberg Wedges with Cherry Tomatoes (page 6)
Raspberry Chocolate Mousse Cakes (page 314)

#18: Spring Salmon Celebration

Kajmak with Herbs (page 53)
Grilled Copper River King Salmon Fillet with Pinot Noir Sauce (page 242)
Grilled Fennel with Oranges (page 1)
Danish Rice Pudding with Fresh Cherries (page 308)

#19: Blue Skies Above, Crisp Leaves Underfoot

Grilled Walnut-Olive Bread with Exotic Mushrooms (page 318)
Grilled Pork Porterhouse with an Apple-Maple-Ginger Glaze (page 120)
Grilled Lacinato Kale Salad (page 6)
Grilled Pears with Honey, Yogurt and Cardamom (page 8)

#20: The Diet Starts Tomorrow

Crisp and Unctuous Pork Belly (page 38), with
Madhur Jaffrey's Fresh Green Chutney (page 349), and
Sauce Chermella (page 353)
Beef Tartare Burger (page 44)
Grilled Corn on the Cob with Chipotle Mayonnaise (page 270)
Crusty Macaroni and Cheese (page 288)
Grilled S'mores (page 9)

CONTRIBUTORS: CURRENT AND FORMER STAFF MEMBERS OF *THE NEW YORK TIMES*

Mark Bittman is the author of *How to Cook Everything* and a dozen other cookbooks. At *The New York Times* he is the Opinion columnist on food and *The New York Times Magazine*'s lead food writer.

Nelson Bryant, who was on *The New York Times* sports staff from 1967 to 1990, wrote the Outdoors column for many years.

Marian Burros, who wrote for *The New York Times* for 27 years, is the author of 13 food and cookbooks, including *Elegant but Easy Cookbook*, *20 Minute Menus,* and *Cooking for Comfort*. Retired but still writing, she lives in Washington, D.C., and Vermont.

Craig Claiborne (1920–2000) was the longtime food editor and restaurant critic of *The New York Times* and author of numerous cookbooks, including *The New York Times Cookbook*.

Melissa Clark, a food columnist of *The New York Times*, has written 34 cookbooks. Her latest is *Cook This Now*. She lives in Brooklyn with her family.

Damon Darlin, currently the international business editor at *The New York Times*, has eaten his way around the world as a foreign correspondent and a technology writer and editor.

Timothy Egan, a former national correspondent for *The New York Times*, is now an online Opinion columnist for *The Times*. He is the author of seven books, one of which, *The Worst Hard Time,* won the 2006 National Book Award for nonfiction.

Florence Fabricant has contributed to *The New York Times* since 1972 and has written regularly for its food sections since 1980. She is the author of 11 cookbooks, including the forthcoming *Wine with Food: Pairing Notes from The New York Times,* written with Eric Asimov.

Pierre Franey (1921–1996) was a noted French chef who wrote *The New York Times 60-Minute Gourmet* for *The Times* and a series of cookbooks that grew out of that feature.

Moira Hodgson is the author of *It Seemed Like a Good Idea at the Time: My Adventures in Life and Food*. She was on staff at *The New York Times* from 1979 to 1981 and later a senior editor at *Vanity Fair* and the restaurant critic of the *New York Observer*.

Nancy Harmon Jenkins is a food writer and an authority on Mediterranean cuisine. The author of a number of cookbooks, including, most recently, *The New Mediterranean Diet Cookbook*, she is currently writing a book on olive oil, to be published in 2015.

Dena Kleiman, a reporter for *The New York Times* from 1975 until 1991, is the author of a bestselling book, *A Deadly Silence.* A freelance journalist and screenwriter, she is currently at work on a play. She continues to enjoy writing about food.

Elaine Louie is the author, most recently, of *The Occasional Vegetarian*, based on The Temporary Vegetarian feature that she wrote for the Dining section of *The New York Times*. She won the 1995 James Beard Journalism Award for a series of articles on ethnic cuisine in New York City.

Bryan Miller is a food and wine writer who was the restaurant critic of *The New York Times* from 1984 to 1993. A recipient of the James Beard Lifetime Achievement Award, he is the author, most recently, of *Cooking Basics for Dummies*.

Julia Moskin is a food writer for *The New York Times* who appears regularly in the Dining section and hosts Recipe Lab, an interactive feature that appears every month. She is the coauthor of eight cookbooks, including, most recently, *CookFight* with Kim Severson.

Molly O'Neill is a former reporter for *The New York Times* and food columnist for *The New York Times Magazine.* Her most recent cookbook is *One Big Table*.

Regina Schrambling, an editor and writer for the Dining In/Dining Out section of *The New York Times* from 1998 to 2002, now has a food website, http://www.gastropoda.com.

Mimi Sheraton, the restaurant critic of *The New York Times* from 1976 to 1994, is the author of the memoir, *Eating My Words: An Appetite for Life*.

Sam Sifton is a senior editor for *The New York Times* and a columnist for *The New York Times Magazine.* Formerly the national editor, restaurant critic, culture editor and editor of the Dining section, he is building a subscription-based cooking service for NYTimes.com.

Alex Ward is the editorial director of book development at *The Times.*

Alex Witchel is a staff writer for *The New York Times Magazine* and the author of *All Gone: A Memoir of My Mother's Dementia. With Refreshments.*

PICTURE CREDITS

With thanks to Jeffrey Roth and William P. O'Donnell of *The New York Times* for their assistance with photo research and production.

PAGE A, fish, vegetables, and fruit on the grill, photo by Francesco Tonelli.

PAGE B, duck à l'orange, photo by Francesco Tonelli.

PAGE C, Beef Tartare Burger, photo by Francesco Tonelli.

PAGE D, Greek-Style Fish with Marinated Tomatoes, photo by Evan Sung.

PAGE E, Top: Grilled Lobster, photo by Fred R. Conrad; Bottom Left: Halibut with Indian Rub and Corn Salsa, photo by Andrew Scrivani; Bottom Right: Grilled Clams, photo by Andrew Scrivani.

PAGE F, Curry-Spiced Lamb Burgers, photo by Francesco Tonelli.

PAGE G, Grilled Sardines, photo by Andrew Scrivani.

PAGE H, Bacon Explosion, photos by Don Ipock.

PAGE I, Top: New Yorkers grilling jerk chicken, photo by Evan Sung; Bottom: Jerk Chicken, photo by Jennifer May.

PAGE J, Grilled Pork Loin with Wine-Salt Rub, photo by Andrew Scrivani.

PAGE K, Top: Steak prepared with a rub, photo by Francesco Tonelli; Bottom: Braised and Grilled Pork Ribs, photo by Andrew Scrivani.

PAGE L, Top: Shu Mai-Style Burger, photo by Francesco Tonelli; Bottom: Japanese Burger with Wasabi Ketchup, photo by Tony Cenicola.

PAGE M, Crusty Macaroni and Cheese, photo by Andrew Scrivani.

PAGE N, Top: Grilled Leeks with Romesco Sauce, photo by Andrew Scrivani; Bottom: Grilled Lamb and Figs on Rosemary Skewers, photo by Evan Sung.

PAGE O, Grilled Peaches with Dukkah and Blueberries, photo by Francesco Tonelli.

PAGE P, Grilled Rose-Water Poundcake, photo by Sabra Krock.

PAGE 10, Master barbecue grill and charcoal briquettes, circa 1949, photo by *The New York Times*.

PAGE 40, Hamburgers on the grill, photo by Bill Aller.

PAGE 68, Odette and Robert Herrmann and sons aboard the *Why Not* in 1968, photo by Arthur Brower.

PAGE 116, Judge samples barbecue at the fifth Annual Taylor (Texas) International Championship Barbecue Cook-off, 1982, photo by Zigy Kaluzny.

PAGE 154, Evan and Judith Jones grilling on their New York City apartment terrace in 1961, photo by Bill Aller.

PAGE 178, Sarrett Rudley preparing an elaborate al fresco meal on her terrace in 1958, photo by Alfred Wegener/The New York Times Studio.

PAGE 210, Joe Lewis buttering buttering shad at Ross Dock in Palisades State Park, New Jersey, in 1959, photo by Eddie Hausner.

PAGE 256, Five famous French chefs—Pierre Franey, Jacques Pepin, Roger Fessaguet, Jean Vergnes and Rene Verdon—on Gardiner's Island, New York, in 1965, photo by Jack Manning.

PAGE 292, Couple dining out on barbecue in 1985, photo by Zigy Kaluzny.

PAGE 326, Judge samples barbecue at the fifth Annual Taylor (Texas) International Championship Barbecue Cook-off in 1982, photo by Zigy Kaluzny.

INDEX

NOTE: Italicized-letter page references in parentheses refer to photo captions on pages A to P.